REV IT UP
• VERSE·BY·VERSE •
VOL I

Revelation Demystified

&

the Future Clarified

D1440852

SAMUEL A. KOJOGLANIAN, MD, FACC

Rev It Up – Verse by Verse
Volume I
By Samuel A. Kojoglanian, MD, FACC

© 2020
Samuel A. Kojoglanian, MD, FACC

Requests for permission to make copies
of any part of the work should be mailed to:
Dr. Samuel Kojoglanian
24868 Apple Street, #103
Santa Clarita, CA 91321

DrK@MenderOfHearts.org

Library of Congress Cataloging-in-Publications Data
Kojoglanian, Samuel A. MD
Revelation Demystified
pp. cm.
Summary: The future is made clear today
1. Rapture is imminent ; 2. Tribulation is real;
3. Christ is sovereign

ISBN 978-0-9989210-4-4

The New King James Version was used for Bible verses.

Published by Dr. Samuel Kojoglanian
Rock Your Planet, Inc

Layout by Lynn Lanning

Cover by Chris Hunter

Printed in the United States of America

Dedication

*To all those whose hearts long for
Christ's imminent return*

Acknowledgments

Dr. Paul Greasley, a God-sent Bezalel; your comments, questions, edits and wisdom has enriched this book immensely.

Laura Jennings, thank you for tirelessly reviewing and verifying each verse.

Lynn Lanning, you've helped me from the very first book; so thankful for your faithfulness and expertise.

Tim Loan, thank you for being a true friend.

Dr. Floyd Moss, your willingness to come alongside humbles my heart.

Jeff and Denise Robertson, thank you for your love and service for Christ.

My Pastor Dudley Rutherford, thank you for your uncompromising teaching and for encouraging my soul.

Mentors I have never met, but am so grateful for their scholarly work:

   Dr. John Ankerberg
   Dr. Donald Grey Barnhouse
   Dr. Jimmy DeYoung
   Dr. Ed Hindson
   Dr. Mark Hitchcock
   Dr. Robert Jeffress
   Dr. David Jeremiah
   Dr. Ron Rhodes

Holy Spirit, the very breath I take is a gift from You; all wisdom and understanding comes from You!

Table of Contents

How Should I Read This Book?

Approximately 66% of the book of Revelation deals with the Tribulation, from chapters six to nineteen. There is much in the book of Revelation that speaks about a future judgment, but the overall theme is Christ, His beauty, His mercy, His victory, and His endless love for you and me!

If you want the bottom line, what we call a "bullet presentation" in medicine, you can simply read the next chapter, "Summary of the Entire Book," and have a firm understanding of the Book of Revelation.

One could also read the chapter summary before delving into each chapter. Chapter summaries are at the end of each chapter. The Table of Contents has page numbers for the first page of each chapter and the first page of each chapter summary.

Another approach is to read specific sections, grasping the sequence of events in chronological order as noted below:

1. Divine Outline of the Book of Revelation. 1:19.
2. The Church Age. 1:12-13. (7 local churches 2:1; 2:8; 2:12; 2:18; 3:1; 3:7; 3:14).
3. Rapture. 3:10; 4:1; 4:4; 13:9; 20:5; 22:12; 22:17; 22:20.
4. Tribulation. 5:1; 5:5 (last paragraph); 6:1-2; 6:3-8; 6:9; 6:12; 6:17; 7:9; 7:15; 8:1; 8:7-13; 9:1; 9:13-18; 11:1; 11:4; 11:7; 11:15; 11:18; 14:4; 14:6.

5. Middle of Tribulation and Satan, the Dragon. 12:1-6; 12:13-14.

6. Great Tribulation. 13:1-6; 13:11; 13:16-18; 14:8; 14:9-10; 14:12; 15:8; 16:2-4; 16:8-12; 16:17-21; 17:1-6 / 17:15-18 / 19:2 (Religious Babylon destroyed); 18:2-8 and 18:12-13 (Commercial Babylon destroyed).

7. Antichrist, the First Beast. 9:11; 13:1-7; 17:8-14; 19:19-20.

8. False Prophet, the Second Beast. 13:11-18; 19:20.

9. Tribulation Martyrs. 15:2-4; 17:6; 19:2; 20:4.

10. Marriage of the Lamb. 19:7-8.

11. Marriage Supper of the Lamb. 19:9.

12. Second Coming of Christ. 19:11-16.

13. Armageddon. 14:19-20; 19:11-16; 19:19-21.

14. Antichrist and False Prophet cast into hell. 19:20.

15. Satan bound. 20:2-3.

16. Millennium. 20:2, 4.

17. Satan temporarily released, then cast into hell. 20:7-10.

18. Great White Throne judgment. 20:11-15.

19. Book of Life. 13:8; 17:8; 20:15.

20. Hades, Death. 9:2; 14:13; 20:5; 20:14; 21:4,8.

21. The Lake of Fire, Hell. 14:11; 19:20; 20:5-6; 20:10; 21:8; 22:15.

22. Heaven and Eternity. 21:1-5; 21:9; 21:18; 21:22-27; 22:1-5; 22:21.

Finally, to truly grasp the beauty of Christ and to draw closer to Him, I recommend you read the entire book, studying it in an expository format, verse by verse in detail. Challenge yourself to read one to two chapters at each setting. At the end of each chapter, you'll find a summary. Because this book is detailed, I recommend that you read the summary of each chapter before and after reading the chapter, getting a fore-taste of what the Spirit of God will unfold in your heart and for your life.

Throughout the book, you'll note highlighted texts that are the author's favorites. You'll also encounter medical and cardiology related analogies as well as geopolitical points of view to better grasp the meaning of the book and better understand how current events are inherently tied to Revelation, a book of prophecy. You could read these sections separately and glean much insight about Christ's unblemished love for you, His ultimate victory, and the shifting sands of our times.

Each of these highlighted texts will have a design and their own font, according to the key shown below.

By God's grace, the future is made clear today!

Key to Highlighted Text

Favorite texts written by the author

Medical and cardiology related analogies

Geopolitical points of view

Summary of the Entire Book

The book of Revelation was written by the 90-year-old Apostle John approximately 95 AD on the Island of Patmos, where he was banished as a political prisoner because Rome considered him a threat for preaching the Gospel of Christ. The book was written not only to reveal that Christ will reign as King of Kings and Lord of Lords in the Millennium and during all Eternity, but also details the course of the events that lead up to His reign.

This book is futuristic, meaning that the events in chapters four through twenty-two have not yet occurred. The symbolism and numbers used are not random; they are all noted in the Old Testament. The "Day of the Lord" does not start with the Coronavirus Pandemic or the blazing turmoil, chaos, and hostility of 2020; it starts with the Rapture and continues through the Tribulation and the Millennium; the Day of the Lord covers the seven-year wrath spoken of by the prophets that will fall upon a God-rejecting, Christ-hating and Holy Spirit-denying world. The reason for the wrath of God is that the iniquity of this world will have reached a breaking point, bringing us to the end of man's rule, and the beginning of Christ's rule on earth.

The book of Revelation is divided into three sections: the past, the present and the future. We learn this in Revelation 1:19, where we are given the divine outline for the entire book.

1. The past (things that were) speaks of Christ's death and

resurrection, His role of prophet while on earth and role of High Priest after His resurrection, noted in chapter one.

2. The present (things that are) speaks of the seven churches in Asia Minor, and the Church Age, each church representing a set period of time including the churches of Philadelphia and Laodicea, the sixth and seventh churches that symbolize today's church. Jesus' present role is no longer a prophet, but a High Priest, interceding on behalf of His Church and believers. The messages to the seven churches are sobering, found in Revelation chapters two to three.

3. The future (things that will be) speaks of Christ as the King of Kings and the Lords of Lords. Christ performs "surgery" to transition from prophet to High Priest to the King of Kings. Though the "surgical report" lasts for a period of seven years, it encompasses the majority of the book of Revelation, the details being disclosed in chapters 4 through 19. This period demarks the last seven years of man's rule and Satan's rule on earth. Chapter 20 exposes the dismantling of Satan, and chapters 21-22 declare the splendor of Eternity for all believers.

We are living in the Church Age today and the next major event on God's prophetic calendar is the Rapture (chapter four), where Christ will take His Church (believers, or Christ-followers) home to heaven. This event is imminent and will occur in the twinkling of an eye, where saints of the Church Age who have died and those who are still alive will receive their glorified bodies and meet the Lord in the air and will be taken to heaven (I Corinthians 15:51-52; I Thessalonians 4:16-18).

For the next seven years believers will be in heaven with the Lord. Those who remain on earth will undergo seven years of horror and judgments, known as the Tribulation. The Tribulation is broken in two halves, each being three and a half years, or 42 months or 1,260 days.

In the first half, judgments released on earth will occur when

Summary of the Entire Book

Christ breaks the seven seals from the scroll which His Father hands Him (Revelation 5:1-7). This age will be dark, the first four seals unleashing the four horsemen:

1. The first seal, the horseman on a white horse. The Antichrist will confirm a covenant with Israel and the Arab world, bringing in "peace." (Revelation 6:1-2).

2. The second seal, the horseman on a red horse. The Gog and Magog war of Ezekiel 38-39 occurs, Israel being attacked by Russia, Iran and Syria with their allies. Five-sixth or 83% of all nations attacking Israel will be wiped out as God protects and defends His nation, Israel. (Revelation 6:3-4).

3. The third seal, the horseman on a black horse. A great famine will follow the war. (Revelation 6:5-6).

4. The fourth seal, the horseman on a pale horse. Death will follow famine, where one fourth of the earth's population will die. (Revelation 6:7-8).

5. When the fifth seal is broken, we see the martyrs who were killed for their faith in Christ, crying out to God and asking for vengeance for their death. They will soon be granted their request! (Revelation 6:9-11).

6. When the sixth seal is broken, we witness unimaginable disturbances such as earthquakes, volcanic explosions, probably nuclear warfare that will turn the sun black and the moon bloody red. Many will still deny God and not turn to Him. (Revelation 6:12-17).

7. We will not see the seventh seal broken until chapter 8:1. The seventh seal will unleash the seven trumpet judgments. Between the sixth and seventh seal, there is an interlude noted in Revelation chapter seven:

   a. 144,000 thousand Jewish evangelists will preach the Gospel worldwide, leading millions of souls to Christ (Revelation 7:1-8).

   b. Martyrs from the Tribulation are taken to heaven in soul and spirit, and worship God (Revelation 7: 9-17).

During the first half of the Tribulation, the seventh seal is broken, leading to the seven trumpets (Revelation 8:1):

1. The first trumpet causes fire, hail and blood to fall on the earth, burning up one-third of trees and green grass (Revelation 8:7).

2. The second trumpet causes a meteor to be cast in the sea, causing one-third of the sea to turn into blood, killing a third of sea life and destroying a third of ships (Revelation 8:8-9).

3. The third trumpet causes another meteor, or "a great star" named "Wormwood" to fall from heaven on the third of the rivers and springs of waters, making the waters bitter and killing "many." (Revelation 8:10-11).

4. The fourth trumpet causes a third of the sun, moon and stars to be darkened (Revelation 8:12).

5. The fifth through seventh trumpets are introduced as three "woes" that will devastate the inhabitants of the earth (Revelation 8:13). The fifth trumpet, or the first woe, unleashes demonic locusts that torment mankind who are not following Christ (Revelation 9:1-12).

6. The sixth trumpet releases four demons at the Euphrates River who cause the River to become dry, preparing the way for two hundred million soldiers to attack Israel in the Campaign of Armageddon. One third of mankind will die during this judgment. By now more than half of earth's population is dead, one fourth dying during the fourth seal (Revelation 6:7-8) and one third of the remaining dying during the sixth trumpet. There are still those who refuse to turn to God and ask for forgiveness! (Revelation 9:13-21).

7. As there was an interlude between the sixth and seventh seals, so too there will be an interlude between the sixth and seventh trumpets, noted in chapter ten. As we'll read below, the seventh trumpet will be sounded in Revelation 11:15-19.

In chapter ten, a mighty "angel" which could be Christ (though Christ is not an angel but is referred to as "the Angel of the Lord" in the Old Testament) hands a little book to John. John witnesses seven thunders but is instructed not to write down what the thunders entail. John is also told to take the book and eat it, which is sweet in his mouth but bitter to his stomach (the Bible is sweet to those who accept it, reaping eternal life, and bitter to those who reject it, reaping eternal death). (Revelation 10:1-11).

In chapter eleven, two witnesses, who are likely Elijah and Moses, preach the Gospel (along with the 144,000 Jewish evangelists) for 42 months or in the first half of the Tribulation. Satan kills the two prophets but in three and a half days, God resurrects them, and all of the people on earth witness the miracle (Revelation 11:1-14).

The seventh trumpet is sounded, which will release the seven bowl judgments in the second half of the Tribulation. But when this trumpet is heard, heaven rejoices, knowing that Christ is soon to reign on earth and for all Eternity (Revelation 11:15-19).

In the midst of the two three-and-a-half-years or 42-month periods, Satan will claim he is God; this action is known as the abomination of desolation, where he desecrates the temple by making his claim (Daniel 9:27). This will usher in the second half of the Tribulation known as the Great Tribulation and will lead to a cataclysmic chain of events.

Chapter twelve marks the middle of the Tribulation. Two signs are seen in this chapter:

1. A woman dressed in the sun and having twelve stars on her head. She represents Israel and not Mary (Revelation 12:1-2).

2. A red Dragon in the sky who wants to devour the woman (Israel) and her child (Christ). The Dragon is Satan (Revelation 12:3-4). Satan chases Israel. The remnant of Israel,

which is one-third of the Jewish population, will escape to Petra, a city in Jordan and will be protected by God (Isaiah 34:6, 63:1; Zechariah 13:8). They will turn to Christ at the end of the Tribulation and look on the One, Jesus, whom they have pierced (Zechariah 12:10; Revelation 12:5-17).

The Great Tribulation, or the last 42 months, or last 1,260 days begins as the abomination of desolation unfolds. We'll see in chapter 13: verses 1-18 that the:

1. Antichrist, the First Beast who rises from the waters, will be given full reign to dominate the world.

2. False Prophet, the Second Beast who rises from the earth, will draw millions astray by leading them to worship the Antichrist.

3. 666 mark will be introduced.

   a. Only those who accept the mark either on their right hand or their forehead will be able to buy or sell.

   b. But anyone accepting the mark will never be able to enter into God's kingdom.

   c. The name of whoever receives the 666 mark was never written in the Book of Life, hates God and will have his eternal abode in the Lake of Fire after the Millennium and the Great White Throne judgment.

There is a shift in the way the Gospel is preached in the last half of the Tribulation, noted in chapter 14.

1. 144,000 Jewish evangelists taken up to heaven and are with Christ (Revelation 14:1-5).

2. An angel flying and proclaiming the Gospel in all the earth to every nation, tribe, tongue and people, inviting the masses to fear God and turn to Him (Revelation 14:6-7).

3. Another angel foretells the fall of Religious Babylon and Commercial Babylon before it crumbles (Revelation 14:8).

4. Another angel warns that if anyone receives the mark of

the Beast, his reward will be the eternal Lake of Fire (Revelation 14:9-11).

5. Jesus is seen wearing a golden crown, sitting on a cloud with a sharp sickle. He thrusts the sickle onto the earth to separate the wheat (Tribulation believers) from the chaff or tares (Tribulation unbelievers). Revelation 14:14-16.

6. Another angel has a sharp sickle. And yet another angel instructs him to thrust his sickle and gather the clusters of vines because the grapes are ripe, meaning it is judgment time for those who have rejected Christ. During the campaign of Armageddon, there will be so much blood spilled that it will run for two hundred miles, at least five feet high (Revelation 14:17-20).

7. Chapter 15 prepares the seven angels for the seven last plagues, known as the bowl or vial judgments.

When the seventh trumpet is blown (Revelation 11:15-19), it initiates the seven bowl judgments which occur at the tail end of the Great Tribulation:

1. The first bowl is poured out on the earth, causing loathsome sores upon mankind who received the mark of the Beast (Revelation 16:2).

2. The second bowl is poured out on the sea, and all of the sea turns into blood and all living creatures in the sea die (Revelation 16:3).

3. The third bowl is poured out on all the world's rivers and springs of water, and they turn into blood (Revelation 16:4-7).

4. The fourth bowl is poured out on the sun, and mankind is scorched with authentic and divine global warming; mankind still refuses to repent (Revelation 16:8-9).

5. The fifth bowl is poured out on the throne of the Beast, with his headquarters being in Babylon, and his kingdom facing darkness; mankind still refuses to repent (Revelation 16:10-11).

6. The sixth bowl is poured out and the Euphrates River dries up, allowing the kings of the East, including China, to march into battle in attempts to devour the land of Israel in the Campaign of Armageddon (Revelation 16:12-16).

7. There is no interlude between the sixth and seventh bowl as there was in the seven-seal series and the seven-trumpet series. The seventh bowl is poured out into the air (the very sphere that Satan rules); an earthquake will shake the entire world. Jerusalem will be divided into three parts. Babylon will fall as noted in Revelation 17 and 18. Hail falls from heaven. Mankind continues to blaspheme God (Revelation 16:17-21).

What will the church be doing in heaven during these seven years?

1. Worshiping God, adoring Him, singing, dancing, rejoicing and enjoying the beauty of Christ (Revelation chapters 4 and 5).

2. Facing the judgment seat of Christ, Bema Seat, where we are rewarded for our works that we did while on earth. This is crucial because it will give us our eternal positions, possessions and the extent of our reign and privileges (I Corinthians 3:12-14; II Corinthians 5:10).

3. Taking part in the Marriage of the Lamb as the Bride of Christ and partaking in the Supper of the Lamb (Revelation 19:7-9).

In order for Christ to reign on earth, the worldly system of man must fall. Religious Babylon, or false religion, collapses in chapter 17. Commercial Babylon, the world's economic, financial, political, governmental system plummets in chapter 18. The fall of Babylon is a consequence of the seven bowls being poured out.

Chapter 19 marks another significant turning point in the book of Revelation. When the church, who was Raptured in chapter four, witnesses the fall of Babylon and anticipates the Second Coming of Christ, it bursts into a joyful song of "alleluia!" (Revelation 19:1-10).

1. Christ returns on a white horse with His Church, His bride, as well as His angels, known as the Second Coming of Christ to fight in the Campaign of Armageddon (Revelation 19:11-16).

2. Christ defeats the Antichrist and the False Prophet as well as all existing world powers (Revelation 19:17-18).

3. The Antichrist and the False Prophet are cast into the Lake of Fire (Revelation 19:19-20).

4. All mankind who took part in the rebellion were killed with the sword, or Word, that came out of Christ's mouth (Revelation 19:21).

5. The remnant of Israel will be saved (Zechariah 12:10).

6. The judgment of the goats and the sheep occur at this point (Matthew 25:31-46).

7. The Old Testament saints along with the martyred saints of the Tribulation will receive their glorified bodies (as their souls and spirits were already in heaven). (Daniel 12:1-2; Revelation 20:4).

The Millennium, when Jesus reigns on earth for a thousand years, will then be ushered in, noted in chapter 20.

1. Satan is bound for a thousand years (Revelation 20:1-3).

2. Christ reigns for a thousand years and His saints with glorified bodies (unable to sin or die) rule and reign with Him (Revelation 20:4-6).

3. The "sheep" along with the Jewish remnant saved at Petra who enter the Millennium do not have glorified bodies but they are able to live for up to one thousand years by eating from the healing leaves of the trees provided by God (Ezekiel 47:12).

4. Satan is released after the thousand years and deceives the children of those who did not receive their glorified bodies, luring them to fight against Christ.

5. Satan is defeated and is finally and forever cast into the Lake of Fire.

6. All the souls and spirits of the wicked (Christ-rejecters), who are kept in tormented Hades now resurrect with their eternal bodies, known as the second resurrection, and face God at the Great White Throne judgment. Hades is a temporary holding place for the wicked but there is no such thing as purgatory as those in Hades will never escape; all will tragically end up in hell. They are judged and sentenced to eternal hell because their names are not found in the Book of Life, and they are cast into the Lake of Fire forever!

7. The paradise side of Hades was empty after the resurrection of Christ, where He went to Hades and took the souls and spirits of Old Testament saints to heaven (Ephesians 4:8). When a believer dies today, his body stays on earth but his soul and spirit bypasses the paradise side of Hades and goes directly to heaven (II Corinthians 5:8). The Rapture, or the first resurrection, is when a believer receives his glorified body, joining his soul and spirit. The Rapture occurs in stages, like a carpool, Jesus Christ being the first of all to be resurrected or Raptured.

The Millennium leads to Eternity, where the New Jerusalem will descend from heaven and will be our new abode. All things will be made new, including a New Heaven and New Earth (Revelation 21). We will live with our Father and our Christ. There will be no more sin, no more sickness, no more viruses, no more heartaches, no more murders, no more injustice, no more corruption, no more greed, and no more death (Revelation 22). Oh, how glorious! Come, Lord Jesus, Come!

Preface

As you read this book, you need to know where you stand in time. What time is it? We are in overtime, which means the Church Age is about to end, the Rapture is imminent, and the rule of mankind will be turned over to the only One who is capable and worthy to rule with love, equity, justice and righteousness, Jesus Christ. It's hard to say whether it's just overtime, double overtime or beyond. Since the fall of man, the world has faced war after war, famines, floods, hardships, heartaches, darkness, sickness, theft, murder and death. I can hardly watch television anymore, being grieved by what mankind is doing to mankind. The fact that the wrong is now called right and the right is now called wrong does not shock me, as the prophet Isaiah proclaimed it 2,600 years ago in Isaiah 5:20, "Woe to those who call evil good and good evil; who put darkness for light, and light for darkness; who put bitter for sweet and sweet for bitter!" Here is where mankind stands: at the end of the ages, scrambling for solutions, deviating in morals, fighting deadly viruses, searching for justice, and desperately running out of hope in overtime.

The world is looking for a global leader, a savior, a hero, a mighty person who is an economic genius, an eloquent soothsayer, a staunch warrior, a slick politician, and a dynamic dignitary. The stage is set for him; he is the Antichrist and he will appear during the seven-year span called the Tribulation, swaying millions to worship him and accept his 666 mark. But the book of Revelation is not about him; it is about Jesus Christ. The Antichrist will be suave, but Jesus is the Way. The Antichrist will be convincing, but Jesus is the Truth. The Antichrist will offer hope, but Jesus is the Life.

We will see Jesus like never before. The days of Jesus the Prophet are history. The days of Jesus the High Priest, our Intercessor, are coming to a close. The days of Jesus who will rule as the King of Kings are soon approaching and planet earth will never be the same.

In this book, we will learn the sequence of future events that will take place as we transition from this short-lived present time to an endless eternity of immortality. We will grasp the gravity of God's wrath that will be poured out during the Tribulation as He "Revs it Up," or intensifies His judgments, and silences those who worship creation and despise the Creator. Finally, as we study the Word together, we will behold the splendor of Jesus Christ and worship Him in awe.

The book of Revelation is the only book in the Bible which has its own divine outline. It is found in chapter one, verse nineteen, when John, the author, is told to "Write the things which you have seen, and the things which are, and the things which will take place after this." That's how simple the book is! It tells of what occurred in the past, what is occurring today, and what horrific events await a God-hating and Christ-rejecting world, as well as what joyous marvels are prepared for those who have accepted salvation through the blood of the Lamb. It is a wonder that a book written 2,000 years ago can so eloquently speak of the past, the present and the future, including what will eventually happen to Israel, Russia, China, and even the United States of America!

It is also the only book in the Bible that promises both the reader and listener a unique blessing. It is found in chapter one, verse three, "Blessed is he who reads and those who hear the words of this prophecy and keep those things which are written in it; for the time is near." To one's delight, the blessing is repeated in chapter twenty-two, verse seven, "Behold, I am coming quickly! Blessed is he who keeps the words of the prophecy of this book." But many Christ-followers, including well-intentioned pastors, are intimidated by the content of Revelation and either dismiss it as incomprehensible, deem it dispensable, skeptically view it as allegorical or complain that it is too judgmental. They tragically miss out on knowing Christ intimately, and forfeit the blessings promised in this book of prophecy.

The book of Revelation was written by John, the Apostle, to reveal the person, the beauty, the power, and the finished work of Jesus Christ. The word "revelation" in the Greek is "apokalypsis," meaning unveiling. The Gospel of John was written so that we may believe that Jesus is the Son of God (John 20:31). The Epistles of John were written so that we may be sure we have eternal life through Jesus Christ (I John 5:13). And Revelation was written by John so that we may encounter Christ in a startling new manner and be prepared for His return (Revelation 1:1).

In the Gospel of John, the Apostle presented Jesus as the much-anticipated Messiah, the perfect divine Son of God, and the breathtaking Lamb of God. John wrote Revelation to "show His servants (God's servants, including us) what must soon take place," and John's emphasis in this book is about future events. It was not written to help us identify the Anti-Christ, survive the tribulation, or escape Armageddon. Although if you miss the Rapture, the next event on the prophetic calendar, this book will be an essential survival guide. John wrote Revelation so that we may encounter Christ the Redeemer, Christ the Resurrected, and Christ the Reigning King. He wrote it so that we may be mindful of our actions because the present days are evil. He wrote it to encourage us to be wise, understanding the will of God, walking in God's favor and continually being filled with the Spirit.

 Revelation unveils the transformation of Jesus from the position of the intercessory High Priest to the reigning King of Kings.

In the Old Testament, there were three offices: prophet, priest and king. Melchizedek was a priest and king of Salem (Jerusalem). David was a prophet, priest and king. Jesus, who is in the order of Melchizedek and from the line of David, holds three offices:

1. While on earth, He was a prophet as He declared, "No prophet is accepted in His own country" (Luke 4:24);

2. While in heaven, He intercedes for us as our High Priest, "we have a great High Priest who has passed through the heavens" (Hebrews 4:14);

3. In this book, we'll see Jesus "shift" from High Priest to King of Kings, where He will strip Satan, the prince of the power of the air (Ephesians 2:2), of his rights (Revelation 19:16). Christ has already redeemed us through the blood of the Lamb, but in Revelation, we'll see Him redeem our planet and everything on it to Himself once and for all.

Before you begin reading this book, I'd like for you to have a bird's eye view of what is to occur in the future. We will relive the past, study the present, and reveal the future. The resurrection and glorification of our Lord Jesus occurred 2,000 years ago. You and I are currently in the Church Age. Below I outline the major future events in chronological order:

1. Rapture of the church, and the departing of the saints (imminent).

2. Tribulation, rise of the Antichrist and his deception (3.5 years).

3. Great Tribulation, and earth's devastation (3.5 years).

4. Second Coming of Christ, and deliverance of Israel (75 days).

5. Armageddon, and the defeat of the Beast's armies.

6. Judgment of sheep and goats.

7. Millennium reign of peace, and the dominion of Christ (1,000 years).

8. Satan's last attempt to overthrow Christ.

9. Final Judgment Seat of God (unbelievers facing the Great White Throne judgment), and the doom of the lost.

10. New Heaven and New Earth, and destruction of the old.

11. New Jerusalem, and the dominion of death shattered.

12. Final state, and our destiny in Eternity.

How should we interpret the book of Revelation?

1. Historically? No. This view falsely states that the contents of the book have been fulfilled throughout history, up to today.

2. Preterist view? No. This view falsely claims that the contents of the book were fulfilled in 70 AD, when Israel's temple was destroyed. Also, followers of this view erroneously believe in Replacement Theology, believing that the church has replaced Israel as God's chosen people.

3. Mid-Tribulation view? No. This view wrongly claims that the church will go through the first half of the Tribulation before we are Raptured.

4. Post-Tribulation view? No. This view inaccurately asserts that the church will go through all seven years of Tribulation before we are Raptured (Revelation 3:10; 4:1).

5. A-Millennial view? No. This view mistakenly ignores the 1,000 years of the literal reign of Christ mentioned six times in Revelation 20:2-7.

6. Allegorical view? No. This view incorrectly states that all of Revelation is symbolic or figurative.

7. Futuristic and literal view? Yes. Yes. Yes. Chapter one of Revelation has already occurred, where Jesus is presented as the resurrected Christ. Chapters two and three not only depict the seven local churches that existed during John's day, but the prophetic present which extends to the current Church Age. Chapters four to twenty-two will occur in the future, with the Rapture triggering all the events. By examining how God fulfilled prophecy in the past, where His Word was spoken, and it ultimately came into being, literally, we can understand how God will fulfill prophecy in the future, that is, literally.

From Genesis to Malachi, more than one hundred specific prophecies were fulfilled regarding Christ's First Coming such as He would be born in Bethlehem (Micah 5:2). According to a wise precept, "When the literal sense makes good sense, seek no other sense, lest it result in nonsense." How do we then interpret the many symbols and signs in the book of Revelation? Where there are symbols, we will apply each symbol to illustrate a literal truth and principle.

The book of Revelation is futuristic because:

a. The Rapture of the church has not yet occurred as noted in Revelation 4:1.

b. The seal, trumpet and bowl judgments have not yet occurred; the 666 mark has not yet been implemented as noted in Revelation 13:18, 19:20.

c. The Second Coming of Christ, which will physically be seen by all the living at the end of the seven-year Tribulation, has not yet occurred as noted in Revelation 19:1-21.

d. The literal third temple that will be built by Israel in Jerusalem has not yet occurred as noted in Revelation 11:1-2.

e. The literal 1,000-year reign of Christ has not yet occurred as noted in Revelation 20:1-7.

f. Satan has not yet been bound for 1,000 years as noted in Revelation 20:2.

g. We are not yet living in a New Earth, New Heaven and New Jerusalem as noted in Revelation 21:1-2.

Do you recall the story that took place on the road to Emmaus found in Luke 24:25-27 where the resurrected Christ walked with two disgruntled disciples? He said to them, "'O foolish ones, and slow of heart to believe in all that the prophets have spoken! Ought not the Christ to have suffered these things and to enter into His glory?' And beginning at Moses and all the Prophets, He expounded to them in all the Scriptures the things concerning Himself." Once we realize that you and I are like the disciples on the road to Emmaus, our eyes will open, and God will reveal His Beloved Son to us in a stunning way as we take this journey together.

Stand firm, open your hearts, be in prayer, read on and anticipate goodness and mercy in your life, knowing that God Almighty, "El Elyon" in Hebrew, has not only declared Christ victorious, but has also anointed you as a priest and declared you as royalty in His kingdom now and forever! (I Peter 2:6-9).

This book was not written so that we may simply acquire knowledge, puffing us up with a prideful attitude. It was not written for us to feel secure about our salvation, and yet at the same time, act with indifferent and calloused hearts toward those who don't know Christ. It was written so that we may be filled with the Spirit of Wisdom and Understanding, the Spirit of Counsel and Might, the Spirit of Knowledge of our Christ, and the Spirit of the Fear of the Lord. It was written to inspire us in pursuing a deeper relationship with Christ. It was written so we would be overwhelmed with God's blessings that will not only fill up our cup without measure but will also run over so that we may bless those around us!

SECTION 1

YESTERDAY

Chapter 1
History, Mystery, Prophecy

The book of Revelation proclaims Jesus Christ in His glory. Christ crucified is Christ magnified. Christ rejected is Christ exalted. Christ in His sufferings is Christ the King of Kings. Christ the slain is Christ in His eternal reign. In this chapter, the Apostle John reveals to us the beauty, the deity, the loyalty and the ministry of Jesus Christ.

Revealing Christ

1:1 The Revelation of Jesus Christ, which God gave Him to show His servants — things which must shortly take place. And He sent and signified it by His angel to His servant John.

The Apostle John is Pastor John, prophet John and poet John all in one, and he wrote Revelation in 95 AD, during the reign of Roman emperor Domitian. Throughout our journey in Revelation, it is my priority to present Jesus, see Him as the central figure of all life and kingdoms, proclaim His goodness, declare His supremacy, and bow down in awe of His splendor. It is not my duty to identify the Antichrist by name or turn over every rock to find the son of perdition. I cannot emphasize this enough: this book is not the Revelation of John or the Revelation of the Antichrist; it is the Revelation of Jesus Christ.

As we dig deeper, our primary aim is not to be enlightened about Bible prophecy. Our main purpose is to encounter Jesus Christ personally.

In 95 AD, Domitian may have been on an earthly throne and viciously persecuting Christians, but John reminds his readers that it is Jesus Christ who is truly on the eternal throne and He is the Comforter and the Ruler of all ages. In fact, in our days, we may be shocked at the political storms that seemingly change by the second, but be of good cheer: Christ was, is and will always be in control and will one day take the reins out of man's greedy hands and carnal hearts, and then, He will rightfully reign for Eternity.

The Apostle Paul presents Jesus Christ in a humble manner in Philippians 2:5-8, where Christ is seen as a servant, making Himself of no reputation. "Let this mind be in you which was also in Christ Jesus, Who, being in the form of God, did not consider it robbery to be equal with God, but made Himself of no reputation, taking the form of a bondservant, and coming in the likeness of men. And being found in appearance as a man, He humbled Himself and became obedient to the point of death, even the death of the cross." Mark this down: this lowly image of Jesus will not be the Jesus you see in the book of Revelation!

While on earth, Jesus grew in wisdom, stature and favor according to Luke 2:52. So too will we grow in grace and be in awe of the glory of Christ as we study this book together. Jesus died and rose from the dead. Though He is God, He has not abandoned His humanity, and according to Hebrews 4:15-16, He remains our compassionate High Priest. He is like us in that He personally relates to us. Don't despair. Don't quit. Don't give up hope. Don't bow your head in defeat. Not now! Not ever! There is a God who became man, and understands all of your shortcomings, sins, habits, brokenness, heartaches and disappointments. Come, and see Christ as He is; your advocate, your warrior, your Savior, your strength and your very hope. He will conquer. He will rule. He will vindicate. He will make all things new!

The revelation of Christ is given to Him by God the Father. Yes, it is given to Jesus! As mentioned in the Preface, the word "revelation" in the Greek is "apokalypsis," that has the meaning of laying bare, making naked, uncovering, disclosing the truth concerning things that were unknown before, manifesting, appearing and coming. Today, when we hear the term "apocalypse," we think of a large-scale catastrophic event that happens to humanity and nature, bringing us to the end of the world. When Jesus appears in the Rapture to take His followers home, the world as we know it will spin on its axis for one "last week," or its last seven years, as stated in Daniel's 9:27 prophecy, facing one tragedy after the other.

God gives the revelation directly to Jesus, not to John. This is important. Jesus receives this revelation and continues to pass it down. Why would God give Jesus the revelation? So that Jesus may "show his servants things which must shortly take place." The order of the revelation starts with God, is handed off to Jesus, then to an angel, then to John, then to His servants which include the seven local churches, then to saints of all times; and finally to us. This last book of the Bible was not written to conceal mysterious symbols; it was written to reveal the end times, to point out our place in Eternity and to magnify the ruling and forever reign of our King, Jesus Christ.

This teaching did not come from man. It came from God. In Galatians 1:1, we read, "Paul, an apostle, not from men nor through man, but through Jesus Christ and God the Father who raised Him from the dead." The revelation of Jesus is not through human intelligence or teachings; it is through God, graciously giving us full disclosure of His Son and what is to come at the end of the age. As Jesus indicated in John 14:16, the revelation comes through the Holy Spirit, "When He, the Spirit of truth, has come, He will guide you into all truth; for He will not speak on His authority, but whatever He hears He will speak; and He will tell you things to come. He will glorify Me, for He will take of what is Mine and declare it to you."

One cannot move the goal post of truth, although it seems history is being deliberately re-written by "enlightened minds." The truth is the truth and even if attempts are made to alter it to ease the conscience of mankind, it will still remain the truth. "But the natural man does not receive the things of the Spirit of God, for they are foolishness to him; nor can he know them, because they (the things of the Spirit of God) are spiritually discerned" (I Corinthians 2:14). Holy Spirit, guide us, instruct us, give us discernment, understanding and counsel, and pour out Your wisdom on us as we study Your Word!

When John says these things that are written "must" shortly take place, what does he mean? We look to Isaiah to interpret this matter. God speaks to the obstinate in Israel before their exile to Babylon, "Remember this, and show yourselves men; recall to mind, O you transgressors. Remember the former things of old, for I am God, and there is no other; I am God, and there is none like Me, declaring the end from the beginning, and from ancient times things that are not yet done, saying, 'My counsel shall stand, and I will do all My pleasure'" (Isaiah 46:8-10). What God has decreed for the end of days will occur. It cannot be altered. It cannot not be averted. God's sovereign plan cannot be stopped!

Approximately 2,000 years have passed since John penned this book; how then can it be said that these things must "shortly" take place? The word "shortly" in the Greek is "tachos." The English word "tachometer" stems from the Greek, meaning to measure the working speed of an engine in revolutions per minute. In our text, "shortly" means quickly, speedily, in haste, where the completion of God's purpose at the end of ages will accelerate rapidly on earth's time-meter. We read in Psalm 90:4, "For a thousand years in Your sight are like yesterday when it is past, and like a watch in the night." Peter reiterates this in II Peter 3:8, "But, beloved, do not forget this one thing, that with the Lord one day is as a thousand years, and a thousand years as one day." In the Lord's eyes, two days (two thousand years for us) have passed since John wrote the book of Revelation! The future events mentioned, once underway, will unfold swiftly and uninterruptedly, transpiring in rapid sequence.

God "signified" His message, in the Greek, "Semaino," meaning to make known, to give a sign, to indicate. Why would God reveal His Word in so many symbols during John's time? There are several reasons:

1. Avoid. To avoid further persecution of the church because the Roman soldiers would likely confiscate this writing and be confused by the symbols, dismissing John as a madman.

2. Aspire. To aspire further investigation as there are over 500 Old Testament symbols that appear in the book of Revelation. These symbols convey the truths of the Old Testament and reveal the glory of Christ.

3. Arouse. To arouse further longing for God's truth as images of seals, horns, fire and beasts stimulate one's devotion to knowing God, being devoted to Him daily.

An angel reveals the prophecy to John. John, therefore, transcribes what he hears and what he sees, a truth which is in line with scripture, II Peter 1:21, "For prophecy never came by the will of man, but holy men of God spoke as they were moved by the Holy Spirit." God's Word is inspired. His Word is infallible. His Word is satisfying to the soul. Be encouraged as you read on!

***1:2** who bore witness to the word of God, and to the testimony of Jesus Christ, to all things that he saw.*

John bore witness to these truths. He witnessed it, recorded it, and was guided by the Holy Spirit to present it to the seven local churches. John will continually proclaim throughout his writings that Christ may have been rejected by man and was slain on the cross, but He will eventually be victorious over His foes and will govern forever as the sovereign ruler over all kings.

What is recorded is inerrant because "In the beginning was the Word, and the Word was with God, and the Word was God" (John 1:1). The very theme of the book is the Word, Jesus Christ; this is prophesied in Psalm 40:7, "Then I said, 'Behold, I (Jesus Christ) come; in the scroll of the book it is written of Me." According to Luke 18:31, "All things that are written by the prophets concerning the Son of Man will be accomplished." Jesus said to His disciples, "These are the words which I spoke to you while I was still with you, that all things must be fulfilled which were written in the Law of Moses and the Prophets and the Psalms concerning Me" (Luke 24:44).

1:3 Blessed is he who reads and those who hear the words of this prophecy, and keep those things which are written in it; for the time is near.

Blessed is the one who reads this book (Revelation), hears the reading of this book, and keeps the words of this book. No other book in the Bible has this promise! If by blessed we mean "happy," which the Greek word "makarios" indicates, then surely someone can be happy by celebrating a birthday, or having their team win the World Series or the World Cup. By extension, "makarios" can also mean fortunate or well off. Instead of happy, fortunate or well off, I believe "rewarded" would be the best explanation for "blessed." The Word of God has eternal significance: eternally rewarded are those who hear it, read it and keep it!

His Word is written and spoken for all to understand. Jeremiah was instructed by God accordingly, "Thus says the Lord, 'Stand in the court of the Lord's house, and speak to all the cities of Judah, which come to worship in the Lord's house, all the words that I command you to speak to them. Do not diminish a word'" (Jeremiah 26:2).

During His First Coming as a man, Jesus made it clear to the Pharisees in John 8:43-47 why they and anyone of this current age do not understand the Word, "Why do you not understand My speech? Because you are not able to listen to My word. You are of your father the devil, and the desires of your father you want to do. He was a murderer from the beginning, and does not stand in the truth, because there is no truth in him. When he speaks a lie, he speaks from his own resources, for he is a liar and the father of it. But because I tell the truth, you do not believe Me. Which of you convicts Me of sin? And if I tell the truth, why do you not believe Me? He who is of God hears God's words; therefore, you do not hear, because you are not of God."

If you are reading and hearing these words, rejoice! You are able to listen to Jesus' words. You are choosing to fulfill the desires of your heavenly Father. You are able to stand in the truth. Not only do you know about the Father, but you believe Him, trust Him, love Him and worship Him. You listen to the conviction of the Holy Spirit. You are of God. And if not, I pray that you will come to know Jesus. Why? Because your Eternity is at stake!

Blessed are those who keep these words. "Keeping" in the Greek is "terao," meaning to handle it constantly, not passively, but actively living in the Word.

 When it comes to God's Word, keep in it, keep at it, keep after it, and keep on it.

That is your path to blessings and a life filled with supernatural joy. Doing the Word is keeping the Word. Desire it, devour it, decide to pursue it, dedicate time for it, and delight in it. We have an investment in this and an admonition, "Therefore, beloved, looking forward to these things, be diligent to be found by Him in peace, without spot and blameless" (II Peter 3:14). Wasted time will be regretted. Time spent in the Word will be rewarded.

 Facts about prophecy will not change your life. Time spent with Christ will.

What does John mean when he writes, "For the time is near?" The right and opportune time approaches. "From the perspective of prophetic anticipation, this period is declared to be near."[1]

When the fullness of time was come, God sent forth His Son 2,000 years ago (Galatians 4:4). When the fullness of time will come, God will initiate the events written in this book, starting with the Rapture. Christ's First Coming as a man was right on time. His Second Coming as King of Kings will be right on cue as He will return when the time is ripe. Concerning the Lord's Second Coming, which is seven years after the Rapture, and at the end of the Tribulation, James writes, "Therefore be patient, brethren, until the coming of the Lord. See how the farmer waits for the precious fruit of the earth, waiting patiently for it until it receives the early and latter rain. You also be patient. Establish your hearts, for the coming of the Lord is at hand" (James 5:7-8).

The time of the Rapture is imminent. The tragedies we see today are nothing compared to the chaos that will afflict the world after the Rapture. You definitely want to miss the Tribulation. But you certainly don't want to miss the Rapture. The question is, where will you be standing at the Rapture? Do you know the Jesus who is the focal point of the Revelation?

Jesus: Slain Savior, Sovereign Lord

1:4 John, to the seven churches which are in Asia: Grace to you and peace from Him who is and who was and who is to come, and from the seven Spirits who are before His throne.

John, the author, or more accurately, the transcriber, is writing the book about 95 AD to the seven local churches that he has overseen, shepherded and ministered to since 66 AD in Asia Minor, known as Turkey today.[2] He greets the congregations, imparting on them grace and peace.

 The members of these churches are not the only targeted audience; these words are as relevant today as they were 2,000 years ago and are directed at us not only for our ears to hear, but in our hearts to hold dear.

The number seven is used 735 times in the Bible including 54 times in the book of Revelation alone. If the words "sevenfold" (used six times) and "seventh" (used 119 times) are included, the total is 860 references to the number seven in the Bible. Seven is the number associated with the foundation of God's word, the number of completeness and perfection, tied directly to God's creation, the complete period of God's work of creating. God created in six days and rested on the seventh.[3]

The seven churches, mentioned in Revelation 1:11 and chapters two and three, represent all churches of all ages. The seven Spirits represent the complete and perfect omniscience, omnipresence and omnipotence of the Holy Spirit.[4] The seven seals, trumpets and bowls which we'll discuss in the ensuing chapters represent the completeness of God's worldwide judgment.[5] The word "created" is used seven times to describe God's handiwork (Genesis 1:1, 21, 27; 2:3, 4). There are seven days in a week and God's Sabbath is on the seventh day.

You cannot read the book of Revelation and miss the number seven:

1. Seven candlesticks or churches (Revelation 1:4, 12, 20).
2. Seven stars or angels (Revelation 1:16, 20).
3. Seven Spirits (Revelation 1:4).
4. Seven lamps of fire or of the Holy Spirit (Revelation 4:5).
5. Seven seals (Revelation 5:1).
6. Seven horns and seven eyes of the Lamb (Revelation 5:6).
7. Seven angels with seven trumpets (Revelation 8:2).
8. Seven thunders (Revelation 10:3)
9. Seven heads of the dragon and seven crowns (Revelation 12:3).
10. Seven heads of the Beast (Revelation 13:1).
11. Seven last plagues (Revelation 15:1).
12. Seven bowls (Revelation 15:7).
13. Seven mountains and kings (Revelation 17:9-10).
14. Sevenfold glory to the Lamb (Revelation 5:12).
15. Sevenfold glory to God (Revelation 7:12).

The number seven is significant in the Bible and especially Revelation.

According to Revelation 1:4, God imparts grace and peace to the believer. Grace is going to keep the believer out of the seven-year Tribulation as a result of the Rapture. Grace will also care for the unbeliever who will go through the Tribulation and turn to Christ. "How so," you ask? There will be the greatest revival the world has ever known during the Tribulation and millions of souls will come to Christ! That, dear reader, is grace, where God extends His love once again to those who have rejected Him in the past!

Only when we embrace grace can we then understand peace. In fact, without grace, there is no peace. If you are filled with anxiety, and long for peace, pursue God's grace, understand that He makes you righteous in Christ, that He does not condemn you, that He loves you, adores you, and embraces you. Know that His grace gives to you what you don't deserve. In fact, that is why so many Christians are anxious and worry. They rely on their own merit, strength, wisdom, experience, talents and understanding. When we abide in His grace, we rely on Him. And once we rely on Him, living and soaking in His grace, then we'll possess peace, which too is a gift. Jesus said, "Peace I leave with you; My peace I give to you; not as the world gives, do I give to you. Let not your heart be troubled, neither let it be afraid" (John 14:27).

Peace for the unbeliever will be of paramount importance during the Tribulation. For those who accept Christ, God will give them the peace to witness the wrath that is poured out on a God-rejecting, Christ-hating, Holy Spirit-bashing world. God will also give them the grace to face unmatched hatred as they are viciously targeted by the Antichrist.

Grace and peace come from Him who is, who was and who is to come. Who is John talking of? The Most-High God, El Elyon. Because He is the same yesterday, today and forevermore (Hebrews 13:8), everything for Him is seen through an eternal lens. According to Ecclesiastics 3:15, that which has been, is now; that which is to be, has already been. When Moses asked God for His name in Exodus 3:14, he heard God from the burning bush say, "I AM WHO I AM." He encompasses all things and all times, and though His saints were and are being martyred and anarchy is showing its ugly head, He is "already on His way and may arrive at any moment."[6]

Here lies the heart of the book: The Rapture is imminent! So why should we care if it's imminent? "Beloved, now we are children of God; and it has not yet been revealed what we shall be, but we know that when He (Christ) is revealed, we shall be like Him (not God, but sons and daughters of God), for we shall see Him as He is. And everyone who has this hope in Him purifies himself (lives a life worthy of God's calling), just as He is pure" (I John 3:2-3).

 Imminency trumps apathy, avoids living destructively, helps us love God intimately, stirs us to serve humanity and inspires purity!

Grace and peace not only come from God, but also come from the "seven Spirits who are before God's throne." The seven Spirits are the illumination or characteristics of the Holy Spirit. We will see this image again in Revelation 4:5, where the Holy Spirit is in the presence of God's throne. We are introduced to the seven characteristics of God's Spirit in Isaiah 11:2. There is only one Holy Spirit, with seven attributes. Here are six: the Spirit of Wisdom, the Spirit of Counsel, the Spirit of Under-standing, the Spirit of Might, the Spirit of Knowledge, and the Spirit of the Fear of the Lord.

When we count the attributes, we only see a total of six; commentators state that the seventh is the "Spirit of the Lord" mentioned in Isaiah 11:2, and it may very well be, but it seems redundant to me. I believe the seventh characteristic is tucked away in Revelation 19:10b, "Worship God! For the testimony of Jesus is the Spirit of Prophecy." The Spirit of Prophecy makes sense since the Holy Spirit is our Advocate who admonishes, teaches, empowers and instructs. According to II Thessalonians 2:6-7, the Holy Spirit is restraining lawlessness from turning into ultimate chaos until the Rapture occurs, "And now you know what is restraining, that he (Antichrist) may be revealed in his own time (during the Tribulation). For the mystery of lawlessness is already at work; only He (Holy Spirit) who now restrains will do so until He is taken out of the way."

 Today's political unrest is minuscule compared to what will be seen in the Tribulation. God will "Rev It Up," pouring out His judgments upon man. Pandemonium will metastasize. Persecution will rise. Prophecy will be fulfilled. Pride of man will be stilled.

1:5 and from Jesus Christ, the faithful witness, the firstborn from the dead, and the ruler over the kings of the earth. To Him who loved us and washed us from our sins in His own blood

John continues to tell us that grace and peace not only come from the Father and the Holy Spirit, but also from Jesus Christ, all three persons making up the Holy Trinity. Jesus said, "Do you not believe that I am in the Father, and the Father in Me? The words that I speak to you I do not speak on My own authority; but the Father who dwells in Me does the works; I and the Father are one" (John 10:30; 14:10). Jesus' divinity will be in full display in this book. We read in John 1:17, "For the law was given through Moses, but grace and truth came through Jesus Christ." We also read in Colossians 3:15, "Let the peace of Christ rule in your hearts." Do you find yourself anxious about events that have not yet occurred? Cast all your cares on Christ because He cares for you! (I Peter 5:7).

In this verse John depicts Christ as the "Faithful Witness." In Revelation 19:11, Jesus is called the "Faithful and True." According to Numbers 23:19, "God is not a man, that He should lie, nor a son of man, that He should repent. Has He said, and will He not do? Or has He spoken, and will He not make it good?" God is proved right when He speaks, and it is impossible for Him to lie (Hebrews 6:18) and God is true while every man a liar (Romans 3:4).

When Jesus became a man, He provided the perfect witness of the true God for mankind. "And the Word became flesh (Jesus born in Bethlehem) and dwelt among us, and we beheld His glory, the glory as of the only begotten of the Father, full of grace and truth" (John 1:14). How is Jesus Christ the faithful witness? Because all that we need to know about God is revealed through Christ. He said to Philip, "Anyone who has seen me has seen the Father" (John 14:9). You can't know God without knowing His Son. You can't love God without loving His Son. You can't come to God without going through His Son! Why? Because Jesus is not only the Faithful Witness revealing God, He is the only Way to God!

Why does John call Christ the "firstborn from the dead?" To

date, Christ is the only one who ever died and resurrected in His glorified body, forever imperishable. "Jesus is the image of the invisible God, the firstborn over all creation" (Colossians 1:15). That does not mean that Jesus was the first of God's creation. That means that Jesus is the first in position in the Father's economy. God called Himself "I AM." Jesus said "I AM" the Bread, the Light, the Way, the Truth and the Life. Jesus also proclaimed, "I am the Resurrection and the Life," and three days after His death, He made good His word and validated His claim by being the first to rise from the dead, and ascended to heaven. Jesus is the firstborn from the dead so that "in all things He may have the preeminence" (Colossians 1:18).

We should remember that John was writing to the persecuted churches. He is letting believers know that despite their imprisonment, being burned in cauldrons of searing oil, being fed to lions, being unfairly targeted and inhumanely treated, that their Savior, who was brutally beaten, crucified and killed, lives and waits to welcome them into His Kingdom!

In Revelation 1:5, we see that Jesus is rightfully the "ruler over the kings of the earth." It may not seem like it when we hear Middle Eastern rulers proclaim death to America and Israel, but the prophet Daniel proclaimed Christ's sovereignty in Daniel 7:13-14, "I was watching in the night visions, and behold, One like the Son of Man (Jesus), coming with the clouds of heaven! He came to the Ancient of Days (God), and they brought Him (Jesus) near before Him (God). Then to Him (Jesus) was given dominion and glory and a kingdom, that all peoples, nations, and languages should serve Him. His dominion is an everlasting dominion, which shall not pass away, and His kingdom the one which shall not be destroyed." "And in the days of these kings (earthly kings) the God of heaven will set up a kingdom (of Christ) which shall never be destroyed; and the kingdom shall not be left to other people; it shall break in pieces and consume all these kingdoms, and it shall stand forever" (Daniel 2:44). Just in case we think that Jesus is ineffective in today's modern world, we need to read Proverbs 21:1, "The king's heart is in the hand of the Lord, like the rivers of water; He turns it wherever He wishes." There is coming a day when Christ will no longer tolerate or extend His mercy to a God-hating, Christ-bashing and Holy Spirit-denying world. We're not far off. We're in overtime and the whistle or trumpet will soon sound.

Jesus is not simply an historic figure who once was alive and tragically died. He is not simply a humble prophet riding on a donkey on Palm Sunday. He is not simply an eloquent teacher who spoke God's Word. He was brutally crucified on a cross and is now risen from the dead. He is alive. And when He returns, all forces, all enemies, all mockers, all skeptics, all the religious and all of mankind from the creation of the world until then will bow before Christ!

 Jesus will rule for all Eternity. There will be no recounts. There will be no independent counsel's investigation as to a "collusion." There will be no FBI inquiry into who gave Jesus the right to be on the throne. Love it or hate it; accept it or reject it; receive it or repeal it; it's gonna happen!

We're only in the fifth verse of the very first chapter of the book of Revelation, and John introduces the blood of Jesus, stating, "To Him who loves us and washed us from our sins in His own blood." To circumvent, modify or ignore this truth is not only negligent but also tragic. You and I cannot have eternal life without the precious blood spilled on our behalf. We can hang up diplomas. We can ride in our new cars. We can hire a shrink to justify our past. We can read self-help books to reach new heights. But we cannot clean our own souls. Only the cross. Only the blood. Only the death and life of Christ!

In all His majesty, His authority, His divinity, Christ loved and died for the whole world selflessly. Christ loved us (and is loving us), not after we became "right or good." He loved us while we were yet sinners; and it was then, in the midst of our shame, our arrogance, our addictions, our lies and our brokenness that Christ died for us. Don't believe for a second that love means we first loved Him; divine love means that He first loved us (I John 4:10). And if Christ loved us while we were dying in our sins, how much more now?

This is the Good News! I know we fail and are critical of ourselves. But it is not about us and our failures. It is about our Father, and His unending, unreserved, unbreakable and unlimited love for us! We read in Colossians 1:12-14, "Giving thanks to the Father who has qualified us to be partakers of the inheritance of the saints in the light. He has delivered us from the power of darkness and conveyed us into the kingdom of the Son of His love, in whom we have redemption through His blood, the forgiveness of sins." It's one thing to create the stars and name each and every one of them; it's another thing to love broken humanity like you and me unconditionally! (Psalm 147:3-4).

Scripture describes God's love eloquently, "For when we were still without strength, in due time Christ died for the ungodly. For scarcely for a righteous man will one die; yet perhaps for a good man someone would even dare to die. But God demonstrates His own love toward us, in that while we were still sinners, Christ died for us. Much more then, having now been justified by His blood, we shall be saved from wrath through Him. For if when we were enemies we were reconciled to God through the death of His Son, much more, having been reconciled, we shall be saved by His life" (Romans 5:6-10). This is a powerful promise that we should always remember.

In His First Coming, Christ died in obedience and in love to save a wretch like you or me. That's a priceless gift. What man does with it is up to him. In His Second Coming at the end of the Tribulation, Christ will pour out His wrath on those who cursed His name, rejected His love, and trampled on His grace.

The gift stands, but since we're in overtime, there is not much time left to make a decision. Take it or leave it. If you take it, you will see Him face to face and bask in His glory eternally. If you leave it, you will mourn your decision.

When my patients present to the emergency room with chest pains, one of the first things our medical team does after questioning them and getting a full history is order a blood panel. The blood will "speak" and point us in the right direction. Is it a heart attack? Is it indigestion? Is it pancreatitis (inflammation of the pancreas)? Is it a pneumonia? If a patient is sluggish and tired, we order a thyroid panel to check thyroid levels, a blood count to check if he is anemic, a metabolic panel to check for diabetes and kidney disease. If numbers don't lie, then the blood "speaks" the truth.

The Bible states that the life of a creature is in the blood (Leviticus 17:11). God created it this way before time began and documented it 3,500 years ago in His Word. I love science and consider myself blessed to study it and apply its findings to better the life of my patients. But it's worth noting that it wasn't until the 1900s that scientists made the discovery about the importance of blood and stopped bleeding people (like they did our first President, George Washington, contributing to his death) and started transfusing people!

May I add that our brain is very small compared to the universe? And God is big enough to create the universe and gracious enough to craft our brains. It is He who gives man the mind for inventions using physical laws that govern the universe. But in the end, man's greatest knowledge is but foolishness to God. I share this to show the importance of God's Word, the frailty of man and the significance of His blood.

In what way do you think Jesus' blood is different than

man's? Let me explain. Jesus was in Mary's womb. In the womb, a mother supplies the child nutrition and receives his waste, but no blood is exchanged. Jesus did not have Mary's blood. Since there were no physical relations between Mary and Joseph, and Jesus was born of the Holy Spirit, Jesus does not have Joseph's blood. Therefore, the blood of Jesus is not marked with sin as ours is with Adam's.

When we accept the shed blood of Christ, the blood of the Lamb, we are completely made righteous. Jesus did not sin, He knew no sin, and in Him was no sin. Yet He became sin by taking on our sin, so that we may take on His righteousness and become the righteousness of God in Christ (II Corinthians 5:21).

 You can choose rejection, religion or a relationship. Rejection requires intellectual pride. Religion requires steadfast pride. Relationship with Christ requires a death to pride.

When you are under the blood of Christ and go to Him and say, "I messed up again, I'm sorry Lord." I am convinced He says, "Again? I don't remember you doing it in the first place!" That is not cheap grace. That's the power of His blood. That is the result of the blood of the Lamb! As far as the East is from the West, He has removed our sins from us (Psalm 103:12). Christ will not remember our sins if we are in Him (Hebrews 8:12). In Christ Jesus, we who once were far off, have been brought near by the blood of Christ (Ephesians 2:13).

 Because of Christ's finished work at Calvary, we are washed from our stains and we are loosed from our chains. There is no condemnation that weighs us down; there is redemption that lifts us up.

There are, however, consequences for our actions and we don't have the license to live in disobedience. In summary, a Gospel without the blood of the Lamb is the bloodless gospel of Cain who offered an unacceptable sacrifice to God, producing an ineffective, hopeless and lifeless gospel. The blood of Christ washes. The blood of Christ forgives. The blood of Christ gives hope. The blood of Christ gives eternal life.

1:6 *and has made us kings and priests to His God and Father, to Him be glory and dominion forever and ever. Amen.*

Herein lies the great substitution. Jesus takes our place on the cross and accepts God's wrath for our sins (I Peter 2:24). We take His place and sit at the right hand of the Father in the heavenly realms with Christ and in Christ (Ephesians 2:6).

There was a king of Judah in II Chronicles 26:16 named Uzziah who made a grave mistake due to pride, "But when he was strong his heart was lifted up, to his destruction, for he transgressed against the Lord his God by entering the temple of the Lord to burn incense on the altar of incense." What was his mistake? Only the priests, the sons of Aaron, were consecrated to burn incense. And because of his transgressions, King Uzziah became a leper, was cut off from the house of the Lord, dwelt in an isolated house, and died as a leper.

The king could not be a priest nor the priest a king. But because of the cross and the blood of the Lamb, Christ has made us both a king and a priest. We are therefore in the royalty and priestly ministry because we are in Christ! John is speaking to the imprisoned, to the brutally persecuted, and is subtly telling them to stand fast, stand firm, and stand tall.

 Things may be rotten for you right now, but remember this: you are a people of great destiny; your Redeemer has given you authority; do not forsake your ministry!

Remember this, loved ones, no matter how overwhelming life has become, no matter how difficult the tide, no matter how wrenching that feeling in your gut, we have a calling to be priests and kings; we are adorned with garments of salvation and purity; we are called to persevere in our earthly bodies and ministries; and one day we will rule on behalf of Christ in glorified bodies. Our present condition does not accurately express our future fulfillment, but make no mistake, our God has spoken, and it will come to pass. When I complain to my Father in heaven, He reminds me that "the sufferings of this present time are not worthy to be compared with the glory which shall be revealed" in you (Romans 8:18). I argue and say, "But how about now, Papa?" He smiles and says, "My child, as you walk through the valley of tears, of fears, of lies, of hardships and of 'unanswered prayers,' I am with you and My grace will carry you!"

The Bible scholar Seiss wrote, "There is not a believer, however obscure or humble, who may not rejoice in princely blood, who does not already wield a power which the potencies of hell cannot withstand, and who is not on the way to possess eternal priesthood and dominion."[7] It was Peter, the fisherman, who walked with Christ. It was Matthew, the tax collector, who spoke His words. It was John, who had no accolades, who was given the privilege to take care of Jesus' mother after Jesus returned to heaven and who wrote the book of Revelation. It is you and I, chosen to perform abundant works for God, in the name of Christ, and by the power of the Holy Spirit. We too, in spite of ourselves, have an amazing calling of being crowned kings and priests today, tomorrow and for Eternity. May our conversations, our conduct and our character support our position.

Revelation 1:6 ends with the phrase, "To Him be glory and dominion forever and ever. Amen" and testifies that Jesus is God. How so? In Isaiah 48:11 God declares that He will not give His glory to anyone. "For how should My name be profaned? And I will not give My glory to another." Because this sixth verse proclaims that to Christ be glory and dominion forever and ever, and God will not share His glory with anyone, Christ is God!

1:7 Behold, He is coming with clouds, and every eye will see Him, even they who pierced Him. And all the tribes of the earth will mourn because of Him. Even so, Amen.

If you were reading a mystery, you would not find this seventh verse till the end of the book. It is the climax which we'll find in chapters 19-22, yet John is unable to restrain himself and shouts it out from the rooftops, "Christ is coming back!" John skips the Rapture, the Tribulation, Armageddon and goes right to the Second Coming of Christ in this verse. I can imagine John saying, "Let me make sure you understand; Christ is coming back! I know you are ostracized; I know you are heartbroken; I know you are on the verge of giving up; I know the numbers don't add up; I know you have not received what you have asked for; I know you are lonely; I too am stuck here on the God forsaken rocky and barren Island of Patmos because I was proclaiming God's Word! But hold! Don't give up, don't cave in; believe the Lord's compassions never fail; be confident of this, He is coming back! And He will make all things new, for the better, forever!"

Even if you think that everything is going "right" in life and you are riding the crest of the rainbow, all is not right; if you are truthful, you feel an emptiness deep in your soul, saying "Something is terribly missing." According to Ecclesiastes 3:11, God has placed Eternity in our hearts and we desperately long to be with Him. Many of you are in the middle of a trial, foreclosure, failure, shortage, chemotherapy, accusation or addiction. There is no minimizing your pain, your dilemma or your lack, but be assured, Christ is coming back! That is what I long for, and thirst for. That's when all things will finally be right. All things will be restored, renewed and reckoned when He comes back. It gets even better for the believer, who has the privilege to forego the Tribulation, meet the Lord in the Rapture, enjoy his presence for seven years, and return with Him in the Second Coming. The Rapture is our blessed hope as noted in Titus 2:13, "Looking for the blessed hope and glorious appearing of our great God and Savior Jesus Christ."

As this verse states, He is coming with clouds. There are over five hundred Old Testament illustrations and images that appear in the book of Revelation, clouds being one of them. As we see in the book of Exodus, clouds are associated with the glory and the presence of the Lord, "Now it came to pass, as Aaron spoke to the whole congregation of the children of Israel, that they looked toward the wilderness, and behold, the glory of the Lord appeared in the cloud" (Exodus 16:10). When God led His children out of Egypt and into the wilderness for forty years, a cloud led them by day and fire by night (Exodus 13:21). When Solomon built his temple, the glory of God was like a cloud filling the temple (II Chronicles 7:1). Today's clouds that loom over us are a bit different. Morals are deteriorating, cultural norms are collapsing, and churches are compromising. Don't look down. Don't look around. Don't look within. Look up. And call on the name of the Lord.

In Daniel 7:13, the prophet stated, "I was watching in the night visions, and behold, One like the Son of Man, coming with the clouds of heaven! He came to the Ancient of Days, and they brought Him near before Him. Then to Him was given dominion and glory and a kingdom, that all peoples, nations, and languages should serve Him. His dominion is an everlasting dominion, which shall not pass away, and His kingdom the one which shall not be destroyed." The Second Coming of Christ with the clouds of heaven was prophesied seven hundred years prior to John's writing. Domitian may have been the emperor with an iron fist during John's time, but there will be One coming in the clouds, Jesus Christ, who will rule with peace and equity.

 With justice, He will vindicate. With righteousness, He will dictate. With loving-kindness, He will administrate. With fury, He will infuriate and incarcerate Satan.

Many are unable to differentiate between the Rapture and the Second Coming of Christ, and some think it is one and the same. They are two separate events, starting with the Rapture, as the next major event in prophetic history, followed by a seven-year span known as the Tribulation, culminating with the Second Coming. Jesus appears in the air at the Rapture whereas Jesus will set His foot on planet earth at the Second Coming. "It has been estimated that one out of every twenty-five verses in the New Testament refers to the Second Coming."[8]

In I Thessalonians, chapter 4:13-18, we read about the Rapture, "But I do not want you to be ignorant, brethren, concerning those who have fallen asleep, lest you sorrow as others who have no hope. For if we believe that Jesus died and rose again, even so God will bring with Him those who sleep in Jesus. For this we say to you by the word of the Lord, that we who are alive and remain until the coming of the Lord will by no means precede those who are asleep. For the Lord Himself will descend from heaven with a shout, with the voice of an archangel, and with the trumpet of God. And the dead in Christ will rise first. Then we who are alive and remain shall be caught up together with them in the clouds to meet the Lord in the air. And thus we shall always be with the Lord. Therefore, comfort one another with these words." In these verses, Paul is talking of the Rapture, when Christ will descend and those who have accepted Christ in the past and have died and those who have accepted Christ presently and are alive will be caught up in the air to meet the Lord.

Paul also writes about the Rapture in I Corinthians 15:51-53, "Behold, I tell you a mystery: We shall not all sleep, but we shall all be changed — in a moment, in the twinkling of an eye, at the last trumpet. For the trumpet will sound, and the dead will be raised incorruptible, and we shall be changed. For this corruptible must put on incorruption, and this mortal must put on immortality."

In the Rapture, the Lord will descend from heaven with a shout, with a voice of an archangel, and with the trumpet of God. We will be taken up along with all the New Testament saints who have passed away (asleep). Jesus comes for His Church, meets us in the air, and we will spend seven years with our Lord in heaven prior to His Second Coming.

We will face the Bema seat during this time found in I Corinthians 3:12-14, "Now if anyone builds on this foundation with gold, silver, precious stones, wood, hay, straw, each one's work will become clear; for the Day will declare it, because it will be revealed by fire; and the fire will test each one's work, of what sort it is. If anyone's work which he has built on it endures, he will receive a reward. If anyone's work is burned, he will suffer loss; but he himself will be saved, yet so as through fire."

The stage set for the Bema seat is not a period of judging the eternal destiny of the saints. Our sins were forever forgiven on the cross. This is the time to receive our crowns, and the works we have done for Jesus as a result of our love for Him will be counted at this time. In the meanwhile, the Tribulation will be occurring on earth for seven years, and yes, this will be a time of "hell on earth" (Revelation chapters six through nineteen).

In the Second Coming, Jesus does not come *for* His Church, He comes *with* His Church to save the nation of Israel. In the Rapture, we will be caught up *in* the clouds. In the Second Coming, He is coming *with* clouds. The prophet foretold in Zechariah 12:10 regarding the Second Coming, "And I will pour on the house of David and on the inhabitants of Jerusalem the Spirit of grace and supplication; then they will look on Me whom they pierced. Yes, they will mourn for Him as one mourns for his only son and grieve for Him as one grieves for a firstborn." Jesus will come with His Church, the Campaign of Armageddon will unfold, the Jewish people, who have fled to Petra during the last half of the Tribulation, will turn to Him and cry out in anguish. Just as Joseph's brothers, who sold

Joseph to Ishmaelite slave traders to die, turned to him after many years and cried, the Jews, who gave Jesus up to die, will turn to Him and cry, beating their breasts, as they see the One whom they pierced! The Gentiles too will cry and mourn, realizing the only truth in life was, is and will always be Jesus Christ. Why weep? Because all will clearly realize that the King does not belong on the cross; He belongs on the throne! On His throne He will be for all Eternity!

The Second Coming is not intended to seek revenge on Israel; it is to save the remnant of Israel. It is, however, the final blow to the careers of the Antichrist and the False Prophet. It finally ushers in the reign of Christ on earth.

Today, if you are bought by the blood of the Lamb, but are facing difficult times, take heart. You may not be happy and you know it, and you're not in the mood for clapping your hands or stomping your feet, but your King is on His way and you will soon be Raptured; your tears, your lack, your addiction, your worries, your fears, your weaknesses and your shame will all be left behind!

For the Jews and the rest of the Gentiles who have not accepted Christ as their Savior, their time on earth will definitely be a taste of hell for seven years. If you look on the bright side, you will still have the opportunity to accept Christ. That would not be "plan A," but if you insist on staying, make sure you never take the 666 mark of the Beast, which is an irrevocable sentence to eternal hell. If you reject the 666, your life on earth will likely be one of a martyr. But that's a "small price" to pay, as it will lead to eternal life with Jesus Christ. This is your warning. Don't cry out and mourn with those people described in this verse when they realize the truth that only Jesus saves!

1:8 *"I am the Alpha and the Omega, the Beginning and the End," says the Lord, "who is and who was and who is to come, the Almighty."*

The title "the Alpha and the Omega, the Beginning and the End" is applied to both the Father (Revelation 21:6) and the Son (Revelation 1:8, 22:13), indicating once again that Jesus is God. Alpha is the first letter in the Greek alphabet and omega is the last letter. God's existence spans pre-time, today in the midst of time, and post-time. God exists outside of what we know as time. The original Greek text has the word "alpha" plainly written out in letters, but the word "omega" is only the symbol, Ω, meaning there is no ending to our God.

In Isaiah 44:6, we hear God, the King of Israel, the Redeemer of Israel and the Lord of Hosts refer to Himself, "I AM the first and I AM the last, and there is no God besides Me." God is known as the Almighty, El Shaddai, and the first mention of this title is found in the Old Testament. God appeared to Abraham in Genesis 17:1 and called Himself El Shaddai.

 El Shaddai is the Almighty, the One who is able to deliver in the midst of bareness, brokenness, and bewilderment.

When Sarah conceived and bore Abraham a son, Isaac, she was 90 years old and he was 99 years old, a miraculous feat orchestrated solely by the hands of El Shaddai.

It is worth emphasizing again that Jesus is God. Isaiah 9:6 states, "For unto us a Child is born, unto us a Son is given, and the government shall be upon His shoulders, and His name shall be wonderful, counselor, the Almighty God, and the Prince of Peace." Jesus is called Almighty God as is His Father. Both are deity, both are divine, and both are equally God. God Himself became man and took our place on the cross by dying for us. When Christ was arrested in the Garden of Gethsemane, His accusers were overwhelmed by His sovereignty, might and command when He said "I AM." This "simple" name, "I AM" was so powerful that its force literally knocked them down to the ground (John 18:6).

Through His title, El Shaddai, the Almighty God, what the Lord is saying to you despite your married life with challenges, single life with solitude, family quarrels, meager bank account, bad business deals, broken heart and sheer loneliness, He is El Shaddai, the Almighty, knowing the beginning from the end.

 For believers, the end is beyond good! Sorrows are gone! Heartaches are done! Tears are none! And victory in Christ is won!

He will place us at His side, as His bride, robed in righteousness. It is finally going to be well when He returns. We need only to believe and trust: first, believe who you are in Christ. You are priests and kings; second, simply trust Him, for not only does He know the beginning from the end, but everything in between. Believe it. Not only will it be well in the future, but in faith you and I can now say, "It is well in my soul!"

 Despite our frailties and Satan's constant attacks and accusations, our Almighty God longs for us to know that even when we are faithless, clueless, or lost, He is faithful, true, and in love with us.

May we remember not only who we are but, more importantly, whose we are in the Almighty, in El Shaddai, in God, Jesus Christ!

Encountering Christ

***1:9** I, John, both your brother and companion in the tribulation and kingdom and patience of Jesus Christ, was on the island that is called Patmos for the word of God and for the testimony of Jesus Christ.*

First, John identifies himself as our brother, not Saint John, not Pope John, not Apostle John, not privileged John, not most holy Reverend John, but Brother John. He is not impressed with himself and is aware of his inadequacy to have received the honor to present this revelation. Seiss wrote that "At the time of the vision, he was the only remaining apostle, and perhaps the only survivor of those with whom Christ had personally conversed. He was therefore the most interesting and exalted Christian then living upon the earth — most revered and venerable man. But he was as humble and meek as he was high in place."[9]

Second, John introduces himself as our companion in tribulation. Satan rages against Christians. The world's system, working as Satan's agent, follows in the same path. The word "tribulation" in the Greek language is "phlepsis," which means pressure. What would you do with a worthless chunk of coal? If there are tons and more tons of "phlepsis" or pressure, along with heat and time, the worthless coal will become transformed into a diamond gem. If you are feeling the heat and pressure, take heart: you are being made into a gem!

One day soon we will reign with Christ in His earthly kingdom during the Millennium for 1,000 years, but according to Acts 14:22, we must first go through many tribulations to enter the kingdom of God. "What good can tribulations and trials be?" you may ask. According to Romans 5:3-5, "But we also glory in tribulations, knowing that tribulation produces perseverance; and perseverance, character; and character, hope. Now hope does not disappoint, because the love of God has been poured out in our hearts by the Holy Spirit who was given to us."

Note, John is not talking about the seven-year Tribulation found in Revelation chapters six through nineteen, but tribulation as in life's daily burdens and hardships. Jesus alludes to this in John 16:33, "In this world you will have tribulation, but take heart, I have overcome the world."

In the Garden of Eden, God gave the deed of this world to man. Man (Adam and Eve) relinquished it to Satan. Because

Satan has free rule (with restrictions imposed by God) he capitalizes on his prize by creating strife, wars, accidents, illnesses, death, murders, rape, and tragedies. Why does God not get rid of all the evil now? Well, then, we'd have no freedom of choice in anything we say or do. We'd be programmed like robots. Where there is no choice, there is no love. We are all given a choice because we are all loved by God. You will never go wrong or regret choosing God, Jesus Christ! The only thing you'll regret is that you didn't choose Him earlier!

The tribulations both the godly and the ungodly face today are because Satan pours out his wrath on this world. The tribulation that the ungodly will face for seven years during the Tribulation is because God will pour out His wrath on an unbelieving, God-hating, Christ-rejecting, Holy Spirit-blaspheming world. God will not allow His children to be slammed from both sides of this equation, today life's tribulations versus the future seven-year Tribulation, and will therefore snatch away or Rapture His Church to heaven right before the seven-year Tribulation.

According to Tertullian, before John was exiled to the Island of Patmos, he was placed in a cauldron of boiling oil as a punishment for preaching the Word of God; it took a miracle for him to not only to survive but to surface unscathed.[10] Unscathed? Yes, just like the three men thrown into Nebuchadnezzar's fiery furnace who were not hurt (Daniel 3:25). John saw Jesus being crucified. He saw the betrayal, the denial, the brutal blows and the unjust sentencing of his Christ. He heard the resurrected Christ say, "Touch my wounded side." John is part of the body of Christ, the church, informing, encouraging, cheering, guiding and inspiring his fellow brothers and sisters while he himself was suffering.

How is John to minister to the churches, his brothers and sisters who were suffering at the time, as well as ministering to you and me today? He does not present himself as one of the "sons of thunder," when as a much younger man he wanted to call down fire from heaven on a village in Samaria. He has become the Apostle of Love! Jesus has transformed him through the trials and the tribulations of life, as He is doing to you and me. John is ministering while he is suffering. You and I should do the same.

 Before God can use us mightily, He will allow us to be hurt deeply.

History is full of examples. The prophet Ezekiel sat where his people sat in exile. The prophet Daniel was exiled as his people were exiled. The prophet Hosea was asked to marry a prostitute to imitate God's relationship with His people. God allows the trouble in our lives, not only to turn coal into diamonds, but that we may be able to comfort those who are deeply hurting (II Corinthians 1:3). Surely we are better able to understand and share the feelings of others as a result of our own troubles.

The V-formation of migrating birds can help us understand this further. The point bird, who is in the front, leads the way and exerts most of the energy. But when he gets tired, he will rotate back with another bird that will take the lead role while he gets refreshed. John is saying that flying solo isn't going to cut it. We're all in this together and we all need to chip in and play our role at the right time.

John is writing in the era where emperors such as Nero would light up his imperial gardens at night by burning Christians hung on posts like torches of fire, riding his chariots and jeering, "You're the light of the world!" John writes this verse to let his fellow believers who were being crucified upside down, dressed up in sheepskins (because Jesus was the Good Shepherd) and devoured by hungry lions, to hold fast. After Nero's death, Domitian, who was responsible for John's exile, also launched persecutions against both Christians and Jews. John wasn't in hiding; he was exiled and felt their pain.

In Revelation 1:9, John, our brother and companion in the tribulations of life, tells us that he "was on the island that is called Patmos for the Word of God and for the testimony of Jesus Christ." The Island of Patmos is ten miles long and five miles wide, located in the Mediterranean Sea approximately 100 kilometers or 63 miles from Ephesus, Asia Minor.[11] It is shaped like a crescent, with its horns facing eastward, making it a safe place for vessels to anchor during storms; it was the last stopping place when traveling from Rome to Ephesus and the first stopping place on a return trip to Rome.[12] Being a rocky and barren place, without trees, rivers, nor any land for cultivation, it was chosen as a punitive settlement by the Romans.[13] Early Christian tradition states that John was sent to Patmos during Domitian's reign (AD 81-96) and was forced to work in mines; when Domitian died, John was permitted to return to Ephesus.[14] John did not find himself in an executive suite with an ocean-front view in a high-rise. He was likely subjected to hard labor up to fourteen hours daily. Sardined in the slave quarters and brutally treated, he may have been exiled up to ten years.

Why was he on the Island of Patmos? For the Word for God, meaning because of the Word of God. He preached and was therefore impeached. Yes, there was enough evidence against him to warrant his arrest as a Christ-follower. I sometimes wonder if there is enough evidence to convict us as Christ-followers.

 John was a man in the Word, of the Word, and for the Word.

Fausset wrote that "Restricted to a small spot on earth, he is permitted to penetrate the wide realms of heaven and its secrets. Thus, John drank of Christ's cup, and was baptized with His baptism."[15]

Why would God allow such a loving apostle to go through this tragedy? Because God is Jehovah Jireh, He is the God who provides, just as He provided the ram for Abraham to sacrifice rather than slay his own son, Isaac. Because God is Jehovah Rapah, He is the God who heals, just as He healed the bitter waters making them life-giving for the children of Israel in the wilderness.

What would you like God to provide for you? Ask Him. What would you like God to heal? Ask Him. Ask for His goodness, His mercy, His favor, His long-suffering, His healing touch, His loving embrace and His will. Ask, believe, and thank Him. Thank Him even if you still have symptoms or still suffer lack. Faith is being sure of what we hope for and certain of what we have not seen (Hebrews 11:1).

Moses did not part the Red Sea until he was trapped by the enemy. Shadrach, Meshach and Abednego did not see Jesus until they were hurled into the fire. Daniel was not saved until he was thrown into the lion's den. The lady with the history of uterine bleeding who touched the hem of Jesus' robe did not receive healing until she suffered with the condition for twelve years. John did not write the book of Revelation until he was banished to the Island of Patmos. When you walk with Jesus, no matter where you are, His peace will overwhelm your soul. We don't blame anyone for praying to get himself out of hardship. But it is in the hardship, the impossible and the pain when Jesus is so near!

 If we don't sense that Jesus is near, it's not that He is not present; it's that we are not in His presence.

John was on the Island of Patmos not only because he preached the Word of God and was therefore incarcerated, but "for the testimony of Jesus Christ." He was in the middle of crushing, fiery, heart-searing heat and pressure, "phlipsis," but he was about to see the King of Kings and Lord of Lords and share the beauty of Christ with us. Because of his testimony, we are able to draw nearer to our Christ.

That is why we go through trials. To have a revelation, a word from God, and a testimony. Truthfully, we don't want the trials. We like the comfortable, pleasant, vacation-like seasons of life. Who doesn't? But without a test, we won't have a testimony. If we stop grumbling, we will take our turn in front of the V-formation, we will take the heat, we will stare down the lions, and we will come out like a gem that not only shines in the light, but also comforts others who are facing immense suffering.

1:10 I was in the Spirit on the Lord's Day, and I heard behind me a loud voice, as of a trumpet,

Though John was not on a beach resort, there is a beauty in his imprisonment: receiving fresh revelation! We don't catch him complaining about being on a barren island. He is in the Spirit on the Lord's Day (not on the Day of the Lord). The Lord's Day is considered to be Sunday (Acts 20:7). The Day of the Lord is considered to be the end days or a period of time including the Rapture, Tribulation and the Millennial Kingdom. John may have been beaten on earth and found himself "down here" physically, but in his heart and soul, he was "up there" with the Lord.

To the dismay of some, I do believe that our Brother John was speaking, praying and singing in tongues, as Apostle Paul had suggested in I Corinthians 14:15, "What is the conclusion then? I will pray with the spirit, and I will also pray with the understanding. I will sing with the spirit, and I will also sing with the understanding."

In order to survive some ordeals in life, you must consider moving out of the rationalized and intellectual spectrum of your previous experience and start praying in the Spirit. This is a glorious place to find yourself in. It does no harm to self. It does no harm to others. You may be in prison, in pain, in perils but when you speak in tongues, you'll find yourself in the presence of the Lord!

A person in the flesh may have a heavy heart, a downcast mind, and plugged ears. But the one in the Spirit, will hear the voice of the Lord. That voice will carry him above his dreadful condition. Paul points to Christ as the source of revelations, "But I make known to you, brethren, that the gospel which was preached by me is not according to man. For I neither received it from man, nor was I taught it, but it came through the revelation of Jesus Christ" (Galatians 1:11-12). And as we will see throughout this book, Peter stated, "Prophecy never came by the will of man, but holy men of God spoke as they were moved by the Holy Spirit" (II Peter 1:21). John, being in the Spirit, discounting his surroundings and recognizing the realities of God, heard a loud voice, as of a trumpet; we'll hear what the voice said in the following verse.

1:11 *saying, "I am the Alpha and the Omega, the First and the Last," and, "What you see, write in a book and send it to the seven churches which are in Asia: to Ephesus, to Smyrna, to Pergamos, to Thyatira, to Sardis, to Philadelphia, and to Laodicea."*

In this verse, Jesus Christ is speaking, designating Himself as the Alpha and Omega, the First and the Last, and instructing John to write down what he witnesses and relay it to the seven local churches in Asia Minor.

In Psalm 90:2, Moses proclaimed regarding the Lord God, "Before the mountains were brought forth, or before You formed the earth and the world, even from everlasting to everlasting, You are God." There is only One God according to Isaiah 43:10, "Before Me there was no God formed, nor shall there be after Me." How then does this everlasting God pay attention to mere mortals like John and you and me? Isaiah answers our question, "For this says the High and Lofty One who inhabits Eternity, whose name is Holy, 'I dwell in the high and holy place, with him who has a contrite and humble spirit, to revive the spirit of the humble, and to revive the heart of the contrite ones" (Isaiah 57:15). David echoes Isaiah's words in Psalm 34:18, the Lord is close to the brokenhearted, and saves those who are crushed in spirit.

In the Old Testament, Habakkuk the prophet asked God some tough questions, "How long shall I cry, and You will not hear? Why do the unjust rule over the righteous? Why do You let the wicked get away with treachery?" In the second chapter, Habakkuk goes up a tower, stands watch, and has a scroll and pen in hand, ready to write, expecting God to give him a vision. And the Lord spoke, instructing Habakkuk to write down the revelation, "Though the vision I show you tarries, it will certainly come to pass; the enemy is puffed up and gathers nations as his captives; but woe to those who prospers by unjust gain, woe to those who shed human blood, woe to those who plot the ruin of others, woe to those who get their neighbors drunk to stare at their nakedness and woe to those who worship idols; their time of plunder approaches as God pours His wrath upon them; but the righteous shall live by faith!" (Habakkuk 2:1-20). The prophet answers in Habakkuk 3:2, "I stand in awe of Your deeds, Lord."

 When you don't expect to hear anything, you won't hear anything. But even in the hard times, dark times, and times of uncertainty, gear up, get a pen in hand, and expect God to speak to you! Expect to hear a revelation worth writing down. Expect God to do the impossible!

That's what John was told. The Lord will speak. Subsequently, John will hear and see visions. He not only records Christ's words to share with the churches, but he also records His words to instruct, inspire and encourage you and me 2,000 years later.

The seven churches existed literally and historically at the time of John's writing in 95 AD; they also prophetically characterize the entire 2,000 years of the Church Age, stages or periods spanning from 33 AD up to today.[16] The seven ages are as follows:

1. Ephesus ....Pretend Church (33 AD – 100 AD)
2. Smyrna............Persecuted Church (100 AD – 313 AD)
3. Pergamos.......Perverted Church (313 AD – 590 AD)
4. Thyatira ....Promiscuous Church (590 AD – 1517 AD)
5. Sardis..............Perished Church (1517 AD – 1790 AD)
6. Philadelphia..Patriotic Church (1730 AD – present)
7. Laodicea.........Passive Church (1900 AD – present)

Christ Glorified

1:12 Then I turned to see the voice that spoke with me. And having turned I saw seven golden lampstands, 1:13 and in the midst of the seven lampstands One like the Son of Man, clothed with a garment down to the feet and girded about the chest with a golden band.

John hears a voice and then turns to see that the One speaking is the Son of Man, found in the midst of the seven golden lampstands. The Son of Man is none other than Jesus Christ. The lampstands represent the seven local churches (Revelation 1:20) but they can also be representative of the people in the churches which we know as the church. Note that the church bears light, but the source of the light is Jesus Christ and not the churches. We know this because Jesus is found in their midst. John states, "In Him (Jesus) was life, and the life was the light of men. And the light shines in the darkness (the world), and the darkness did not comprehend it" (John 1:4-5). The One standing in the midst of the seven lampstands is the High Priest, Jesus Christ, who intercedes on our behalf. According to Hebrews 4:15-16, "For we do not have a High Priest who cannot sympathize with our weaknesses, but was in all points tempted as we are, yet without sin. Let us therefore come boldly to the throne of grace, that we may obtain mercy and find grace to help in time of need." Why seven churches? Because seven is the number of complete fulfillment; where Jesus is involved, it will always be whole and ultimately prove to be perfect and just.

Jesus *intervenes* for us, just as He did in the Upper Room when He took a towel and washed His disciples' feet. According to John 13:3-5, "Jesus, knowing that the Father had given all things into His hands, and that He had come from God and was going to God, rose from supper and laid aside His garments, took a towel and girded Himself. After that, He poured water into a basin and began to wash the disciples' feet, and to wipe them with the towel with which He was girded." He does for us what we are unable to do for ourselves.

Because He is in the midst of His Church, He also *inspects* and *instructs*. In Matthew 11:1, Jesus gave instructions to his disciples: "Now it came to pass, when Jesus finished commanding His twelve disciples, that He departed from there to teach and to preach in their cities."

In contrast to the Old Testament Menorah, made of a single central shaft to which six or eight branches were joined, John sees seven individual lampstands representing the actual historical churches as well as the symbolic church of today. John has shown us in the Gospel that Jesus, who is in the midst of the seven lampstands, is the source of light and life; "I am the light of the world. He who follows Me shall not walk in darkness but have the light of life" (John 8:12); "I am the vine and you are the branches. He who abides in Me, and I in him, bears much fruit; for without Me you can do nothing" (John 15:5). Some believe that separate lampstands represent the dispersion of the Jews around the world. Bullinger writes "So that just as the one lampstand represents Israel in its unity, the seven lampstands represent Israel in its dispersion; and tells us that

Jehovah is about to make Jerusalem again the center of His dealings with the earth."[17] In my view, the lampstands represent His Church, whether a person is Jew or Gentile, if he is in Christ, he is an integral part of the church and his light will shine throughout the world.

Many complain about the church because of hypocrites within its walls. But you must identify where Jesus stands: in the midst of His Church! Yes, there are hypocrites in the church. There are also hypocrites outside the church. In one way or another, we are all hypocrites. Simply, if you want the dog, you've got to take the fleas! Not one Christian is guiltless. Not one pastor is spotless. Not one man is righteous.

Since there were a myriad of churches during John's time, do you ever wonder why these specific seven churches? I believe God uses signs in the sky to tell us stories because He declared it in Genesis 1:14, "Let there be lights in the firmament of the heavens to divide the day from the night; and let them be for signs and seasons, and for days and years." I do not subscribe to astrology or horoscopes, believing it to be of Satan. I do believe in studying astronomy because the universe is God's creation. I do not worship the created, including the stars; I only worship one Creator, the triune God, Jesus Christ and the Holy Spirit.

The constellation Taurus (bull) has a cluster of stars designated as the Pleiades, known as the Seven Sisters. "Coincidently," the Taurus mountains are found in Asia Minor or Turkey, and in its outskirts stand the seven churches. Is this truly all a "coincidence?" I'll let Psalm 19 answer the question, "The heavens declare the glory of God; the skies proclaim the works of His hands. Day after day they pour forth speech. Night after night they display knowledge. There is no speech or language where their voice is not heard." Though there are more than 500 stars in Pleiades, there is a central star named Alcyone, that shines more brightly within the cluster of seven large stars. The image is likened to Jesus, the Light of the World, amongst the seven churches.[18]

Jesus is presented in Daniel 7:13 as the Son of Man; this title is one of the most frequently used titles Christ applied to Himself, depicting Him as human and approachable rather than a fearful supernatural being. When speaking of His Second Coming, Jesus said, "And you will see the Son of Man sitting at the right hand of the Power and coming with the clouds of heaven" (Mark 14:62). Though He is the Son of God, He relates to us on a personal level by calling Himself the Son of Man. As the Son of God, He is divine. As the Son of Man, he comes from the line of David, Abraham and Adam (Luke 3:31-38). As the Son of God, He is the Alpha and Omega, the Beginning and the End. As the Son of Man, He is our kinsman-redeemer, buying us out of the slave market of sin. According to I Timothy 2:5, "For there is one God and one mediator between God and men, the Man Christ Jesus," His divinity, virgin birth and sinless life providing the perfect means of atoning for our sins.

 The Son of God became a man, so that the sons of man can become sons and daughters of God.

In verse thirteen, the long robe Christ is wearing is typical of the garments the High Priest wore as he ministered in the Holy Place. The hem of the High Priest's robes was adorned with bells of gold. When a priest went into the Holy Place before the Lord, the absence of bell sounds would indicate the priest died and the Lord was displeased with him (Exodus 28:31-35). Jesus is the High Priest and will never die again; He has become a priest, not on the basis of his lineage or ancestry like Aaron, but on the basis of the power of an indestructible life (Hebrews 7:16). Therefore, there are no bells of gold around the hem of His robe. In John 13:4-5, Jesus took off His outer garments and served His disciples in the Upper Room by washing their feet. On the cross, He hung naked. John now sees Him, not as a servant and not as a sacrifice, but as the

Son of God, robed with dignity and deity. The golden sash around His chest is a symbol of authority, yet also depicts the tenderness of our Jesus' heart.

 Jesus is God and His appearance is overwhelming, but always remember, He has a heart of gold which is long-suffering, patient, understanding, and ready to forgive us of anything.

Don't miss this. God is the "Papa" that ran to the prodigal son, to embrace him, welcome him, cover him and love him. He is the good Shepherd who sought the one lost sheep, to carry him gently on His shoulders. He is the Redeemer who went the distance to find a demoniac, an oppressed and shackled man in Gadarenes, to give him healing, hope and life. He is the Savior who hung on the cross so that you and I may be free from our sins and may soar in the midst of our sorrows. He is the only God that came to earth to meet us where we are while all other "gods" demand mankind to search the heavens and perhaps one day, if they are lucky, gain eternal life. The golden sash around his chest is a reminder of Isaiah 40:11, "He gathers the lambs in His arms and carries them close to His heart." Jesus! Only Jesus!

1:14 His head and hair were white like wool, as white as snow, and His eyes like a flame of fire.

This is a different image of Christ than we're accustomed to seeing. We know Jesus as the gentle Shepherd, carrying and tending to His flock, you and me. He is the compassionate healer, touching the leper who was deemed an outcast. He is the tender caregiver, holding children in his arms, and blessing them. He is the affectionate God, crying over Jerusalem because His own people rejected Him. As we're about to see, He is so much more!

According to Hebrews 13:8, He is the same yesterday, today and forever. Let's look closer and see what John saw. In these few verses, John is actually saying that Rome or any power in the past or any power that is to come in the future is nothing compared to our Lord Jesus Christ, who is the King of Kings! Rome may have persecuted the early Christian believers, but behold, hold fast, look and see, we will be rejoicing in our King and with our King who is to come.

The imagery of His head and hair as white as wool and white as snow indicates righteousness spoken by the prophet in Isaiah 1:18, "Come now, and let us reason together," says the Lord, "Though your sins are like scarlet, they shall be as white as snow; though they are red like crimson, they shall be as wool." It also speaks of Christ's eternal existence for He is not only the Son of God, but as a part of the Trinity, He is equal with God the Father. God is depicted as the Ancient of Days, with clothing as white as snow and hair white like wool, as described in Daniel 7:9-13. The fact that Jesus bears the same image in Revelation 1:14 proves His deity and His identity as God.

While on earth, Jesus prayed to God, "And now, Father, glorify Me together with Yourself, with the glory which I had with You before the world was" (John 17:5). The white hair is not a description of age or wisdom, but of sinless purity and God's glory. "How then shall we explain this hair 'white like wool'? It is a part of the transfiguration in light of the glorified person of the Redeemer; a transfiguration so complete that it reaches to the extremities, to the very hairs of the head."[19]

His eyes were as a flame of fire, which speaks of His piercing insight into the matters of the church, uncovering all intentions and sins. He sees all. He sees our motives. He sees our hearts. He even sees how much we put in His treasury. Moses said of Him in Psalm 90:8, "You have set our iniquities before You, our secret sins in the light of Your countenance." David was in awe as he wrote Psalm 139:1-10, "O Lord, You have searched me and known me. You know my sitting down and my rising up; You understand my thought afar off. You comprehend my path and my lying down and are acquainted with all my ways. For there is not a word on my tongue, but behold, O Lord, You know it altogether. You have hedged me behind and before and laid Your hand upon me. Such knowledge is too wonderful for me; it is high, I cannot attain it. Where can I go from Your Spirit? Or where can I flee from Your presence? If I ascend into heaven, You are there; if I make my bed in hell, behold, You are there. If I take the wings of the morning, and dwell in the uttermost parts of the sea, even there Your hand shall lead me, and Your right hand shall hold me."

Never forget this: no matter where you are and what dilemma you find yourself in, our God is not looking for you in order to punish you; He seeks you because He loves you, desires to instruct you, lead you, help you, sustain you and uphold you with His righteous right hand!

"And there is no creature hidden from His sight, but all things are naked and open to the eyes of Him to whom we must give account" (Hebrews 4:13). Let's make it plain. If you know Him, your name will be written in the Book of Life, and He will see the blood of Christ covering you and your sins. If you choose not to know Him, your name will not appear in the Book of Life but will be in the Books of Deeds (Revelation 20:12), and you will be judged according to your works, which will amount to a pile of dirty rags compared to Christ's sin-cleansing work on the cross.

Christ looked straight in the eyes of Peter when he denied Him three times (Luke 22:61), and I am convinced that the look was that of forgiveness and grace; not condemnation. As far as our hidden motives, the deep secrets and greatest failures, He is aware of all the facts, and continues to call us, love us and embrace us. Oh, what a Savior! That love, that look, that compassion is extended to you until your last breath. Here's a simple warning: Since you don't know the hour of your last breath, it is wise to heed His calling and surrender your life to Him today.

1:15 *His feet were like fine brass, as if refined in a furnace, and His voice as the sound of many waters.*

Burnished brass in the Bible is symbolic of judgment. When Samson went astray and Delilah lulled him to sleep, he was captured by the Philistines, who took him and put out his eyes, "bound him with bronze fetters (shackles)," and placed him in prison (Judges 16:18-21). When King Nebuchadnezzar invaded Judah and defeated it, burning down its temple, he captured the last king of Israel, Zedekiah, killed his sons, put out his eyes, "bound him with bronze fetters," and exiled him to Babylon (II Kings 25:1-7). The brazen altar outside the tabernacle (Exodus 27:1-8) represented the cross, where innocent lambs were slain, foreshadowing the crucifixion of the Lamb of God. Our sins and judgments fell on Jesus at the cross of Calvary and He bore them all; past, present and even future. This, however, does not stop Him from evaluating, directing and admonishing His Church. Because Jesus is all-knowing, He is more than capable of leading, cautioning and encouraging His Church.

Have you ever imagined where His feet walked? Through the Red Sea, leading the exiles. Through the Babylonian exile. Through the fire with Shadrach, Meshach, and Abednego. The feet of Jesus may be burnished brass, ready to judge the unjust, but they are feet that will carry you when you can no longer carry yourself. We read about God's grace in Isaiah 46:4, "Even to your old age, I am He, and even to gray hairs I will carry you! I have made, and I will bear; even I will carry, and will deliver you."

His voice is as the sound of many waters, one of thunderous authority. It is the same voice that called this universe into existence, the voice that will Rapture His Church out of this sinful world, and the voice that calls out your name in love. The call of entertainment, parties, materialism, education, psychology, philosophy, and money seem to take precedence over the voice of Jesus Christ today. But there will come a day, when all these voices will be silenced by the resounding voice of the Son of God.

 M.D.'s, Ph.D.'s, Th.D.'s, Pharm.D.'s, Ed.D.'s, J.D.'s, and all intellectuals with degrees will hush before the Doctor of all Principalities!

If you've ever been to the edge of Niagara Falls, all other sounds are engulfed by the deafening roar of the crashing waters. So too will the thunderous voice of the Son of Man drown out all others on the day of judgment for those who rejected Him. His voice, however, is a sweet, compassionate and warm melody for all those who accept Him.

 And that is the Gospel in summary. It is sweet as honey to those who taste and embrace it, yet bitter like wormwood to those who reject it. It gives life to those who accept it, yet death to those who refuse it. It offers eternal hope to those who welcome it, yet everlasting grief to those who spurn it. Get it?

Revelation presents Jesus more majestically than any other book in the Bible. He was despised and rejected by men and He was a man of sorrows according to Isaiah 53:3. But when He returns, He will be revered and worshiped by everyone, for He will come with power and great glory (Luke 21:27). It will mean eternal hell for those who reject Him. At the name of Jesus, every knee will bow, and every tongue will confess that He is Lord (Philippians 2:9-11). No other name. No other god. No other way.

When He was on earth, Jesus asked, "Who do men say that I am?" Some said He was just a teacher, a rabbi, a prophet, a healer, a good man, or a mad man. His next question was directed to His disciples, "But who do you say that I am?" (Matthew 16:13-15). Peter, who was inspired by the Holy Spirit, proclaimed, "You are the Christ, the Son of the living God."

Truly, who do you say that He is? Jesus is the great High Priest, in authority, in holiness, in judgment, and most importantly, in love. But He will not return as the High Priest. He will return as the King of Kings. That means all dominion in heaven, on earth, in the sea and all of the universe will lay prostrate before Him.

There will be no usurper.

There will be no Hollywood director desecrating Christ's name in his movie picture.

There will be no Tinseltown actor reveling as His mocker.

There will be no dictator or prime minister who will be able to defeat the Master.

There will be no man who will violate the Scripture.

There will be no one who will be able to eclipse the Savior.

No. No one will outwit the Mighty God, the Everlasting Father and the wonderful Counselor!

You'd be so terrified if you were to lose your house or your freedom. I implore you to ask yourself if you are willing to lose your soul. Your choice should be voiced with urgency because your choice determines your eternal destiny.

1:16 He had in His right hand seven stars, out of His mouth went a sharp two-edged sword, and His countenance was like the sun shining in its strength.

As we saw in Revelation 1:13, Jesus is in the midst of the lampstands, which represents His Church. Jesus holds seven stars in His right hand; the right hand is a symbol of favor and honor. Christ-followers during John's time, therefore, understood that despite unbearable persecutions, nothing was able to remove them out of God's loving and protective hand, even if they were martyred! In John 10:28-30, Jesus said, "And I give them eternal life, and they shall never perish; neither shall anyone snatch them out of My hand. My Father, who has given them to Me, is greater than all; and no one is able to snatch them out of My Father's hand. I and My Father are one." As we've discussed, the Lord's compassion for His children is unmatched, "He will feed His flock like a shepherd; He will gather the lambs with His arm, and carry them in His bosom, and gently lead those who are with young" (Isaiah 40:11). Comfort! Security! Beauty!

We shall see that our Lord Himself interpreted the meaning of the seven stars in verse 20, "The seven stars are the angels of the seven churches." The meaning in Greek for angels is messengers. This likely refers to the local pastors and not angelic beings. But some view the angels as supernaturally created beings assigned to each church. Just as children have guardian angels (Matthew 18:10), and we have guardian angels (Psalm 91:11), so too the churches have guardian angels. In our context, however, I believe the seven stars are seven pastors. Churches fail for many reasons, one of them being that the pastors or messengers reject the Holy Spirit's leading and tone down, neglect or twist the clear message of the cross!

The sharp two-edged sword coming out of the Lord's mouth is the Word of God illustrated in Hebrews 4:12, "For the Word of God is living and powerful, and sharper than any two-edged sword, piercing even to the division of soul and spirit, and of joints and marrow, and is a discerner of the thoughts and intents of the heart." The Apostle Paul also clarified this truth in Ephesians 6:17, "and the sword of the Spirit, which is the Word of God."

Christ, the suffering servant, spoke of Himself in Isaiah 49:2, "And He (God) has made My (Christ's) mouth like a sharp sword; in the shadow of His hand He has hidden Me, and made Me a polished shaft; in His quiver He has hidden Me." The future battle between Christ and the Antichrist (Revelation 19) will conclude with the sword or Word of Christ. Satan will find himself indefensible against the Word and will be bound in chains for a thousand years before His final rebellion and his ultimate destiny in hell forever and ever.

 Many have a lighthearted perception of Christ.
Just to clarify, He is not sleeping in a manger.
He is not a pushover.
He is not an idol to be placed on a shelf or a church pedestal.
He is not a curse word or an object of words that are vulgar.
He is not just a prophet or a good man, a mere man or a teacher. He is the one and only sin-atoning Savior.
He is God and will not give His glory to another.
He not only speaks the Word, but He wrote the Word and He is the Word, for He is the life-giving Author.
You will forever be changed once you encounter the Master!

Despite His fierce appearance in the book of Revelation, He is majestic as described in Song of Solomon 5:16, "His mouth is most sweet; yes, He is altogether lovely." He speaks to you gently and carries you with His strong and tender arms; He *is* the language of love!

On the Mount of Transfiguration, Christ was transfigured before Peter, James and John and His face shone like the sun, and His clothes became as white as the light (Matthew 17:2). The three disciples saw Jesus in His divine glory, just as John saw Him in this vision in Revelation chapter one. Jesus is God, radiant, splendid, pure, righteous, and holy, shining like the sun in its full strength. We read in I Timothy 6:16 about the King of Kings and Lord or Lords, Jesus Christ, "Who alone has immortality, dwelling in unapproachable light, whom no man has seen or can see, to whom be honor and everlasting power. Amen."

As the sun disperses the darkness, so too the Son of Man conquers sin. In Isaiah 9:2, Christ is seen as the light that overcomes the darkness in this world, the darkness in a man's mind and the darkness in a man's heart, "The people walking in darkness have seen a great light; on those living in the land of deep darkness a light has dawned." According to Psalm 84:11, the Lord is our sun and our shield. How is He like the sun? To shine on those who live in darkness and in the shadow of death, to guide their feet into the path of peace (Luke 1:78-79).

What's there not to like about the sun? Its scorching heat. During the Tribulation, climate change advocates will finally feel the heat, literally, not because of their faulty Melankovitch scientific analysis, but because of God's sovereign purpose.[20] Today's climate change rhetoric has escalated beyond an environmental issue and has transformed into a moral issue, known as climate justice. Some proponents view those who do not agree with their line of thinking as "evil" and "racists." Children around the world are being indoctrinated into believing that climate change is an existential threat to our well-being. They are purposefully taught by activist adults to school and shame unbelieving adults in hopes of converting them into believing adults.

But rest assured: God will take care of His planet until His return. God delights in His creation for when He created the earth, He called it "good" (Genesis 1:10). He destroyed it by a flood not because man trampled the earth but because man rejected His Word. After the flood, God assured Noah that seedtime and harvest, cold and heat, winter and summer, day and night will not cease while the earth remains (Genesis 8:22). The earth's climate does change but it is not unstable. Why? Two reasons. First, our God is stable, solid and sovereign, known as the Rock (II Samuel 22:32). Second, the earth is the Lord's,

and everything in it is in His hands (Psalm 24:1; 95:4).
Do we then ignore caring for the earth? No, we have
been given dominion over it and are asked to be good
stewards (Genesis 1:26). As stewards of the earth,
we have a responsibility, but to treat it as a religion is
blasphemy. The earth will one day be destroyed again
by fire during the Tribulation, compliments of God,
not because man desecrated the earth with its carbon
dioxide emissions, but because man trampled on the
Word, Jesus Christ! (II Peter 3:10).

Christ-followers should not be panicked over the issue
of climate change because much of that alarmism is
coming from an evolutionary point of view that denies
God's sovereignty over His creation. To the utter shock
of climate change advocates, climate change and global
warming will strike during the Tribulation. When the
fourth bowl judgment is unleashed, mankind will be
scorched by the sun's intense heat and will curse God
(Revelation 16:8-9). Science? No, try the Creator of
science! You can count on it! Christ, whose countenance
is like the sun shining in its strength, will "bump up"
the heat and He alone will "Rev it Up!"

1:17 And when I saw Him, I fell at His feet as dead. But He laid His right hand on me, saying to me, "Do not be afraid; I am the First and the Last.

We are called sons of God, heirs of God and joint-heirs with
Christ in Romans 8:17. But despite this, it is clearly understood
that we will never be divine or "deities" even in our glorified
bodies given to us at the moment of the Rapture. John, the
very disciple who laid his head on Jesus' breast in the Upper
Room, prostrated himself at the feet of the resurrected Christ,
astonished by Jesus' glory. As we'll see, this response is not
the exception. It is the rule.

When Isaiah saw the Lord, he exclaimed, "Woe is me, for I am undone! Because I am a man of unclean lips, and I dwell in the midst of a people of unclean lips; for my eyes have seen the King, the Lord of hosts" (Isaiah 6:5). Ezekiel describes the same reaction in Ezekiel 3:23, "So I arose and went out into the plain, and behold, the glory of the Lord stood there, like the glory which I saw by the River Chebar; and I fell on my face." Daniel states, "Therefore I was left alone when I saw this great vision, and no strength remained in me; for my vigor was turned to frailty in me, and I retained no strength" (Daniel 10:8). A word to those who are currently cavalier, jeering Christ: you will bow, and lay prostate, in complete fear and honor when you meet your Maker.

There is always a wonderful balance found in Christ. He is the Lamb, yet the Lion. He is the meek, yet the strong. He is the Creator of the stars, yet close to the brokenhearted. Though He is God, He became a man and has the capacity to understand man's hearts. Though He shines like the sun in its radiant power, He gives strength to the weary and increases the power of the weak.

On many occasions while in His incarnate state, Jesus told His twelve disciples, "Do not be afraid," "Peace be with you," and "Do not let your heart be troubled, nor let it be afraid" (Matthew 10:31, John 14:27, John 20:19). The same admonitions apply to us today. While giving His Church the Great Commission, He comforted us by saying, "And surely I am with you always" (Matthew 28:20).

When John fell as if he were dead, the Lord touched him with His right hand, restoring him, strengthening him, accepting him, encouraging him, and uplifting him with His righteous right hand. With the threat of nuclear weapons in the hands of terrorist nations, those without Christ have every reason to fear for they are unsure of their future. But those who love

Christ should walk with courage, "For God has not given us a spirit of fear, but of power and of love and of a sound mind" (II Timothy 1:7). We too can proclaim like David, "I have set the Lord always before me; because He is at my right hand I shall not be moved" (Psalm 16:8).

Why would John fall at the feet of Christ as if he were dead? After all, he was the same apostle John who laid his head on Jesus' chest during the Last Supper.

 Simply, when one comes face to face with Christ, his sheer unworthiness and unholiness is laid bare in the midst of the glorified, resurrected, holy and omnipotent Jesus, who is overwhelming to behold and worthy to be worshiped!

"The beloved disciple, who had physically touched the Word of life, laid on his Lord's bosom in the days of his flesh, can as little as any other person endure the revelation of His majesty."[21]

Jesus is the "First and the Last," noted in Colossians 1:16-17, "For by Him all things were created that are in heaven and that are on earth, visible and invisible, whether thrones or dominions or principalities or powers. All things were created through Him and for Him. And He is before all things, and in Him all things consist." There was no one before Him and there will be no one after Him. The Antichrist and the False Prophet will soon appear and be in control of this world for seven years, but their time will end. Satan's years of dominion will too come to term. There will be no Pharaoh, no Nebuchadnezzar, no Cyrus, no Alexander the Great, no Nero, no tyrant nor any hero who will be able to crush Jesus Christ.

The reason why there is so much chaos today is because man has free will and Satan has been given a temporary and limited influence over the earth. Jesus is still in control and will soon take over and reign in righteousness, but patiently awaits His appointed time in human history. We are not to fear because our Christ not only created us, but cares for us. In contrast, we do fear Him in reverent awe, not in fear of His vengeance or punishment, but in approaching Him with complete honor and worship.

1:18 I am He who lives, and was dead, and behold, I am alive forevermore. Amen. And I have the keys of Hades and of Death.

Jesus touched John and gave him four reasons not to fear. He does the same for you and me today. 1) He is the First and the Last. 2) He is the Living One. 3) He was dead, but behold, He is alive forevermore. 4) He holds the keys of Hades and of Death. Yes, all things at all times are in His loving hands.

We have studied why Christ is called the First and the Last. But why does He call Himself the "Living One?" He willingly gave up His life as a sacrificial atonement for your sin and my sin, and rose on the third day, conquering sin, death, and all of hell's powers. Prior to Christ, every High Priest, through the Levitical lineage, made atonement for his people, but eventually died. Goats and calves were offered continually to signify the blood spilled of an innocent animal that covered the sins of the guilty people. But the blameless Lamb of God, Jesus Christ, offered Himself only once, and unlike the previous sacrifices and the previous High Priests, Jesus died and rose leaving an empty grave, and cleansed our conscience from dead works so that we may serve the living God and have the promise of eternal life (Hebrews 9:11-15).

Though once dead, He is "alive forevermore." In I Peter 3:18 we read, "For Christ also suffered once for sins, the just for the unjust, that He might bring us to God, being put to death in the flesh but made alive by the Spirit." He died just once; He does not need to and will not die again. "And being found in appearance as a man, He humbled Himself and became obedient to the point of death, even the death of the cross. Therefore, God also has highly exalted Him and given Him the name which is above every name" (Philippians 2:8-9). He will not bow His head on the cross again. All will bow to Him.

He ends the statement "I am He who lives, and was dead, and behold, I am alive forevermore" with an "Amen," which means "so be it, verily, true," or "truly" (literally "truth"). Amen is a declaration or affirmation of what was just spoken or written. King David exclaimed in Psalm 41:13, "Blessed be the Lord God of Israel from everlasting to everlasting! Amen and Amen."

In Hebrews 2:14-15, we read, "Inasmuch then as the children have partaken of flesh and blood, He Himself likewise shared in the same, that through death He might destroy him who had the power of death, that is, the devil, and release those who through fear of death were all their lifetime subject to bondage."

 The keys of death and Hades that Jesus holds are a symbol of release and not imprisonment. He does not want to lock us up, He wants to set us free.

The Christ-follower need not fear death or Hades. Hades is the unseen abode of the unbelieving dead, awaiting judgment at the Great White Throne that will sentence them to eternal hell, the Lake of Fire. The one who rejects Christ should fear both physical death and then Hades, and even worse, the Lake of Fire, which is the second death (eternal death noted in Revelation 20:14).

John 3:16 tells us that Jesus Christ died for the sins of the whole world. Not all will be saved, for every person is given a choice and free will to decide, whether to embrace or reject the greatest gift of Jesus Christ and His atoning blood. We are so privileged because the Word of faith which the apostles preached is recorded and near us today. If we confess with our mouths that Jesus is Lord and believe in our hearts that God raised Him from the dead, we will be saved. And if we believe in Him, we will not be put to shame. (Romans 10:8-13). He says to you, "I, the source of all life, stooped even to taste of death" just for you.[22] I urge you to ask Christ to come into your heart, cleanse you from all your sins, and save your soul eternally. He has the universe to control and governments to steer, but at the same time, He is deeply concerned for you and madly in love with you!

Divine Outline

1:19 Write the things which you have seen, and the things which are, and the things which will take place after this.

This is important! This verse unveils the mystery of the entire book of Revelation! It is the key that unlocks the fastened doors. It is the divine outline that explains the pages of this book. John is instructed to write down:

1. The events he has seen in the past;
2. The events which were in John's present time;
3. The events which will take place in the future.

Walvoord instructs that "This outline is the only one which allows the book to speak for itself without artificial manipulation and which lays guidelines of sufficient importance so that expositors who follow this approach have been able to establish a system of interpretation of the book of Revelation."[23]

What has John seen that is in the past? He saw the glorified, mighty, reigning, radiant and risen Christ we are studying in chapter one.

What does John see regarding his present to our current present? The events that are unfolding are the churches, chapters two through three. We will discuss seven messages to the seven churches of Asia Minor and study the different eras of church history up to the point of the Rapture.

What does John see regarding the future? The events that will transpire "after this," or "meta tauta" in the Greek, which hereafter are found in chapters four through five, where the church is Raptured and will be safe with Christ for seven years. Along with chapters four through five, it includes chapters six through nineteen, where the ungodly remain on earth and suffer the Tribulation. It is seven years of bliss and a honeymoon in heaven for those of us who will be raptured, and it will be seven years of hell on earth for those who remain. "Meta tauta" also includes chapters twenty through twenty-two, where we will see the Second Coming of Christ, the Campaign of Armageddon, Christ ruling for a thousand years, Satan being defeated and cast in hell, the making of a new heaven and new earth, and finally, God's children living happily ever after.

Why do I believe that the church will escape the Tribulation? One of the reasons is very subtle. You will see the seven messages to the churches all end with the phrase "He who has an ear, let him hear what the Spirit says to the churches." But we find during the time of Tribulation (Revelation 13:9), God says, "If anyone has an ear, let him hear." The difference may be a moot point, but it has huge implications: God left out the phrase "what the Spirit says to the churches" in chapter thirteen because the church is no longer on earth! More to come about the Rapture later on in this book! (chapter 4: verse 1).

It seems as if everything in this life is broken or breaking. Hearts are broken, health is broken, marriages are broken, memories are broken, 401K's are broken, ministries are broken, churches are broken, backs are broken, people are broken. But there is still a blessed hope! The solution is not found in more education, information, reformation, motivation, compensation, innovation or inspiration.

The single and universal problem in our world is sin. The single and universal answer to the problem is Jesus Christ.

The solution will be unfolded in its fullness during the coming of the King of Kings and Lord of Lords. Fix your eyes on Him. Don't let your hearts be troubled for He has given you the Holy Spirit so you can stand firm and live in victory despite the brokenness all around you.

1:20 The mystery of the seven stars which you saw in My right hand, and the seven golden lampstands: The seven stars are the angels of the seven churches, and the seven lampstands which you saw are the seven churches.

It is best to let the Bible interpret the Bible as we read it in this verse.

 It is humbling to acknowledge that the mystery is made clear solely because God revealed it and not because man searched for it.

The seven stars are the messengers or pastors of the seven churches. However, note that the "angel" is not in charge nor is he the "new sheriff in town" as some view themselves. The pastors are in Jesus' right hand. A pastor is accountable to Christ and will be corrected by the Lord, but that certainly does not give us the right to criticize the pastor. In Psalm 105:15 we read, "Do not touch My anointed ones, and do My prophets no harm."

Where can you find Jesus? He is in the midst of the seven lampstands or in the midst of His Church (as we noted in Revelation 1:13). Jesus is involved in the church. He shares the Word because He is the Word. He guides the pastors. He has them in His right hand even though all human endeavors fall short of the glory of God. He'll deal with his messengers, as we read in James 3:1, "My brethren, let not many of you become teachers, knowing that we shall receive a stricter judgment." Will the messengers be judged? Yes, but they will be judged in love.

 Mysteries will be solved by God's atoning.
Answers we will be receiving.
Hearts will be mended by Christ's healing.
The tears of the night will turn to the joys of the morning.
The righteous will be rejoicing.
The unbelievers will be cringing.
Jesus is soon coming.
We should all be planning.
The Rapture is nearing.
Our hearts for His return are longing.
Jesus will settle the score, appearing in majesty, as the Lion of the Tribe of Judah, roaring!

REV IT UP & SUM IT UP – CHAPTER ONE:

The book of Revelation was written to reveal Jesus Christ in all His glory. He is the central person of the book. The purpose of the book is to unveil the mysteries and prophecies of the future to His servants. The apostle John penned the book in 95 AD on the Island of Patmos (off the West coast of Turkey, in the Mediterranean Sea) where he was exiled as a prisoner, punished for preaching the Gospel. While in chains, praying in the Spirit, he saw visions of the risen and reigning Savior and he witnessed what the righteous and the wicked will encounter in the future.

John sees Jesus amongst the seven golden lampstands, as He is holding the seven stars in His right hand. The lampstands not only depict the seven churches in Asia Minor of John's time, but each church also represents an era or period of time, ranging from 30 AD to the present, culminating at the Rapture. It is critical to note that Jesus is standing in the midst of the churches and is also holding the stars (messengers or pastors that minister to the church) in His hands. He is in complete control and completely in love with His Church even though we may be out of control and incompletely in love with Him.

When Jesus was crucified, He was stripped and naked on the cross. In Revelation, He is dressed as a king, a priest and a judge in royal clothes. He once hung on a tree in shame. Here He appears in glory. On the cross He had hair dripping in crimson blood. Here, His hair is whiter than snow, which shows His righteousness and purity. He once had eyes filled with tears, crying out to save those who rejected Him. Here, His eyes are like flames of fire, piercing the motives of the heart. Spikes once nailed His feet to the cross. Here, His feet are like molten brass, as judgment is nearing. A spear once severed his side, where water and blood poured out. Now He has a sword, the Word of God, coming out of His mouth. Once His face was battered, bruised and mutilated. Here, His face shines like the sun, even brighter than the noon-day sun.

Glory and honor and praise belong to our Lord, indeed! The days of Satan's reign on earth are coming to an end. We are in "overtime." The clock ticks its last ticks, the whistle will blow, the trumpet will sound, and our Lord will return to take His children home. Blessed are those who hear these words and take them to heart!

SECTION 2

TODAY

Chapter 2
The Church's Report Card

We will study four of the seven churches in this chapter. The first congregation, Ephesus, lost their first love, serving Christ yet forgetting to love Him. The second, Smyrna, lost their lives, denying the world and staying loyal to Christ. The third, Pergamos, lost their character, marrying the Spirit of Christ with the spirit of Balaam, a false prophet. The fourth, Thyatira, lost their purity, joining ranks with Jezebel, the false prophetess. In the midst of all the churches stands Christ, extending His grace, strength, admonition and encouragement.

The Pretend Church

2:1 *"To the angel of the church of Ephesus write, 'These things says He who holds the seven stars in His right hand, who walks in the midst of the seven golden lampstands:'"*

According to our divine outline, John wrote about events that occurred in the past in chapter one. In chapters two to three, he wrote about the events that are in the present. Thereafter, starting in chapter four, he wrote about the events that will be in the future. Because the seven churches existed in John's days and because they represent today's Church Age, chapters two and three which cover all seven churches are considered to be in the present age. As we'll shortly read, Ephesus, the first of the churches, is considered to be the Pretend Church because it had the appearance of perfection yet was missing its deep love for Christ.

The message to each church was to be shared amongst all seven churches. The churches listed are in the same order as the Roman postal circuit in which mail was delivered, starting at Ephesus and ending at Laodicea.[1] John is not only addressing a specific message to each church, but he is also revealing that each church represents an era or stage in history.[2]

 The discourse in the churches is like a pep talk at half time, where the game is not progressing as planned. The fumbles, interceptions and injuries have plagued the team in the first half and the coach is glaring into the eyes of each player and instilling hope, courage, guidance and tenacity in their hearts.

What has happened has happened. It's not time to throw in the towel. It's not time to retreat. It's not time to bow your head in shame. It's time to make critical changes. It's time to work wholeheartedly. It's time to cast aside complacency. It's time to remember why we're here, why we do what we do, and how to do it for the sake of honoring the team and not ourselves. It's time for every single member of the team to step up and contribute beyond his ability. Listen intently: you and I are the players, and Jesus has sound advice for us so that we may remember to walk with Him closely and serve mankind humbly.

In John's days, the seven churches existed locally, and were founded and oddly grew because of persecutions of Christ-followers; their account speaks to us ecclesiastically and historically, spanning every church from past to present; we are able to apply the plan, pattern and paradigm of each church to our lives personally; we are given insight prophetically, reflecting with a panoramic outlook of what was, what is and what is to be.

We'll address the churches in order, and focus on Ephesus at the beginning of this chapter:

1. **Ephesus....... Pretend Church (33 AD – 100 AD)**
2. Smyrna............Persecuted Church (100 AD – 313 AD)
3. Pergamos.......Perverted Church (313 AD – 590 AD)
4. Thyatira ....Promiscuous Church (590 AD – 1517 AD)
5. Sardis...............Perished Church (1517 AD – 1790 AD)
6. Philadelphia..Patriotic Church (1730 AD – present)
7. Laodicea.........Passive Church (1900 AD – present)

We'll also learn about each church using the following seven characteristics:

1. Churches' identification
2. Christ's characterization
3. Cheering affirmation
4. Constructive admonition
5. Curative instruction
6. Call to action
7. Coming restoration

For the church in Ephesus, the Loveless or Pretend Church, the seven characteristics are:

1. Church's identification: Ephesus

2. Christ's characterization: Found in verse one, "These things says He who holds the seven stars in His right hand, who walks in the midst of the seven golden lampstands."

3. Cheering affirmation: Found in verses two, three and six, "I know your works, your labor, your patience, and that you cannot bear those who are evil. And you have tested those who say they are apostles and are not and have found them liars; and you have persevered and have patience and have labored for My name's sake and have not become weary. But this you have, that you hate the deeds of the Nicolaitans, which I also hate."

4. Constructive admonition: Found in verse four, "Neverthe-

less I have this against you, that you have left your first love."

5. Curative instruction: Found in verse five, "Remember therefore from where you have fallen; repent and do the first works, or else I will come to you quickly and remove your lampstand from its place — unless you repent."

6. Call to action: Found in verse seven, "He who has an ear, let him hear what the Spirit says to the churches."

7. Coming restoration: Found in verse seven, "To him who overcomes I will give to eat from the tree of life, which is in the midst of the Paradise of God."

Ephesus was the chief city of the province of Asia, called "the Light of Asia," adorned with white marble streets, beautiful buildings, temples and amphitheaters; the city was centered on the worship of the goddess Diana.[3] The city was famous for its Temple of Artemis, 425 feet long by 220 feet wide with each of its 127 columns donated by a king, one of the seven wonders of the world.[4] The temple was considered sacred, attracting vast commerce, and thus propelled Ephesus to the primary banking center in Asia Minor. Paul spent three years ministering in Ephesus, the longest he stayed in any one city on his journeys. Paul who wrote the letter to the Ephesians, also wrote I & II Timothy, addressing his protégé Timothy. John later ministered in Ephesus until he was exiled to Patmos. Ephesus was an important city in the early growth of Christianity.

The attributes given in each letter that describe Jesus are derived from Revelation 1:12-18 and are purposely and precisely applied to each church. The fact that Christ holds the seven stars in His right hand describes Him as the Sovereign ruler, the loving caretaker, the constant supporter, and the gentle protector of the church's angel, orator, pastor or minister. According to Paul in Ephesians 5:32, "This is a great mystery, but I speak concerning Christ and the church." The church, defined as the body of Christ, was not revealed to mankind until after

Christ came. Daniel the prophet was blinded to it, for he fore-saw the coming of the Messiah and the seven-year Tribulation but was not allowed to see the Church Age in which we now live. Christ loves the church to the point that He died for us. We see this in Ephesians 5:25 where Paul states, "Husbands, love your wives, just as Christ also loved the church and gave Himself for her."

Since Christ will do anything to help, guide, give, support, and love His "Loveless or Pretend Church," the Church of Ephesus, He walks in the midst of her. According to Psalm 46:4-5, "There is a river whose streams shall make glad the city of God, the holy place of the tabernacle of the Most-High. God is in the midst of her, she shall not be moved; God shall help her, just at the break of dawn." God's word and ordinances are like tidings of rivers and streams with which God makes His saints glad in grim and dark days. The streams that make glad the city of God are not rapid, but gentle. God is also preparing a heavenly Zion, the New Jerusalem, a peaceful abode, a place of broad rivers and streams for His followers (Isaiah 33:20-21). The spiritual comforts for today and the future are relayed to the saints by soft and silent whispers and are more than suffi-cient to offset the loudest threats of an angry world and bitter circumstances.

The fact that He walks in the midst of the seven golden lamp-stands, or the churches, describes the church as His cherished bride, His protected companion, the apple of His eyes, and the pleasure of His soul. God assures His Church of His special presence with her; His honor sojourns in her. He has set up His tabernacle in her and secures her integrity, and therefore she shall not be moved. She will not be destroyed nor removed as the earth will be one day. The church is built on the Rock, Jesus Christ, and the gates of hell shall not prevail against it (Matthew 16:18). Despite the "mess" we find in many churches today, it is comforting to know that Christ has sovereign, providential and ultimate control over His Church and its leaders.

2:2 *"I know your works, your labor, your patience, and that you cannot bear those who are evil. And you have tested those who say they are apostles and are not, and have found them liars;"*

The Church of Ephesus was the early church of 33 AD, following Pentecost, which we see in the book of Acts as a place of fire, zeal and energy. It was the Apostolic Church, abiding in the teachings of Christ and His apostles. But when the book of Revelation was written in 95 AD, this church had already diminished in power and love. In plain terms, by the end of the first century, the church was messed up, pretending to be what it used to be!

Jesus is omniscient and knew that the Ephesian congregation would be hard-working and is not fooled by false religious people, fabricated religions, or strange doctrines. In Galatians 6:9, Christ-followers are encouraged not to "grow weary while doing good, for in due season we shall reap if we do not lose heart." We are encouraged to do good, "But as for you, brethren, do not grow weary in doing good" (II Thessalonians 3:13). There is a promise in Isaiah 40:31 for those who have been toiling, waiting, believing and trusting upon the Lord, "But those who wait on the Lord shall renew their strength; they shall mount up with wings like eagles, they shall run and not be weary, they shall walk and not faint."

One of the most misunderstood verses in the Bible is found in Matthew 7:1, "Judge not, that you be not judged." We are not to judge in condemnation, but we are encouraged to judge in identification. The Church of Ephesus was encouraged for identifying, or judging, false apostles and not allowing them to infiltrate the church! They did not allow evil doctrine to be sown amongst them, were not influenced by secular culture and did not bow to the pressure of political correctness. How did the Church of Ephesus identify the false teachers? "Beware of false prophets, who come to you in sheep's clothing, but inwardly they are ravenous wolves. You will know them by their fruits" (Matthew 7:15-16). Paul warned the church of these wolves, "For I know this, that after my departure savage wolves will come in among you, not sparing the flock. Also, from among yourselves men will rise up, speaking perverse things, to draw away the disciples after themselves. Therefore, watch and remember that for three years I did not cease to warn everyone night and day with tears" (Acts 20:29-31). The Church of Ephesus was awake, watching and identifying!

In II Peter 2:1-3, we read that false teachers deceive with words and even deny Christ, "But there were also false prophets among the people, even as there will be false teachers among you, who will secretly bring in destructive heresies, even deny-ing the Lord who bought them, and bring on themselves swift destruction. And many will follow their destructive ways, because of whom the way of truth will be blasphemed. By covetousness they will exploit you with deceptive words; for a long time, their judgment has been idle, and their destruction does not slumber." In our present time, deception is getting worse by the day, "But evil men and impostors will grow worse and worse, deceiving and being deceived" (II Timothy 3:13). Though the Church of Ephesus did not follow the false teachers, many do today. It will neither go well with the false teachers nor their followers. How can the church identify false teachers today? Be leery of those who omit from the Word and of those who add to the Word. Of course, that implies that the Christ-follower knows the Word!

2:3 *"and you have persevered and have patience, and have labored for My name's sake and have not become weary."*

The Church of Ephesus sounds like the prototype of perfec-tion, working hard, laboring for Christ, serving the people, having patience, and not putting up with strange teachings. They were not fooled. They were active. They were dynamic, dedicated, determined, disciplined and discerning. You cannot persevere in the absence of obstacles and if everything is going your way. You cannot overcome if the road is smooth and down-hill. You cannot develop pristine character unless you push through failure, hardship, lack, loss, slander and persecution. Hardships and tribulation produce perseverance; in turn, perseverance creates good character.

The Church of Ephesus remained adamantly faithful amid their suffering and followed Christ, bearing their cross. There-fore, the church developed strong character in Christ. They can be likened to believers spoken of in Titus 3:14, "And let our people also learn to maintain good works, to meet urgent needs, that they may not be unfruitful." Mass persecution occurred under Roman rule: Nero, the sixth emperor of Rome, perpetrated the first mass oppression, set Rome aflame and blamed the Christians in 67 AD, and illuminated his gardens at night by setting Christians aflame; persecution continued under Domitian in 81 AD, where Christians were blamed for everything, including earthquakes, and put to death![5] Plow-ing through tribulation, being patient in persecution and persevering in difficulties were trademarks for the Church of Ephesus. As we work today, let us not only do it in the name of Christ, but also let us do it in His character and with a deep love for Him. For some of us, that is going to take a lot of work!

2:4 *Nevertheless I have this against you, that you have left your first love.*

Despite all their impeccable attributes, the Church of Ephesus had left its first love, and was therefore declining in influence. Despite their faithfulness to sound doctrine, they still needed correction. They served God in the name of Christ, but they forgot to love Christ while serving Him! Amazing that just thirty years prior, when Paul wrote the book of Ephesians, he stated, "Ever since I heard about your faith in the Lord Jesus and your love for all God's people, I have not stopped giv-ing thanks for you, remembering you in my prayers" (Ephe-sians 1:15-16). When John wrote the book of Revelation, the passion, the patience and the perseverance in good works and service were all intact, but the love for Christ was missing! How tragic!

You may have seen it; a church full of activities with a corporate structure; but the love, the thirst, the desire and the longing for Christ alone was somehow secondary, if not dead. One can allow culture to influence him to the point of being well known for his good works; but being well known ends abruptly; while a deep love for Christ endures eternally.

I Corinthians 13:1-3 demonstrates what Ephesus was like, "Though I speak with the tongues of men and of angels, but have not love, I have become sounding brass or a clanging cymbal. And though I have the gift of prophecy, and understand all mysteries and all knowledge, and though I have all faith, so that I could remove mountains, but have not love, I am nothing. And though I bestow all my goods to feed the poor, and though I give my body to be burned, but have not love, it profits me nothing." These verses disturb me, and admonish me to look in the mirror, asking myself if I am merely a clanging cymbal. Am I? Are you?

Martha and Mary illustrate the struggle between the human effort versus the longing heart. Martha was not only busy making food for Jesus, but she was livid that Mary was not helping her. Mary, on the other hand, had finished her duties, left the kitchen and was sitting at the feet of Jesus to listen and receive anointing. Martha pointed fingers at Mary and Jesus, "Do You not care that my sister has left me to serve alone? Therefore, tell her to help me" (Luke 10:38-40). Martha was saying, "Tell her to work; Tell her to exert some energy; I'm dying in the kitchen already! Tell her to pull her own weight; Tell her to move it!" Jesus answered her, "Martha, Martha, you are worried and troubled about many things. But one thing is needed, and Mary has chosen that good part, which will not be taken away from her" (Luke 10:41-42). Jesus was saying, "Chill, be still; don't sweat this; I'd rather Mary commune with me, learn from me, sit with me, than entertain me." Yes, we are called to serve our Lord and people with compassion and zeal, but more importantly, we are called to love our Lord and people with passion and fervor. Without the love, the service turns into a clanging cymbal and a life of pretense.

2:5 *Remember therefore from where you have fallen; repent and do the first works, or else I will come to you quickly and remove your lampstand from its place — unless you repent.*

Jesus asks them to remember, repent and redirect:

1. Remember. Remember His goodness. Remember His love. Remember His loving kindness. Remember His grace. Remember His sacrifice. Remember His wonders. Remember how you used to love Him, adore Him and enjoy Him. And come back into His forgiving arms. And when you remember, keep on remembering!

2. Repent. Repent and change your mind. Repent and change your conversation. Repent and change your conduct. Repent and change your character. When Jesus started His ministry on earth, He stated, "Repent, for the kingdom of heaven is at hand" (Matthew 4:17).

3. Redirect. Redirect your mind. Redirect your motives. Redirect your heart. Redirect your actions and do what you used to do; do what you were called to do; do what the Lord asks you to do; but whatever you do, do it by loving and honoring the Lord. Jesus did not ask them to increase their service; they toiled and labored for His name's sake and did not become weary. "The first works are the going forth of affection to Christ, freely, devotedly."[6]

 Remember, repent and redirect, and in so doing, alter your focus from the thorns of life to the throne of the Lord, from the sweat of your brow to the sweet fellowship at His feet.

If the church did not repent, Jesus said He would remove their lampstand quickly; the Lord will not stay where He is simply tolerated; He will not stay where He is not loved; He will not stay where He is not welcomed. Today, the light of Christ no longer shines in Ephesus. "I have before me a picture of the Ephesus of today — a ruined archway ... a forbidding castle, 'midst desolate hills. No lampstand for Christ where once Paul labored three years, night and day with tears!"[7]

 When a relationship with Christ turns into a religion, service for Christ turns into a profession, and passion for the Savior turns into a robotic compulsion, then the conclusion of the matter is the Lord's exclusion.

2:6 *But this you have, that you hate the deeds of the Nicolaitans, which I also hate.*

To their credit, the Church of Ephesus hated what God hates: the Nicolaitans doctrine, which is in stark contrast to the third of the seven local churches, Pergamos, which wholeheartedly held to the Nicolaitans teachings. The word Nicolaitans stems from "Nikao," which means to conquer; and "laos," which means the people. It means victory over people; "this view considers the Nicolaitans as the forerunners of the clerical hierarchy superimposed upon the laity and robbing them of spiritual freedom."[8] There were likely clergy at that time who said, "Submit to us because we have authority over you! We'll tell you how to dress, what to eat, and how and when to conduct your business." No man should rule over another in this way, and to their credit, the Church of Ephesus refused this kind of rule! It is dangerous, self-serving and an abomination, where man not only rules over man, but attempts to take the place of God. Paul wrote it eloquently in Galatians 3:28, "There is neither Jew nor Greek, there is neither slave nor free, there is neither male nor female; for you are all one in Christ Jesus."

2:7 *"He who has an ear, let him hear what the Spirit says to* *the churches. To him who overcomes I will give to eat from the tree of life, which is in the midst of the Paradise of God.'"*

When Jesus says, "He who has an ear, let him hear what the Spirit says to the churches," He is talking about the "blood-tipped ear." In Exodus 29:20, we read, "Then you shall kill the ram, and take some of its blood and put it on the tip of the right ear of Aaron and on the tip of the right ear of his sons, on the thumb of their right hand and on the big toe of their right foot, and sprinkle the blood all around on the altar." In order to consecrate the priest, blood had to be placed on the tip of his right ear (a symbol of being touched by the Father's love, cleansed by the blood of Christ, and an anointing of hearing the counsel of the Holy Spirit and acting on His truth).

We hear sounds all day long, but we may miss the message. In John 14:26, Jesus said, "But the Helper, the Holy Spirit, whom the Father will send in My name, He will teach you all things, and bring to your remembrance all things that I said to you." The phrase, "He who has an ear, let him hear what the Spirit says to the churches," will be used for all seven churches, so their dull ears may become attentive. Because the Holy Spirit, the third person of the Trinity, is God, inspires all Scripture, is the Spirit of truth, guiding us in all truth and bringing to remembrance what Christ has taught us, His Word is refined and trustworthy since it flows from the very throne of God (John 16:12-15).

The overcomers will eat from the Tree of Life, which is in the midst of the Paradise of God. After the Fall, man was forbidden to eat of the Tree of Life, as recorded in Genesis 3:22-24. There is coming a day that the "no trespassing" sign will be removed, and Christ-followers will have the privilege of eating of the Tree of Life in the garden of heaven, the New Jerusalem, as noted in Revelation 22:2. Not only will we have streets of gold, but also a garden of greenery with this tree bearing fruit, bursting forth with juices of abundant life. Where exactly is the Paradise of God? It is now lost but will be renewed in the New Earth and New Heaven. During Adam and Eve's days of innocence, it was in the Garden of Eden. "From Adam until the Ascension of Jesus, Paradise was in Abraham's Bosom. From the Ascension of Jesus until the end of the Millennium Paradise is in heaven. Then, after the Millennium and for all Eternity, Paradise will be in the New Jerusalem on the New Earth."[9]

The Church of Ephesus at first sounds electrifying and impeccable, possessing admirable characteristics including her relentless work ethic, discernment and perseverance. But a closer look, with divine surgical magnifying glasses, shows that the Church of Ephesus had tragically lost her sincere love for Christ; she was going through the motions, checking off the boxes, appearing flawless. She was advised to repent or completely lose her influence. We will next read about Smyrna, the Persecuted Church, having a poor congregation, yet being deemed rich by Christ for their faithfulness.

The Persecuted Church

2:8 *"And to the angel of the church in Smyrna write, 'These things says the First and the Last, who was dead, and came to life':"*

We'll now assess the second church, Smyrna.

1. Ephesus .... Pretend Church (33 AD – 100 AD)
2. **Smyrna .... Persecuted Church (100 AD – 313 AD)**
3. Pergamos .... Perverted Church (313 AD – 590 AD)
4. Thyatira .... Promiscuous Church (590 AD – 1517 AD)
5. Sardis .... Perished Church (1517 AD – 1790 AD)
6. Philadelphia .. Patriotic Church (1730 AD – present AD)
7. Laodicea .... Passive Church (1900 AD – present AD)

For the church in Smyrna, the Persecuted Church, the seven characteristics are:

1. Church's identification: Smyrna

2. Christ's characterization: Found in verse eight, "These things says the First and the Last, who was dead, and came to life."

3. Cheering affirmation: Found in verses nine and ten, "I know your works, tribulation, and poverty (but you are rich); and I know the blasphemy of those who say they are Jews and are not but are a synagogue of Satan. Do not fear any of those things which you are about to suffer. Indeed, the devil is about to throw some of you into prison, that you may be tested, and you will have tribulation ten days."

4. Constructive admonition: None.

5. Curative instruction: None.

6. Call to action: Found in verse eleven, "He who has an ear, let him hear what the Spirit says to the churches."

7. Coming restoration: Found in verses ten and eleven, "Be faithful until death, and I will give you the crown of life. He who overcomes shall not be hurt by the second death."

The word Smyrna means "myrrh" or bitter and has the connotation of suffering in Christian literature.[10] Smyrna represents the "Persecuted or Martyred Church," covering the period of 100 AD to 313 AD. The city of Smyrna (modern Izmir) was 35 miles north of ancient Ephesus (modern Selçuk) and was founded 1,000 years before Christ.[11] Many writers during John's time referred to Smyrna as the loveliest city in Asia, known as "the Ornament of Asia," "the Crown of Asia," or "the Flower of Asia;" boasting a hill covered by temples and noble buildings known as Pagos; the locals called the buildings encircling this hill the "crown of Smyrna."[12] It was destroyed in 600 BC only to be rebuilt with architectural wonder and aesthetic beauty, courtesy of Alexander the Great's generals around 300 BC. A Greek city of trade on the Aegean Coast,

Smyrna was also noted as a center of learning, especially in science and medicine.[13] Polycarp, one of the most notable leaders in the early post-apostolic church, was one of the "angels" or pastors of Smyrna and died a martyr's death at age 86 in 168 AD because he refused to deny Christ.[14]

Smyrna received its name from one of its principal commercial products, myrrh, a gum resin taken from a shrubby tree. Myrrh was one of the elements used to make sweet smelling incense unto the Lord (Exodus 30:23); to make perfumes for the bridegroom and the bride (Psalm 45:8); for the purification of women (Esther 2:12); to embalm the dead (John 19:39).[14] "And Nicodemus, who at first came to Jesus by night, also came, bringing a mixture of myrrh and aloes, about a hundred pounds. Then they took the body of Jesus and bound it in strips of linen with the spices, as the custom of the Jews is to bury" (John 19:39-40). Ignatius, who was martyred in Rome 108 AD wrote about the Smyrna Christians, "I observed that you are established in an unshakable faith, having been nailed, as it were, to the cross of the Lord Jesus Christ in both body and spirit and firmly established in love by the blood of Christ."[16]

In this verse, we find that Christ is the "First and the Last, who was dead, and came to life." Christ is the eternal God, who existed before time and will exist beyond time, from Eternity to Eternity.

 His crucifixion was a gift of salvation and His resurrection was a resounding proclamation, that He, the Lord Jesus Christ, will remain unshaken!

2:9 *"'I know your works, tribulation, and poverty (but you are rich); and I know the blasphemy of those who say they are Jews and are not but are a synagogue of Satan.*

In Matthew 2:11, the wise men brought to baby Jesus, gold, myrrh and frankincense. Gold symbolizes royalty, fit for the

King of Kings. Frankincense symbolizes the priesthood, fit for the great High Priest. Myrrh symbolizes the martyred prophets, fit for the slain Lamb of God. Myrrh is extracted through repeatedly bleeding the tree by damaging the bark. And a sweet aroma is released by the crushing of the indigenous plant. In the Greek the crushing is known as "thlipsis," tribulation, or intense pressure, such as placing a boulder on a person's chest until it crushes him to death.

As mentioned, myrrh had several purposes: medicinally (wound dressing), for perfume, embalming, and incense. It reminds us of the passion or suffering of Christ, and how everlasting life arose like sweet aroma from the bruising, crushing and crucifying of our Savior. Christ-followers needed to know that it was Christ who was in charge and who not only knew of their suffering but allowed it; they were brutally battered but their testimony lives throughout history, giving hope to countless disciples who are being martyred today for the name of Christ. These souls will not be forgotten, their lives will not be in vain and they will receive the Crown of Life, presented to them by their Savior.

As we'll also see for the sixth church (The Church of Philadelphia), Christ did not have anything negative to say about Smyrna. It is worth reminding ourselves that Jesus is introduced to the Church of Smyrna as the "First and the Last, who was dead and came to life." Jesus' death which was accented by his resurrection must have resonated in the hearts of the Smyrna's congregation. The victory Jesus had over death became an emblem of hope in the hearts of the congregation of Smyrna Church who faced martyrdom. They therefore would stay faithful to death, holding on to the promise of the "Crown of Life" (Revelation 2:10).

Smyrna was plundered, "died" in 600 BC and "came back to life" in 300 BC; Jesus was scourged, died and resurrected from the dead; so too the congregation of Smyrna would be persecuted, martyred and rise to meet their Redeemer and receive the Crown of Life. The devil could destroy their body but could not touch their spirit (Luke 12:4).

All Roman citizens were obligated to love Rome, love its emperors and worship them. Since these faithful Christ-followers were loyal to Christ, and refused to bow the knee to Rome, they were deemed disloyal and were tortured terribly for their faith by being burned alive, fed to lions, boiled in cauldrons, limbs torn off, burned slowly at the stake, and crucified.[17] Those who remained alive were banned in the city from earning a living and were robbed of what they had, and the Lord knew of their poverty and their destitute state. The Christ-followers of Smyrna knew if they denied Caesar, they would be denied bread on their table, and though they be martyred, they would rather be covered by the blood of the Lamb rather than have a roof over their heads. "We know that they put first things first."[18]

 They had less in their pockets, but God had more of their lives.

Why were they considered to be rich while living in poverty and persecution? They were storing up eternal treasures in heaven! We read in Matthew 6:19-20, "Do not lay up for yourselves treasures on earth, where moth and rust destroy and where thieves break in and steal; but lay up for yourselves treasures in heaven, where neither moth nor rust destroys and where thieves do not break in and steal."

The math of heaven is usually the inverse of what we tally on earth, "For you know the grace of our Lord Jesus Christ, that though He was rich, yet for your sakes He became poor, that you through His poverty might become rich."

 Nowhere in the Bible does it state that riches or money are bad; the reality is that "moths," or scavengers, are present

*on earth and many times not only do "moths" eat away at
the riches, but riches eat away at one's heart.*

We'll see in Revelation 3:17 that the last church, Laodicea, had
great wealth but according to Christ were "wretched, miserable,
poor, blind, and naked," not because they had material prosperity, but because the material prosperity had them. Biblically,
there is poverty which translates into riches and there are
riches which translate into poverty.

In verse nine, we find a statement that attests to the book of
Revelation being far from politically correct; "I know the blasphemy of those who say they are Jews and are not but are a
synagogue of Satan." This is not identity politics; this is the raw
truth. Jews and Gentiles who converted to Christianity were
attacked by apostate Jews who hated them for worshiping
Jesus Christ. These renegades may have been Jews by their
genotype (family lineage), but their pagan hearts did not know
the way of the God of Abraham, Isaac and Jacob. Having been
deceived by the false religion of the culture, they served as
Satan's tool to martyr God fearing Jews and Gentiles who
swore their allegiance to Christ. "For he is not a Jew who is
one outwardly, nor is circumcision that which is outward in
the flesh; but he is a Jew who is one inwardly; and circumcision is that of the heart, in the Spirit, not in the letter; whose
praise is not from men but from God" (Romans 2:28-29).

The Jews who were from the "synagogue of Satan" were not
branded as such because they did not convert to Christianity;
they were designated as such because they identified, slandered and treated Christ-followers with venomous malice.
They joined their heathen counterparts in gathering wood
and burning alive a Christ-follower named Polycarp, who was
a pastor in Smyrna and a pupil of the apostle John.[19]

We see evidence of this kind of slander throughout the book
of Acts in the Apostolic Church Age, "But the Jews stirred up

the devout and prominent women and the chief men of the city, raised up persecution against Paul and Barnabas, and expelled them from their region" (Acts 13:50). Rome gave Jews a special privilege of worship in Judaism, an exemption from worshiping Roman gods and participating in the Greco-Roman cults. Christianity was considered part of Judaism at least through 70 AD, and also benefited from this privilege. However, the followers of Judaism struggled earnestly to separate themselves from Christianity and informed the Roman Empire that Christians were not only counterfeit Judeans, but they were menaces in a cult called Christianity.[20]

When I was a cardiology fellow (in training), I recall seeing a 16-year-old teenager, Ben, who complained of being short of breath after minimal activity. This was unusual as he was an athlete, a pitcher, and already was being scouted by colleges. He had been visiting doctors for three months and was diagnosed with asthma, given inhalers and steroids, with no relief of symptoms. When he came to me, I listened to his story, and when I listened to his lungs, and saw his condition, I admitted him to the ICU. He had idiopathic dilated non-ischemic cardiomyopathy, which is a fancy way of saying his heart's horsepower had given up and he was in heart failure and no one knew why. He was such a clean kid: no tobacco, no alcohol, no cocaine, no heroin, no marijuana, no codeine, no drugs ever, a straight-A student, a class act, serving his community. A simple common cold, three months before, caused his condition, which quickly deteriorated, and we placed this fine young man on a heart transplant list.

You talk about a shock! An aspiring major league pitcher who was fearless, and who was going to be offered scholarships, was fighting for his life, scared and shattered! It took three months on a waiting list for Ben to get his new heart, and his life changed drastically. Ben suffered an episode of transplant rejection and was treated with immunosuppressants. Up to 90% of heart transplant patients live one year after their surgery and do well, especially if they are young, but tragically, Ben did not make it. We were all broken and in tears. Ben, a kind soul, a clean kid, a wonderful son, an amazing young man slipped out of our hands without doing anything wrong. That's not exactly how we'd draw it up in the ninth inning for Ben.

The persecution in Smyrna is not how Christ-followers would have drawn up their scenario. They would have settled for food on the table, getting along with their next-door neighbor, not to be subjected to the literal fire, nor be under the whip of the flogger, nor come under the hammer, nor be downtrodden by the harasser, nor to be under constant pressure, nor face unimaginable torture, nor fall in the hands of a traitor, nor to die as a martyr. That is definitely not how they'd draw it up as the ninth-inning gamekeeper!

2:10 *Do not fear any of those things which you are about to suffer. Indeed, the devil is about to throw some of you into prison, that you may be tested, and you will have tribulation ten days. Be faithful until death, and I will give you the crown of life.*

While the "ninth inning" seemed to be nothing short of cruel for Smyrna, Christ told the church to be fearless. Despite the "ten days of persecution," which realistically is a span of two hundred years with ten waves of overwhelming oppression that took place under ten pagan Roman emperors, Christ is Lord over all of life's circumstances. The ten rulers with their approximate time of rule are as follows:

1. Nero 64-68 AD. He burned Rome and blamed Christians; executed Paul and Peter.

2. Domitian 90-96 AD. He banished John to the Isle of Patmos.
3. Trajan 104-117 AD. He outlawed Christianity.
4. Marcus Aurelius 161-180 AD. He beheaded Christians.
5. Severus 200-211 AD. He crucified Christians.
6. Maximinus 235-237 AD. He executed Christians.
7. Decius 250-253 AD. He attempted to wipe out Christianity.
8. Valerian 257-260 AD. He too attempted to wipe out Christianity.
9. Aurelian 270-275 AD. He persecuted Christians.
10. Diocletian 303-312 AD. He burned the Scriptures.[21]

The number ten is used 242 times in the Bible and "10th" is used 79 times, bringing the total to 321 times; ten is viewed as a complete and perfect number as are three, seven and twelve.[22] There are ten commandments, and the number ten signifies the testimony, law, responsibility and the completeness of order. The phrase "God said," is used ten times in Genesis one, a testimony of His creative power. A tithe is a tenth of one's earnings, and when given, it is a testimony of one's faith in the Lord. The Passover lamb was selected on the tenth day of the first month (Exodus 12:3) as was Jesus, the Lamb that takes away the sins of the world (John 1:29). The ten days of suffering does not demark the Tribulation period of seven years as the church will not go through this horrid time; it denotes the complete washing and purification of the church.

Make no mistake: Satan is the crafty instigator, the true adversary, the vicious prosecutor and the deadly persecutor. He unleashed all the forces of hell in an effort to stamp out the Church of Smyrna. Satan hates. Satan kills. Satan steals; he will "Rev Up" all his tactics of destruction during the Tribulation but will always be on a leash; he has and will always be "Out-Revved" by God! During the Smyrna era, Christ-followers were mocked, slandered, beaten, jailed, tortured, burned and crucified, and yet stood fast during this horrendous "cleansing" period because they were promised the Crown of Life, an appropriate reward for those who lived in the city known as the "Crown of Asia."

There are at least five crowns that overcomers since the beginning of time will receive when we are with Christ:

1. The Imperishable Crown (I Corinthians 9:24-27). Olympians may get gold, but their metal's glory and memory fades. As we run the spiritual race, not under the law, but under grace, aiming to honor God by serving Him and serving mankind, we aim to acquire a prize that is eternal. Given to Christians who persevere.

2. The Crown of Rejoicing or Exaltation (I Thessalonians 2:19-20). Given to evangelists, who preach the Gospel to nonbelievers.

3. The Crown of Life (James 1:12; Revelation 2:10). Given to martyrs and those who have endured trials.

4. The Crown of Righteousness (II Timothy 4:8). Given to Christ-followers who long for His appearing, and while waiting, desire intimacy with God.

5. The Crown of Glory (I Peter 5:2-4). Given to the shepherds, pastors and messengers who guide the church with love.

When will the crowns be handed out? We'll study this more in depth in chapter four, but after the Rapture, all believers will face Christ at the Bema seat or the judgment seat of Christ (Romans 14:8-10; I Corinthians 3:1-10; II Corinthians 5:10). This is not when one is judged to go to heaven or hell; he is already in heaven! This is when believers either receive or forfeit rewards, depending on their works for Christ while they lived on earth.

One of my favorite verses that I recite daily is Isaiah 41:10, where the Lord encourages us, "Fear not, for I am with you; be not dismayed, for I am your God. I will strengthen you, yes, I will help you, I will uphold you with My righteous right hand." Knowing our God is carrying us with His righteous right hand, despite our circumstances and our heartaches, gives us great courage. We may see our pain in a different light if we consider II Corinthians 4:8-9,17, "We are hard-pressed on every side, yet not crushed; we are perplexed, but not in despair; persecuted, but not forsaken; struck down, but not destroyed. For our light affliction, which is but for a moment, is working for us a far more exceeding and eternal weight of glory." Our suffering has Godly purpose. "The time of interim suffering is likely to terminate in actual death, not the mere threat of it, but that death for the Christian is the prelude to life."[23]

Christ tells the church to be faithful, even unto death. Here lies the beauty of Christ found in II Timothy 2:13, "If we are faithless, He remains faithful; He cannot deny Himself." But we, who are His children, can grow under faith so that we may abandon fear.

 We may never get to the point of being "fearless," but we can, by His grace, fear less!

No matter how small our faith, our Shepherd will always hold us. These precious believers may have lived in Smyrna, but they were citizens of an even greater kingdom whose King was, is and will always be the eternal God. Since our Christ gained victory over death, we shall not fear hardships, frivolous lawsuits, the horror of addictions, divorce, failure and even death. Christ knew exactly what they were facing. He knows what you are facing right now. He knows. He sees. He loves. He will never forget you nor forsake you. He will always love you and provide for you. Hold on! Fight on! Stand firm! Look up! He will see you through!

The words spoken by Christ to the church are not empty promises or mere words. Christ gave up the riches of heaven and had nowhere to lay His head (Matthew 8:20); He knew and experienced poverty. He also endured slander and false accusations, and was brutally whipped and murdered. He is not an outsider looking into the church with an attempt to offer empty and insincere condolences. He is the slain Lamb of God who is our High Priest, sympathizing with our weaknesses, and understanding our difficulties (Hebrews 4:15). Ten days may have been 200 years, but there was still a limit placed on suffering. For the child of God, suffering will not last forever. God's purpose will stand. God's help will sustain. God's love will endure.

2:11 *"He who has an ear, let him hear what the Spirit says to the churches. He who overcomes shall not be hurt by the second death."*

As mentioned, Smyrna was one of the loveliest cities in Asia Minor, known as "the Crown of Asia." The overcomer may have faced the first death, or physical death, but he would receive the heavenly "Crown of Life" and escape the second death, or eternal death. The first death is the death experienced at the end of our earthly lives. The second death is for unbelievers, those who have rejected Christ and are sentenced to an eternity apart from God's presence. The first death is unavoidable. The second death can be bypassed by accepting the redemption and final work of Christ on the cross.

 The first death separates the soul and spirit from the body. The second death separates the soul and spirit from God, eternally. The world lives to die, but the believer will die to live.

If you are born once, you will die twice, the second being eternal hell. If you are born twice, physically and born again spiritually, you will only die once. There will be Christians who will bypass even the first death because they will be alive when the Rapture takes place and caught away directly into heaven.

No matter the circumstance and wherever you may find yourself, you will be able to cope, to stand, to persevere and to be victorious in Christ. You don't have to fight for your life; Jesus was dead, is alive, and fights for you. You don't have to get victory; victory was already won for you at Calvary. It is done. It is finished. Be aware of who you are in Christ!

The Church of Ephesus appeared faultless but lacked love for Christ. The Church of Smyrna was bombarded by slander and was about to face immense suffering. As the Great Physician placed His divine surgical magnifying glasses on, He gave Smyrna her diagnosis and prognosis: you will be tested to the point of death; take heart, remain faithful and you will receive the crown of life. We will next read about Pergamos, the Perverted Church, caught up in idolatry and sexual immorality.

The Perverted Church

2:12 *"And to the angel of the church in Pergamos write, These things says He who has the sharp two-edged sword."*

We'll now discuss the third church, Pergamos.

1. Ephesus..........Pretend Church (33 AD – 100 AD)
2. Smyrna............Persecuted Church (100 AD – 313 AD)
3. **Pergamos.... Perverted Church (313 AD – 590 AD)**
4. Thyatira...........Promiscuous Church (590 AD – 1517 AD)
5. Sardis...............Perished Church (1517 AD – 1790 AD)
6. Philadelphia..Patriotic Church (1730 AD – present AD)
7. Laodicea.........Passive Church (1900 AD – present AD)

For the church in Pergamos, the Compromising Church, the seven characteristics are:

1. Church's identification: Pergamos

2. Christ's characterization: Found in verse twelve, "These things says He who has the sharp two-edged sword."

3. Cheering affirmation: Found in verse thirteen, "I know

your works, and where you dwell, where Satan's throne is. And you hold fast to My name and did not deny My faith even in the days in which Antipas was My faithful martyr, who was killed among you, where Satan dwells."

4. Constructive admonition: Found in verses fourteen and fifteen, "But I have a few things against you, because you have those who hold the doctrine of Balaam, who taught Balak to put a stumbling block before the children of Israel, to eat things sacrificed to idols, and to commit sexual immorality. Thus you also have those who hold the doctrine of the Nicolaitans, which thing I hate."

5. Curative instruction: Found in verse sixteen, "Repent, or else I will come to you quickly and will fight against them with the sword of My mouth."

6. Call to action: Found in verse seventeen, "He who has an ear, let him hear what the Spirit says to the churches."

7. Coming restoration: Found in verse seventeen, "To him who overcomes I will give some of the hidden manna to eat. And I will give him a white stone, and on the stone a new name written which no one knows except him who receives it."

Pergamos, modern day Bergamo, was the capital of Rome's government in Asia Minor, 60 miles north of Smyrna and fifteen miles east of the Aegean Sea which is a part of the Mediterranean Sea; if Ephesus was the "Light of Asia" and Smyrna was the "Crown of Asia," then Pergamos was the "Big Apple of Asia."[24] It was a university city, famous for its library of 200,000 parchment scrolls, second only in size to the library of Alexandria in Egypt; the Egyptian king banned the export of papyrus to Pergamos when he found that the Alexandrian librarian was enticed to head the library of Pergamos; scholars in Pergamos therefore invented parchment which is a writing material made from untanned skins of animals, which subsequently played a big role in preserving the Bible.[25]

As we shall see in the next verse, the Church of Pergamos, the "Perverted Church," was mixed, contaminated with men of corrupt minds, who did what they could to defile both the faith and manners of the church. Christ in turn resolved to fight against them by the sword of His mouth, or by the Word of God. The sword is sharp, able to cut through the hardest of hearts. Not only does the Word have an edge to wound (it convicts and cautions man because of their unbelief and pride), but it also has a second edge to open a festered wound in order to allow healing (it convicts and converts man because of their belief and humility). "For the Word of God is living and powerful, and sharper than any two-edged sword, piercing even to the division of soul and spirit, and of joints and marrow, and is a discerner of the thoughts and intents of the heart" (Hebrews 4:12).

"In the beginning was the Word, and the Word was with God, and the Word was God; and the Word became flesh and dwelt among us, and we beheld His glory, the glory as of the only begotten of the Father, full of grace and truth" (John 1:1,14). Jesus, full of grace and truth, was the Word, is the Word, and will always be the Word. Jesus is the Son of God, and He is God. All religions try to reach a god or something beyond themselves. Jesus Christ became flesh, dwelt among man and reached us, introducing God as our Father.

Why is the Bible a two-edged sword? The number two conveys the meaning of a union, division or verification.

1. Union: There is a union between Christ and the church (I Corinthians 12).

2. Division: The Bible is divided into the Old and New Testaments. The first man, Adam, sinned and brought death and destruction into the world. Jesus, the second or last Adam, brings the hope of eternal life (I Corinthians 14:21-22, 45-49). Those who refuse to repent and obey God will be thrown into the Lake of Fire, which is

the "second death" according to Revelation 21:8. This will divide those who are righteous from the unrighteous.

3. Verification: The testimony of at least two people was needed in the Old Testament to convict a person of a crime (I Timothy 5:19). Jesus sent His disciples out to preach, teach and heal in groups of two (Mark 6:7-13). Two witnesses, Elijah and Moses, will appear in Revelation chapter eleven to speak God's truth and resist the lies of Satan.[26]

One reason why people reject God, His Word, Jesus Christ is because they don't want to know the truth about themselves. We are all sinners and have fallen short of God's glory. But if people would just listen, they would realize how much God loves them! The image of Christ with a sword in His mouth, the symbolism of the Word, depicts His displeasure with this compromising church and His petition for the church to hear the truth and repent.

 Being the Great Physician, Jesus handles the scalpel skillfully. His cut is precise and is intended not to bring misery in your life but to promote healing for your soul.

2:13 *"I know your works, and where you dwell, where Satan's throne is. And you hold fast to My name and did not deny My faith even in the days in which Antipas was My faithful martyr, who was killed among you, where Satan dwells.*

When John wrote the book of Revelation, Satan's headquarters was in Pergamos, Turkey. Some believe Satan resides in hell, but they are mistaken. Satan will not be thrown into hell, or the Lake of Fire, until the end of time (Revelation 20:7-10). Today, Satan camps out on earth, and as the prince of the world, controls kingdoms, roaming around to and fro like a roaring lion, seeking to devour (I Peter 5:8). Since Satan goes about to and fro, he can change his central location; in the future, it will be in Babylon as we shall discuss in Revelation 17 and 18, where I'll pinpoint who and where Babylon will be.

Pergamos was the center of emperor worship, boasting the largest altars of worship in honor of the emperors or Caesars of that time. Citizens were required to pledge their allegiance once a year and offer a pinch of incense at Caesar's altar and profess that he is Lord.[27] Pergamos was decorated with pagan temples: the temple of Athena, the great temple of Caesar Augustus, Hadrian's great temple, the great altar to Zeus, and the temple of Dionysius.[28] Dionysus, also known as Bacchus, is the god of wine, the goat-god, depicted with horns. His upper part is a man's figure and his lower part as a goat, with cloven feet and a tail. The most popular image of Satan comes from the god Bacchus, from Pergamos, and not the Bible.

The word "Pergamos" has its root in "per" and "gamos," "per" meaning unacceptable or inappropriate (such as per-vert) and "gamos" meaning marriage: unacceptable or objectionable marriage. This church represents the era of 313 AD to 590 AD. After Domitian's reign, two leaders contended to become the next emperor: Constantine, who was the underdog, and Maxentius who was set to win the battle. On the night before the major Battle of the Milvian Bridge, Constantine saw a vision of the cross in the sky and was convinced that he was to "conquer." Constantine won the battle, instantly declared himself a Christian and made Christianity the official religion of the Roman Empire, protecting Christians. He recruited all the pagan priests of that time and "changed" them to Christian priests. The priests of Jupiter, Juno, and Venus who were on the imperial payrolls quickly changed their temples into churches.[29]

Many question his conversion to Christianity, but Christians joined him by the droves, and gained great political advantage that ended their persecution. Unfortunately, if you change your garment without changing your heart, you have only changed your appearance but not your person.

When I had just graduated from medical school, I entered into a residency program, an essential steppingstone for me to become a cardiologist. I recall being on a team and taking care of a patient who had severe cardiomyopathy (heart failure, leading to fluid in the lungs). One of my colleagues asked the team leader if he could use both a beta blocker and dobutamine on this patient at the same time. The team leader went ballistic, asking my colleague which medical school he graduated from, and "Did you even *go* to medical school?" It was an embarrassing moment for us all.

Beta blockers (blockers inhibit a physiological function) are used in many cases, including in patients who have high blood pressure, history of strokes, history of heart attacks, and even history of heart failure that is chronic or under control. Dobutamine is partially a beta agonist (agonists stimulate a physiological function) and is used in the intensive care unit, where a patient's symptoms of heart failure are so severe that he may die without this agent on board. The two are diametrically opposed. If you're using dobutamine to save someone's life, you don't use beta blockers at the same time. They don't mix. The beta blocker will make the frail patient's condition worse and cause great harm. When you have a Christ-centered church, there is no mixing. You've got to go with all the Word; if you don't, then compromising with the culture and the fear of losing your reputation will undermine Christ's redemption.

Christ had words of affirmation for this church. Some held fast to His name and did not deny their faith even in the midst of persecution. In an era where citizens would take incense, offer it on the altar and shout, "Caesar is Lord," Antipas, a faithful defender of the truth, firmly held on to his belief in the only true God and refused to participate. He was placed in a brazen bull-shaped altar that was hollowed out, placed over a fire, burned to death, and made an example to the whole city of what would happen to those who did not bow the knee to the emperor in 92 AD. No wonder Satan felt at home! Targeting Christians, making a spectacle out of them, censoring them, harassing them, shunning them, and taking their very lives from them! But Antipas' testimony was dramatic, and the knowledge and news of his sacrifice became widespread.[30]

 You can kill a Christian, but you can't kill the Christ who lives in him!

2:14 *But I have a few things against you, because you have those who hold the doctrine of Balaam, who taught Balak to put a stumbling block before the children of Israel, to eat things sacrificed to idols, and to commit sexual immorality.*

We read in Numbers 22-24, Balak, the king of Moab, hired Balaam, a false prophet and a sorcerer, to curse the people of Israel prior to their entry into the land of Canaan. Balaam, unable to curse Israel because of God's intervention, taught Balak the way to corrupt Israel was by intermarrying them with Moabite women. The Moabites introduced idolatry and sexual immorality into the hearts and lives of Israel. A little mixing won't hurt anyone, right? Just ask your friendly virus as it mixes in the blood stream. It may be a minuscule, microscopic agent. But it will certainly cause colossal illnesses!

The error of Balaam was that he thought God would curse Israel because they were sinners. God even had Balaam's donkey speak to him and "teach" him the ways of God! But Balaam's greed would not allow him to obey God. To his dismay, every time he tried to curse, a blessing came out of his mouth. The way of Balaam was to covet as he sought to curse a nation, willing to sacrifice them to gain great rewards from Balak.

Just as Balaam compromised the faith of the Israelites, so too the influence of Rome compromised the faith of the Christian church. Civil and religious life were intertwined; for believers to accept social engagements meant involvement with pagan-ism.[31] The church is no longer a church when it integrates itself into culture; it must set itself apart; otherwise, it's just a club. Let the culture integrate itself into the cross, where only the blood of Jesus is able to take away man's sins.

 Culture cannot correct Christ. Christ, however, can heal the culture and Christ-followers can influence it for the good with service and love!

2:15 Thus you also have those who hold the doctrine of the Nicolaitans, which thing I hate.

Constantine married paganism to Christianity and took on the title Pontifex Maximus, becoming the first pope of the Roman church. Rags of persecution changed overnight into plush silk priestly robes. Great cathedrals were built. Robes were swishing. Incense was rising. And dazzling hats were displaying. All of Rome's pagan culture penetrated the church. The Roman Empire engulfed the Christian church and made it into the Roman church. The pagan priests took over as the new "Christian" priests. One can profess to be a believer, but actions speak the truth. The Nicolaitans were not an outside force in the city; they were from within the church. They held in their hearts a spirit of mastering others: they conquered the people, ruling over their minds and their very existence. They ate food sacrificed to idols and also engaged in idolatry and fornication. According to Galatians 5:9, a little yeast will work through the whole batch of dough. A "little" sin may seem harmless and allowed to be tolerated, but it can weaken and destroy the church.

 In cardiology, it's the smallest things that cause the greatest problems: salt is notorious for worsening hypertension in many patients; sugar is key in causing diabetes; nicotine in cigarettes and vaping devices may not be seen, but this foul stimulant causes havoc to the entire body, including heart attacks. Small matters with big consequences? You betcha!

2:16 *Repent, or else I will come to you quickly and will fight against them with the sword of My mouth.*

Christ warns the church to turn from the way of perversion, idolatry and adultery. Neither the word of the Nicolaitans nor of Balaam holds up to the Word of God. The Sword of the Spirit, or the Word, will confound any false teaching or relativism. Antipas was burned alive under Rome's sword, but some of the members of the Pergamos Church were warned that they were about to encounter Christ's sword unless they repented. Christ promised to enter into Pergamos' affairs judicially, personally and swiftly.

2:17 *"He who has an ear, let him hear what the Spirit says to the churches. To him who overcomes I will give some of the hidden manna to eat. And I will give him a white stone, and on the stone a new name written which no one knows except him who receives it."*

"He who has an ear, let him hear what the Spirit says to the churches," is now used in the reading of the third church, as an encouragement so that believer's dull ears may become attentive. "To him who overcomes I will give some of the hidden manna to eat." In contrast to the foods sacrificed to pagan gods, God assured the overcomer heavenly manna. The Israelites had bread called manna that rained down from heaven while they were in the wilderness for forty years. Moses said to the Israelites in Exodus 16:15, "This is the bread which the Lord has given you to eat." In John 6:32-35, Jesus said, "I am the bread of life." If you come to Him, you will never hunger and if you believe in Him, you will never thirst. The reason the manna is "hidden" is because it represents the person of Jesus

Christ, interceding for us in the tabernacle of God, and thereby sustaining us day to day. Those who ate the manna in the wilderness died; those who eat of the Bread of Life will live eternally.

In Revelation 2:17, we continue to read, "And I will give him a white stone, and on the stone a new name written which no one knows except him who receives it." During court trials, if a judge handed a white stone to the defendant, he was deemed innocent. If he handed a black stone, the defendant was guilty.[32] We will not be black balled in heaven. No one will hand us a negative vote and reject us. We who are washed by the blood of the Lamb and do not bow to any other god, will be accepted into the loving arms of our Good Shepherd who laid down His life for the sheep.

We will get a new name, like a nickname, known only to the recipient and to Christ. According to Revelation 19:12, Jesus will have a new name as well, "He had a name written that no one knew except Himself." We are so unique and so loved by God, that we will still have our own special identities handed to us by the One who has written our names in the palm of His hands (Isaiah 49:16).

 Come to Him! He will embrace you. He will accept you. He will acquit you. He who has called you by name will make you altogether new!

The Church of Pergamos held fast to Christ with one hand and to the teachings of Balaam and the Nicolaitans on the other, transforming itself as a "hybrid" church, partially good and partially bad. As the Great Physician placed His divine surgical magnifying glasses on, He called the Church of Pergamos out for mixing Christ's teaching with idolatry and sexual immorality. We will next read about Thyatira, the Promiscuous Church, caught up in Jezebel's wicked spell.

The Promiscuous Church

2:18 *"And to the angel of the church in Thyatira write, 'These things says the Son of God, who has eyes like a flame of fire, and His feet like fine brass'"*

We'll now discuss the fourth church, Thyatira.

1. Ephesus .... Pretend Church (33 AD – 100 AD)
2. Smyrna .... Persecuted Church (100 AD – 313 AD)
3. Pergamos .... Perverted Church (313 AD – 590 AD)
4. **Thyatira .... Promiscuous Church (590 AD – 1517 AD)**
5. Sardis .... Perished Church (1517 AD – 1790 AD)
6. Philadelphia .. Patriotic Church (1730 AD – present AD)
7. Laodicea .... Passive Church (1900 AD – present AD)

For the church in Thyatira, the Corrupt Church, the seven characteristics are:

1. Church's identification: Thyatira

2. Christ's characterization: Found in verse eighteen, "These things says the Son of God, who has eyes like a flame of fire, and His feet like fine brass."

3. Cheering affirmation: Found in verse nineteen, "I know your works, love, service, faith, and your patience; and as for your works, the last are more than the first."

4. Constructive admonition: Found in verses twenty through twenty-three. "Nevertheless, I have a few things against you, because you allow that woman Jezebel, who calls herself a prophetess, to teach and seduce My servants to commit sexual immorality and eat things sacrificed to idols. And I gave her time to repent of her sexual immorality, and she did not repent. Indeed, I will cast her into a sickbed, and those who commit adultery with her into great tribulation, unless they repent of their deeds. I will kill her children with death, and all the churches shall know that I am He who searches the minds and hearts. And I will give to each one of you according to your works."

5. Curative instruction: Found in verses twenty-four through twenty-five. "Now to you I say, and to the rest in Thyatira, as many as do not have this doctrine, who have not known the depths of Satan, as they say, I will put on you no other burden. But hold fast what you have till I come.

6. Call to action: Found in verse twenty-nine. "He who has an ear, let him hear what the Spirit says to the churches."

7. Coming restoration: Found in verses twenty-six through twenty-eight. "And he who overcomes, and keeps My works until the end, to him I will give power over the nations — 'He shall rule them with a rod of iron; They shall be dashed to pieces like the potter's vessels' — as I also have received from My Father; and I will give him the morning star."

Thyatira is known as the "Adulterous or Promiscuous Church," and though it was an actual church in John's days, it represents the Church Age from 590 AD to 1517 AD. This period is known as the Middle Ages or Dark Ages in world history.

Thyatira was located in a valley between Pergamos (the third church) and Sardis (the fifth church we'll see in the next chapter). Even though it had no natural fortifications, and some consider it to be the least important of the seven cities, it received the longest of the letters addressed to the seven churches.

Thyatira was famous for a purple dye manufactured from the madder root, which was a cheap rival for the expensive Phoenician murex dye made from shellfish.[33] It was the home of Lydia, mentioned in Acts 16:14, a business woman and a dealer of purple cloth. She traveled to Philippi, Macedonia (Greece), on business, and while there, met the apostle Paul, accepted Christ and became the first recorded Christian convert in Macedonia.[34] She returned to Thyatira with the Gospel burning in her soul and established a church in her home city.

However, Lydia faced a difficult religious environment in Thyatira. The mystical Babylonian system and religion had entrenched itself in Rome and its territories. The celebration of gods such as Baal, Ashtoreth, Nimrod and Tammuz was prevalent. The Saturnalia on December 25th was kept but called Christmas. The Ishtar during Spring was kept but called Easter. The Queen of Heaven was exalted, and Mary became greater than Jesus. Bridges were built between people and God, known as the Pope and the hierarchy of priests. In their practice, Christ was to be sacrificed continually during mass, and is still considered dying every time a priest blesses the bread and wine. However, the Bible states that Jesus died once and only once to break the power of sin (Romans 6:10).

Thyatira represents the Roman Catholic Church. I am not questioning today's congregation's salvation; that's in God's hands and in the people's hearts. If one wishes to remain Biblically Correct, then he needs to abide by what the Bible states: "For there is one God and one Mediator between God and men, the Man Christ Jesus" (I Timothy 2:5). That's how simple it gets. No man, including the Pope, and no woman, including Mary, the mother of Jesus, can be our intercessor to God. Why? Because they were not the ones who died on the cross for our salvation!

Dark shadows swamped the church during the Middle Ages because the Bible that gives light, life and liberty was not the basis for life. Power was maintained in the church, but darkness ruled the land. This was definitely not the church of Acts! It doesn't matter if a church is Catholic or Protestant. One is not better than the other. One is not "more right" than the other. What matters is if Christ is being preached. It matters if the blood of the Lamb has cleansed you from all your sins. It matters if Jesus is your Savior, Lord, and the love of your life. No mass, no churchgoing, no Sunday school, no man, no woman, no denomination, no choir, no pastor, no priest, no Pope, no priestly mediator, nothing is greater than Christ and nobody can take His place. There are no bridges to God except through Christ. No man can bridge you to God or forgive you of your sins because he, no matter what his title or his apparel, is a sinner himself and needs to be redeemed by the blood of the Lamb. A man, a Pope, a rabbi, a pastor is not the final word. Christ, the living Word, is the final word!

Jesus reveals Himself to this church as "the Son of God, who has eyes like a flame of fire, and feet like fine brass." Note that He did not call Himself the Son of Man, a name which He repeatedly referred to in the Gospels. He called Himself the Son of God. Son of Man is tied to Jesus' humanity, while Son of God speaks of His deity. Since the Church of Thyatira faced the Son of God, it added a weighty seriousness to the problems in the church. Those reading and hearing these words would fully comprehend that Christ was making an unequivocal claim to be God. During Jesus' early ministry, the Jewish leaders not only began to persecute him but wanted to kill him because He was "breaking" the Sabbath, and calling God His own Father, making himself equal with God (John 5:16-18). Jesus called Himself God because He is God.

The problem in the church in Thyatira may not have been in plain sight, but because Jesus has the eyes like a flame of fire, signifying His omniscience as God, He can see right through the smokescreen. What is done in secret will be revealed; what is hidden in darkness will be exposed; and what is swept under the carpet will be uncovered. Yes. The timeworn saying is still true: you can run, but you can't hide!

The feet of fine brass reveal the judgment of Christ. The translation of the original word for "brass" is curious because it's used in only one other place in the New Testament. It's the Greek word "chalkolibanon," a composite of the words "chalkos" and "libanos." The word "chalkos" describes the metal brass as a copper alloy, primarily mixed with zinc. The word "libanos" is the Greek word describing frankincense. If we recall that priests used frankincense (Leviticus 2:1-2) in their priestly ministry, the meaning becomes clear when we picture Jesus as our High Priest. Although Christ was coming with judgment, His feet of brass were soaked in frankincense. In other words, because Jesus did not want to condemn His Church, even His judgment was immersed in prayer and mercy.

A quality well known about the metal brass is that it is heavy. If someone's feet were made of brass, he wouldn't be able to do much running. Although Jesus was coming to admonish His Church, He was moving very slowly. All the churches that received a warning from Jesus would have ample time to respond to Him and repent before He arrived in judgment. What action would He take when He arrived at the church?

 Christ will be coming with feet of brass bathed in frankincense, not to devour, but to correct. Not to devastate, but to direct. Not to destroy, but to perfect. Blessed be the name of the Lord!

2:19 *"I know your works, love, service, faith, and your patience; and as for your works, the last are more than the first.*

According to Galatians 5:22-23, the fruit of the Spirit is love, joy, peace, patience, kindness, goodness, faithfulness, gentleness, and self-control. Thyatira had strong faith, love and patience as evidenced by their works or service. We read in Titus 3:8, "This is a trustworthy saying. And I (Paul) want you to stress these things, so that those who have trusted in God may be careful to devote themselves to doing what is good. These things are excellent and profitable for everyone." Good works are evidence of a heart that has been transformed by Jesus.

In I Corinthians 3:12-15, we read, "Now if anyone builds on this foundation with gold, silver, precious stones, wood, hay, straw, each one's work will become clear; for the Day will declare it, because it will be revealed by fire; and the fire will test each one's work, of what sort it is. If anyone's work which he has built on it endures, he will receive a reward. If anyone's work is burned, he will suffer loss; but he himself will be saved, yet so as through fire." These verses refer to the Bema Seat of Christ where all Christ-followers will be judged just after the Rapture during the seven-year Tribulation period. We will have been raptured immediately to heaven, while a Christ-rejecting, God-hating, Holy Spirit-blaspheming souls will be left on earth to face the Tribulation during the same seven-year period.

Christ-followers will not be judged whether or not they make it into heaven; they are already in the presence of their Master and Savior! We will be judged for our works, the resources and time and gifts given to us and how we gave back to build Christ's Kingdom. All carnal works or wasted efforts will be burned up; all that was for His glory will be turned into a reward or one of the five crowns. Christ not only sees our works, but He also sees our true motives.

When we hear Jesus say, "I know your works, love, service, faith, and your patience; and as for your works, the last are more than the first," we should all be going to this church! They outdid themselves and continued to surpass in their work day to day. This was a laboring church, a loving church, a loyal church and a long-suffering church. But whenever you have something good, Satan schemes to make it bad. The Garden of Eden was good; Satan made it a place of disobedience. Health is good; Satan introduced sin and now we need hospitals and heart doctors. Life is good; Satan introduced death. Thyatira was a good church; as we'll see, Satan made it his business to undermine its ministry by introducing the spirit of Jezebel.

2:20 Nevertheless I have a few things against you, because you allow that woman Jezebel, who calls herself a prophetess,

to teach and seduce My servants to commit sexual immorality and eat things sacrificed to idols.

Holiness was the major ingredient lacking in the Church of Thyatira. Though the church displayed many good traits such as having love, it tolerated evil, the self-crowned prophetess, Jezebel, in its midst. This is the exact opposite of the church of Ephesus, the first church, which could not bear evil but had no love.

Thyatira was a spineless church which tolerated immoral behavior because it was caught in the foolish game of political correctness. It was a church which was guided by Matthew 7:1, "Judge not, that you be not judged" but intentionally overlooked John 14:6, "Jesus said, 'I am the way, the truth and the life. No one comes to the Father except through Me.'" It was a church that allowed culture to control its speech, tragically changing the message of the sacred Gospel. Unlike the church in Ephesus, the church in Thyatira failed to test the false apostles and erroneously attributed Jezebel's spiritual power to God. She wielded spiritual powers, but her influence and gifts "reached her from beneath" and did not descend on her from above.[35] John wrote in his epistle, I John 4:1, "Beloved, do not believe every spirit, but test the spirits, whether they are of God; because many false prophets have gone out into the world."

It concerns me that we have many pastors that bend the Word, twisting it to align with the heart of today's culture. They are tickling the ears of the people instead of touching the hearts of the broken. Only the Word of God, spoken in its unadulterated manner, with the cross and the blood of the Lamb, can heal the hearts and souls of mankind. There is coming a time in the near future where pastors will be forced to stop speaking the truth because their rhetoric is a matter of "public safety." But then again, legislators don't even have to worry; there are many teachers who are already amending, adding and subtracting from the Word. By modifying the Bible, these "men of God" are attempting to "tame" God, increase their followers, and bolster their fame. What a shame!

In the Old Testament, Jezebel was the wife of Ahab, the wicked, idolatrous and spineless king of the ten Northern tribes of Israel. Her father, Ethbaal king of the Sidonians (I Kings 16:31), was a priest of a cult that endorsed idolatry and glorified sexual immorality with temple prostitutes during worship. Jezebel married Ahab and enticed Israel to engage in Baal worship (I Kings 16-19). She threatened and killed God's messengers and built an army of false prophets, 450 of Baal and 400 of Ashtoreth. She hired two thugs as false witnesses to have a man (who had a beautiful garden) killed so her pouting husband could get this innocent man's garden. She was like Delilah who seduced a prophet and a judge named Samson, taking him from God's gracious hands into her intoxicating influence.

The spirit of Jezebel is a demonic spirit. It seduces, meaning it causes one to stray and be led aside from the right way.[36] It refuses to admit guilt, takes prideful credit for everything, demeans people, ignores people, discredits people, criticizes everyone, upstages people, manipulates people, meddles with people's hearts and their relationships, uses people for its gain, intimidates people, belittles people, yells at people, silences people, controls people, mocks people, betrays people, confuses people, lures people, deceives people, never takes blame, thirsts for more power, is vengeful, is demonically spiritual, will kill anyone who gets in its way and will kill anyone to get its way. Her character was incompatible with Christianity. "They (Jezebel and her followers) held banquets in a temple, beginning and ending with a ritual sacrifice to the gods, so the meat eaten at the event was offered to idols; the functions also included drunken revelry and slack morality."[37] Jezebel's great deception was that you can engage in sins in your body without injuring your soul and spirit. Impossible!

When the spirit of Jezebel infiltrates the mind and soul of a person, that soul becomes purely evil, vile, prideful, seductive, narcissistic, demanding, cold, ruthless, cunning, combative, cheating, hating prayer, and able to give false testimony and false prophecy. It can suck the very life out of you and make you feel depressed and suicidal as it did to God's prophet, Elijah, when he killed all of Jezebel's prophets and she came after him with a vengeance! (I Kings 19:1-18).

Just as King Ahab "ignored" or feared Jezebel and did not rebuke her or stand up to her, the church leaders of Thyatira also took on a passive role and gave Jezebel a pass! The "prophetess'" name may very well have been Jezebel, or she simply was a Jezebel-like woman of the Old Testament. This church allowed a satanic spirit to infiltrate and introduce idolatry and sexual immorality through Jezebel. When the Spirit of the Lord warned this "prophetess" in the church of Thyatira and convicted her to repent, she refused. God therefore was about to move in and "cast her into a sickbed" or afflict her with a horrible sickness. But God is merciful, giving ample time for us to repent. According to Isaiah 48:9, God refrains and defers His judgment for His own name's sake for His own praise. Let's not spurn His goodness and grace, and let's not confuse His forgiveness for weakness.

The pleasures of sin are fleeting. Paul also reminds us in Galatians 6:7 regarding consequences, "Do not be deceived, God is not mocked; for whatever a man sows, that he will also reap." Therefore, "her bed of whoredom will be changed into a bed of anguish."[38] God is holy and will not allow rebellion forever. Hebrews 10:31 reminds us: "It is a fearful thing to fall into the hands of the living God."

2:21 *And I gave her time to repent of her sexual immorality, and she did not repent.*

According to II Peter 3:9, God is patient and is not willing that anyone perish, but longs that the lost come to repentance. He gave her time. How much time? I guess as much time as He gave to Pharaoh to change his heart; but just as Pharaoh hardened his heart (Exodus 7:13), so too did Jezebel because she did not recognize the grace, the kindness and the goodness of God. Ezekiel was instructed by God to speak to Israel in Ezekiel 33:11, "Say to them, 'As I live,' says the Lord God, 'I have no pleasure in the death of the wicked, but that the wicked turn from his way and live. Turn, turn from your evil ways! For why should you die, O house of Israel?'" John wrote in I John 1:9, "If we confess our sins, He is faithful and just to forgive us our sins and to cleanse us from all unrighteousness." God is faithful. He is just. He is forgiving. He is simply waiting for you and me to come in response to His invitation!

2:22 *Indeed I will cast her into a sickbed, and those who commit adultery with her into great tribulation, unless they repent of their deeds.* **2:23** *I will kill her children with death, and all the churches shall know that I am He who searches the minds and hearts. And I will give to each one of you according to your works.*

The warning extended not only to the "prophetess" Jezebel, but also to those who indulged in her sin and wickedness; those who committed adultery with her were going to be cast into great trials, sicknesses, and torment unless they repented. Again, notice the restraint of our God! Psalm 86:15 states, "But You, O Lord, are a God full of compassion, and gracious, long-suffering and abundant in mercy and truth." He is so patient! He is so kind! He is so willing to forgive us and break the bonds of oppression which deceitfully and momentarily appear to be "tassels of freedom."

But if there is no repentance, there will be a sentence. Her bed of passion and pleasure was about to become the bed of pestilence and pain.

Christ stated, "I will kill her children with death, and all the churches shall know that I am He who searches the minds and hearts. And I will give to each one of you according to your works." Jezebel's children may be her physical children born of her immorality or her spiritual children who were caught in the web of her deception. She is like the harlot Babylon we'll meet in Revelation 17:1-2, "who sits on many waters, with whom the kings of the earth committed fornication, and the inhabitants of the earth were made drunk with the wine of her fornication." Both Jezebel and the harlot Babylon will pay the price of eternal death. The deceived "believers" of apostate churches will be immersed into a time of unparalleled sorrow, either reaping what they sow, or even worse, suffering in the Great Tribulation, the last horrific half of the Tribulation. A word to the wise found in Romans 2:4, "Do you despise the riches of God's goodness, forbearance and long-suffering, not knowing that the goodness of God leads you to repentance?"

Wisdom, the person of Christ, speaks in Proverbs 8:32-36, "Now therefore, listen to Me, My children, for blessed are those who keep My ways. Hear instruction and be wise, and do not disdain it. Blessed is the man who listens to Me, watching daily at My gates, waiting at the posts of My doors. For whoever finds me finds life and obtains favor from the Lord; but he who sins against Me wrongs his own soul; all those who hate Me love death." The patience of God seems endless, but the judgment of God is swift. He will warn. He will plead. He will advise. He will wait. But if our ears continually and intentionally mute His voice, He will "Rev it Up" and intercede with the hand of justice.

The Son of God, who has eyes like a flame, not only searches the hearts and minds of mankind, but knows our real motives to the core. This is beautifully stated in Jeremiah 17:9-10, "The heart is deceitful above all things, and desperately wicked; who can know it? I, the Lord, search the heart, I test the mind, even to give every man according to his ways, according to the fruit of his doings." According to John 2:23-25, Christ not only knows all of mankind, but He knows what is in the heart and mind of each man.

After the Millennium, the resurrection of the unsaved dead will occur as they appear before the Great White Throne judgment of God. These souls will be judged according to their works, "And I saw the dead, small and great, standing before God, and books were opened. And another book was opened, which is the Book of Life. And the dead were judged according to their works, by the things which were written in the books." You've got a choice. You can either be judged by your own works as compared to that of Christ's or you can receive Christ as your Savior, and have your name written in the Book of Life, obtain God's righteousness through faith in Jesus and escape the Lake of Fire. Simple!

 Tragically, the proud heart will not allow the willing mind to submit to God.

I've tried all my life to give. My time to serve. My life to heal. My money to tithe. There are two ways of looking at this. One, if I sum it all up and compare it to the works of Christ, it adds up to "filthy rags." According to Isaiah 64:6, "But we are all like an unclean thing, and all our righteousness are like filthy rags; we all fade as a leaf, and our iniquities, like the wind, have taken us away." Two, under the blood of the Lamb, I am encouraged to work and press on. "Therefore, my beloved brethren, be steadfast, immovable, always abounding in the works of the Lord, knowing that your labor is not in vain in the Lord" (I Corinthians 15:58). "And let us not grow weary while doing good, for in due season we shall reap if we do not lose heart" (Galatians 6:9). I commit to staying under the blood of the Lamb, knowing it's His sacrifice that makes me righteous, apart from any of my works, and knowing that my works, done in His name, are pleasing to Him!

In medicine, skin wounds can involve the invasion of deeper tissues, causing abscesses, and can jeopardize a limb or even become life-threatening. Because the dead tissue inhibits the development of healthy new tissue and makes the affected area more susceptible to further infection by bacteria, it must be removed. If not removed, the pocket of exudate (pus) will increase, invade deeper tissues (including bone), and become resistant to antibiotics. Debridement is the medical removal of the infected, damaged and dead tissues to improve the healing potential of the remaining healthy tissue. Removal is usually surgical, using sharp tools to cut and discard the damaged tissue.

In the church of Thyatira, the source of infection was Satan. The bacteria in play was Jezebel. The affected tissue was Thyatira. And the deep tissue full of pus was the members of this church. The only way of healing was to take Jezebel out, but because she was resistant to the antibiotics (God's word and admonition), then she had to be removed surgically (death bed). Not only was she to be removed, but all the tissue (church members) she infected. What a horrible tragedy! Let the doctor be the doctor. Let the patient pay attention. And Let the Word of God stand!

2:24 *"Now to you I say, and to the rest in Thyatira, as many as do not have this doctrine, who have not known the depths of Satan, as they say, I will put on you no other burden. 2:25 But hold fast what you have till I come.*

There was a remnant in this church who held on to the Word, refused to succumb to the teachings of Jezebel, and did not know the depths of Satan. God told them that He did not require anything else from them except to stand firm and resist evil until His return. During Thyatira's era, some "believers" felt that they could attend festivities honoring Caesar as god, partaking in food offered to idols, indulging in sexual immorality in order to enable them to grasp knowledge and senselessly and preposterously "to know the satanic opponent's deceptive methods so well that they could all the better defeat Satan in the future."[39]

Don't underestimate the appetite of the flesh and the schemes of Satan. We are complete in Christ as Paul articulates in Colossians 2:8-10, "Beware lest anyone cheat you through philosophy and empty deceit, according to the tradition of men, according to the basic principles of the world, and not according to Christ. For in Him dwells all the fullness of the Godhead bodily; and you are complete in Him, who is the head of all principality and power." In all this, the antidote is not the Word of God in our ears; it is holding on to the Word of God in our hearts! "I have chosen the way of truth; Your judgments I have laid before me. I cling to Your testimonies; O Lord, do not put me to shame!" (Psalm 119:30-31).

In an era where church-goers are grasping onto an open-minded or enlightened view of doctrine, the church is accepting practices that would have been unthinkable a few decades ago. Wherever we are, let's draw a line and let's make that line the inerrant Word of God, refusing to cross over and impeding any "bacteria" from infiltrating the healthy members, speaking, working and living in Christ and His love. You can try to frame me as an intolerant bigot; you'd be mistaken. You would not knowingly allow bacteria to grow in your body, desperately asking the doctor for antibiotics. If I may, it's time to evaluate your own hypocrisy.

2:26 And he who overcomes, and keeps My works until the end, to him I will give power over the nations — 2:27 He shall rule them with a rod of iron; They shall be dashed to pieces like the potter's vessels' — as I also have received from My Father; 2:28 and I will give him the morning star.

As lawlessness abounds in our modern world and the love of many grows cold, we are asked to keep God's work until the end. What exactly does that mean? By keeping His Word, and abiding in Him, we are able to keep His works. Jesus said, "I am the vine, you are the branches. He who abides in Me, and I in him, bears much fruit; for without Me you can do nothing" (John 15:5). Those who sought Jesus asked Him near the shores of Galilee, "What shall we do, that we may work the works of God?" Jesus answered them, "This is the work of God, that you believe in Him whom He sent" (John 6:28-29).

 Doing works for God is not doing any work; work is simply believing in Christ whom the Father sent. Believe in Him. Trust Him. Walk with Him. Adore Him. Worship Him. Call on Him. Submit to Him. Honor Him. Love Him. And in so doing, you will have done great works for Him!

Christ makes an enormous promise that those who overcome will reign over many nations, by quoting Psalm 2:9, "He (Christ) shall rule them with a rod of iron; they (nations who fight against Christ) shall be dashed to pieces like the potter's vessels." As He rules with an iron rod, He will give us the same power to rule with Him during the Millennium and throughout all Eternity (Revelation 17:14, 19:14). This is a chain reaction according to Luke 22:29, "And I (Jesus) bestow upon you (His followers) a kingdom, just as My Father bestowed one upon Me."

The illustration of smashing a potter's vessel resonated loudly to those who read John's book due to the existence of a guild of potters and craftsman in the city of Thyatira.[40] According to

Isaiah 29:16, the clay is intended to be formed and fashioned according to the purpose of the potter. But according to Isaiah 41:25, "Woe to those who quarrel with their Maker," and because the clay refuses to serve the potter, it is the right of the potter to dash the clay into pieces.

When will we receive the privilege of reigning with Christ? The Rapture must first occur; the dead in Christ and those alive in Christ will rise from the earth to meet Christ in the clouds (I Thessalonians 4:15-18). Believers will then stand before the Bema seat judgment (I Corinthians 3:11-15), where we will be given crowns and learn the capacity of our future positions. We will remain in heaven for seven years while the Tribulation occurs on earth. Then we will return with Christ (the Second Coming), witness the Campaign of Armageddon, after which Satan will be bound for a thousand years. During the thousand years that follow, known as the Millennium, we will reign and rule with Christ, and "the greatness of the kingdoms under the whole heaven, shall be given to the people, the saints of the Most High" (Daniel 7:27). How do we know that the reign will not end at the Millennium? Revelation 22:5 verifies it, "There shall be no night there: they need no lamp nor light of the sun, for the Lord God gives them light. And they (His saints) shall reign forever and ever."

Those who are faithful will also receive the morning star. We'll read in Revelation 22:16 that Jesus is the "Bright and Morning Star." The morning star serves as an indicator of the approaching dawn, encouraging onlookers that the long night is nearing its end, ushering in the sun to shine in its brilliance as it dismisses the darkness. The Church Age, between Christ's ascension from the dead and the Rapture, represents the "darkness." When Christ reigns, no wrong will govern, no bribe will be allowed, and no injustice will be perpetrated. Isaiah speaks of the glory of Jesus that will overtake the darkness in the Millennium, "Arise, shine; for your light has come! And the glory of the Lord is risen upon you. For behold, the darkness shall cover the earth, and deep darkness the people; But the Lord will arise over you, and His glory will be seen upon you. The Gentiles shall come to your light, and kings to the brightness of your rising" (Isaiah 60:1-3).

The first time we hear about a morning star, however, is referenced to Satan, "How you have fallen from heaven, O morning star, son of the dawn! You have been cast down to the earth, you who once laid low the nations!" (Isaiah 14:12, NIV). This is referring to Satan falling as he is being thrown out of heaven (Luke10:18). According to John 12:31, Satan is the ruler of this world; he is the god of this world, having power in government, health, spiritual forces and religion (II Corinthians 4:4; Matthew 4:8-9; Luke 13:10-17; Jude 9; Ephesians 6:11-12; Revelation 2:9, 3:9). The last we hear about the morning star is referenced to Christ: "I, Jesus, have sent My angel to testify to you these things in the churches. I am the Root and the Offspring of David, the Bright and Morning Star." Why would Jesus and Satan both be referred to as the morning star?

Let's dig deeper. There is another concept in the Bible, the image of a lion, that is also applied to both of them. In Revelation 5:5, Jesus is the "Lion of the tribe of Judah" while in I Peter 5:8, Satan is compared to a roaring lion, seeking to devour. Jesus is like a lion in that He is the King of Kings, adorned with royalty, majesty and authority. Satan too is like a lion in that he desires to devour other creatures. That's where the comparison ends. Jesus is of sheer purity and Satan is of utter immorality.

The morning star is a star that outshines all the other stars. According to Ezekiel 28:12, Satan was created with full of wisdom and perfect beauty. He surpassed any other angel and was a bright and morning star. However, Jesus, who is God made flesh, God incarnate, is not "a" bright and morning star, He is "the" bright and Morning Star. Though they may both be referred as "bright and morning stars", there is no equality between Jesus and Satan. Satan was created. Jesus is the Creator. And according to John 9:5, Jesus is the Light of the World. Satan may be a bright and morning star and he may transform himself as the "an angel of light" (II Corinthians 11:14), but he is only an imitation. He ain't the real thing! He's a counterfeit. He's pretentious. He's a liar. He's a thief. He's the instigator of all violence, rage, rape, sickness and murders because he is the very origin of hatred and death. Jesus, on the other hand, is the truth, the life, your advocate, your hope, your peace and the lover of your soul!

2:29 *He who has an ear, let him hear what the Spirit says to the churches.*

When Jesus spoke of the parable of the sower with the four seeds in Mark 4:1-9, He said, "He who has ears to hear, let him hear!" All have ears, but not all ears hear the calling of the Spirit. Even if the natural man heard with his ears, he would refuse the truth of the Spirit of God because it would sound like gibberish, madness, and altogether irrational. Strange that God's truth and His love sound like blubbering babble to many while Satan's lies and his deceit ring like the truth. The sound waves have been emitted. You choose what you will. One choice leads to goodness and mercy. The other, to death upon death. I'm not a rocket scientist, but it sounds like a no-brainer to me!

The Church of Thyatira poured their heart and soul into their work, with love, faith and patience, but tolerated the "prophetess" Jezebel who encouraged sexual immorality and sacrifice to idols. As the Great Physician placed His divine surgical magnifying glasses on, He first extended His grace and mercy and waited for her and her followers to repent; if they refused to accept His admonitions, they would be handed the sentence of sickness and death. In the next chapter, we will study three churches, Sardis, Philadelphia and Laodicea, a dead church, a faithful church and a lukewarm church, respectively.

REV IT UP & SUM IT UP – CHAPTER TWO:

The church in Ephesus represented the first-century Apostolic Church. In the beginning, she was on fire as we see in the book of Acts: boldness, conversions, healings, unity and love. However, she lost the reason for her very existence; she lost her love for Christ, and became the "Pretend Church."

The church in Smyrna represented the second and third century suffering church in the Roman Empire, enduring the tragic killings of five million Christians and yet staying true to the Word of God. The "Persecuted Church" stood fast and received only praise from Christ.

Beginning in the fourth century, the church in Pergamos represented the compromised and corrupted church, or "Perverted Church" under the ruler Constantine. The church brought the world's jingles into her sanctuary instead of taking her song into the world. If you want to change your method that's one thing, but when you change the message, Christ the Word, the Son of God, and God Himself, that is church suicide!

The church in Thyatira was commended for its love. In fact, what was declining in Ephesus was churning in Thyatira. However, Thyatira, the "Promiscuous Church," was known for its immorality, tolerating Jezebel, the false prophetess. She had her way among certain members of the church, introducing the "deep secrets" of Satan to "better equip" Christ-followers to defeat Satan, but in turn, lead them to their death.

If Satan is unable to conquer the church by the temptation of colossal work (Ephesus), the application of political pressure (Smyrna) or the propagation of intellectual heresy (Pergamos), he will lure the people with the presentation of immoral actions (Thyatira). If he can't persecute from the outside as he did in Smyrna, he will infiltrate the ranks spiritually from the inside as he did in Thyatira.

Each trait that Jesus characterizes Himself for the church in question fits the need of that church. He is the keeper of the church, the intimate counselor, the source of life. Though He came as a babe in Bethlehem, rode on a donkey in Jerusalem, and died on the cross of Calvary, He rose and will return victoriously on a white horse. He has a sharp two-edged sword that cuts deep. He is the Son of God with eyes that see all and feet of brass symbolizing that He judges all. But don't forget, He is also the Son of Man, our High Priest who constantly intercedes for us, and despite the rebelliousness found in our hearts, II Peter 3:9 describes Him beautifully: "The Lord is not slack concerning His promise (His Second Coming), as some count slackness, but is long-suffering toward us, not willing that any should perish but that all should come to repentance." As He gave the churches time to repent, He also extends His grace, mercy and kindness toward you and me today.

Chapter 3
The Church's Destiny

We will study the last three of the seven churches in this chapter. The fifth congregation, Sardis, kept their way, serving their own interests and dying *in* their faith instead of *for* their faith. The sixth, Philadelphia, kept their faith, persevering and staying in God's Word. The seventh, Laodicea, kept their pride, becoming lukewarm, and blindly lived in shame.

The Perished Church

3:1 And to the angel of the church in Sardis write, "These things says He who has the seven Spirits of God and the seven stars: 'I know your works, that you have a name that you are alive, but you are dead.'"

We'll now discuss the fifth church, Sardis.

1. Ephesus..........Pretend Church (33 AD – 100 AD)
2. Smyrna............Persecuted Church (100 AD – 313 AD)
3. Pergamos.......Perverted Church (313 AD – 590 AD)
4. Thyatira...........Promiscuous Church (590 AD – 1517 AD)
5. **Sardis .... Perished Church (1517 AD – 1790 AD)**
6. Philadelphia..Patriotic Church (1730 AD – present AD)
7. Laodicea.........Passive Church (1900 AD – present AD)

For the church in Sardis, the "Dead or Perished Church," the seven characteristics are:

1. Church's identification: Sardis.

2. Christ's characterization: Found in verse one, "These things says He who has the seven Spirits of God and the seven stars."

3. Cheering affirmation: Found in verse four, "You have a few names even in Sardis who have not defiled their garments; and they shall walk with Me in white, for they are worthy."

4. Constructive admonition: Found in verse two, "I know your works, that you have a name that you are alive, but you are dead."

5. Curative instruction: Found in verse three, "Remember therefore how you have received and heard; hold fast and repent. Therefore, if you will not watch, I will come upon you as a thief, and you will not know what hour I will come upon you."

6. Call to action: Found in verse six, "He who has an ear, let him hear what the Spirit says to the churches."

7. Coming restoration: Found in verse five, "He who overcomes shall be clothed in white garments, and I will not blot out his name from the Book of Life; but I will confess his name before My Father and before His angels."

Sardis, the capital of the ancient kingdom of Lydia, was the oldest city of Asia Minor, founded in 2,000 BC; today, it is known as Sart, 50 miles east of Smyrna and 30 miles southeast of Thyatira.[1] The city sat on a spur of the Tmolus Mountains, surrounded on three sides by huge, impenetrable cliffs; the fourth side was approachable only by a narrow isthmus that was insurmountable for the enemy to enter; the city was considered impregnable.[2] Croesus was the greatest king of Sardis, possessing copious riches, yet the downfall of Sardis occurred on his watch. "Sardis epitomized the complacency, softness and degeneration which invariably ultimately accompany wealth."[3]

In 546 BC, Cyrus the Persian launched an invasion to besiege Sardis and Croesus' great wealth. While surrounding the city and keeping watch, a Persian soldier witnessed a soldier of Sardis accidentally dropping his helmet over the edge of the wall. The soldier of Sardis then appeared at the base of the cliff, retrieved his helmet and then disappeared. How did he get down and back up? The Persian soldier deduced that there must be a cleft in the wall, and therefore, a passage-way in the midst of the impenetrable rock! That same night, the Persian soldier led a group of his men to the base of the cliff where they found the mysterious crack in the wall. The soldiers of Sardis were completely unguarded; the Persians marched in, opened the gates of Sardis allowing the entire Persian army to easily charge in and capture the city.[4]

In his arrogance, Croesus never bothered to guard the isthmus to Sardis or the cleft. 335 years later, in 214 BC, the same had occurred, when Antiochus III discovered the existence of the secret cleft.[5] Twice Sardis failed to be vigilant, twice it failed to be on the lookout, and twice it was captured due to arrogance and laziness. The church of Sardis was also not vigilant! The city's demise symbolizes the church's lackadaisical attitude, leading to the church's spiritual death.

There were, however, a few who had "not defiled their garments" in the Sardis church and were alive! In the prophetic church timeline, Sardis represents the Reformation Period (AD 1517–1790). Leaders such as Martin Luther came out of the Roman church in search of true Biblical doctrine. While the church of Thyatira, or the Roman Catholic Church, said that the Pope can dictate doctrine that may not be found in the Bible, the church of Sardis, or the Protestant Church of the Reformation period, said, "sola scriptura," or "Scripture only." Not tradition. Not the Pope. Not a Cardinal. Not a man. But the Bible alone. It was not through Pontifex Maximus. It was not for the glory of church leaders. It is by grace, through faith, in Christ, by the power of the Holy Spirit and for God's glory.

Every man is flesh, frail and flawed. We are to fix our eyes on Jesus, talk about Jesus, walk with Jesus, lift up Jesus and lean on Jesus. The reformers said, "No!" to idolizing men with high hats and fancy clothes.

Jesus, who has the "seven Spirits of God" and the seven stars (messengers or pastors of each church) in His right hand, spoke. The phrase "seven Spirits of God" appears in the Book of Revelation in four places, verses 1:4, 3:1, 4:5, 5:6. In Revelation 4:5, the phrase describes the seven lamps blazing before the throne of God, and in Rev. 5:6 it refers to the seven eyes of the Lamb. Because there is only one Holy Spirit, the "seven" is referring to the sevenfold characteristics of the Holy Spirit. Seven refers to perfection and completion; God created the world in six days and rested on the seventh, making His work complete. The phrase "seven Spirits of God" is not referring to seven different spirits of God, but the perfect and complete Holy Spirit with seven distinct attributes.

As we've already studied in Revelation 1:4, the sevenfold qualities of the Holy Spirit are outlined in Isaiah 11:1-3, resting on the Messiah. "There shall come forth a Rod from the stem of Jesse, and a Branch shall grow out of his roots. The Spirit of the Lord shall rest upon Him, the Spirit of wisdom and understanding, the Spirit of counsel and might, the Spirit of knowledge and of the fear of the Lord. His delight is in the fear of the Lord." The Spirit of the Lord is described with six definite attributes, perhaps seven in these verses: wisdom, understanding, counsel, power, knowledge, and a fear of the Lord, with either the Spirit of the Lord" or "a delight in the fear of the Lord" as the seventh attribute.

What then is the seventh attribute? There is a verse in Revelation 19:10b that may help us, "Worship God! For the testimony of Jesus is the spirit of prophecy." It is not inconceivable that the seventh trait is the spirit of prophecy and is a concrete demonstration of the knowledge, counsel and understanding that rests upon Christ and His followers. Jesus said of the Holy Spirit, "I tell you the truth. It is to your advantage that I go away; for if I do not go away, the Helper will not come to you; but if I depart, I will send Him to you" (John 16:7). The Holy Spirit is our Advocate, our burden bearer, our guide and our source of wisdom.

Though this church had an outward veneer of liveliness, it was inwardly withered and dead. The congregation bore the name "Christian," but the Spirit of God did not rest upon them. It is like Jesus' description of the Pharisees in Matthew 23:27, whitewashed tombs; beautiful outside, but full of dead men's bones inside. "They can pontificate about the amazing grave rather than preaching amazing grace. They exist as a social organization without a Spirit-led life. Why is there no persecution of this church? Satan need not bother with a dead church! Go throughout Christendom and you will often find the Gospel in a coffin."[6] "There may be prayers, vigils, fasts, temples, altars, priests, rites, ceremonies, worship, and still be no true piety. Heathenism has all these."[7] Just because one looks the part, speaks the part and plays the part doesn't mean he truly is the part!

3:2 *Be watchful, and strengthen the things which remain, that are ready to die, for I have not found your works perfect before God.*

Just as Croesus and his men were slumbering and careless, the church at Sardis was being inattentive. Christ told Sardis to be continually watchful. Paul tells us in I Thessalonians 5:6, "Therefore let us not sleep, as others do, but let us watch and be sober." Our calling is not only to be awake, but to "be sober, be vigilant; because your adversary the devil walks about like a roaring lion, seeking whom he may devour" (I Peter 5:8).

 We find ourselves in an era when many churches do not preach about the life-giving blood and health-restoring stripes of Jesus Christ. Words like "Satan, Devil, sin, hell, salvation, the blood of Jesus, the cross" may even upset the majority of congregations today. Outwardly alive, but inwardly dormant, drowsy and dead.

In I Thessalonians 5:2, we are told that the Day of the Lord will come like a thief in the night. The day of His vindication is on its way. The day of our victory draws nigh. Do not be afraid. Do not be downcast. Do not be dismayed. Cry out to God and say, "I am so weak Lord, and my circumstances are crushing me. My mind is restless, and my heart is heavily burdened with anxiety. Holy Spirit guide me. Father have mercy on me. Deepen my love for You and Your Word. Keep me away from temptations. Guard me from the evil one. I call on You. I look to You and You alone. I worship You. I trust You. Help me keep my eyes on You. In Jesus' name. Amen and amen!"

 When a patient undergoes surgery, he is not "placed under" all at once. The anesthesiologist takes extreme measures to administer his medications slowly and gradually:

1. There is stage one, known as induction, where the patient can still carry on a conversation.
2. This leads to stage two, the excitement stage, the period following loss of consciousness, with potential uncontrolled movements, irregular heart and respiratory rate.
3. Stage three, known as surgical anesthesia, is where the skeletal muscles relax, respiratory depression occurs, and eye movements slow down and stop. The patient is unconscious and ready for surgery.
4. Stage four, is known as overdose, when too much anesthesia is given, where there is respiratory cessation and potential cardiovascular collapse.

This stage is lethal without cardiovascular and respiratory support.

I believe Satan uses a similar method to influence our minds and actions. He does not come and say, "Hey, how you doing? I'm gonna entice you; lie to you; confuse you; snatch you; hurt you; and drag you down to hell!" We'd all run away! He is an angel of light, a liar, a deceiver, and a hater of God and Christ-followers. Satan slowly lulls us to sleep until he overdoses us with his poison. He introduces his timeless agents: jealousy and envy, which often lead to hatred and murdering someone in our hearts; promiscuity and lewdness, which often lead to adultery and perverted sexuality; selfish ambitions, which often lead to broken families, broken churches, dissensions and heresies; idolatry, which often leads to sorcery; drunkenness, which often leads to revelries; ungodly influence and uncensored social media, which often lead to a life drowning in deadly addictions.

Do you know the secret to Satan's work? It's simple. He encourages Christ-followers to marginalize God's Word. When that happens, the spiritual anesthesia process begins! When the church alters or aborts the Bible, it removes the Holy Spirit's paramount tool of transforming believers into the image of Christ. Christ encourages His Church to hold fast, or keep, honor and obey the Word of God. Pushing it aside simply leads to spiritual death. What Paul wrote to the church of Ephesus in Acts 20:29-31 applies to all churches and is worth repeating, "For I know this, that after my departure savage wolves will come in among you, not sparing the flock. Also, from among yourselves men will rise up, speaking perverse things, to draw away the disciples after themselves. Therefore, watch and remember that for three years I did not cease to warn everyone night and day with tears." Be watchful! Be diligent! Be alert! Be on guard! Be faithful!

The Sardis church was completely inept and powerless to strengthen the faith that scarcely remained except for a new reliance upon the Holy Spirit. Since the fall of Adam and Eve, man is burdened under the curse of sin and is unable to do anything to merit salvation. Though he is a free agent, he is unable to originate the love of God in his heart. "As a bird with a broken wing is 'free' to fly but not able, so the natural man is free to come to God but not able."[8] This bothers our critics of evangelical Christianity, for they believe they can achieve all things by sheer will, intellect and tenacity. This is what tempts the Christ-follower: I can; I am able; I will achieve with my mind, with my might, with my skills; with my charisma; with my diploma; with my achievements; I am able to achieve anything. As we've seen, the math of heaven is precisely opposite. I cannot; but with God, I am able to do all things (Philippians 4:13).

Why had Christ found their "works not perfect before God"? Glitter before man is impressive and will give anyone a good name, but it is fatally flawed. Follow Cain; he had property. Follow Samson; he had strength. Follow Solomon; he had wisdom. Follow Herod; he had wealth. Follow Judas; he had knowledge. Each of them impressive in his own right. Each had a name that was alive outwardly, but each was dying in his soul. According to Matthew 23:5, the religious leaders of Jesus' day did all their works to receive the recognition of man. Even though they appeared righteous outwardly, they were full of hypocrisy and lawlessness inwardly (Matthew 23:28).

 Before man, the Pharisees' works received the "wow" factor, but before God, the "woe" factor.

3:3 *Remember therefore how you have received and heard; hold fast and repent. Therefore, if you will not watch, I will come upon you as a thief, and you will not know what hour I will come upon you.*

Christ is not giving them an option. He is giving them a command, just as He did to the Church of Ephesus, to remember what they first heard: how we were chosen, how we were saved, how we are set apart, how we are to serve, how we are to love, how we are to be Christ-like and how we are to wait for the coming of Christ! Paul wrote in Hebrews 2:1, "Therefore we must give the more earnest heed to the things we have heard, lest we drift away." What exactly are we to watch for? The return of Christ. Aimlessly looking up in the skies? No. Wholeheartedly seeking His Word, serving others, and awaiting the day when He will make all things new! We are exhorted in I Corinthians 16:13-14, "Watch, stand fast in the faith, be brave, be strong. Let all that you do be done with love."

Christ warns Sardis that He will come unexpectedly as a thief if they do not watch. A thief doesn't announce when he'll strike; his visit is a surprise. "The first phase of the Lord's coming is as a bridegroom and the second phase is as a thief. He does not come upon His bride as a thief and he does not come upon the apostates and unregenerate world as a bridegroom."[9] In this case, the "thief in the night" does not refer to the Rapture, but to the coming judgment on the Church of Sardis, which can be averted by repenting. The reference to a "thief" is a reminder drawn from the embarrassing history of the city, being plundered twice, first by Cyrus and second by Antiochus due to Sardis' indifference.[10]

Matthew 24 speaks of the "thief in the night," as we'll study in chapter six, but it is worth noting, to the surprise of many, that the content of Matthew 24 does not deal with the Rapture, but of Christ's Second Coming. "But as the days of Noah were, so also will the coming of the Son of Man be. For as in the days before the flood, they were eating and drinking, marrying and giving in marriage, until the day that Noah entered the ark, and did not know until the flood came and took them all away, so also will the coming of the Son of Man be. Then two men will be in the field: one will be taken and the other left.

Two women will be grinding at the mill: one will be taken and the other left. Watch therefore, for you do not know what hour your Lord is coming. But know this, that if the master of the house had known what hour the thief would come, he would have watched and not allowed his house to be broken into. Therefore, you also be ready, for the Son of Man is coming at an hour you do not expect." Those taken are the wicked. Jesus is not a thief, but His appearing will be like a thief in that the date of His coming cannot be predicted accurately by mankind. Again, Christ's coming as a thief does not refer to the Rapture of the church but to His Second Coming. We will cover this subject more completely in chapters six and nineteen.

3:4 *You have a few names even in Sardis who have not defiled their garments; and they shall walk with Me in white, for they are worthy.*

There were a few in the church who had not defiled themselves, who had not gone under general anesthesia, who refused to be intoxicated with Satan's serum of sloppiness. They would one day walk with Christ in the New Jerusalem dressed in the white clothing of righteousness. One's rejection of Christ is characterized by defiled garments and has hideous consequences. The acceptance of Christ has enormous benefits, including an eternity of full fellowship with God as Adam and Eve once had before their fall. Being worthy is not found in ourselves; it is found in Him in whom we believe! My prayer for you and me is that we ask the Spirit of the Lord, especially the fear (reverence) of the Lord, to consume us; in that way, we will love our Lord so much that deep love and reverence will take precedence over our inclination to sin. I pray that we will repent, changing our minds, turning around, and face a God who welcomes us with open arms.

3:5 *He who overcomes shall be clothed in white garments, and I will not blot out his name from the Book of Life; but I will confess his name before My Father and before His angels.*

The Reformation, like any other revival, has a pattern, starting out with one man (like Martin Luther or John Calvin). The man is given a ministry, which churns into a movement, which if not moderated, will become a machine and sadly turn into a monstrous grave site. Even today? Yes, many are adopting a "cultural perspective" and happily abstaining from being called bigots, homophobes, narrow-minded and intolerant, and therefore accepting all kinds of practices including having pastors who practice perverse sexuality as a lifestyle. Many churches are rethinking the Genesis story, including creation and sexuality. They are encouraging people to satisfy their urges! Seriously? What if their urge is to molest a child? Is that okay? No, never! The only true framework of life is the Bible; it calls sin what it's supposed to be called: sin. It also shares the unending love of God, freely given to those who turn to Him. Stick to the Bible. If something is new, it ain't true! And if it's true (such as God's Word), it ain't new!

It's time to reverse the anesthesia and come back to the land of the living!

1. Those who overcome shall be clothed in white garments. The image of wearing white and walking with Christ represents how His blood has cleansed us, and how the Spirit of God helps us stay faithful and true to His Word.

2. It appears that everyone born from the foundations of the earth has his name written in the Book of Life. There is one exception: those who will accept the 666 mark of the Beast during the Tribulation were never written in the Book (Revelation 13:8 and 17:8).

Who **will not** be blotted out of the Book of Life?

   a. Those who overcome shall not have their names blotted out from the Book of Life. Salvation cannot be lost;

once you are truly under the blood of the Lamb, you are cleansed eternally, and your name remains in the Book of Life. Christ paid the price with His life so you and I can be written in the Book of Life. The overcomer is the true believer who remains faithful after accepting Christ as his Savior.

b. Those who overcome shall have Christ confess their names before His Father and before His angels. The redeemed will be introduced by Christ to His Father and His angels by having their names read out of the Book of Life, proclaiming them as valiant and faithful followers. In Matthew 10:32, Jesus proclaimed that if we acknowledge Him before men, He will acknowledge us before His Father.

c. Children who die before they reach the age of accountability or babies who are murdered by abortion. According to Luke 18:15-16, when people brought infants to Christ so that He may touch and bless them, the disciples rebuked the people. But Jesus said, "Let the little children come to Me, and do not forbid them; for of such is the kingdom of God." Those who have not reached the age of accountability will not be blotted out.

Who *will* be blotted out of the Book of Life?

a. According to Psalm 69:28, David asks the Lord to blot out the unrighteous (those who reject God's goodness and persecute God's chosen).

b. According to Revelation 22:19, those who dilute, take away, delete from the Book of Revelation.

c. According to Luke 12:10 and Mark 3:28-29, those who refuse to listen to the wooing of the Holy Spirit and reject Christ (the unpardonable sin).

d. According to Hebrews 6:4-6, those who actually were enlightened of God's grace, tasted the heavenly gift of Christ, became partakers of the Holy Spirit, but fall away and willfully reject God's good Word and His powers.

e. According to Exodus 32:33, those who chose gods over God, attributing their journey in life to gods (such as a golden calf) rather than the true God.

f. In summary, those who reject God the Father, God the Son and God the Holy Spirit.

Will your name remain in the Book of Life? This is not the time to say, "I hope so!" This is the time to come under the blood of the Lamb and proclaim, "Yes! Forevermore!"

***3:6** "He who has an ear, let him hear what the Spirit says to the churches."*

What was heard in Sardis was also heard in all seven churches. The shortcomings of each church were broadcast throughout, not to marginalize that church but to bolster and encourage it to walk closer to Christ, listen to His Word and watch for His coming. Every word John wrote was conceived by the Holy Spirit (II Peter1:21) and faithfully transcribed by John. All Scripture is inspired by God; it instructs us to walk in the paths of righteousness; it restores our soul; it equips us, corrects us and imparts to us wisdom (II Timothy 3:15-17). That is one voice you don't want to place on mute!

The Church of Sardis was in a spiritual coma. As the Great Physician placed His divine surgical magnifying glasses on, He revealed that the church appeared alive, but its vital signs attested that she was in critical condition and dying. Christ admonished the congregation to repent and keep their names in the Book of Life. Next, we will study the Church of Philadelphia, the church that kept God's Word and did not deny the name of Christ.

The Patriotic Church

***3:7** "And to the angel of the church in Philadelphia write,*

These things says He who is holy, He who is true, He who has the key of David, He who opens and no one shuts, and shuts and no one opens'"

We'll now discuss the sixth church, Philadelphia.

1. Ephesus .... Pretend Church (33 AD – 100 AD)
2. Smyrna .... Persecuted Church (100 AD – 313 AD)
3. Pergamos .... Perverted Church (313 AD – 590 AD)
4. Thyatira .... Promiscuous Church (590 AD – 1517 AD)
5. Sardis .... Perished Church (1517 AD – 1790 AD)
6. **Philadelphia . Patriotic Church (1730 AD – present AD)**
7. Laodicea .... Passive Church (1900 AD – present AD)

For the church in Philadelphia, the Faithful or Patriotic Church, the seven characteristics are:

1. Church's identification: Philadelphia

2. Christ's characterization: Found in verse seven, "These things says He who is holy, He who is true, He who has the key of David, He who opens and no one shuts, and shuts and no one opens."

3. Cheering affirmation: Found in verses eight through ten, "I know your works. See, I have set before you an open door, and no one can shut it; for you have a little strength, have kept My word, and have not denied My name. Indeed, I will make those of the synagogue of Satan, who say they are Jews and are not, but lie — indeed I will make them come and worship before your feet, and to know that I have loved you. Because you have kept My command to persevere, I also will keep you from the hour of trial which shall come upon the whole world, to test those who dwell on the earth."

4. Constructive admonition: None

5. Curative instruction: Found in verse eleven, "Behold, I am coming quickly! Hold fast what you have, that no one may take your crown."

6. Call to action: Found in verse thirteen, "He who has an ear, let him hear what the Spirit says to the churches."

7. Coming restoration: Found in verse twelve, "He who overcomes, I will make him a pillar in the temple of My God, and he shall go out no more. I will write on him the name of My God and the name of the city of My God, the New Jerusalem, which comes down out of heaven from My God. And I will write on him My new name.

The ancient city of Philadelphia, meaning brotherly love, is on the site of the modern city of Alaşehir in Turkey, and is twenty-seven miles southeast of Sardis.[11] It was established in 189 BC by King Eumenes II of Pergamon (reigned 197-159 BC). His successor was his brother, Attalus II, who refused Rome's offer to betray Eumenes; this love for his brother made their story famous. Attalus was nicknamed Philadelphus, brotherly love, where the city derives its name.[12] On our prophetic timeline, Philadelphia represents the "Evangelistic or Patriotic Church" (1730 AD through the present day and up to the Rapture), embodying the modern church that currently focuses on spreading the Gospel around the world. Prophetically, it overlaps the period of Laodicea, the last church.[13]

As Jesus addresses the Church of Philadelphia, we see Him as our High Priest, holy and as our Advocate, true. He is set apart, stands as the only begotten Son of God, and is the only means to gain access to God. His title is not given to Him through the Levitical priesthood but in the order of Melchizedek as both priest and king. The Levitical line is based on a strict regulation of ancestry. Jesus is from the line of eternal hope, based on a power of indestructible life, through which we draw near to God (Hebrews 7:11-19).

According to Hebrews 7:27, no other man could bear the sins of mankind because he could not bear his own sin. God makes a reference to His own deity and name in Isaiah 40:25, "'To whom then will you liken Me, or to whom shall I be equal?' says the Holy One." According to Isaiah 6:3, only God is holy as we witness the angelic cherubim fall before Him and proclaim, "Holy, Holy, Holy is the Lord of hosts. The whole earth is full of His glory!" Jesus, the second member of the Trinity, in a Godhead of One, calls Himself "He who is holy, He who is true." He designates to Himself the same attribute that belongs to His Father, revealing that Jesus is God. Despite His glory and perfect holiness, Jesus is our compassionate intercessor, who understands our weaknesses and forgives our shortfalls (Hebrews 4:15). How can we not love Him!

According to Hebrews 6:18, it is impossible for God to lie, a distinct attribute of the Trinity. Jesus can forgive. He can avenge. He can judge. And He can rule because He is true and in Him there is no lie. His yes is yes, and His no is no. True to His God, true to His Word, and true to you and me, with unbending compassion, unfailing love, unmatchable grace and unadulterated trustworthiness.

In this verse, we also see Him as our King, having the Key of David. To hold a key indicates authority. Having the Key of David gives Christ control over King David's domain, Jerusalem, the City of David, the kingdom of Israel during the Millennium; He will then rule with His Father from the New Jerusalem during all of Eternity.

According to Genesis 49:10, the "scepter shall not depart from Judah," the ancestral line of David and of Christ. This key is not handed to anyone else. You and I cannot somehow desire and acquire this key, or become enlightened, and through hard work, possess this eternal position of power! In turn, what Christ opens, no man, no power, no demon, no principalities, no forces, no armies can shut. He has opened the door of salvation and global evangelism as witnessed in our day. Subsequently, what He closes, no one can blast open. Beware, take note, be sober, and contemplate with great alarm, the door of evangelism will be shut one day! Today is the day of your salvation! Because you cannot control if you are granted your very next breath or very next heartbeat, you should pay attention. Jesus is Holy and Mighty. He is simply Sovereign. He is mighty to save. But always remember, He is not mad at you, but madly, madly, madly in love with you! Come as you are and accept His gift of eternal life!

The Old Testament reference to the Key of David is found in Isaiah 22:22, "The key of the house of David I will lay on his shoulder; so he shall open, and no one shall shut; and he shall shut, and no one shall open." Here, during King Hezekiah's reign, the prophet Isaiah tells the palace secretary Shebna that he will be replaced by Eliakim. Eliakim, who was to hold the key, would have the authority over Israel's treasury, the temple's gold, silver, precious oils, spices and armory; he was raised by God because of his humility, diligence and faithfulness while Shebna fell because of his sinful pride, vanity and sense of entitlement. Eliakim did not undermine Shebna nor take Shebna's position; God gave it to him. Eliakim foreshadows Christ, who is the Heir of the throne of David, and who shall supplant all of earth's unworthy stewards, having abused their privileges.

In Matthew 23:13, we read that Jesus chastised the leaders of Israel, "But woe to you, scribes and Pharisees, hypocrites! For you shut up the kingdom of heaven against men; for you neither go in yourselves, nor do you allow those who are entering to go in." The authority was then entrusted to simple fishermen; Jesus said to Peter in Matthew 16:9, "And I will give you the keys of the kingdom of heaven, and whatever you bind on earth will be bound in heaven, and whatever you loose on earth will be loosed in heaven." Today, the authority to preach the Gospel of Jesus Christ is entrusted to the church. Ultimately and for Eternity, the authority will justly, righteously, perfectly and solely be Jesus Christ.

The Key of David was promised to the Messiah in both the Old and New Testaments. We read in Isaiah 9:6-7, "For unto us a Child is born, unto us a Son is given; and the government will be upon His shoulder. And His name will be called Wonderful, Counselor, Mighty God, Everlasting Father, Prince of Peace. Of the increase of His government and peace there will be no end (His reign and peace will be unending), upon the throne of David and over His kingdom, to order it and establish it with judgment and justice from that time forward, even forever. The zeal of the Lord of hosts will perform this." Jesus will sit on the Throne of David, and His reign will never end. In Luke 1:32, we read, "He (Jesus) will be great, and will be called the Son of the Highest; and the Lord God will give Him the throne of His father David."

3:8 *"I know your works. See, I have set before you an open door, and no one can shut it; for you have a little strength, have kept My word, and have not denied My name."*

When Christ states, "See, I have set before you an open door, and no one can shut it," the open door depicts an opportunity for ministry. In Colossians 4:2-4, Paul exhorts the congregation to continue earnestly in prayer, giving thanks, and praying that God would "open to us a door for the word, to speak the mystery of Christ, for which I am also in chains, that I may make it manifest, as I ought to speak." Philadelphia was strategically located as a gateway city to a large region that included other cities in the region. Christ reminded this church that they were given an enormous privilege to evangelize. On the other hand, they had little strength to pursue this opportunity.

 Because this church had little power, she was encouraged to rest in God's power. Why is that a good place to find yourself? So that when you achieve what you achieve, the Lord will receive what He alone should receive: all glory, honor and praise!

This is made evident by Paul's statement in II Corinthians 12:9,

"And He (Christ) said to me, 'My grace is sufficient for you, for My strength is made perfect in weakness.' Therefore, most gladly I will rather boast in my infirmities, that the power of Christ may rest upon me."

The church in Philadelphia kept the Word of God and in so doing showed their devotion and love for Him. Jesus said in John 14:23-24, "If anyone loves Me, he will keep My word; and My Father will love him, and We will come to him and make Our home with him. He who does not love Me does not keep My words; and the word which you hear is not Mine but the Father's who sent Me."

We sense the tide shifting today. Christ-followers are jeered, ridiculed, demonized and ostracized more and more if we bring up the Bible or God's point of view by a crowd who not only rejects the Bible as truth but views us as intolerant, out of touch with reality and a dangerous cult. "We are asked by some to abandon Genesis to 'science,' salvation by redemption to anthropology, the life of the Spirit to psychology, the very Word itself to higher criticism."[14] The Church of Philadelphia did not deny the name of Christ; but there is coming a time, in the Tribulation, when man will outright deny His name. It is already in full swing today! Jesus prophesied this in John 5:43, "I have come in My Father's name, and you do not receive Me; if another comes (Antichrist) in his own name, him you will receive."

This church may have been small with little strength, but it had kept God's Word and had not denied His name. If God's Word is removed or diluted from the pulpits of churches, morals will erode. If Christians don't recognize God's standards, they will become as blind men leading the blind. The church in Philadelphia not only kept God's Word, but also remained faithful to Him, refusing to deny His name. They refused to participate in the Caesar worship of the time and in the face of persecution from both Jews and Gentiles, they stayed true to God the Father. They did not generate the power but relied on God's power. That's when the weak become strong. That's when the fool becomes wise. That's when the lowly is lifted up. If all fails and all hell breaks loose, remember the words of Christ, "My strength is made perfect in weakness" (II Corinthians 12:9). Stand firm!

3:9 *Indeed I will make those of the synagogue of Satan, who say they are Jews and are not, but lie — indeed I will make them come and worship before your feet, and to know that I have loved you.*

The same group of Jews that attacked the church in Smyrna was attacking the church in Philadelphia, the church having both Jewish and Gentile followers of Christ. The attackers were Jews who claimed to be serving God under false pretenses. They were Jews by lineage and descendants of Abraham, but not really Jews in the true spiritual sense; they were apostates who were sharp tools in Satan's hands. Jesus not only referred to them as "the synagogue of Satan," but He was going to humble them before the faithful in the Church of Philadelphia.

There comes a point when Christ will no longer tolerate apostasy. This does not sound politically correct, and it isn't; it is, however, Biblically accurate. Examine Saul on his way to Damascus to persecute the church; God blinded him and totally changed his way of life. As Christ sets before Philadelphia an open door of evangelism, some of the greatest Jewish adversaries of this church were going to repent, as Paul had done, and obey Christ. Their worshiping before the church's feet expresses the convert's willingness to forsake their past wickedness and take the very lowest place in the church, submissively honoring those whom they once persecuted. "In the Church Age, God elevates the faithful, both Gentile and Jew, over the national Jew who rejects Messiah Jesus."[15]

According to Paul in Romans 11:11, the salvation the church enjoys is intended to provoke the unbelieving Jewish nation to jealousy. Ultimately, these renegade Jews would (or will at the Great White Throne judgment) understand how much God values His Church.

Interestingly, the opposite will be true in the Millennium, when Gentiles who receive Christ, and who somehow make it through the Tribulation and Armageddon, will enter into the thousand-year reign of Christ with an unglorified body. They will be able to live for centuries without death due to a changed environment, which includes tree leaves with healing properties, found along the banks of the river which flows from the sanctuary of Christ (Ezekiel 47:1-12). They will have children who will not know the saving power of Christ. Many of the Gentiles will latch onto the faithful Jews alive at that time and ask them to be led to the Messiah who will be reigning in Jerusalem. Thus says the Lord of hosts: "Peoples shall yet come, inhabitants of many cities; the inhabitants of one city shall go to another, saying, 'Let us continue to go and pray before the Lord, and seek the Lord of hosts. I myself will go also.' Yes, many peoples and strong nations shall come to seek the Lord of hosts in Jerusalem, and to pray before the Lord." Thus says the Lord of hosts: "In those days ten men from every language of the nations shall grasp the sleeve of a Jewish man, saying, 'Let us go with you, for we have heard that God is with you'" (Zechariah 8:20-23).

3:10 *Because you have kept My command to persevere, I also will keep you from the hour of trial which shall come upon the whole world, to test those who dwell on the earth.*

In verse ten, God unveils a promise that indicates the church will escape the Tribulation, "Because you have kept My command to persevere, I also will keep you from the hour of trial which shall come upon the whole world, to test those who dwell on the earth." Simply, the church will be spared from the seven-year Tribulation period. While there is Tribulation on earth, the church is in heaven with Christ and this verse explains the churches' absence. God is not sparing the church in Philadelphia from a local persecution and the Christians today are not spared from times of persecution. The trial God's Church will avoid is one that will come "upon the whole world." Philadelphia is not representative of the "whole world."

The "hour of trial" refers to the seven-year Tribulation that will follow the Rapture of the church and will precede Christ's Second Coming. The church is not kept through the hour of trial; it is kept from the hour of trial. It is troublesome that many sincere followers of Christ still believe that the church will remain on earth and go through the most distressing period in history.

 The church is the bride of Christ. If Christ left His bride on earth to receive the wrath of God, that would best be described as divine domestic violence. Absurd! There is no condemnation in Christ, and there is no seven-year Tribulation for His Church.

If this verse meant that the church would remain on earth and kept safe during the Tribulation, then the rest of Revelation would contradict itself. Throughout the Tribulation, we'll read that there will be new converts who are martyred on a colossal scale, noted in Revelation 6:9-11; 11:7; 12:11; 13:7; 13:15; 14:11; 17:6 and 18:24. For instance in Revelation 18:24, we read, "And in her (Babylon) was found the blood of prophets and saints, and of all who were slain on the earth." When Christ states, "I also will keep you from the hour of trial which shall come upon the whole world," He is speaking to the church and not the new converts or believers of the Tribulation. If the church were to remain on earth and endure all the horrors of the Tribulation, Christ-followers would be martyred and not kept from the hour of trial! The words "keep you from the hour of trial" would then be meaningless, contradictory and a lie, which stand against God's attribute of honesty!

The new converts, new worshipers and new saints are the ones who will go through the Tribulation and will certainly face horrible death! "Only if church saints and Tribulation saints are kept distinct does the promise of Revelation 3:10 make any sense."[16] Furthermore, the fact that the Tribulation "shall come upon the whole world" negates the erroneous Preterist belief that this trial already occurred in 70 AD with the Roman destruction of Jerusalem. Remember, when the literal sense makes good sense, seek no other sense, lest it result in nonsense!

It is worth noting that Christ will keep us from the hour. The definite article, "the," tells us that Christ will not keep us from an hour of the Tribulation, or a partial time period, as is believed by the Mid-Tribulation and Post-Tribulation adherents, but He will keep us from the entire hour. According to Romans 5:9, we as believers who have been justified by the blood of Christ, shall be saved from wrath through Him. Paul continues to drive this point home in I Thessalonians 1:9-10 and 5:9, stating that Jesus, whom we wait for and whom God raised from the dead, will deliver us from the wrath to come; indeed, we who obtained salvation through our Lord Jesus Christ are not appointed to God's wrath.

After the Rapture of the church, the wrath of God will pour out on all "those who dwell on the earth" who are the unbelieving, God-hating, God-mocking, God-blaspheming and God-rejecting world, globally. Jesus said in Matthew 24:21-22, "For then there will be great tribulation, such as has not been since the beginning of the world until this time, no nor ever shall be. And unless those days were shortened, no flesh would be saved; but for the elect's sake those days will be shortened." The concepts of "upon the whole world," "no flesh would be saved," "those who dwell on the earth," the seven seals, the seven trumpets and the seven bowls all argue for a global event. How can one stand against God as He "Rev's It Up" and unleashes inexplicable tragedies that will make Pharaoh's devastating ten plagues look trivial?

3:11 Behold, I am coming quickly! Hold fast what you have, that no one may take your crown.

Christ promises that He will come quickly: "Behold, I am coming quickly! Hold fast what you have, that no one may take your crown." There will be scoffers who will say, "Ah, two thousand years have passed, and He still hasn't come! Some prophet this Jesus guy you worship!" Quickly does not refer to when Christ will come back, but how He will come. He will come "in a moment, in the twinkling of an eye, at the last trumpet" according to I Corinthians 15:52. Christ encourages us to hold fast to the faith, the truth, the beauty of grace, the zeal and the love to the brethren. Hold fast and do not let go! Keep believing. Keep trusting. Keep sharing. Keep praising. Keep praying. Keep interceding. Keep crying out for mercy. Don't give up. Don't weaken in your resolve.

 If you and I don't evangelize, we will fossilize! If you and I don't live by Scripture, we will be tossed about by the winds of culture. Stand on Christ, the sure anchor, and remain faithful!

We will not lose hope! We will not quit! We will trust Him! We will give thanks to the Lord for He is good … His love endures forever!

Which crown will these believers receive? It is not made clear in this verse. If they are holding fast to what they have, they are persevering, and will get the Imperishable Crown, given to those who run the race and aim to acquire a prize that is eternal (I Corinthians 9:24-27). They may also receive the Crown of Glory we spoke of in Revelation 2:10, which is given to those who desire intimacy with God and long for His coming.

3:12 He who overcomes, I will make him a pillar in the temple of My God, and he shall go out no more. I will write on him the name of My God and the name of the city of My God, the New

***Jerusalem, which comes down out of heaven from My God.
And I will write on him My new name.***

Just as two pillars (Boaz, which means strength; and Yakin,
which means established) adorned Solomon's temple in
I Kings 7:15-22, so too we who are caught up in the Rapture
will form the footings and be included in the community of
God's heavenly temple."[17] This is a fitting reward for the Philadelphia overcomer: he has had a little strength, so he is made
a pillar of strength." Magistrates in Philadelphia were honored
by having a pillar placed in a temple in their name; Jesus is
encouraging the believers that they too will be honored in a
better heavenly realm.

 *God's Church will be planted firmly, with stability, and for
Eternity.*

We read in Revelation 3:12, that the saints will "go out no more."
Adam and Eve walked right into Satan's scheme, and consequently were sent out of the Garden. Abraham temporarily
walked out of God's will and bore a child out of God's promise.
David walked onto his balcony, took a look at Bathsheba, and
briefly walked out of God's protective plan. Peter, who walked
on water, walked right into denying Jesus, taking steps to temporarily break his fellowship with God. All of us have fallen. All
of us continue to fall short of God's glory. But there is coming
a day when we "shall go out no more!" We read in Revelation
21:3, "And I (John) heard a loud voice from heaven saying,
"Behold, the tabernacle of God is with men, and He will dwell
with them, and they shall be His people. God Himself will be
with them and be their God." To that we say, "Hallelujah! Amen
and amen!"

When I visited Ivory Coast, Africa, to preach the Gospel of
Christ, my friends took me to tour the Basilica in the city of
Yamoussoukro. This massive six hundred-million-dollar build-
ing is said to be the largest cathedral in the world. It has 272

Doric columns or pillars in its circular colonnade. What surprised me as I stood at the base of an enormous pillar were its cracks and imperfections. That's the frail earth we live in, filled with its blemishes. There will be no flaws in heaven; no weathered pillars; no broken fragments; no chipped paint; no missing pieces. As we'll see in Revelation 21:22, there will not even be a temple in Eternity because the triune God is its temple! We will be in our glorified bodies, pillars for Christ, with no "cracks" and no brokenness! Again, I say amen!

When you are a son or daughter of God, you bear His name. We will bear God's name, the name of His city — the New Jerusalem — and Jesus' new name. They will be written on us and we will be known, just as a tree is known by the fruit it bears. The 144,000 Jewish evangelists will bear the name of God on their foreheads during the Tribulation, not allowing Satan to touch them. During the Tribulation, Satan, the master deceiver, will also unleash his 666 mark and place it on the foreheads or right arms of his followers.

We read in Genesis 4:8-15 that after Cain killed his brother Abel, God designated him to be a restless wanderer on the earth. When Cain lamented that his punishment was too great and that he'd have a target on his back to be hunted and killed, the Lord put a mark on him that would prevent others from murdering him.

 The mark of God is given with great mercy. It is His holy name, taking away our shame. The mark of Satan is forced maliciously. It is his vicious aim, to kill and maim.

We get into heaven solely by accepting the finished works of the Lord Jesus Christ, dying on the cross and being raised from the dead after three days. We cannot arrive at the "pearly gates" and convince Peter, Paul or John to get us into heaven. There is no such thing as "What's the 'password?'" or "Why should I let you get in?"

You must declare your loyalty to Christ while on earth to receive your citizenship in heaven.

Prior to Eternity, we'll spend a thousand years with Christ on a rehabilitated earth. The restored Jerusalem will then be called "the Throne of the Lord" and "the Lord is There" (Jeremiah 3:17; Ezekiel 48:35). After the Millennium, Christ rejectors will face the Great White Throne judgment and will be cast into hell; believers will live throughout Eternity on a brand-new earth, in a brand-new heaven and in the heavenly brand-New Jerusalem, which will descend from heaven (Revelation 21:1-2).

We will not only bear the name of God, the name of His new city, the New Jerusalem which Jesus spoke of making for us in John 14:1-3, but we will also bear the new name of Christ. What will His new name be? It does us no good to guess, but it will express an undisclosed character of Jesus Christ; it will therefore encompass His compassion, servant's heart, love, forgiveness, gentleness, patience, humility, glory, honor and power. The fact that the overcomer in Philadelphia and all believing overcomers of all time will concurrently bear the name of both the Father and His Son through the power of the Holy Spirit is an unflinching and clear statement of Christ's deity; God the Father would never share ownership with any other entity except God!

Bearing the name of God makes us family, heirs, co-heirs, sons, daughters and the beloved of Christ. There will be no outcasts. There will be no loneliness. There will be no homeless. There will be no abandonment. There will be no orphans.

 Safety! Security! Sanctity! Serenity!
You belong permanently! Glory!

3:13 *"He who has an ear, let him hear what the Spirit says to the churches."*

The message of God is not spoken to one church alone. This letter was directed to the church in Philadelphia, but all seven churches got the memo and all the churches were faced with a decision. The same message rings true today! It is not dead. It is not medieval. It is not outdated. It is not abstract. It is relevant. It is reliable. It is refining. It is this message, the Gospel, the Good News, the life-giving Word that brings healing, cultivates joy and fosters true hope. It is proclaimed to all people of all ages and of all time. All creation and the entire universe proclaim the glory of God and the works of His hands. Let him who has an ear, hear what the Spirit is saying to you!

The Church of Philadelphia kept the Word of God and did not deny the name of Christ. As the Great Physician placed His divine surgical magnifying glasses on, He noted that the church had little strength but was faithful and persevered; He promised them that He'd keep them out of the Tribulation. Lastly, we will study the Church of Laodicea, the lukewarm church that was about to be spit out.

The Passive Church

3:14 *"And to the angel of the church of the Laodiceans write, 'These things says the Amen, the Faithful and True Witness, the Beginning of the creation of God.'"*

We'll now discuss the seventh and final church, Laodicea.

1. Ephesus .... Pretend Church (33 AD – 100 AD)
2. Smyrna .... Persecuted Church (100 AD – 313 AD)
3. Pergamos .... Perverted Church (313 AD – 590 AD)
4. Thyatira .... Promiscuous Church (590 AD – 1517 AD)
5. Sardis .... Perished Church (1517 AD – 1790 AD)
6. Philadelphia .. Patriotic Church (1730 AD – present AD)
7. **Laodicea ..... Passive Church (1900 AD – present AD)**

For the Church in Laodicea, the "Passive Church," the seven characteristics are:

1. Church's identification: Laodicea

2. Christ's characterization: Found in verse fourteen. "These things says the Amen, the Faithful and True Witness, the Beginning of the creation of God."

3. Cheering affirmation: None

4. Constructive admonition: Found in verses fifteen through seventeen. "I know your works, that you are neither cold nor hot. I could wish you were cold or hot. So then, because you are lukewarm, and neither cold nor hot, I will vomit you out of My mouth. Because you say, 'I am rich, have become wealthy, and have need of nothing' — and do not know that you are wretched, miserable, poor, blind, and naked."

5. Curative instruction: Found in verses eighteen through twenty. "I counsel you to buy from Me gold refined in the fire, that you may be rich; and white garments, that you may be clothed, that the shame of your nakedness may not be revealed; and anoint your eyes with eye salve, that you may see. As many as I love, I rebuke and chasten. Therefore, be zealous and repent. Behold, I stand at the door and knock. If anyone hears My voice and opens the door, I will come in to him and dine with him, and he with Me."

6. Call to action: Found in verse twenty-two. "He who has an ear, let him hear what the Spirit says to the churches."

7. Coming restoration: Found in verse twenty-one. "To him who overcomes I will grant to sit with Me on My throne, as I also overcame and sat down with My Father on His throne."

To all the preceding churches, God said, "And to the angel of the church in Ephesus, Smyrna, Pergamos, Thyatira, Sardis, Philadelphia, write." To Laodicea, God said, "And to the angel of the church of the Laodiceans write." What's the difference between "in" versus "of"? This church is "of" the Laodiceans and, therefore, belongs to the Laodiceans, not God. "Laodicea" means "people ruling." This is set in contrast to God's ruling in the church. It is a church entirely ruled by men, for the Holy Spirit is not present and doing His ministry of guiding."[18] Simply, Christ was not welcome there. This church made Christ sick, in a manner of speaking, and harsh language rang loudly as He addressed the congregation. Despite it making Him sick, we must remember, He still "walks in the midst of all lampstands," and longs to heal His Church.

Laodicea was originally known as Diospolis, the City of Zeus, founded between 261 and 253 BC by Antiochus II of Syria and named in honor of his wife, Laodice. The city later fell into the hands of Rome in 133 BC.

Laodicea was one of the wealthiest city of Asia Minor, wealth coming from three sources: banking, textiles, and medicine.

1. The city was at the crossroads of north-south traffic between Sardis and Perge and east-west from the Euphrates to Ephesus, making it a busy and prosperous metropolitan center, and one of the most prosperous cities of the ancient world.[19] It was perfectly situated as the financial center of Asia Minor.

2. It was a great center for the manufacturing of clothing. The black sheep that grazed in the Lycus Valley produced soft raven-like black wool, and the people wore black clothes with pomp. It was the fashion center of Asia Minor.

3. It was well known for its school of medicine. The city had an ophthalmology center, producing eye salve made of oil and colander seed. It was the medical center of Asia Minor.[20]

Two major cities lay near Laodicea: Colossae eight miles to the southeast and Hierapolis six miles to the north. Colossae was known for its cold refreshing waters from the northern mountain tops and Hierapolis was known for its many hot springs. Because Laodicea lacked a natural water supply, it was dependent on its neighbors. By the time water reached Laodicea from the hot springs or cold mountain springs via underground aqueducts, it was dirty, tepid and lukewarm.[21]

From a prophetic perspective, the Laodicea Church represents the renegade church at the end of the Church Age (1900 AD to the present time, leading up to the Rapture). We are now living in the era represented by this apathetic, smug and lukewarm church! Christ has little to commend the church that will exist when He returns. Following the evangelistic movement of the Philadelphia Church, there exists a lukewarm attitude in the church. Since the 1920s there have been stubborn voices within the church that refuse to accept the Bible literally. In a post-modern world, some church leaders have become cynical and believe there is no absolute truth, there are no rules, there is nothing good or bad, and sins should be tolerated.

Many pastors today are failing to tell their congregations that we are sinners desperately in need of redemption through the work of God who loves us; failing to tell us that salvation is through the sacrifice of Christ alone; failing to utter the consequences of rejecting Christ and the reality of hell; and failing to truthfully speak about the cost of being a Christ-follower. They are, however, "successful" not only in their embrace of culture instead of souls but also in their attempt to change the Gospel into a watered-down bloodless version of the truth. If you don't have the blood of the Lamb, you've got inspiration, motivation and education, but you're flat out missing salvation!

"Scripture is given by inspiration of God, and is profitable for doctrine, for reproof, for correction, for instruction in righteousness, that the man of God may be complete, thoroughly equipped for every good work" (II Timothy 3:16-17). Then why is it not being preached in that way? Because today's congregations, as was true in Laodicea, want it their way! "For the time will come when they will not endure sound doctrine, but according to their own desires, because they have itching ears, they will heap up for themselves teachers; and they will turn their ears away from the truth and be turned aside to fables" (II Timothy 4:3-4).

Have we changed that much? You be the judge: "But know this, that in the last days perilous times will come: for men will be lovers of themselves, lovers of money, boasters, proud, blasphemers, disobedient to parents, unthankful, unholy, unloving, unforgiving, slanderers, without self-control, brutal, despisers of good, traitors, headstrong, haughty, lovers of pleasure rather than lovers of God, having a form of godliness but denying its power. And from such people turn away!" (II Timothy 3:1-5).

People like to look fancy in their Sunday clothes. Church attendance? Check. Community service? Check. Nice smiles while greeting others? Check. Raising the hand and saying, "Amen?" Check. But taking part in ungodly activities and supporting a platform of death over life? Check! Wearing a cross around your neck doesn't get you into heaven. Just calling yourself a Christian doesn't mean you are forgiven. Attending church doesn't get you a free pass out of eternal damnation. If you straddle the fence, you're going to self-destruct in your own rebellion.

In this verse, we are introduced to four attributes of Jesus Christ: The Amen, the Faithful, the True Witness, and the Beginning of the creation of God. The Amen, the unblemished

God, who reaches out to the spiritually blind. The Faithful, who searches out the unfaithful. The True Witness, the only true God whose words are infallible, and ways are trustworthy. The Beginning of all creation, who offers His healing touch to the sick church and woeful world.

Jesus is the "Amen." The word "amen" means "so be it," or "with complete assurance." In Isaiah 65:16, God is said to be "the God of truth;" in the Hebrew text, it is written as "the God of amen." Jesus is truly God, as He shares the same name as God, "the Amen." Jesus is absolutely, verily and completely supreme, and there is no shadow of uncertainty in Him. Amen speaks of integrity and certainty. He is the cornerstone. He is the capstone. He is the reason the universe exists and is held together. And His Word is the DNA and backbone of our whole being. Anything other than His Word, and anything other than the Amen, is incompatible with our existence. According to Colossians 1:17, "He is before all things, and in Him all things consist."

 The reason people who hate or reject Christ are still breathing is because of His favor, not because they are self-made and are able to make it on their own and conquer!

The Amen, the unblemished God, reaches out to the spiritually blind and continues to extend His grace to all of us who are undeserving.

Jesus also called Himself the "Faithful." This is in stark contrast to the Church of Laodicea, the unfaithful and deceitful, in contrast to Christ, who is faithful. "Christ's attributes of sincerity and truth come to the forefront as He deals with those whose alleged devotion to Him is only superficial and not substantial."[22] Jesus is faithful to His Father. He is faithful to His Church. He is faithful to His Word. He is faithful to His promises. He is faithful to you and me. He is faithful and absolutely reliable.

How humbling it is to know that the Faithful searches out the unfaithful, bringing hope and joy!

He is the "True Witness." Three things are necessary for Jesus to meet this requirement: First, He bears witness to all events and can testify with exact reliability; Second, He is able to relate the message for others flawlessly; Third, He is willing and bound to do so truthfully. In addition, it's worth repeating that Jesus is God, for He possesses the same attributes of God mentioned in Jeremiah 42:5, where God is "the true and faithful witness." In Christ all these conditions meet. He witnessed creation for He is the Creator. He witnessed the crucifixion, for He was the One nailed to the cross. He witnessed the resurrection, for He Himself is the Resurrection. He does not change. He does not waver. He does not shift like shifting shadows. He is the True Witness, the only true God whose words are infallible, and ways are trustworthy. And that is why you can trust Him with your pain, your life, your will and your future!

Jesus is "the Beginning of the creation of God." This does not mean that He was the first created being; it means that He is the author, the first cause, the source, the architect and ruler of all creation. He is the origin of all creation, the "supreme authority over the creation of God."[23] "In the beginning was the Word (Jesus), and the Word was with God, and the Word was God. He was in the beginning with God. All things were made through Him, and without Him nothing was made that was made" (John 1:1-3). According to Colossians 1:16, "For by Him (Christ) all things were created that are in heaven and that are on earth, visible and invisible, whether thrones or dominions or principalities or powers. All things were created through Him and for Him." The Beginning of all creation offers His healing touch to the sick church and His gentle love to a woeful world.

Here stands our Creator. His name is the Word, Jesus Christ, who crafted the universe with a simple command. Unfortunately, many in the church today believe that the Genesis story is allegorical and not a literal account of creation. As a man of science, I'm here to tell you that there is no process of natural selection or evolution as they teach in schools today. Evolution, as it is currently taught, is at best a theory, and is not scientifically proven.

 There are at least one hundred billion galaxies in our observable universe, and a mind the size of a dust mite is going to allegorize the creation? The Darwinian "expert" who calls himself clever is an impostor and in danger of heading towards eternal disaster.

3:15 *"I know your works, that you are neither cold nor hot. I could wish you were cold or hot.* **3:16** *So then, because you are lukewarm, and neither cold nor hot, I will vomit you out of My mouth.*

The church in Laodicea was conceited, compromising and Christ-less. The Word of God was not the standard; the people decided what was right. Resembling the water supply of the city, which was neither hot, like the healing springs of Hierapolis, nor cold, like the refreshing waters of Colossae, so too was this church, lukewarm. To please the congregation's ears, God's Word was diluted, made lukewarm.

 When you bend the Word not to offend anyone, there comes a point where it does not affect anyone!

Their wealth, arising from the excellence of its city's textile wools, led to a self-satisfied, lukewarm state of complacency that lulled them into a spiritual coma. Just as their water was lukewarm, so too were their hearts.

"The hot are the truly saved believers. The cold are those who are not believers and do not claim to be believers. The lukewarm are those who do claim to believe in Jesus but are not truly regenerate believers."[24]

In God's economy, if you are hot, like Peter, He can use you. If you are cold, like Saul of Tarsus, He can convict you, break you and mold you into a godly instrument. If you are lukewarm, He will spew you out of His mouth.

The hot are empowered by the fire of the Holy Spirit. The cold are untouched by the power of God's love. The lukewarm have tasted the heavenly gift, the good Word of God, but have failed to be stirred by grace. In Jesus' time, "the publicans and harlots were 'cold,' the Apostles 'hot.' The Scribes and Pharisees were 'lukewarm.'"[25] The brethren in Laodicea were not accused of apostasy nor idolatry, but of being a lukewarm congregation. Christ will not put this matter on the back burner. He will vomit forth the lukewarm, denoting a distaste that causes emesis, a visceral emotion of extreme disgust and rejection. This is the only church about which Christ had nothing good to share!

3:17 *"Because you say, 'I am rich, have become wealthy, and have need of nothing' — and do not know that you are wretched, miserable, poor, blind, and naked."*

"The Christians of Laodicea shared the self-sufficiency of their fellow-townsmen and carried it into the sphere of their relations with God and Christ."[26] Riches in themselves are not bad, but when riches enter the heart, so does pride. In 60 AD, an earthquake leveled Laodicea; the Roman Emperor Nero offered financial assistance in the reconstruction, but the proud citizens of Laodicea rejected the offer and rose from the wreckage by their own strength. The attitude of "I am rich, have become wealthy and have need of nothing" is one of hoarding the blessing but denying God, the very One who gave the provision!

In the center of Asia Minor's financial headquarters, this congregation assimilated seamlessly with the culture of pride and self-assurance. They boasted of their wealth blatantly, yet surprisingly, they were assessed as being poor. With "state of the art" medications in the heart of a medical powerhouse, they, who perceived themselves as having 20/20 vision, were diagnosed as being blind. Posing on the front cover of "Vogue©," they, who thought of themselves as fashionable, were told they were naked.

Vanity leads our hearts to miss the truth by blinding us. Being blind leads us to compromise. Compromise leads us in the paths of blunders. Blunders leads us to the cliff of depravity. Unbeknownst to us, the cliff of depravity leads to a Christ-less, wretched, miserable, poor, blind and naked state of thinking, living and being, which entices us to leap carelessly into the hands of death.

What is tragic is that the Laodicean church was unaware of its status. When God spoke of Israel prior to their Babylonian exile, He said, "Seeing many things, but you do not observe" (Isaiah 42:20). Though used as the golden standard today, ministry statistics and pragmatic measures cannot accurately diagnose the condition of a church's heart. Only the Word of God can. The Church of Laodicea had no idea they were lukewarm; tragically, neither does today's church.

3:18 *I counsel you to buy from Me gold refined in the fire, that you may be rich; and white garments, that you may be clothed, that the shame of your nakedness may not be revealed; and anoint your eyes with eye salve, that you may see.*

Here is the goodness of Christ. He does not taunt. He does not abandon. He does not give up on His Church, His bride. He not only makes the correct diagnosis, but He also dispenses the right medication: Himself, the Great I AM, God Almighty, who is not only willing, but able to heal them with His relentless love!

They were rich indeed and took great pride in their financial wealth. But money is useless when one is spiritually lukewarm and unaware of his status. Money cannot buy salvation nor sanctification. Spiritual wealth comes only through Christ. Christ challenges those who are thirsty to come to the waters in Isaiah 55:1-3. Just as He offers those who thirst to buy wine and milk without pay, He offers the Laodicean church to buy gold without money. His gold, purified in the fire, immersed in suffering and obedience, offers the church spiritual wealth, transforming them into a devoted and dedicated congregation on fire.

 Gold prices on earth fluctuate by the minute. Gold from God is tested, pure, and a sure bet. It does not change, it cannot fluctuate on a Dow Jones investment portfolio, and it will not be devalued.

They were dressed elegantly, walked in splendor but were shamefully naked spiritually. Nakedness in the Bible symbolizes defeat and humiliation. It is not Christ that made them naked. Christ offered to clothe them with white righteous garments. "My soul shall be joyful in my God; For He has clothed me with the garments of salvation, He has covered me with the robe of righteousness," exclaimed the prophet in Isaiah 61:10. Just as the fig leaves weren't good enough to cover Adam and Eve, expensive Laodicean wool wasn't good enough to cover this church. Why? Atonement for sin was needed. Atonement is not earned but given as a gift to those who accept Christ and His finished work on the cross. There is work to be done after we are saved, but that work does not earn God's love nor buy our salvation. Our work is to be performed wholeheartedly, out of adoration and service to the One who loved us first and who we follow.

 Christ-followers, praying earnestly, serving graciously, doing God's work passionately, will be clothed with fine white linen righteously (Revelation 19:8).

Laodicea was famous for its eye salve with medicinal benefits. Though the city physicians were experts in treating eye problems, the "patients" completely blind spiritually. Christ makes a culturally relevant reference to drive the point home. They didn't need man-made eye salve; they needed the truth of God which would give sight to their lukewarm hearts. God's anointing oil, the Holy Spirit, would give them sight so they would not call good evil and evil good (Isaiah 5:20).

Oh, the sweet nudging of the Holy Spirit that opens our eyes and leads us to repentance! God is good. He is not cruel. He is not a tyrant. He is not deceptive. He has torn the temple veil and allows us to enter into the Holy of Holies and see His goodness. In Isaiah 42:16 we read, "I will bring the blind by a way they did not know; I will lead them in paths they have not known. I will make darkness light before them, and crooked places straight. These things I will do for them, and not forsake them." Praise Him!

3:19 *As many as I love, I rebuke and chasten. Therefore, be zealous and repent.*

Rebuking and chastening speak of Jesus' love and are not an insincere approach. If you were going down the road and a bridge was out, you'd appreciate a sign that reads, "Road closed. Bridge out. Detour ahead." Some get mad that signs are up, feverishly yelling, "That's intolerant! That takes away my rights!" You've got a bridge out; the sign is saving your life! It's the same with Jesus. He tells us that He is the way to the Father and our only means to heaven. And people shout, "Intolerant! Bigotry! Hateful! Exclusive! Disrespectful! Narrow-minded!" The blind will be blind. If they, however, continue to reject His light, they will feel the heat of His punishment.

We read in Hebrews 12:5-8, "And you have forgotten the exhortation which speaks to you as to sons: 'My son, do not despise the chastening of the Lord, nor be discouraged when you are rebuked by Him; for whom the Lord loves He chastens, and scourges every son whom He receives.' If you endure chastening, God deals with you as with sons; for what son is there whom a father does not chasten? But if you are without chastening, of which all have become partakers, then you are illegitimate and not sons."

Personally, I don't like to be rebuked, but God sees it differently. If I'm his son, then I will be rebuked by Him, not out of cruelty, but out of His love for me. Throughout this book we'll continue to see that the mathematics of heaven is different than yours and mine. Jesus longs to embrace you, care for you, honor you, uplift you and guide you — when instead, He could have just said, "Go to hell!" He is a gentleman. He steps back and lets you have a free choice. You decide whether to heed the signs. You decide whether to become zealous and repent, or unreceptive and rebel. If you are from the "Laodicean descent," ask Him to transform your cold or lukewarm heart to one of burning passion for God!

3:20 *Behold, I stand at the door and knock. If anyone hears My voice and opens the door, I will come in to him and dine with him, and he with Me.*

We are in the Laodicean age. Jesus is knocking at the door of His Church and of our hearts. Despite the closed, self-absorbed, entitled demeanor of the church, Christ will not break the door down. He will not force us to open the door. What's ironic is that the church belongs to Jesus; He is the rightful owner; He is the rightful Shepherd; He is the rightful King; yet He is thrown out of His own Church! This is not an evangelical call for those outside the church; this is a plea motivated by love for those who are posing as Christ- followers. They profess to know Christ, yet they don't possess the virtues of Christ. He stands outside, and longs to be invited in. He calls each individual personally. He wants to dine with you. He wants to dine with me. This is not a cheap date; it is intimate companionship.

The invitation extends across the globe to anyone who has an ear to hear. In Luke 19:1-9, we meet Zacchaeus, a hated tax collector, who was filthy rich, and who happened to hear the knocking at his door. There is no mention of Jesus telling Zacchaeus what he must do to change. But once Love sits with the one who is broken, hopeless and grieved, that breathtaking Love turns the man into a new creation! Jesus longs to come in and dine with us. He does not want to beat us up. He does not want to hang our faults before us for all to see. He does not want to demolish our place. He longs to bring comfort. He longs to bring hope. He longs to bring joy. He longs to bring healing. As said of Zacchaeus, may it be said of us, "Today Salvation has come into this house" (Luke 19:9).

3:21 To him who overcomes I will grant to sit with Me on My throne, as I also overcame and sat down with My Father on His throne.

If you've ever wondered what grace looks like, this statement seals the deal. "Those who were about to be spewed from His mouth are invited to sit with Him on His throne."[27] Paul wrote of this in I Corinthians 6:2, "Do you not know that the saints will judge the world? And if the world will be judged by you, are you unworthy to judge the smallest matters?" Overcomers will sit in the throne room, to dine with Him, to fellowship with Him, not to be judged by Him, but to judge with Him. In II Timothy 2:12, those who endure will reign with Christ. May the Lord make our backs stronger, our faith deeper, and our hearts purer!

Do you ever wonder why Christ doesn't just pull the plug on Satan? Satan has already been defeated. Christ was crucified, and it was Satan who was horrified when Christ rose from the grave. Satan "rightfully" offered the kingdoms of this world to Christ when tempting Him. "Again, the devil took Him (Christ) up on an exceedingly high mountain and showed Him all the kingdoms of the world and their glory. And he said to Him, 'All these things I will give You if You will fall down and worship me.' Then Jesus said to him, 'Away with you, Satan!' For it is written, 'You shall worship the Lord your God, and Him only you shall serve'" (Matthew 4:8-10).

Notice Christ did not argue that Satan had a temporary hold of this world! Satan is allowed to run the gamut, with limitations set by God, so that you and I would have the freedom to choose. All are offered the love of Christ. Absurd to some. Precious to His followers. Christ is currently seated at the right hand of the Father on the Father's throne, "Who is even at the right hand of God" (Romans 8:34). But the time will come when Jesus will rule. After the Rapture He will, as we'll see in chapter five, take the scroll from His Father and begin to execute judgment on this world.

According to II Samuel 7:12-13, Christ Himself will gloriously reign from the Davidic throne, and that divinely scheduled office will arrive at the right time. When will that be?

1. After the seventh trumpet is sounded and the seven bowls of God's final wrath are executed (Revelation 15-16).

2. After the interdependent Religious, Economic, Political and city of Babylon are destroyed (Revelation 17-18).

3. After the Second Coming of Christ to save Israel and defeat the world leaders at the Campaign of Armageddon (Revelation 19:11-16).

4. After the Antichrist has his seven year "day" during the Tribulation and is slain, "its body destroyed and given to the burning flame" (Daniel 7:11-14).

5. After Satan is thrown into the Bottomless Pit and bound for 1,000 years (Revelation 20:1-3).

6. When the Son of Man comes in His glory (Second Coming), and all the holy angels with Him, *then He will sit on the throne of His glory.* All the nations will be gathered before Him, and He will separate them one from another, as a shepherd divides his sheep from the goats" (Matthew 25:31-32). This is the judgment of sheep and goats prior to the Millennium, where Christ judges those who either cared for or showed total disdain for His Tribulation saints

and the remnant of Israel. This is not the Great White Throne judgment; the White Throne will occur after the Millennium, where the wicked dead are raised and judged and sentenced to the Lake of Fire.

7. The judgment of the sheep and goats will be followed by the Millennium, where Christ will reign on earth and His saints will reign with Him. Finally, Christ will take up the throne that rightfully belongs to Him. "I (Daniel) was watching in the night visions, and behold, One like the Son of Man (Christ), coming with the clouds of heaven! He came to the Ancient of Days (God), and they brought Him (Christ) near Him (God). Then to Him (Christ) was given dominion and glory and a kingdom, that all peoples, nations, and languages should serve Him. *His dominion is an everlasting dominion,* which shall not pass away, and His kingdom the one which shall not be destroyed" (Daniel 7:13-14). "I (Daniel) was watching; and the same horn (Antichrist) was making war against the saints, and prevailing against them, until the Ancient of Days (God) came, and a judgment was made in favor of the saints of the Most High, *and the time came for the saints to possess the kingdom*" (Daniel 7: 21-22).

8. The Millennium will usher in the Great White Throne judgment, which leads to eternal death for Christ-rejecters and eternal life for the saints of Christ. The Lake of Fire will host Satan and his followers, where there will be excruciating pain and gnashing of teeth; The New Jerusalem will host Christ-followers, where there will be no tears, no fears and no death. In the eternal state, the throne of God and Christ are one in the same: "And he (the angel) showed me (John) a pure river of water of life, clear as crystal, proceeding from the throne of God and of the Lamb" (Revelation 22:1).

Let's review the chronological order of rewards and when they are originally mentioned, spanning from Ephesus to Laodicea, covering the span from the birth of man to the eternal life of man:

1. Ephesus: Tree of Life. Dates back to the beginning of mankind, Adam and Eve, when they were in the Garden of Eden with access to the Tree of Life.

2. Smyrna: No second death. Adam and Eve faced death because of sin. Those in Christ will not face the second death, or the Lake of Fire.

3. Pergamos: Manna. The children of Israel tasted heaven's bread, manna, while in the wilderness. Overcomers in Christ will taste of the heavenly manna for Eternity.

4. Thyatira: Rule with an iron rod. In His First Coming, Christ died on the cross, but after His Second Coming, His rule will be indestructible during the Millennium and beyond.

5. Sardis: Name in the Book of Life. Those who reject Christ will face the Great White Throne judgment after the Millennium and will be cast into the Lake of Fire because their names will not be found in the Book of Life.

6. Philadelphia: New Jerusalem. The New Jerusalem will descend from heaven and believers bought by the blood of the Lamb will live with Christ forever.

7. Laodicea: Sit on God's throne. We will reign with Christ for all Eternity.

3:22 *"He who has an ear, let him hear what the Spirit says to the churches."*

This will be the last time we read the word "church" in God's Word until we get to Revelation 22:16. The omission of the word "church" is intentional, signifying that the church saints will not experience the Tribulation (chapters 6-19) because they will be caught up into heaven during the Rapture. The newly converted saints during the Tribulation, however, will face horrible events, including decapitation. We'll read in Revelation 20:4, "And I (John) saw thrones, and they (saints) sat on them, and judgment was committed to them. Then I saw the souls of those who had been beheaded (new converts during the Tribulation) for their witness to Jesus and for the Word of God, who had not worshiped the Beast or his image, and had not received his mark on their foreheads or on their hands. And they lived and reigned with Christ for a thousand years."

This is the seventh time we'll read, "He who has an ear, let him hear what the Spirit says to the churches." The Holy Spirit is no less than God; He is God. In Acts 5:3-4, we find that Ananias, who lied to the Holy Spirit, was actually lying to God. We are in an age of grace, where goodness and mercy flows from God's heart. "The sevenfold call still sounds, and the Spirit still speaks."[28] It is critical to note that it is not psychology, philosophy, society, culture sensitivity or money that is calling out to the churches; it is the Spirit of the living God. If you've got an ear, listen closely! The Holy Spirit is tenderly calling your name.

The Church of Laodicea considered herself to be wealthy, lacking nothing, yet as the Great Physician placed His divine surgical magnifying glasses on, He called her "wretched, miserable, poor, blind and naked." He despised her lukewarm state yet informed her of His ever-present help. Just as He did for the Church of Laodicea, Christ is knocking at your heart's door. No matter who you are, no matter what you've done, no matter what you're going through and no matter where you find yourself, He comes to you, longing to heal, to love and to comfort you. Won't you let Him in?

REV IT UP & SUM IT UP – CHAPTER THREE:

In this chapter, we span from the 1500s to the present age, examining three churches, Sardis, Philadelphia and Laodicea.

Sardis represents the Dark Ages and is the "Dead or Perished Church" from 1517 to 1790 AD. Without the Bible, people are the walking dead. Many boast that they are better off without God's Word "meddling" in their lives; they feel free, independent, resilient and happy, stating they don't follow anyone "blindly." One day they will bow the knee when they see God's glory and face Jesus who is worthy; the Lake of Fire will not be funny, but as they'll find out, it will be an eternal tragedy, with misery added upon misery. Spoiler alert: The Lord will return like a thief in the night. Therefore, rise from your apathetic state, be cleansed under the blood of the Lamb, and be an overcomer in Christ. Only then, will your name will be found and remain in the Book of Life, and you will receive white garments of righteousness, living eternally with Christ.

Philadelphia represents the "Faithful or Patriotic Church," with the explosion of evangelism from 1730 AD to the present. God promises to keep His followers out of the seven-year Tribulation, "Because you have kept My command to persevere, I also will keep you from the hour of trial which shall come upon the whole world, to test those who dwell on the earth" (Revelation 3:10). Christ-followers will bear the name of God and will enjoy Eternity with Him forever.

Laodicea represents the "Lukewarm or Passive Church," with an indifferent approach to Christ, spanning from 1900 AD to the present age. Its assessment of itself reaches an all-time high narcissistic posture: "I am rich, have become wealthy, and have need of nothing." Christ's assessment, however, is quite the opposite, "You are wretched, miserable, poor, blind and naked."Their church became a club where religious snobs got together and told each other how great they were. Self-reliance and pride lead to spiritual blindness; Christ-reliance and humility lead to eternal richness.

Section 3

TOMORROW

Chapter 4
I Fly Sky High

Chapter four demarks a pivotal point in the course of human history, the Rapture, the next significant event in God's time-line of prophesy. John is snatched up to heaven and beholds the glory of God, the four cherubim worshiping God, and the 24 elders, representing the Raptured church, joining in and singing praises to God.

Snatched Up to Heaven

4:1 *After these things I looked, and behold, a door standing open in heaven. And the first voice which I heard was like a trumpet speaking with me, saying, "Come up here, and I will show you things which must take place after this."*

John is moved in two directions: upward in space to heaven and forward in time to the Day of the Lord, which includes the Rapture, just prior to the Tribulation period. He has already written about things which were in the past (Jesus' resurrected body and glory) in chapter one, and which are in the present (the Church Age) in chapters two and three. He has witnessed what was and what is, and "after these things," or "meta tauta" in the Greek, meaning afterward, following, hereafter, John will write concerning what is to come. The door of heaven opened, and John heard a voice likened to a trumpet, welcoming him to God's throne so he could witness visions and share it with us today.

Two thousand years have passed since John penned these words and scoffers mock in these last days, cynically asking, "Where is the promise of His coming? For since the fathers fell asleep, all things continue as they were from the beginning of creation" (II Peter 3:3-4). Just as scoffers laughed at the time it took Noah to build the Ark prior to the flood, they laugh today, blinded that the next event in prophecy is the Rapture of the church, followed by fiery judgment on the earth targeting its ungodly people (II Peter 3:7).

The dilemma is quite simple. When Jesus spoke to the Samaritan woman at the well in John chapter four, He spent two days with the Samaritans and then went back to the Jewish people. Does it not fascinate you that He spent two days versus one, or three or more? He spent two days with the Samaritans, the "non-Jews," (considered by Jews to be "half-breeds") and then went back to the Jews. To the Lord, one day is a thousand years, and a thousand years as one day (Psalm 90:4). If one day is a thousand years, then two days are two thousand years. The Lord is not slack concerning His promise, but is merciful toward us, not willing that any should perish but that all should come to repentance (II Peter 3:9). Therefore, He has spent two thousand years with the Gentiles, non-Jews, and has given life to the church. The two days are coming to an end. Let the scoffers scoff. Let the believers believe. Let the unsaved come to Christ. Let the saved stop being careless and abide in Christ. The day of the Lord will soon come as a thief in the night (II Peter 3:10). We're in overtime!

Just as Enoch was caught up to heaven before the judgment of the flood, John was caught up to the third heaven before he saw the visions of the Tribulation judgments that were to ensue. "These are the types (pre-figures or events in the Old

Testament). The anti-type (an event that occurs in the New Testament era) lies in the fact that all believers will be caught up to heaven before the judgment is actually poured out upon the earth."[1]

The church will have been caught up into heaven before the hell on earth is unveiled. Why do I believe this? Because the church is called the bride of Christ. To allow the church to undergo the Tribulation would be likened to, as we've discussed, an abusive, controlling, manipulative and violent relationship. We will escape this seven-year barrage of assaults. I often kid with Southern Californian people, stating, "If you can't handle the 405 in your air-conditioned car (the 405 is one of the worst traffic-jammed freeways in America), how will you be able to handle the Tribulation when God "Rev's Up" the heat and you find yourselves in a real jam?"

Because there are significant parallels between verse one and the Rapture, I believe what occurred to John is not just an isolated event, but a foreshadowing of what the church will experience:

1. Just as John, the believers will hear a spoken command at the Rapture: "For the Lord Himself will descend from heaven with a shout, with the voice of an archangel, and with the trumpet of God. And the dead in Christ will rise first" (I Thessalonians 4:16).

2. Just as John, the believers will be Raptured to heaven: "Then we who are alive and remain shall be caught up together with them in the clouds to meet the Lord in the air. And thus, we shall always be with the Lord" (I Thessalonians 4:17).

3. Just as John, the believers are in Christ: "For as the body is one and has many members, but all the members of that one body, being many, are one body, so also is Christ. For by one Spirit we were all baptized into one body — whether Jews or Greeks, whether slaves or free

— and have all been made to drink into one Spirit" (I Corinthians 12:12-13).

4. Just as John, the believers will hear the sound of a trumpet: "In a moment, in the twinkling of an eye, at the last trumpet. For the trumpet will sound, and the dead will be raised incorruptible, and we shall be changed" (I Corinthians 15:52).

5. Just as John, the two witnesses found in Revelation chapter eleven will hear the command, "Come up here!" as they are resurrected: "And they heard a loud voice from heaven saying to them, "Come up here." And they ascended to heaven in a cloud, and their enemies saw them" (Revelation 11:12).[2]

 The Rapture will be in a sequential order, such as a carpool, where people are not all picked up at the same time, but all will arrive at the same destination.

Jesus was the first to be Raptured or resurrected (the word "resurrection" is at times used interchangeably for the word "Rapture") from the dead and received His glorified body; followed by the next event on the prophetic calendar, the Rapture of the church when believers after Christ's crucifixion will receive their glorified bodies; followed by the Tribulation converts who will be beheaded during the seven year period; followed by the Old Testament saints before the Millennium; followed by Jews and Gentiles who entered the 1,000 year period in their unglorified bodies and remained true to Christ, occurring after the Millennium.

What exactly is the Rapture? It is "harpazo" in the Greek, "rapturo" in Latin and "caught up" in English. It means to seize, carry off by force, to snatch out or away. God will finally take believers home to heaven where the soul, the spirit and the glorified body will unite and be forever in His presence.

We find it in Paul's writings. "Behold, I tell you a mystery (the

Rapture was not fully revealed until Paul's ministry; Jesus only mentioned it in John 14:1-3). We shall not all sleep (physical death for the believer), but we shall all be "changed "("allasso" in Greek, meaning to transform, or get our glorified bodies) — in a "moment" ("atamos" in Greek, meaning so minute that it cannot be cut in two), in the twinkling of an eye, at the last trumpet. For the trumpet will sound, and the dead will be raised incorruptible (be caught up in the air, meet the Lord, be taken to heaven, given immortal bodies that are unable to be sick, sin or die), and we (believers who are alive) shall be changed (get their glorified bodies and bypass death)!" (I Corinthians 15:51-52).

 After we do an angiogram on a patient, we look closely at the images on a computer. But sometimes the heart is beating so fast that we are unable to decipher whether there is a true blockage or not; we slow down the images and use the keyboard to view the artery frame by frame. And then it becomes clear! This is what Paul has done for us in I Corinthians 15:51-52. The Rapture will occur in a twinkling of an eye, in an atomic second! But Paul helps us see the images frame by frame to better understand what will happen to believers during the Rapture. He does so in his letter to the Corinthian Church and as we'll now see, to the Thessalonian Church.

"For this we say to you by the word of the Lord, that we who are alive and remain until the coming of the Lord will by no means precede those who are asleep (believers in Christ who have already died). For the Lord Himself will descend from heaven with a shout, with the voice of an archangel, and with the trumpet of God. And the dead in Christ will rise first (those who were Christ-followers and have died; their old bodies will be glorified and meet their souls and spirit which are already in heaven). Then we who are alive and remain shall be caught up (if the Rapture were to happen right now, Christ-followers who are alive will be caught up by instantly receiving their glorified bodies) together with Him (Christ) in the clouds to meet the Lord in the air. And thus, we shall always be with the Lord (in heaven)" (I Thessalonians 4:15-17).

How can we be sure that believers will be going to heaven? Jesus said in John 14:1-3, "Let not your heart be troubled; you believe in God, believe also in Me. In My Father's house are many mansions; if it were not so, I would have told you. I go to prepare a place for you. And if I go and prepare a place for you, I will come again and receive you to Myself; that where I am, there you may be also." Simple! We will be with Christ in our Father's house, heaven, for seven years, then accompany Christ in His Second Coming to earth, not for the battle of Calvary but for the Campaign of Armageddon. This discredits the Post Tribulation theory which states that the Rapture occurs at the end of the Tribulation, and the Rapture and the Second Coming of Christ occur simultaneously. After the Second Coming, believers will spend a thousand years with Christ on a renovated earth, followed by Eternity with God in the New Jerusalem and in a new earth and a new heaven.

Before the cross, when people died, their bodies were buried, but their souls and spirits went to a place called Hades in Greek or Sheol in Hebrew (Luke 16:19-31). Hades is not purgatory; the Bible speaks of no opportunity for redemption after death. There are two compartments in Hades, separated by a great chasm: one is a place of torment and houses unbelievers and the other was a place of rest for the believers while they waited for the resurrection. When Jesus died on the cross, was buried and resurrected on the third day, He went to hell, or Hades, and "led captivity captive" meaning He went to the restful side, collected the believers, who were "held captive," and took them (their souls and spirits) to the Father in heaven (Ephesians 4:8-10). After the cross, when a believer dies, his body is buried, but his soul and spirit go straight to heaven and no longer to the restful side of Hades. To be absent from the body is to be present with the Lord (II Corinthians 5:8). Therefore, the restful side of Hades is now completely empty! More importantly, our Christ's "soul was not left in Hades, nor did His flesh see corruption" (Acts 2:31). He is risen indeed! He lives!

When an unbeliever dies, his soul and spirit go to the torment side of Hades. These souls will never have another chance to accept Christ. In fact, after His resurrection, Jesus visited this side of hell as well: He went and preached (proclaimed) to the spirits in prison (I Peter 3:19). However, He did not preach the message of salvation. He made it clear that He is Salvation! "Having disarmed principalities and powers, He (Christ) made a public spectacle of them triumphing over them in it" (Colossians 2:15). The unbelievers' soul and spirit are in Hades and in a temporary holding place of sheer torment; but oh, how they wish that were the end of their journey; because their soul and spirit will be joined to their bodies in the "second resurrection" when death and Hades will deliver up the dead, having then received their eternal bodies, and they will be judged before the Great White Throne (after the Millennium) and will then be cast into the Lake of Fire (ultimate and eternal hell, the second death). Each unbeliever will live in his dying torment forever as he will also be given an eternal body to unite his soul and spirit (Revelation 20: 11-15).

The Rapture spoken of in I Corinthians 15:51-52 and I Thessalonians 4:15-17, is therefore only for believers in Christ (those who came to Christ after His First Coming). The believers (in soul and spirit) will unite with their buried bodies, but their bodies will be transformed, never again to sin or die. The believers who are alive when the Rapture occurs, will be changed in a "twinkling of an eye," and receive their glorified bodies instantaneously. We will meet the Lord in the air. We will be escorted to heaven. All believers will be judged at the Bema Seat, the judgment seat of Christ (II Corinthians 5:10). This is not a judgment for our sins; our sins were all forgiven on the cross as Jesus absorbed God's wrath, the punishment we deserved (I Peter 2:24). We did not earn our salvation; Jesus did. The Bema seat is a judgment for our works to the Lord; crowns will be handed out to us; we will cast our crown back at the feet of Christ in adoration (Revelation 4:10); I personally don't feel like going to this party empty-handed! According to Daniel 12:1-2, each believer from Adam up to the time of Christ, whose soul and spirit are already with the Lord, will be resurrected from the dead and receive their glorified bodies after the Tribulation and before the Millennium.

The Rapture is not the Second Coming of our Christ. The events in chronological order are as follows: The Rapture (instantaneous); the Tribulation (seven years); the Second Coming of Christ (total 75 days as we'll study later, which includes the Campaign of Armageddon; the 75 "extra" days added to the 1,260 days of the second half of the Tribulation is found in Daniel 12:12). The church will miss the Tribulation entirely as we'll be in heaven with our Lord, singing praises to Him and receiving our crowns, white robes of righteousness, and partaking in the Lamb's supper. Boring? No! Music. Food. Singing. Laughter. Joy. No doctors dispensing medications. No lawyers chasing ambulances. No mechanics fixing cars. What a party it will be to carry us into the Millennium and into Eternity!

What happens to the United States of America after the Rapture? Since millions of Christ-followers will suddenly disappear, much about America will change. The establishment who have been pursuing the new world order — One-World-Government — will hail their new world leader, the Antichrist; no one will be able to withstand his might, being lured by his charm and his deceit.

The United States of America will transform overnight into a second-rate country. Do you think it's the brilliant minds of people who sustain this country?

Think again. It's the prayers of faithful servants of God who intercede for the protection and the blessings of this land! It's the Holy Spirit who holds up the pillars of this country! It's God's extended gentle grace that guards the very foundation of this nation! How will the media report millions missing? "Mother Earth finally purged herself of these intolerant heretics by natural selection."

When the Coronavirus Pandemic hit the United States of America in 2020, it unraveled the raw emotions of fear and panic, displayed in full fashion by people hoarding sanitizers, toilet paper, food and water and leaving shelves empty in grocery stores. The Rapture will take millions of Christ-followers home, to heaven, but those left behind will find themselves in such hysteria during the Tribulation that the dire and tragic Coronavirus Pandemic will look like a picnic, and the lawlessness on our streets will skyrocket. We'll study the Antichrist's 666 mark in chapter 13. People will need the mark, a sign of allegiance to the Antichrist during the Tribulation that will preclude the recipient from ever going to heaven, to buy essential supplies of bread and water; how will they respond? Chilling!

There are different views of the Rapture:

1. Pre-Tribulation (Pre-Trib): The Rapture occurs before the Tribulation and will include all the believers of the Church Age. This is a theologically sound viewpoint and I'm a strong proponent of it.

2. Partial Rapture: The Rapture is for the faithful Christians, and not the carnal Christians, who will be left behind and will experience the seven-year Tribulation.

3. Mid-Tribulation (Mid-Trib): The Rapture occurs after three and a half years of the seven-year Tribulation and before the second half, the Great Tribulation.

4. Post-Tribulation (Post-Trib): The Rapture occurs after the seven-year Tribulation. God worst wrath will be poured out only at the end of the Tribulation. This is like a "yo-yo" view, where the Rapture occurs, believers who are kept from harm during the Tribulation, will be caught up, meet Christ, and then make a U-turn, returning to earth for Christ's Second Coming.

5. Pre-Wrath or Three Fourths Rapture: The Rapture occurs when three-fourths of the Tribulation is complete, and then God pours out His wrath in the last one-fourth of the Tribulation, between the sixth and seventh seal. This theory is flawed for many reasons, one being that the sixth and seventh seals occur in the first half of the Tribulation. If I may, this viewpoint is theologically unsound, as are the Partial, Mid and Post beliefs.

In his book, *The End*, author Dr. Mark Hitchcock masterfully outlines why the Rapture will be Pre-Tribulation.[3] In a simple acronym, "R-A-P-T-U-R-E," I will offer seven reasons why the Rapture will be Pre-Tribulation: **R**emoved Church, **A**ppraising Church, **P**ower Church, **T**hankful Church, **U**nited Church, **R**ole of Church, **E**xpecting Church. I am not referring to the word "church" as a building where believers gather; I am referencing it to true believers and true Christ-followers who make up the church.

1. **R**-A-P-T-U-R-E. **R**emoved Church. The word "church" is mentioned twenty times in the book of Revelation, nineteen times in the first three chapters. It is absent from chapters four to twenty-one; the Tribulation wrath unfolds from chapters six to nineteen. The church is mentioned again in Revelation 22:16.

   The removal of the word "church" helps us understand why the Rapture will occur, ushering in the Tribulation, which is also called the "time of Jacob's Trouble" (Jeremiah 30:7), in the most horrid seven-year span. The Tribulation will also be a time of unparalleled evangelism where millions including unbelieving Jews will turn to Christ. We read in Romans 11:25-26, "blindness in part has happened to Israel until the fullness of the Gentiles has come in. And so all Israel will be saved, as it is written: 'The Deliverer will come out of Zion, and He will turn away ungodliness from Jacob.'" In order to turn to God, the nation of Israel will face dreadful times.

 The Tribulation unfolds not only to bring Gentiles to God, but also the remnant of Israel to God. It is not to bring the church to God; the church will already be in heaven during the Tribulation!

We read seven times, "He who has an ear, let him hear what the Spirit says to the churches" in Revelation 2-3. In Revelation 13:9, during the middle of the Tribulation, we read "If anyone has an ear, let him hear." That's it. It ends there. It does not say "Let him hear what the Spirit says to the churches" because the church is gone! In Revelation twelve, Satan persecutes Israel. Why not the church? Because the church is already removed. It is Raptured!

2. R-**A**-P-T-U-R-E. **A**ppraising Church. Though many commentators note that there are no specific signs given for the Rapture, and that is technically true, there actually are four signs that we find in Genesis chapter six: godlessness, shamelessness, viciousness and population explosiveness. We will study these four signs later in this chapter. The Appraising Church, or alert, evaluating, diligent, Holy Spirit-led and ever-watching church will detect and understand these signs.

    On the other hand, there are specific signs given for Christ's Second Coming, which occurs seven years after the Rapture. These include the signs spoken of in Matthew 24:4-28. There will be false prophets who will deceive many; wars will escalate; nations will rise against nations; there will be famines, pestilence and earthquakes. Newly born-again believers will be martyred; lawlessness will abound; the love of many will grow cold; the Gospel will be preached in all the world; the Antichrist will desecrate the third Jewish Temple. If these signs, except the last one mentioned, seem to be occurring today, how much more intense will they be during the Tribulation!

Only believers will see and take part in the Rapture; everyone on earth will see the Second Coming. In the Rapture, Jesus comes *for* his saints; in the Second Coming, He comes *with* His saints. We meet the Lord in the air in the Rapture and it occurs suddenly; Christ comes back to earth in the Second Coming and it occurs over a period of time. There is a gap between the two events to allow the wrath of God, the seven seals, the seven trumpets, and the seven bowls of God's final wrath to take their course on earth; the Post-Tribulation view cannot account for these events. The Rapture and the Second Coming are entirely different and separate events and cannot be integrated.

3. R-A-**P**-T-U-R-E. **P**owered Church. The church is powered by the Holy Spirit. In Zechariah 4:6, we read, "This is the word of the Lord to Zerubbabel, 'Not by might, nor by power, but by my Spirit,' says the Lord of hosts." When Zerubbabel, Governor of Israel, and Joshua, the High Priest of Israel were overwhelmed in rebuilding Solomon's temple after the Babylonian exile, God gave them the answer to their problems. Be led and empowered by the Holy Spirit!

In chapters three and four, each church was told, "He who has an ear, let him hear what the Spirit says to the churches." It was the Spirit's voice that was moving in the hearts of the believers and enabling them to overcome.

In II Thessalonians 2:5-7 we read, "Do you not remember that when I (Paul) was still with you I told you (church believers) these things? And now you know what is restraining, that he (Antichrist) may be revealed in his own time. For the mystery of lawlessness is already at work; only He (Holy Spirit) who now restrains will do so until He (Holy Spirit) is taken out of the way."

Today, the Holy Spirit is holding back the Antichrist. Today, the Holy Spirit of God permanently indwells the believer (Romans 8:9). When the Spirit is "taken out of the way" so too is the church filled with believers taken out of the way! Once the church is removed, God will allow Satan to proliferate his evil schemes through the Antichrist.

The church that is powered today by the Holy Spirit will no longer be here because the Holy Spirit which indwells the believer will be "taken out of the way." Will there be no Holy Spirit on earth during the Tribulation? Because there will be millions who come to Christ during this horrid time, the Holy Spirit must be playing a critical role, wooing, calling, convicting, but not indwelling the church, since there no longer is a church on earth.

4. R-A-P-**T**-U-R-E. **T**hankful Church. The church will be thankful because it will not go through the wrath of God! In I Thessalonians 1:10, we read, "And to wait for His Son from heaven, whom He raised from the dead, even Jesus who delivers us from the wrath ("orge" in the Greek) to come." In Revelation 6:16-17, 11:18, 15:1, 7, and 16:19 the word "wrath" is the same Greek word, "orge," to describe God's wrath denoting the Tribulation! For instance, in Revelation 6:16, we hear the torment of earth-dwellers screaming as they plead to the mountains and rocks, "Fall on us and hide us from the face of Him (God) who sits on the throne and from the wrath, "orge," of the Lamb."

In I Thessalonians chapter five, Paul distinguishes the believers from unbelievers, calling the believers "you" the sons of light, and the unbelievers "they" of the darkness.

In 5:3, he states, "they (unbelievers) shall not escape" the Day of the Lord which includes the Tribulation. "For God did not appoint us (believers) to wrath ("orge;" the context talks of the Day of the Lord and not eternal hell), but to obtain salvation through our Lord Jesus Christ, who died for us, that whether we wake or sleep (die), we should live together with Him" (I Thessalonians 5:9-10).

We read in Romans 5:9, "Much more then, having been justified by His blood, we shall be saved from wrath ("orge") through Him."

 Christ-followers don't get to "escape" daily tribulations (John 16:33), man's wrath (II Timothy 3:12), Satan's wrath (Ephesians 6:11-12) nor the world's wrath (John 15:18-19); but they do get to escape God's wrath, the Tribulation!

If a professor promises the "A" students that they will be exempt from the final exam and maintain their "A," but tells them to come to the exam and take part in it, then they are still going through the exam and that is likened to the Post-Tribulation view; which makes no sense.

If the professor tells the "A" students not to come to the exam at all and still maintain their "A," then that is likened to the Pre-Tribulation view.

I believe that true believers who disagree with the Pre-Tribulation view are going to be pleasantly surprised at the time of the Rapture because they too will be caught up! Believers are not "A" students, nor do they belong to a specific political party, but they are washed in the blood of the Lamb. And that's their passport and exemption papers from the Tribulation!

5.   R-A-P-T-**U**-R-E. **U**nited Church. The awake church is united in having a blessed hope. According to Titus 2:13, we are "Looking for the blessed hope and glorious appearing of our great God and Savior Jesus Christ." In I Thessalonians

4:17-18, we read, "Then we who are alive and remain shall be caught up together with them in the clouds to meet the Lord in the air. And thus, we shall always be with the Lord. Therefore, comfort one another with these words."

The Pre-Tribulation view is the only "comforting" perspective with a "blessed hope." All the others plant fear, judgment and condemnation in one's heart. When Christ spoke of the Rapture in John 14:1-3, he said "Do not let your hearts be troubled." How can you comfort the church by saying, "You're going to get your head chopped off because the Antichrist is furious and will hound you, imprison you, mistreat you and then kill you on earth during the Tribulation?" Yes, then tell them, "Be of good cheer! May the Lord bless your day as you contemplate your future!" Seriously? Think about it! That's absurd! It makes zero sense!

 The Pre-Tribulation view is the only reassuring perspective with a blessed hope; all the other views offer "blasted hope!"

6. R-A-P-T-U-**R**-E. **R**ole of the church. In the Rapture, Christ will come for His Church. In His Second Coming, Christ will come with His Church to save Israel. The roles the church plays are strictly by God's grace, but they do differ between the two events. Moreover, after the Rapture, believers will face the Bema Seat, where we will be judged for our works, receiving our rewards and crowns. There needs to be a gap of time to fill the period between the Rapture and the Second Coming.

We simply cannot be Raptured and make a U-turn, coming back to earth for the Second Coming as believed by the Post-Tribulation camp. In Matthew 25:31-46, Jesus will separate the sheep from the goats at the end of the

Tribulation during His Second Coming; if all believers are taken up at the end of the Tribulation, how will the sheep be on earth? The church believers will be taken up in the Rapture prior to the Tribulation. New converts who are not martyred during the Tribulation will remain on earth and will be designated as sheep in the Second Coming of Christ, being able to enter the Millennium.

What's more, if all believers were taken up at the end of the Tribulation as believed by the Post-Tribulation view, and get their glorified bodies, how will there be believers who make it through the Tribulation and enter the Millennium with their natural bodies and procreate?

7. R-A-P-T-U-R-**E. E**xpecting Church. The living church is expecting the Rapture to occur at any second, deeming it imminent. Christ can come at any time! That is our living hope! "Blessed be the God and Father of our Lord Jesus Christ, who according to His abundant mercy has begotten us again to a living hope through the resurrection of Jesus Christ from the dead, to an inheritance incorruptible and undefiled and that does not fade away, reserved in heaven for you, who are kept by the power of God through faith for salvation ready to be revealed in the last time" (I Peter 1:3-5). So, what do we do in the meantime? "Wait for His Son from heaven, whom He raised from the dead even Jesus who delivers us from the wrath to come" (I Thessalonians 1:10). We wait because we expect.

It's worth reviewing Titus 2:13, "Looking for the blessed hope and glorious appearing of our great God and Savior Jesus Christ." We are to be waiting earnestly, and we are to be looking expectantly for His coming.

The Pre-Tribulation view is the only outlook where believers can say, "Jesus can very well come today!" All other views are unable to proclaim the imminence of Christ's coming.

The Mid-Tribulation viewpoint requires the church to go through three and a half years of the Tribulation, and because of that, Jesus cannot possibly come now, at any time; He'd have to wait three and a half years after the Tribulation starts. The Post-Tribulation supporters have to go through seven years of hardship, and for them, therefore, Jesus cannot come today. The same holds true for the Partial-Rapture or the Pre-Wrath (Three-Fourths Rapture); according to these erroneous beliefs, Jesus cannot come today, in a blink of an eye, making His imminent return impossible.

The Pre-Tribulation believers are looking for Christ today and if not today, then tomorrow because "our citizenship is in heaven, from which we also eagerly wait for the Savior, the Lord Jesus Christ" (Philippians 3:20).

 The Rapture will be a glad day, a happy day, a blessed day! Why is that so important? Because we are looking for Christ. The Mid-Tribulation, Post-Tribulation, Pre-Wrath, and Partial-Tribulation will be looking for the Antichrist!

Because we look for Christ today, we are motivated to please Him with our words and action; and because we are heartbroken for those who don't have Christ, we evangelize!

There is another nugget that we should discuss. Specific order in the Bible cannot be changed. For instance, in regard to salvation, you first have redemption, followed by justification, followed by sanctification, followed by glorification. You cannot be sanctified before you are justified.

So too is the order of the seven Jewish feasts. There are four Spring festivals:

1. Passover. Signifying redemption. Israel escaped the hands of Pharaoh by applying the blood of a lamb on their doorposts. So too the Lamb of God is slain to save

us from the clutches of Satan. Commemorated on Good Friday, when Jesus died on Calvary's cross.

2. Feast of Unleavened Bread. On the evening after Passover God told the Hebrew people exiting Egypt not to allow their bread to rise (in their haste, exclude leaven from bread, not letting leaven toughen the dough, just bake it and go; leaven symbolizing sin which spreads quickly). While Passover is commemorated for 24 hours, the Feast of Unleavened Bread starts right after Passover and lasts for seven days. It symbolizes the purging of evil. Symbolically, Jesus lay in the tomb sinless.

3. Feast of First Fruits. The first grain of the harvest was given to God as an offering, highlighting that the seed that was buried in the ground gave life to the grain that sprouted. It is celebrated on Resurrection Day or Easter. Symbolically, Jesus was the first to resurrect from the dead.

4. Feast of Weeks, Shavuot. The day the Law of Moses was given to Israel. Pentecost, fifty days after First-Fruits; the Holy Spirit fell upon the believers on the fiftieth day after Christ rose from the dead. Currently, we are in the dispensation of grace under the guidance of the Holy Spirit.

The first three feasts are already fulfilled in the prophetic timetable. We are currently and symbolically in the tail end of the fourth feast, when the Church Age and the restraint of the Holy Spirit exists but will soon end.

These are followed by the three Autumn festivals:

1. The Feast of the Trumpets. Rosh Hashanah yearly marks the beginning of the Jewish civil calendar and falls on the first day of the Jewish seventh month, usually the end of September or beginning of October. The shofar was sounded, heralding a solemn time of preparation for the Day of Atonement. Symbolically, for those who rejected Christ, the trumpet will sound for the Rapture but

they will remain on earth for the "Day of Atonement."

The Trumpet Feast begins on the day of a new moon, but initiating it is not exact as the clouds and weather conditions may interfere with the accuracy of blowing the trumpets on time. No one knows the exact time of the Rapture!

2. Day of Atonement. The high priest offered sacrifices for the people of Israel, falling on the tenth day of the seventh month. This symbolizes the Tribulation, a "day" (seven years) of purification. The remnant of Israel will see the One they pierced (Jesus), recognizing and accepting Him as their Messiah at the end of the Tribulation.

3. Feast of the Tabernacles. It falls on the fifteenth day of the seventh month. Known as the Feast of Booths, to remind Israel that they lived in booths or tents in the wilderness, protected by God after they left Egypt. This is symbolic of being with Christ in His Millennial Kingdom on earth and for all Eternity in the New Jerusalem.

The order of these feasts cannot be changed. Neither can the Tribulation (Atonement) precede the Rapture (Trumpet)!

We noted above that there are no specific signs to tell us when the Rapture will occur but there are specific signs as outlined in Matthew 24 that precede the Second Coming of Christ. Let's review the four "signs" indicating that the Rapture is imminent, using symbolic parallels derived from two world events: the flood in Noah's day and the destruction by fire of Sodom and Gomorrah in Lot's day.

It is worth reading II Peter 2:5-9, where we find God "did not spare the ancient world, but saved Noah, one of eight people, a preacher of righteousness, bringing in the flood on the world of the ungodly; and turning the cities of Sodom and Gomorrah into ashes, condemned them to destruction, making them an example to those who afterward would live ungodly; and delivered righteous Lot, who was oppressed by the filthy conduct of the wicked (for that righteous man, dwelling among them, tormented his righteous soul from day to day by seeing and hearing their lawless deeds) — then the Lord knows how to deliver the godly out of temptations and to reserve the unjust under punishment for the day of judgment."

As God saved righteous Noah and backsliding carnal Lot (who was considered righteous by God), so too He will save His Church from the Tribulation. The people who saw the ark Noah built, mocked him; God sent the rains suddenly and globally, and the flood wiped out all mankind and creatures on earth. The people of Sodom and Gomorrah were bent on carrying out their wicked plans; they were consequently blinded by God, and the Lord rained brimstone and fire on Sodom and Gomorrah. The state of man's heart and his depraved mind that prevailed prior to these events are palpably conspicuous today and are clear indicators that the Rapture is imminent:

1. Godlessness: people refused to repent in Noah's days. "Then the Lord saw that the wickedness of man was great in the earth" (Genesis 6:5). The same spirit of rejecting Christ and refusing to accept His love is present today.

2. Shamelessness: peoples' hearts were seared in Noah's days. "Every intent of the thoughts of his heart was only evil continually" (Genesis 6:5). Not only were they godless, but they were hardened, unapologetic and defiant, flaunting their obscenities. The same spirit of obstinance, calling a strike a ball and a ball a strike, and threatening the well-being of those who don't agree, is present today.

3. Viciousness: violence against the godly in Lot's days heightened. "All the men of Sodom, both old and young surrounded Lot's houses and said to him regarding the two visiting angels, "Where are the men who came to you tonight? Bring them out to us that we may know them carnally" (Genesis 19:5). These men ascended in a mob-like fashion to gang rape the two male angels and

then planned to turn their sights on Lot. The same spirit of violence and anarchy is displayed today, allowed by an establishment of legislatures who desire to change the laws of the land. The current fury seen on America's soil is only a foreshadowing of the destruction to come.

4. Population explosiveness: earth's population grew exponentially during Noah's days. "Now it came to pass, when men began to multiply on the face of the earth" (Genesis 6:1). In an era of pharmaceutical wonders and medical advances, the world population is again growing exponentially.

Look to the left. Look to the right. Look upside, downside, inside. Look here, there and everywhere. People are treating sin with an attitude that's cavalier.

 When the world least expects it, Jesus will appear. Let those who have an ear, hear. The Lord's coming is very near. Oh, what a glorious day when true believers will "disappear!"

The Glory of God

4:2 *Immediately I was in the Spirit; and behold, a throne set in heaven, and One sat on the throne.*

As we read in Revelation 1:10, John was "in the Spirit on the Lord's Day." Here he was caught up in soul and spirit into heaven and the first entity John saw was God on His throne. When you look at a Christmas tree, before you focus on the ornaments on the tree, the gifts under the tree, or the angel on top on the tree, you see the brilliant lights detailing the tree. John first sees the Creator, the Redeemer, our Father, who is the source of light sitting on His throne. Isaiah described a similar awe stirring experience, "I saw the Lord sitting on a throne, high and lifted up, and the train of His robe filled the temple" (Isaiah 6:1).

We will see John being transported in the Spirit multiple times and each time we gain a deeper understanding of Christ's and the Father's attributes:

1. Waging Warrior: John was in the Spirit on the Lord's Day on the Island of Patmos and Christ spoke to him saying, "I am the Alpha and the Omega, the First and the Last" (Revelation 1:9-20). Here we see Christ as a warrior who will purify His Church and purge the wicked, appearing with eyes like a flame of fire and feet like fine brass.

2. Rightful Ruler: John was immediately in the Spirit, being transported to the third heaven (Revelation 4:1-2). Here we see God residing over heaven, earth, sea and the universe.

3. Undisputed Conqueror: "So he (the angel) carried me away in the Spirit," John being carried into the wilderness to witness Babylon's fall (Revelation 17:3). Here we see Jesus, the Victor and the Conqueror; Babylon will fall suddenly, and Christ will reign eternally.

4. Glorious Father: "And he (the angel) carried me away in the Spirit." John was carried to a great and high mountain, and was shown "the great city, the holy Jerusalem, descending out of heaven from God, having the glory of God" (Revelation 21:10-11). Here we see God's glory, His majestic city and His endearing and eternal rule.

John's focus will be on Jesus Christ in chapter five, but in chapter four, we will see the Father in His Glory. In Psalm 110:1, we read God saying to Jesus, "Sit at My right hand, till I make Your enemies Your footstool." We also see in Acts 7:55, that as Stephen was being persecuted, he saw "the glory of God, and Jesus standing at the right hand of God." To this day, Christ lives to make intercession for us as our Mediator and High Priest, at the throne of grace (Hebrews 4:15-16). In chapters 6-19, we'll see Christ being occupied with judgment of the unbelievers instead of interceding for the believers. The day is coming when Jesus will not occupy the right hand of His Father's throne; that's why God states in Psalm 110:1, "Sit at My right hand, until (intercession changes to judgment) I make Your enemies Your footstool."

The image of God sitting on His throne signifies His complete rule and control over what was, what is and what is to come. Satan is the god of this age, but without God's permission, he is unable to do anything (Job 1:6, 12; 2:6)! Satan, the Antichrist and the False Prophet will rule on earth for seven years, but they will do so only because it is authorized by God; their final manifestation of evil depends on the permission granted by God. According to Psalm 24:1, "The earth is the Lord's, and all its fullness, the world and those who dwell therein." Jude 1:25 declares, "All glory, majesty, dominion and power belong to the only wise God, our Savior."

Daniel describes the throne of God where "the Ancient of Days was seated; His garment was white as snow, and the hair of His head was like pure wool. His throne was fiery flame, its wheels a burning fire; a fiery stream issued and came forth from before Him. A thousand thousands ministered to Him; ten thousand times ten thousand stood before Him" (Daniel 7:9-10). This is no small matter.

Isaiah describes our God in a majestic manner, "Have you not known? Have you not heard? Has it not been told you from the beginning? Have you not understood from the founda-tions of the earth? It is He who sits above the circle of the earth, and its inhabitants are like grasshoppers, who stretches out the heavens like a curtain, and spreads them out like a tent to dwell in. He brings the princes to nothing; He makes the judges of the earth useless. Scarcely shall they be planted, scarcely shall they be sown, scarcely shall their stock take root in the earth, when He will also blow on them, and they will wither, and the whirlwind will take them away like stubble" (Isaiah 40:21-24).

God's throne is not a place where we sit and sip coffee and casually say, "Oh, hey God, what's up!" This is a place of glory, beauty, purity, reverence and complete astonishment. Those who witnessed it, such as Isaiah; Ezekiel; Daniel; Peter, John and James; Paul and John; all collapsed in the presence of God's glory (Isaiah 6:5; Ezekiel 1:28, 3:23; Daniel 10:8; Matthew 17:6; Acts 9:4; Revelation 1:17). This is actual, physical and material. "There must be a material heaven or there was no ascension, and if there was no ascension, there was no resurrection, and if there was no resurrection, there is no salvation."[4]

4:3 *And He who sat there was like a jasper and a sardius stone in appearance; and there was a rainbow around the throne, in appearance like an emerald.*

God is likened to a jasper stone, the stone being clear as crystal (Revelation 21:11) and depicting the glory, purity and the holiness of God. The walls of the New Jerusalem will be made of jasper; of its twelve foundations, the first is also made of jasper (Revelation 21:18-19). It is likened to a diamond.[5] Sardius stone is red in color, likely a carnelian, depicting Christ's blood spilled to cleanse the sins of mankind. Of the twelve foundations of the New Jerusalem, the sixth is made of sardius (Revelation 21:19).

Prior to his fall, Lucifer was adorned with twelve stones, two of them being jasper and sardius (Ezekiel 28:13-14). Sardius was the first of the twelve stones (representing Reuben the first born) and jasper the last of the twelve stones (representing Benjamin the last born) mounted on the breastplate of the high priest, representing the twelve tribes of Israel (Exodus 28:17-20); God who is likened to sardius and jasper is the First and the Last, the Alpha and Omega, the Beginning and the End, He is all in all, first of all, in the midst of all, and the last of all, no one coming before Him and no one going after Him.

A rainbow usually follows a storm. Noah was given this sign after the flood, a reminder that God will never gain destroy all flesh with a flood (Genesis 9;13-16). We'll see starting in chapter six that the Lord will destroy the earth with fire (II Peter 3:5-7). The church believers have been removed from the storm, the Tribulation, and they are beholding an emerald-green rainbow of eternal life. The apostle Paul declared in Romans 6:23, "For the wages of sin is death, but the gift of God is eternal life in Christ Jesus our Lord." The rainbow around God's throne implies a full circle like a halo.[6] When we study chapter 10, we'll see a mighty angel, whom I believe is Jesus Christ, we'll see the second person of the Trinity, "a rainbow was on his head, his face was like the sun, and his feet like pillars of fire."

Unless we can measure the waters of the sea in the hollow of our hands, or mark off the heavens, or measure the dust of the earth, or weigh the mountains on scales, counsel God, instruct Him, and teach Him the path of justice, knowledge and understanding, it would be best to be still and know that He alone is God! (Isaiah 40:12-14; Psalm 46:10).

The Raptured Church

4:4 *Around the throne were twenty-four thrones, and on the thrones, I saw twenty-four elders sitting, clothed in white robes; and they had crowns of gold on their heads.*

At this point, believers have been Raptured, they have received their glorified bodies, and are in heaven, beholding the beauty of their God the Father. There is no judgment of death; there is only the verdict of life. The 24 elders and thrones represent the church, which is made up of believers. We'll see later how the 24 embody the New Jerusalem (Revelation 21:12-14), the wall of the city with 12 gates (12 tribes of the children of Israel), and the 12 foundations of the city (12 apostles of the Lamb). These elders are not angelic beings because angels don't wear crowns, don't age, don't sit on thrones and don't place themselves among the redeemed (Revelation 5:9). The elders represent the redeemed of the Church Age.[7]

It is doubtful the Old Testament saints are among the elders in their glorified or resurrected bodies. A passage such as Daniel 12:1-2 implies that the Old Testament saints do not receive their glorified bodies until the time of Jacob's Trouble, or the Great Tribulation, is over. We must however understand that the souls and spirits of the Old Testament saints are in heaven at this time; they will receive their glorified bodies and rewards after the Tribulation and before the Millennium.

"The coronation time is the resurrection time; and no one can be crowned until he is either resurrected if dead or translated if living."[8] The Old Testament saints' bodies will be resurrected seven years after the Rapture because they are not in Christ, meaning that they were not baptized into His body and were not part of the church from the Day of Pentecost (I Corinthians 12:13). The fact that the church takes part in worship and praise in chapter five prior to the judgments in chapter six is yet another proof that the church does not take part in the Tribulation.[9]

Believers are clothed in white robes, which is the righteousness of Christ. Our most "righteous" acts on earth are likened to filthy rags in God's sight (Isaiah 64:6). But because of God's grace and loving-kindness, He clothes us with the garments of salvation and covers us with the robe of righteousness (Isaiah 61:10).

Our Father gives the believers, the church, crowns of gold. We will be kings and priests (Revelation 1:6). We will rule with an iron rod with Christ (Revelation 2:27). We will judge angels (I Corinthians 6:3). We will rule with our Christ in the Millennium (Revelation 20:6).

God not only forgives our sins, but He takes away our shame. You can drown yourself in alcohol, drugs, cigarettes, entertainment, food or lies. You can become an addict, alcoholic, narcissistic or atheistic, but that will not lighten your load!

The scars, the pain, the past, the memories, the mistakes, the regrets can all be forgiven and forgotten at the cross of Calvary. And it doesn't stop there. God keeps on giving. He gave His only Son. He gives us joy. He gives us peace. He gives us strength. He gives us wisdom. And one day, He, the God of all gods, the Ruler of all rulers and the King of all kings will give us crowns! Joy unspeakable! Delight unstoppable! Life eternal!

Holy Spirit Fire

4:5 And from the throne proceeded lightnings, thunderings, and voices. Seven lamps of fire were burning before the throne, which are the seven Spirits of God.

The overpowering lightning, thunder and voices are celestial fireworks depicting the judgment that is to befall Satan's empire and the entire world of unbelievers in the next seven years of the Tribulation following the Rapture. When Israel was to receive the law on Mount Sinai, there was thunder and lightning and a voice like a trumpet, so that all the people who were in the camp trembled (Exodus 19:16). Why did the Israelites hear the thunder, lightning and voice at Mount Sinai? It was an ominous sign of the impending sentence upon Israel proceeding from God's throne because of their inevitable disobedience. The letter of the law kills, but the Spirit gives life according to II Corinthians 3:6. In our text, "The voices are not merely the claps of thunder but are the articulate announcements of the judgment of God which the earth will soon feel."[10]

The seven lamps of fire depict only one Holy Spirit who has a perfect seven-fold character in carrying out the purpose of God; these lamps are not the seven lampstands representing the seven churches in Revelation 1:12. To recap, six of the Holy Spirit's characters are given in Isaiah 11:2, The Spirit of wisdom and understanding, the Spirit of counsel and might, the Spirit of knowledge and of the fear of the Lord. "Where is the seventh," you may ask? I believe it is revealed in Revelation 19:10, the Spirit of prophecy.

The Holy Spirit is spoken of as a source of light which signifies His oneness with the Father who is the source of light and His oneness with Jesus Christ who is the Light of the world. We'll see in Revelation 21:23 that the glory of God enlightens the Holy City (the New Jerusalem) and the Lamb (Christ) is the divine light thereof. The source of heaven's light therefore is three-fold and yet, One!

The Holy Spirit is also spoken of as a source of fire throughout the New Testament. When John the Baptist spoke of Christ, he stated, "I baptize you with water for repentance. But after me comes one who is more powerful than I, whose sandals I am not worthy to carry. He (Christ) will baptize you with the Holy Spirit and fire" (Matthew 3:11). At Pentecost, "they (believers) saw what seemed to be tongues of fire that separated and came to rest on each of them. All were filled with the Holy Spirit and began to speak in other tongues as the Spirit enabled them" (Acts 2:3-4).

The Holy Spirit is like a fire in that He brings God's presence, God's purpose and God's purity. According to Romans 8:9 and II Corinthians 5:1, the Spirit indwells the heart of a believer and represents God's presence and the character of Jesus Christ. Do you remember the two traveling disciples talking with the resurrected Christ? They said that their hearts were "burning within us" as Christ spoke of Himself, revealing His person and purpose (Luke 24:32). God longs to purify us, and the agent of our sanctification is the Holy Spirit. Paul says of the believers in Thessalonica, "God chose you as first fruits to be saved through the sanctifying work of the Spirit and through belief in the truth" (II Thessalonians 2:13). The dross from precious metal is purged out by fire; so too our sins are removed by the loving fire of the Holy Spirit (Psalm 66:10).

Four Creatures Worshiping God

4:6 Before the throne there was a sea of glass, like crystal. And in the midst of the throne, and around the throne, were four living creatures full of eyes in front and in back.

We'll find in Hebrews 9:23 that the tabernacle built by Israel on earth was a copy of the true tabernacle in heaven. Before entering the Holy Place, there stood a laver (washing place) covered with mirrors and filled with water in the outer court; the priests saw their reflection, witnessed their impurities, cleansed themselves with the water and entered into the Holy Place. Today, we are able to do the same; if we confess our sins, God is faithful and forgives our sins and cleanses us from all unrighteousness (I John 1:9). Because of the cross, we're justified, or "just-as-if-I'd" never sinned.

After being justified, we are being sanctified on a daily basis, cleansed by the Word of God. That's why Jesus did not want to pour water on Peter's head and hands; Peter was already justified; he needed to be sanctified (set apart, cleansed daily) just as you and I need to be. But in heaven, we will be pure, justified, sanctified and glorified; therefore, this sea appears as crystal or crystalized, picturing the permanent washing away of uncleanness by the atonement of Christ. There will be no more sin! There will be no more temptations! There will be no more fall! There will be no more guilt! There will be no more feelings of condemnation! There will be no more need for cleansing by the laver! We will be with God, who will bestow unto us unblemished goodness, wholeness and beauty. That is heaven! Glory, glory, hallelujah!

There are four living creatures full of eyes in the midst of the throne and around the throne. We'll learn more about them in the verses that follow. The number four is "the signature of the world or of global effect."[11] We will soon see the four horsemen in Revelation chapter six whose actions have worldwide effects. The cross has four points, facing in all directions. For

God so loved the world that He gave His only begotten Son to die on the cross. Whoever, wherever and whenever someone believes, trusts and hopes in Him will never perish but have everlasting life (John 3:16). The global association is derived from the four directions of the compass, North, South, East and West. The four living creatures have eyes in front and back, their foresight encompassing the entire earth. These creatures are similar to the cherubim seen by Ezekiel, both holding different offices, but both representing the throne of God and revealing the glory of God (Ezekiel 1:10-12; 10:14-17).

4:7 The first living creature was like a lion, the second living creature like a calf, the third living creature had a face like a man, and the fourth living creature was like a flying eagle.

These four living creatures are cherubs, or cherubim, winged angels of high rank who worship God, represent His majestic glory and characterize His throne. Lucifer, before his fall, was an anointed cherub "who covered," "cacak" in Hebrew, meaning to protect, to defend or to hedge in as a guardian (Ezekiel 28:14). We see the same word, "cacak" being used in Exodus 25:20, "And the cherubim shall stretch out their wings above, covering, "cacak," the mercy seat with their wings, and they shall face one another; the faces of the cherubim shall be toward the mercy seat."

The Ark of the Covenant in the Holy of Holies, built during Moses' leadership, had a mercy seat with two golden cherubim overseeing, covering and protecting the Ark. Blood was sprinkled on the Mercy Seat on Atonement Day. It was the blood of an innocent slain sacrificed animal on Abel's altar or Mercy Seat, and the blood of the slain Messiah on the cross that prevented God's judgment falling on Abel or on us, "covering" us (Exodus 25:20, 22). "Much more then, having now been justified by His blood, we shall be saved from wrath through Him." (Romans 5:9).

When Adam and Eve sinned in the Garden of Eden, they were

"covered" by the skin of an animal, courtesy of a loving God. Blood had to be shed, which is the foreshadowing of Christ dying on the cross for our sins. When God sent the couple out of the garden, He placed cherubim at the east entrance. A flaming sword, turning every way, guarded the way to the Tree of Life, preventing Adam, Eve and their offspring from entering the garden. This may seem excessively cruel, but it is an act of deep mercy. How so? If Adam and Eve had access to the Tree of Life, and ate of it, they would have lived forever in their sinful state. But God's plan was forgiveness of sin through the life, death and resurrection of His Son.

The cherubim in Genesis 3:24 served another purpose. The altar where Abel made his animal sacrifices was outside the garden. The cherubim likely guarded the altar from Satan's evil hands. The reason why I propose this is because the Ark of the Covenant also had two golden cherubim overlooking the Mercy Seat, where blood was sprinkled on Atonement Day. It is the cherubim who guard the sacrifice. How so? When Mary Magdalene ran to the tomb of Christ on Sunday, she found it to be empty. She saw two angels in white sitting, one at the head of and the other at the feet, where the body of Jesus had lain. This too is the image of Abel's altar and the Ark of the Covenant, all pointing to the greatest sacrifice, Jesus Christ. Jesus, the Mercy Seat, the Redeemer, the sacrificial Lamb of God, who was slain, who shed his blood for you and me, had an angel where His head was lain and an angel where His feet were lain! It was the blood of a slain sacrificed animal on the altar or the Ark that prevented God's judgment from falling on man (Exodus 25:20, 22). It is the sacrifice of the Lamb that keeps judgment from falling on us (Romans 5:9).

It is important to emphasize that these four angels are living creatures. We read in Nehemiah 9:6 about God's creation, "You alone are Lord; You have made heaven, the heaven of heavens, with all their host, the earth and everything on it, the seas and all that is in them, and You preserve them all. The host of heaven worships You."

One creature is like a lion, the second like a calf or ox, the third like a man, and the fourth like a flying eagle, but they are not monstrosities in heaven. They are "four which take the first place in this world: men among the creatures, the eagle among birds, the ox among cattle and the lion among wild beasts."[12] The book of Revelation reveals the cohesiveness of the Old and New Testament: these creatures are noted in Ezekiel's prophecy and their symbolism is displayed in the four gospels:

1. Matthew: presents Jesus as the King, the Lion of the tribe of Judah, the King of Kings, tracing His genealogy back to David and Abraham (Matthew 1:1).

2. Mark: presents Jesus as the Servant, the ox, serving all, not tracing the genealogy of Christ.

3. Luke: presents Jesus as the Man, above all men, yet the Son of Man who understands all our heartaches. His genealogy is traced back to Adam (Luke 3:38).

4. John: presents Jesus as God, the eternal Word who was in the beginning with God. His genealogy is not only traced as being the Son of God, but being God Himself (John 1:1, 14).

 This is Christ: As the Lion, He roars; As the Servant, His life He pours; As the Son of Man, He restores; As the Eagle, He soars!

4:8 *The four living creatures, each having six wings, were full of eyes around and within. And they do not rest day or night, saying, "Holy, holy, holy, Lord God Almighty, who was and is and is to come!"*

The four cherubim represent the Sovereignty of God.

1. Omniscient God. Other gods have eyes, but they cannot see. Without fail, God is all-knowing at all times. "But our God is in heaven; He does whatever He pleases. Their idols are silver and gold, the work of men's hands. They

have mouths, but they do not speak; eyes they have, but they do not see; they have ears, but they do not hear; noses they have, but they do not smell; they have hands, but they do not handle; feet they have, but they do not walk; nor do they mutter through their throat. Those who make them are like them; so is everyone who trust in them" Psalm 115:3-8.

Man may try to predict the weather, the stock market or even the winds of war. God knows the beginning from the end. "Remember the former things of old, For I am God, and there is no other; I am God, and there is none like Me, declaring the end from the beginning, and from ancient times things that are not yet done, saying, 'My counsel shall stand, and I will do all My pleasure'" (Isaiah 46:9-10).

Omnipresent God. In medicine, we diagnose and treat, but are blessed with countless tools such as angiograms, ultrasound and cat scans so that we may be able to "see." God is the source of all knowledge; His eyes see everything, everywhere, every time, for He is all-present. "Oh, the depth of the riches of both the wisdom and knowledge of God! How unsearchable are His judgments and His ways past finding out!" (Romans 11:33). David exclaimed in Psalm 139:7-10, "Where can I go from Your Spirit? Or where can I flee from your presence? If I ascend into heaven You are there. If I make my bed in hell, behold, You are there. If I take the wings of the morning, and dwell in the uttermost part of the sea, even there your hand shall lead me, and Your right hand shall hold me."

2. Omnipotent God. Observe the prophets such as Isaiah and Daniel who beheld His holiness: completely prostrate and powerless in the presence of an all-powerful God. We read in Daniel 4:35, "All the inhabitants of the earth are reputed as nothing; He does according to His will in the army of heaven and among the inhabitants of the

earth. No one can restrain His hand or say to Him, 'What have You done?'" Jeremiah was in awe of God's power as he proclaimed in Jeremiah 32:17-19, "Ah, Lord God! You have made the heavens and the earth by Your great power and outstretched arm. There is nothing too hard for You … You are great in counsel and mighty at work."

These four creatures characterize God's rule and dominion over all beings. As we'll soon see, they are ready to carry out the judgment of God on the world. Twice we read that they are filled with eyes (verses 6 and 8), meaning that they are not blind instruments who act like robots; they see, they understand, they discern, and they obey our sovereign God.

Unlike the cherubim in Ezekiel who had four wings (Ezekiel 1:11-12), these cherubim have six wings like the seraphim which Isaiah saw attending the throne (Isaiah 6:2, 6). Angels hold different offices and are ranked in a specific hierarchy; this will also hold true for every believer in heaven, each individual being rewarded according to his devotion to God's calling.

Many falsely believe that everyone is equal in heaven; that is not the case as there is no Socialism/Globalism in heaven, just as there will be no Socialism/Globalism in hell. God "will render to each one according to his deeds … for there is no partiality with God" (Romans 2:6-11). In Revelation 20:12 Jesus said, "And behold, I am coming quickly, and My reward is with Me, to give to everyone according to his work."

The four creatures have numerous eyes, positioned in such a way that they are able to move their wings without ever disrupting their vision.[13] "These creatures are near the apex of God's created order (Ezekiel 28:12-15)."[14]

Twice we see the song, "Holy, holy, holy" in the Bible, once in the Old Testament and the other in the New Testament, giving us assurance that God is sovereign over all things and of all times. The first incidence is seen in Isaiah 6:3 when Isaiah was taken up to heaven in a vision; he saw the Lord in His glory and witnessed a seraph proclaim, "Holy, holy, holy is the Lord of hosts. The whole earth is full of His glory!" We hear the same proclamation in Revelation 4:8. With all reverence, with profound humility, with utmost honor, heaven's citizens declare the holiness of our God! The three-fold repetition signifies reverence to each of the persons of the Trinity: holy is God, the Father; holy is Christ, the Son; holy is the Holy Spirit, the Counselor.

The Psalmist even chimes in by stating, "The heavens declare the glory of God; the skies proclaim the works of His hands" (Psalm 19:1). God is called Almighty a total of 56 times in the Bible. No one can match His power, no one can hold back His hand, no one can counter Him, and nothing is too difficult for Him. (Psalm 147:5, II Chronicles 20:6, Ephesians 1:19-21, Genesis 18:14). Just in case you'd like challenge Him, read Isaiah 14:27 first, "For the Lord Almighty has purposed, and who can thwart Him? His hand is stretched out, and who can turn it back?"

We will note in chapter thirteen that the 666 mark is a three-fold repetition of six, six denoting the incomplete number of mankind, and 666 denoting the mark of the Beast. Three is a perfect number, completing the Trinity. Satan imitates God in forming his own unholy trinity, Satan, the Antichrist and the False Prophet. The four creatures worship God, who is, who was, and who is to come. Worship is a major theme of the Bible. "Give to the Lord the glory due His name; bring an offering and come before Him. Oh, worship the Lord in the beauty of holiness!" (I Chronicles 16:29). "Who is like You, O Lord, among the gods? Who is like You, glorious in holiness, fearful in praises, doing wonders?" (Exodus 15:11). A phrase such as "Who is like You" is not just a rhetorical question; it is asked in complete admiration, astonishment, humility and submissiveness.

The Raptured Church Worships God

4:9 Whenever the living creatures give glory and honor and thanks to Him who sits on the throne, who lives forever and ever, 4:10 the twenty-four elders fall down before Him who sits on the throne and worship Him who lives forever and ever, and cast their crowns before the throne, saying: 4:11 "You are worthy, O Lord, to receive glory and honor and power; for You created all things, and by Your will they exist and were created."

The church joins the four living creatures in their praise to the One who lives forever and ever. God is eternal. He existed before the beginning and He will exist after the end! He is, He was, and He will always be.

 Many are in the category of "who is." Many are also in the category of "who was." Many will one day be in the category of "who is to come." But no one can be in the category of all three at one time, in Eternity past, Eternity present, and Eternity future but God alone! Praises to His name!

The twenty-four redeemed saints, representing the church, fall and worship God as they witness the cherubim prostrate themselves before God. The crowns, the rewards given to the believers, are given back to God; our crowns rightfully belong to God, and the significance of giving them back is an act of worship and adoration. We do not arrive in heaven for our glory, but by the grace of God and for His glory.

According to Isaiah 44:24, God made all things. All three persons of the Trinity were involved in the creation: The Father (I Corinthians 8:6); the Son (Colossians 1:16); and the Holy spirit (Psalm 104:30). He is our Creator and our appropriate response is to worship Him as seen in Psalm 95:1-7, "Oh come, let us sing to the Lord! Let us shout joyfully to the Rock of our salvation. Let us come before His presence with thanksgiving; let us shout joyfully for Him with psalms. For the Lord is the great God, and the great King above all gods. In His hand are the deep places of the earth; the heights of the hills are His also. The sea is His, for He made it; and His hands formed the dry land. Oh come, let us worship and bow down; let us kneel before the Lord our Maker. For He is our God, and we are the people of His pasture, and the sheep of his hand."

"For by Him all things were created that are in heaven and that are on earth, visible and invisible, whether thrones or dominions or principalities or powers. All things were created through Him and for Him. And He is before all things, and in Him all things consist. And He is the head of the body, the church; He is the beginning and the firstborn from the dead, that in all things He may have the preeminence" (Colossians 1:16-18).

 We live not because of our craftiness but because of God's craftsmanship.

God is seated on His throne with absolute sovereignty. Isaiah attests to His power in Isaiah 14: 24, "The Lord of hosts has sworn, saying, 'Surely, as I have thought, so it shall come to pass, and as I have purposed, so it shall stand.'" Along with the creatures' song in verse eight, these are the first of many praises sung in the book of Revelation, including 4:8,11; 5:9-13; 7:12-17; 11:15-18; 12:10-12; 15:3-4; 16:5-7; 18:2-8; 19:2-6. Why is God the recipient of praises, glory, honor and power? Because He is from everlasting to everlasting, abides forever, is the King eternal and He alone is immortal! We join the four living creatures, the church, and the Apostle Paul, and proclaim, "Now to the King eternal, immortal, invisible, to God who alone is wise, be honor and glory forever and ever. Amen" (I Timothy 1:17).

The Psalmist in Psalm 99:9 proclaims, "Exalt the Lord our God, and worship at his holy hill; for the Lord our God is holy."

 This worship is voluntary. It is done wholeheartedly. It reflects God's majesty. It will be sung for all Eternity.

Worshiping God may even seem boring to Christ-followers. But worship in heaven transcends all our understanding: there will be joy upon joy, laughter upon laughter, freedom upon freedom, love upon love, hope upon hope, and a heart that is continually communed in God's goodness, grace and glory!

In the following chapters, the righteous judgment of God is about to be poured out. But for what reason? It is for the "removal of the curse (Genesis 3:14-19); and of all unholiness from the earth; and the ending of creation's groaning and travail."[15] The eternal plan of God will stand before all Satan, demons and unbelievers. We will witness creation, which has been subject to Satan since the fall, being redeemed. According to Romans 8:21, "creation itself also will be delivered from the bondage of corruption into the glorious liberty of the children of God." We will sing the song of believers as we observe the Lamb overcome the curse of creation with His gift of redemption and His iron fist of justice.

REV IT UP & SUM IT UP – CHAPTER FOUR:

There is a major shift in the book of Revelation, as "what was" and "what is" now transitions into "what is to come." From chapter four onward, we are discussing events that have not yet taken place. The Rapture of the church occurs in this chapter and sets believers free of the horrid seven-year Tribulation that will plague unbelievers.

Several views are presented regarding the timing of the Rapture, three of the most popular being 1) Pre-Tribulation, 2) Mid-Tribulation, and 3) Post-Tribulation. The Pre-Tribulation view correctly states that the Rapture will occur before the Tribulation. All other views including Mid-Tribulation (Rapture will occur after three and a half years of the Tribulation, at its mid-point) and the Post-Tribulation (Rapture will occur at the end of the seven-year Tribulation) are at best erroneous. The only solid perspective that supports Jesus' coming for the believer as imminent is the Pre-Tribulation view.

After the Rapture, believers will face the Bema Seat, the judgment seat of Christ, where we will be judged for the service we have done for Christ on earth after we received salvation. The crowns we obtain as rewards will be cast back at the feet of Christ, giving Him glory and honor.

The twenty-four elders seen around the throne, worshiping God in white robes and golden crowns, represent believers of the Church Age. The seven lamps before God's throne represent the seven characteristics of the Holy Spirit, who illuminates the glory of God. The crystal sea before God's throne represents the complete and permanent cleansing of our sins, as we will have our glorified bodies, having overcome sin, sickness and death. The four living creatures before God's throne are cherubim who represent God's sovereignty, omniscience, omnipotence and omnipresence.

The cherubim and the redeemed church fall before God and worship Him, the Son and the Holy Spirit. Day and night the cherubim proclaim, "Holy, holy, holy, Lord God Almighty, who was and is and is to come!" Believers join in the proclamation that our God alone is worthy to receive glory, honor, power and praise. He alone is the immutable, immortal, and eternal God. He alone is the Creator and the Redeemer, and all of creation exists not only through Him, but for Him. Blessed be the name of our Lord!

Chapter 5
Slain Savior Secures Seals

Why has the Church Age lasted for 2,000 years? To give mankind the opportunity to turn their hearts towards Christ. Why will the Rapture of the church take place? To spare God's children from the appalling judgments that are to befall mankind. Why is it necessary to pour God's wrath on those who remain on earth during the seven-year Tribulation? We'll now study the significance of the seals that Christ unseals, not only unleashing wrath upon wrath on the godless, but also to bring Satan down to his knees and cast him into his ultimate and eternal destination: hell. As we continue to study, we'll see that all thrones and kingdoms will fall, and only Christ will stand!

Unsealing the Seals

5:1 And I saw in the right hand of Him who sat on the throne a scroll written inside and on the back, sealed with seven seals.

John begins to shift his attention from God's glorious throne, the living creatures and the elders to the right hand of the Father who is holding a scroll with seven seals. The breaking of the seals will initiate the time period knows as the Day of the Lord. The church Age is over. The Rapture has taken place. The believers in Christ have their glorified bodies. The redeemed sing songs of praises to Christ. We are dealing with future events. Christ will no longer hold His office of intercession. He will rise from the right hand of the Father and do something that believers from all ages have been longing for: He will administer justice with righteousness upon the unjust, unleashing wrath unseen, unheard, and unimaginable!

We see God holding a scroll in His right hand. The right hand is considered the side of honor, favor and strength, the same side on which the Son is seated next to His Father before He rules in the Millennial Kingdom (Psalm 110:1). We read in Psalm 20:6, "Now I know that the Lord saves His anointed; He will answer him from His holy heaven with the saving strength of His right hand." And in Psalm 98:1, "Oh, sing to the Lord a new song! For He has done marvelous things; His right hand and His holy arm have gained Him the victory."

The Father rules the affairs of the universe from His throne (Psalm 47:8), and we'll see in verse seven that the Father will honor His Son by handing Him the scroll and allowing Him to open its seals. Daniel was told to shut up the words of prophecy, "But you, Daniel, shut up the words, and seal the book until the time of the end; many shall run to and fro, and knowledge shall increase" (Daniel 12:4). Many "run to and fro" today via multiple means of transportation, and knowledge has catapulted into a class of colossal heights; therefore, we stand at the door of the "time of the end," or end times. We are in overtime! The hour of the Rapture is imminent, and the opening of the seals will follow thereafter! "We take it therefore that the opening of the seals of this book is the enlargement, development, and continuation of the Book of Daniel, describing, from God's side, the judgments necessary to secure the fulfillment of all that He has foretold."[1]

The Father is holding a "book," "biblion" in the Greek, a document written on a scroll. The scroll is sealed, indicating that it contains prophecy previously unrevealed. Interestingly, as we'll see in Revelation 5:9, this scroll is inherently related to the redeeming blood of the Lamb. Psalm 2:1-3 explains how the rebellious forces of the earth will gather in an attempt to prevent Christ from taking possession of the earth. But Christ will take what the Father has given to Him and destroy all the rebellious who come against Him (Psalm 2:4-12) and will rule from His eternal throne. Once the seals are opened, the fulfillment of the prophecy begins, "Ask of Me (The Father tells the Son to ask), and I (God) will give You (Christ) the nations for Your inheritance, and the ends of the earth for Your possession" (Psalm 2:8).

We'll soon see the Lamb breaking the seals, which not only exposes the contents of the scroll but the activation of its words. The scroll contains a series of judgments that will occur in the future and will also reveal a deed of purchase. Long strips of papyrus sheets were used in the first century as writing tools and were glued end to end to make the scrolls longer. The scroll was then rolled up and sealed to protect its contents. Usually both sides of the papyrus were used to write on, with the detailed text of the document on the inside of the scroll and the summary of its contents on the outside. Vital documents were often sealed seven times at the edge of each roll within the scroll.[2]

The sealed scroll in the right hand of the Father is the deed of purchase for Christ's ultimate rule over the earth, which Adam and Eve forfeited to Satan when they sinned. A priceless purchase of the scroll was made when Christ paid the redemption price by shedding His blood on the cross to take back Satan's possession of the earth. Since then, two thousand years have passed; why then hasn't Christ taken His rightful place as the ruler of the earth?

A purchase was made at the cross, and after the Rapture, the scroll, or deed of the purchase, will be claimed by its rightful owner. Let's look at Jeremiah's acquisition of a deed which aligns with Christ's securing of this deed and explains the time lag from purchase to possession. Jeremiah was instructed by God to purchase his cousin's land in Israel even though Babylon had already seized Israel in 586 BC. Why buy the land when the enemy occupies it and Jeremiah will not be able to settle in it? The purchase was a sign that God is faithful, and He would restore Israel back to their land (Jeremiah 32:14-15; 43-44). Jeremiah made a purchase in advance and a period of seventy years of captivity ensued before the possession was fully accepted, awarded and acquired. Actual possession of Israel's land could not be met until the Babylonian rule ended because the enemy, Babylon, had usurped the land (Jeremiah 32:28-36).

The Messiah's purchase is quite similar. Christ was instructed by God to purchase the souls of mankind while Babylon, or Satan, had usurped the honor, dignity, soul, life and even the land of mankind. The purchase was a sign that God is faithful, and he would restore mankind back to his original walk with Him if they agreed to follow His Son. God made a purchase in advance; a period of 2,000 years has passed; and possession of this earth is still not fully awarded to the Son. The actual possession of the land cannot be met until the Babylonian rule has come to an end (Revelation 17-18). The possession includes not only the title deed of the earth, but His eternal kingdom (Psalm 2:6-8).

Moses was given two tablets, and the Ten Commandments were written on both sides of the tablets (Exodus 32:15-16). Ezekiel was also given a book which contained writings of lamentations and woe on both sides (Ezekiel 2:10). Jeremiah's legal purchase deed was written on both sides (Jeremiah 32:10, 12). So too is the scroll in the hands of the Father. Until the seals are broken, the contents remain a mystery (Isaiah 29:11). But we are about to witness the unveiling of the future so that the future may become clear today!

There are seven seals, the number seven denoting completion. Why is seven considered "complete"? It refers to the seventh day of rest, finalizing God's six-day work of creation. All seven seals will be broken by the Lamb of God, which will result in Christ taking permanent possession of the earth and establishing His throne and rule from Jerusalem.

The seven seals contain appalling judgments, and the seventh seal will unleash the seven trumpet judgments; the seventh trumpet will subsequently unleash the seven bowl judgments. When Christ opens all seven seals, He will pour out His wrath against an unbelieving, Christ-rejecting world and crush Satan's empire. This will fulfill the 70th week of Daniel, or seven years known as the Tribulation, occurring from the time of the Rapture up to Christ's Second Coming.[3]

 Prophecy will be revealed. God's work will be complete. Satan will face his final defeat. Unbelievers will live in hell's unimaginable fire and heat. The redeemed will possess Eternity and worship forever at Christ's feet.

5:2 *Then I saw a strong angel proclaiming with a loud voice, "Who is worthy to open the scroll and to loose its seals?"*

A mighty angel shouts out a challenge and though he asks a question, it is a rhetorical one. The answer is, "No one!" Right off the bat, I'll tell you that there are many who would be willing to open the scroll, but there is only One who is worthy! No one else but Christ has the authority or righteousness for such an undertaking; there is no one in heaven, not the Archangel Michael, not the Messenger Gabriel, not the four living creatures, not the 24 elders or the redeemed in Christ, nor the thousands upon thousands of angels who serve God in adoration. "All the righteous of all the ages, including Abraham, Isaac, Jacob, Joseph, Job, Moses, David, Solomon, Elijah, Elisha, Isaiah, Jeremiah, Ezekiel, Daniel, Peter and the rest of the apostles, Paul, and all the others from the Church Age, say nothing."[4] No one below the earth, on the earth, or above the earth is able to respond.

"The person who undertakes this tremendous task must be absolutely courageous and absolutely compassionate."[5] Only Christ possesses the necessary credentials:

1. Faultless Judge. "But with righteousness He shall judge the poor and decide with equity for the meek of the earth; He shall strike the earth with the rod of His mouth" (Isaiah 11:4). He is the only judge who has the precise blend of justice and compassion, delivering with perfect mercy and righteousness.

2. Faultless Kinsman-Redeemer. A kinsman redeemer is one who has the responsibility to act for a relative who is in trouble, danger or need of vindication. Christ needed to be a rightful relative of all mankind, who were dead in their sin; therefore, the Lord His God, sent His Son to earth, born of a woman to die on the cross for our sins. No angel, no man, no spirit nor any being can fulfill that requirement except Christ who is not only God's Son but is God incarnate and yet, the Son of Man! "And you know that He (Christ) was manifested to take away our sins, and in Him there is no sin" (I John 3:5). Only a sinless man is able to redeem a sinful man. The sinless man is the Son of Man, Jesus Christ, our kinsman-redeemer.

3. Faultless Savior. The payment for what was lost, earth's deed and man's soul, stands on Calvary's hill. Our Savior was stripped, accused, mocked and beaten beyond recognition! There is no one who has ever faced such gross hardship, accepting the wounds of betrayal, accepting the stripes of denial and accepting the pounding of the nails on the cross to absorb all our sins and sicknesses on His physical body. He shed His innocent blood to purchase us from Satan's grasp. Christ didn't owe Satan anything! We owed God, but we could not pay. To mock Christ is to mock your greatest advocate. To ignore Christ is to reject your greatest love.

Give thought to where you stand. Give thought to how you think. Give thought to what you say. Give thought to how you choose. It will not only determine your destiny, but it will seal your Eternity!

4.   Faultless Master. The Creator is the only One who can make material exist out of the immaterial and out of the nonexistent. The Redeemer is the only One who not only speaks the truth but is the Truth! The Author of life is the only One who is able to bestow physical life and the gift of eternal life. To match Him is impossible. To attempt to surpass Him is irrational and futile. Christ, the First and the Last, is immovable, immutable, insurmountable and unstoppable. Christ is the only One who is both able and worthy to break the seals, revealing God's plans and orchestrating them with perfect timing.

Why Christ? He is the unblemished Lamb who died so we may live. People do things to get things. Christ died so that we may have life. That is what separates Him: He is not self-serving. His goal is to serve His Father and to seek and save the lost, not for His gain, but for the glory of His Father and for our eternal good. Praise Him alone!

5:3 *And no one in heaven or on the earth or under the earth was able to open the scroll, or to look at it.*

Solomon asked a rhetorical question in Proverbs 20:9, "Who can say, 'I have made my heart clean, I am pure from my sin'"? The answer is, "No one!" Solomon follows this train of thought in Ecclesiastes 7:20, "For there is not a just man on earth who does good and does not sin." He must have learned this from his father, David, who said in Psalm 14:2-3, "The Lord looks down from heaven upon the children of men, to see if there are any who understand, who seek God. They have all turned aside, they have together become corrupt; there is none who does good, no, not one." According to Romans 5:12, through one man, Adam, sin entered the world, and death through sin, and thus death spread to all men, because all have sinned. Sin disqualifies all of us. But since Christ had no sin (II Corinthians 5:21) and was sent by God as the Son of Man to bear our sins, He is the only one qualified to open the seals!

Getting into medical school is no easy task. One is judged on grade point average, ability to pass the Medical College Admission Exam with a high score, and ability to communicate. He cannot gain access on the basis of enthusiasm or intent or because he is sincere about helping others. He must prove worthy to enter. Even after 27 rejection letters over a period of three years, and counselors turning their backs on me, with one emphatically stating, "Son, you don't have what it takes to be a medical doctor," I never gave up. With sheer determination, studying, sweating, growing, correcting my shortcomings, and by God's gracious blessings, I was accepted into the University of Southern California Medical School! I had finally proven myself to be worthy.

But let's be clear. No zeal, no intention, no sincerity, no drive, no determination, no passion, no purpose nor any planning will catapult any one of us into the position of our Redeemer. No amount of politics, science, philosophy, religion, education, money, power or crowns can enable us to reach the throne of God. Those who are willing will never be worthy! All of our qualifications would end up disqualifying us because we are all born hopelessly lost in our sin (Romans 3:9). Satan attempted to usurp God's throne and since has tempted a host of individuals to try and become the god and ruler of this world, including Egypt's Pharaoh, Assyria's Sennacherib, Babylon's Nebuchadnezzar, Persia's Cyrus, Greece's Alexander the Great, Rome's Nero,

France's Napoleon, Russia's Stalin, and the Ottoman Empire's Young Turks who inhumanely massacred one and a half million out of three million Armenians in 1915.

 No created being in the universe is qualified to open the seals. Only Christ has the authority, the ability and the purity; He alone stands distinctly. All others, yesterday, today and tomorrow, must and will bow humbly!

Whether one is willing or not, there will come a time when all will humbly bow before God including today's shameless mockers, "That at the name of Jesus every knee should bow, of those in heaven, and of those on earth, and those under the earth, and that every tongue should confess that Jesus Christ is Lord, to the glory of God the Father" (Philippians 2:10-11).

Weeping in Heaven

5:4 So I wept much, because no one was found worthy to open and read the scroll, or to look at it.

When John realizes that no creature in all the universe is able to open the seals, he begins to weep. He has not yet set his eyes on the Lamb of God but has scanned all the universe, past, present and future, and has come up with the realization that no one is worthy! If no one were able to open the seals, then sin, sickness, sorrow, shame, pain, loneliness, murder and death would linger endlessly.

We are unable to overcome on our own. Christ, driven by His love for you and me, overcame on the cross. If the seals remain closed, then all the written prophecies remain hidden and the hopes of all believers of all times would come to naught. John's tears represent the tears of God's elect through all of history. They are the tears of Adam and Eve as they were cast out of the Garden of Eden. They are the tears of Israel as they were forced out of their land, being exiled into Assyria and Babylon. They are the tears of all God's people today who suffer, who are martyred, who bear heartaches, experience loneliness, face divorce, disappointments, disease and death.

John knows that the failure to identify the Redeemer means that greed, lies, death, destruction and damnation would reign forever in the hands of the usurper, Satan the Devil, the wicked Dragon. History changed 2,000 years ago: Christ was born to a virgin, without bearing the tainted blood of mankind. It was His precious shed blood that was the payment for our sin debt! It will be the opening of the seals by the only Redeemer, Jesus Christ, that will lead to the realization of eternal glory that believers will finally inherit.

***5:5** But one of the elders said to me, "Do not weep. Behold, the Lion of the tribe of Judah, the Root of David, has prevailed to open the scroll and to loose its seven seals."*

As John continued to sob, one of the elders consoled him to stop weeping, directing him to look upon Jesus. That is the secret of life! We don't need the seven steps to ultimate success or the three secrets about how to possess wealth. We don't need to look at our broken reality and pity ourselves. We don't need to look around and compare ourselves to our neighbors. We only need to lift our eyes to Jesus, from whom our strength and our hope comes! The elder in our text is not identified. And that's the point; let the central and utmost focus of your life be Christ, and not any other!

The church is the catalyst, directing you and me to Christ. If we find that Christ is not presented as the only means of salvation, we are in the Church of Laodicea, and we should graciously leave. Nothing in life will satisfy. Entertainment, sports and parties may temporarily give us a high, but our hearts still run on empty as our insatiable human appetites constantly demand for more. We are in search of lasting fulfillment. And our bodies desperately need rest and relaxation, but according to Ecclesiastics 3:11, God has placed Eternity in our hearts, and no matter what we run after, only God can fill the void; no matter what this world has to offer us, only fellowship as a part of the church on earth will satisfy, and Eternity with Him in heaven will provide us complete joy! Oh, what a day that will be when my Jesus I shall see!

In John 1:29, when John the Baptist saw Jesus Christ he exclaimed, "Behold! The Lamb of God who takes away the sins of the world!" Some seventy years later, as John the Apostle continues to weep, the elder exclaims, "Behold!" and consoles John, "Do not weep. Behold, the Lion of the tribe of Judah, the Root of David, has prevailed to open the scroll and to loose its seven seals."

 For us who are facing impossibilities, we don't need to "be-told" about a guru's seven steps of overcoming; we need to "be-hold" the Lamb's suffering and the Lion's conquering the very struggle of living and sting of dying.

The One who has triumphed, and conquered sin, sickness and death is Jesus Christ, and we, the believers who will be Raptured, will witness Him loosening and opening up the seals. There will be shouts of joy and festivities like never before. Why? Because unbelievers will face horrific judgments? No, that's heartbreaking! It's because we will finally witness Christ assume His role as the righteous judge who dispenses undeniable justice. It's because we will see atrocious wrongs become right. It's because we will see the wicked whacked and Satan sacked!

Christ is not only known as the Lamb of God who was stripped, spit upon, and slain, but He is seen and worshiped as the "Lion of the tribe of Judah." Why the lion? According to Genesis 49:9, Judah "lies down as a lion, and as a lion, who shall provoke him?" In Luke 3:33, we read that Jesus was born in the line of Judah, and the right of kingly rule fell in Judah's lap because Reuben, who had firstborn rights, sinned, sleeping with his father's concubine, Bilhah, and was discredited (Genesis 35:22; 49:3-4). Reuben's brothers, Simeon and Levi, the next in line to firstborn rights, were also discredited due to their swords that were blood-stained with murder in Shechem (Genesis 34:25; 49:5-7). Therefore, Reuben's rights were divided amongst his other brothers:

1. Material birthright with a double share was given to Joseph who was shackled, sabotaged, sold and nearly slain by his older brothers (Deuteronomy 21:15-17; I Chronicles 5:1-2). It was Joseph's two sons, Ephraim and Manasseh, who reaped the double portion.

2. Priestly birthright was given to Levi as the redeemed firstborn son because of his family's obedience. When Moses faced rebellion, he charged, "Whoever is for the Lord, come to me," and the Levites did as Moses commanded (Exodus 13:2, 15; 32:26-38). The Lord said, "I have taken the Levites from among the Israelites in place of the first male offspring of every Israelite woman. The Levites are mine" (Numbers 3:12, 45).

3. Kingship birthright was given to Judah, Jacob's fourth son (I Chronicles 5:2), because he took responsibility for his youngest brother's Benjamin's life. When the famine was severe in the land of Canaan, Jacob was forced to send his sons to Egypt to buy wheat; what the brothers did not know was that Joseph, the very brother whom they had sold, had become second in command to Pharaoh! On their first visit to Egypt, Joseph recognized his brothers and called them spies and demanded to see their youngest brother Benjamin who had not come with them. To secure their return, Joseph kept Simeon as collateral.

When the brothers needed more wheat the second time, they could not convince their father Jacob to send Benjamin with them. They needed to visit Egypt's prime minister once again but were blinded to the fact that it was Joseph. Judah said to his father Jacob, "Send the boy (Benjamin) along with me and we will go at once, so that we and you and our children may live and not die (due to the famine). I myself will guarantee his safety; you can hold me personally responsible for him. If I do not bring him back to you and set him here before you, I will bear the blame before you all my life" (Genesis 43:8-9).

The prophecy and blessing which Jacob spoke concerning Judah is directly linked to Christ the Messiah, "Judah, your brother will praise you; your hand will be on the neck of your enemies; your father's sons will bow down to you. You are a lion's cub, Judah; you return from the prey, my son. Like a lion he crouches and lies down, like a lioness — who dares to rouse him? The scepter will not depart from Judah, nor the ruler's staff from between his feet, until he to whom it belongs shall come and the obedience of the nations shall be his. He will tether his donkey to a vine, his colt to the choicest branch; he will wash his garments in wine, his robes in the blood of grapes" (Genesis 49:8-11).

According to Genesis 49:9, therefore, the tribe of Judah is the kingly tribe because the term "lion" symbolizes strength, fierceness, nobility, sovereignty, dignity and victory. This designation of "lion" points to no one other than Jesus Christ, the Messiah, and seamlessly consolidates Christ as holding the scepter, with a ruler's staff. He will wash his garments in wine, depicted by the crucifixion of the innocent and obedient Lamb of God. Yet, as the Lion of Judah, He will also wash his robes in the blood of grapes, depicted by pouring out His wrath on the God-hating, Christ-rejecting, Holy Spirit-mocking world during the Tribulation.

In Revelation 19:13-15, we find, "He (Christ) was clothed with a robe dipped in blood, and His name is called the Word of God. And the armies in heaven, clothed in fine linen, white and clear, followed Him on white horses. Now out of His mouth goes a sharp sword, that with it He should strike the nations.

And He Himself will rule them with a rod of iron. He Himself treads the winepress of the fierceness and wrath of Almighty God." This is Christ with His saints in His Second Coming, ready to engage in the Campaign of Armageddon and to overcome!

 The Lamb was slain, but the Lion will rule!

As John kept weeping, the elder pointed him to the Lion of the tribe of Judah who had prevailed to open the scroll and to loosen its seven seals. We read in Isaiah 9:6-7, that Jesus is the Wonderful, Counselor, Mighty God, Everlasting Father, and Prince of Peace; and "of the increase of His government and peace there will be no end, upon the throne of David and over His kingdom, to order it and establish it with judgment and justice from that time forward, even forever. The zeal of the Lord of hosts will perform this."

 God will see to it that His Son will not only reign in the Millennium, but throughout all of Eternity! In all ways, Christ is perfect. In Sonship. In Godship. In genealogy. In history. In prophecy.

We find in Revelation 22:16 what at first glance seems to be contradictory: "I, Jesus, have sent My angel to testify to you these things in the churches. I am the Root and the Offspring of David, the Bright and Morning Star." Jesus as the "Offspring of David" or "son" of David means He comes from the lineage of David. Jesus was born in the line of Jesse whose son was David; this lineage presents Jesus as the "son of David" and "Offspring of David" (Matthew 1:1, 16, 17, 20). Isaiah prophesied about Jesus' lineage, "There shall come forth a Rod (Jesus) from the stem (root) of Jesse (David's father)" (Isaiah 11:1).

How can Jesus, being the "Offspring of David," be the "Root of David?" Jesus is not only from the line of David, making him the "son" of David, but He is "Root of David, making Him David's Father! Isaiah prophesied about this in Isaiah 11:10, "And in that day there shall be a Root of Jesse (Jesus), who shall stand as a banner for the people; for the Gentiles shall seek Him, and His resting place shall be glorious." When speaking with the Pharisees, Jesus said, "'What do you think about the Christ? Whose Son is He?'" They said to Him, 'The Son of David.' He said to them, 'How then does David in the Spirit call Him "Lord," saying: 'The Lord (God) said to my Lord (Christ),''Sit at My right hand, till I make Your enemies Your footstool'" (Matthew 22:42-46; Psalm 110:1). David called Jesus "Lord," meaning Jesus is greater than David, and Jesus was asking the Pharisees how could He be both the "Son of David" and the "Root of David" and how can a son be greater than his father?

If this is confusing, consider Romans 11:36, "For of Him (Christ) and through Him and to Him are all things." Think about it. David existed only through Christ. But physically speaking, Jesus came through the line of David. We will visit Colossians 1:15-18 multiple times as it contains the essence of Christ, "He is the image of the invisible God, the firstborn over all creation. For by Him all things were created that are in heaven and that are on earth, visible and invisible, whether thrones or dominions or principalities or powers. All things were created through Him and for Him. And He is before all things, and in Him all things consist. And he is the head of the body, the church, who is the beginning, the firstborn from the dead, that in all things He may have the preeminence."

Jesus has overcome and is able and worthy to open up the seals! In John 16:33, Jesus said, "These things (about His death and resurrection) I have spoken to you, that in Me you may have peace. In the world you will have tribulation (life's trials, not referring to the seven-year Tribulation); but be of good cheer, I have overcome the world."

"That's fine and dandy," you say, "but how about me? How can I overcome?" John gives us the answer in his epistle, in I John 5:4, "For whatever is born of God overcomes the world. And this is the victory that has overcome the world — our faith." He continues to say in I John 5:5, "Who is it that overcomes the world? Only the one who believers that Jesus is the Son of God." According to Colossians 2:13-15, it is because of what Christ has done that makes us overcomers, "And you, being dead in your trespasses and the uncircumcision of your flesh, He has made alive together with Him, having forgiven you all trespasses, having wiped out the handwriting of requirements that was against us, which was contrary to us. And He has taken it out of the way, having nailed it to the cross. Having disarmed principalities and powers, He made a public spectacle of them, triumphing over them in it."

Believe in Him, be crucified on the cross with Him, be forgiven by Him, rise with Him, be born of Him, be alive in Him, walk with Him, commune with Him, speak about Him and be in love with Him. It's all about Him and what He did for you. You are an overcomer in Him!

When Christ defeated Satan with the redemption price of His shed blood, He gained the right to take possession of this earth away from Satan and to rule on earth as the First and the Last. Jesus said in Revelation 22:12-13, "And behold, I am coming quickly, and My reward is with Me, to give to everyone according to his work. I am the Alpha and the Omega, the Beginning and the End, the First and the Last." In just a short time, Christ will exercise the right he gained at the cross to eternally damn Satan, the usurper, and his forces. The rule with full authority will be given to the One who has all rights, Jesus Christ, as God has ordained in His sovereignty and His perfect timing at the Second Coming of Christ (Ezekiel 25-27).

The Father will not open the seals, because He has entrusted this unique privilege to His Son, "For the Father judges no one, but has committed all judgment to the Son, that all should honor the Son just as they honor the Father. He who does not honor the Son does not honor the Father who sent Him"

(John 5:22-27). According to Anderson, "God the Father Himself will not break a single seal of it, for the Father has ceded the prerogative of judgment."[6]

Why Jesus? Because He was made sin on our behalf and has earned the right to loosen the seals, "All we like sheep have gone astray; we have turned, every one, to his own way; and the Lord (God) has laid on Him (Christ) the iniquity of us all" (Isaiah 53:6). Because He bore all our judgments, He is able to deliver judgment on those who continue to reject His gift of salvation.

To bring the kingdom of God to earth requires that the kingdom of Satan be overthrown. What unfolds with the opening of the seals initiates the process of overthrowing Satan's rule, and in its finality, launches the rightful rule of Jesus Christ! Time is in the hands of God. He created it. "At the proper time, determined sovereignly by God, Christ will exercise the right He gained at the cross to throw out the usurper."[7] This will be the sequence of events:

1. The loosening of the first six seals results in preliminary judgments including the decrees of the four horsemen (Revelation 6:1-17).

2. The loosening of the seventh seal results in more pronounced judgments because the seventh seal contains the seven trumpet judgments, and the seventh trumpet judgment contains the seven bowl judgments (Revelation 8:1-6).

3. When the seventh seal is opened, the first four trumpets are sounded (Revelation 8:7-12).

4. There is a pause before the fifth, sixth and seventh trumpets are sounded because of their severity (Revelation 8:13).

5. The fifth and sixth (the first two of the final three trumpets) trumpets sound (Revelation 9:1-21).

6. The final (seventh) trumpet is sounded and there is a declaration made in anticipation of Christ's rule, "And there were loud voices in heaven, saying, 'The kingdoms of this world have become the kingdoms of our Lord and of His Christ, and He shall reign forever and ever!'" (Revelation 11:15). Because of the finality of this declaration, the seven bowls which follow, will proceed out of the seventh trumpet.

7. The seals and the trumpets occur during the first half of the Tribulation, the first three and a half years. The bowls occur at the second half of the Tribulation, known as the Great Tribulation, the last three and a half years.

8. The bowls conclude the wrath of God poured out on an unbelieving world who trusts the Antichrist over Jesus Christ (Revelation 16:1-21).

9. Finally, after the destruction of Babylon (Revelation 17-18), and the Campaign of Armageddon (Revelation 16:12-16; 19:11-21), Christ retakes what He has already purchased at Calvary, where He proclaimed, "It is finished!" (John 19:30). Note, the road to repossessing the earth will require massive "bombs," starting out with seals, then trumpets, then bowls, and then the Campaign of Armageddon where Satan will challenge Christ by drawing together all the rulers and armies of the world into the land of Megiddo. The destruction of Babylon and the Campaign of Armageddon are the consequences of the fifth, sixth and seventh bowls being dispensed over the earth.

10. Satan along with his armies will lose their wretched hold on possessing the earth and ruling over it. Satan will then be locked up for 1,000 years in the Bottomless Pit before God temporarily releases him to attempt to fool unbelievers who are alive and reside in the Millennium Kingdom (Revelation 20:3, 7-10). The ultimate victory is won when Christ breaks them with a rod of iron and

dashes them to pieces like a potter's vessel (Psalm 2:9). Satan and his followers will be cast into the Lake of Fire and Christ will rule with righteousness as the Lion of the tribe of Judah and the Root of David! (Revelation 20:11-15)

Roaring Lion, Gentle Lamb

5:6 And I looked, and behold, in the midst of the throne and of the four living creatures, and in the midst of the elders, stood a Lamb as though it had been slain, having seven horns and seven eyes, which are the seven Spirits of God sent out into all the earth.

John is desperately seeking for the One who can open the seals, and in the midst of all who are present around the throne, including the four living creatures and the elders, John beholds the Lamb of God who was slain. In the previous verse, the elder instructed John to behold the Lion, "Behold, the Lion of the tribe of Judah, the Root of David, has prevailed to open the scroll and to loose its seven seals."

Isn't it curious that John sees the Lamb instead of the Lion? There is a series of events that must occur in a specific sequence: The Lamb must first be slain in order to purchase redemption for mankind and earn the rights to judge and to rule as a Lion! This is a beautiful picture of God's character: grace and mercy precede His judgment!

 Before Christ rules victoriously, He sacrificed profoundly.

"In one brilliant stroke John portrays the central theme of New Testament revelation — victory through sacrifice."[8]

John will call Christ by His title, the "Lamb," "arnion" in the Greek, or "little lamb." Isaiah referred to our Christ as the sacrificial lamb in Isaiah 53:7, "He was oppressed, and He was afflicted, yet He opened not His mouth; He was led as a lamb to the slaughter, and as a sheep before its shearers is silent, so He opened not His mouth." The apostle Philip taught the Ethiopian eunuch about the Lamb of God (Acts 8:32-35). Peter calls Christ the Lamb without blemish and spot, the perfect Passover Lamb (I Peter 1:19). According to Exodus 12:4, the Passover lamb was not to have any of its bones broken; that foreshadowed the Roman soldiers not breaking the legs of Christ as they did to the two thieves who hung on either side (John 19:33-36). Paul spoke of Christ, "our Passover who was sacrificed for us" (I Corinthians 5:7). Jesus is aptly called the Lamb twenty-eight times in the final book of the Bible, more than any other title of Christ![9]

It is the blood of the Lamb:

1. That allows us to overcome Satan's attacks here and now and helps the new converts during the Tribulation to overcome Satan (Revelation 12:11).

2. That forgives us of all our sins, known as justification.

3. That cleanses us daily from sin, known as sanctification.

4. That allows our bodily transformation during the Rapture, known as glorification.

5. That entitles believers to wear the white linen of righteousness (Revelation 19:8).

6. That qualifies believers to have their names written in the Book of Life (Revelation 13:8).

7. That places a "red stain" on Calvary's hill, spilling over into our hearts, giving us hope to carry on, endure and stand firm in our troubled circumstances until our Lord appears!

We have a considerable number of "lambs" today presenting themselves as friends of the people, speaking words that tickle the ear and soothe the heart. Some sit on church boards. Some sit on corporate boards. Some sit on school boards. Be leery, even the third person of the unholy Trinity, the "Second Beast" looks like a lamb … but speaks like a dragon (Revelation 13:11).

What distinguishes Christ from any other is that He acts under His Father's sovereignty and in the best interest of humanity, you and me, instead of acting on His own behalf selfishly!

The Lamb who has been sitting for 2,000 years at the right hand of His Father now stands, takes the scroll from the Father, and initiates a succession of unalterable events that will conclude in His Millennial Kingdom reign. According to Hebrews 10:11, "and every priest (Jewish priest of the Old Testament) stands ministering daily and repeatedly offering the same sacrifices, which can never take away sins. But this Man (Jesus Christ), after He had offered one sacrifice (Himself on the cross) for sins forever, sat down at the right hand of God, from that time waiting till His enemies are made His footstool." After the Rapture, the clock starts! It's Jesus' time to stand! It's Jesus' time to open the seals! It's Jesus' time to rule! This gentle Lamb is about to roar as the Lion and soar as the Eagle!

When Jesus was slain, "His visage was marred more than any man, and His form more than the sons of men" (Isaiah 52:14). The whips lashing across His back not only tore His skin but shredded His back muscles. The crucifixion on Calvary's hill was the most brutal slaughter known to mankind. Surprising to some, Christ's scars will always remain, and they will serve as a sure testimony of His loving sacrifice for you and me. Those will be the only scars in heaven! In John 20:27, after His resurrection, Jesus said to doubting Thomas regarding His scars, "Put your finger here; see my hands. Reach out your hand and put it into my side. Stop doubting and believe."

God's plan for the salvation of mankind was not conceived in the middle of history; God foreknew all things from the beginning (Isaiah 45:21). When Abraham was lost for words, he told his son Isaac, "God will provide for Himself the lamb" (Genesis 22:8). According to I Peter 1:20, Jesus was "foreordained before the foundation of the world but was manifest in these last times for you." Every eye will see Him in His Second Coming, and will mourn (Zechariah 12:10, Revelation 1:7).

 Don't bet on yourself, your strength, your smarts or your bank accounts. Don't bet on any horse. Bet on the One, Jesus Christ, who will be riding the white horse! (Revelation 19:11).

The Lamb of God has "seven horns and seven eyes, which are the Spirits of God sent out into all the earth." The horn, used as a weapon amongst the animal kingdom, is a biblical symbol of power, might and government (I Samuel 2:10; Psalm 132:13-17). In the prophetic books of Daniel and Revelation, the horn represents dominion, kings and kingdoms (Daniel 7:8; Revelation 13:1,11; 17:3-16). As discussed, the number seven is the number of completeness and perfection. Christ's seven horns represent His complete dominion of the world, and His omnipotence.

 Christ and His Kingdom will reign forever perfectly and permanently. No one can veto Him. No one can impeach Him. No one can overthrow Him. No one can outwit Him. No one sue Him. No one can threaten Him. No one can bribe Him. No one can overcome Him.

His everlasting dominion will never be destroyed. All other horns, or governments, will arise and then be defeated. "And in the days of these kings (worldly powers spoken of in Daniel) the God of heaven will set up a kingdom (Christ's) which shall never be destroyed; and the kingdom shall not be left to other people; it shall break in pieces and consume all these kingdoms, and it shall stand forever" (Daniel 2:44). "Then to Him (Christ) was given dominion and glory and a kingdom, that all peoples, nations, and languages should serve Him. His dominion is an everlasting dominion, which shall not pass away, and His kingdom the one which shall not be destroyed" (Daniel 7:14).

We can reference the seven horns of the Lamb to Joshua's story. To accomplish the conquering of Jericho, Joshua was instructed to hand the priest seven trumpets of rams' horns, blow the trumpets, let the Israelites shout and witness the walls tumble down! (Joshua 6:1-5). By now you should not be surprised that Satan, the counterfeit and fallen angel, will appear as the red dragon with seven heads and ten horns, and seven diadems or crowns on his heads. He has always tried to eclipse God. The number of Satan's heads and horns are not accidental, but they will all be systematically crushed by Jesus Christ. After the power of Satan is finally and completely crushed, believers will enter into eternal rest just as Israel was allowed to enter into the land of Canaan when the horn of Jericho was broken.

The seven eyes of the Lamb are the seven Spirits of God. Seven reminds us "of the sevenfold plenitude of the One Spirit of Jehovah."[10] There is only one Holy Spirit, but He has seven inherent traits. Isaiah writes in Isaiah 11:1-2, "There shall come forth a Rod from the stem of Jesse (Christ), and a Branch shall grow out of his roots. The Spirit of the Lord shall rest upon Him (Christ), the Spirit of wisdom and understanding, the Spirit of counsel and might, the Spirit of knowledge and of the fear of the Lord." As discussed earlier, I only count six, unless one deems the "Spirit of the Lord" as a trait. I believe the seventh is hidden in Revelation 19:10 and is revealed as the "Spirit of Prophecy"; in that verse, we'll witness the angel deterring John from worshiping him: "Worship God! For the testimony of Jesus is the spirit of prophecy."

The seven eyes are sent out over all the earth. The eyes indicate:

1. God's Omniscience. The Holy Spirit knows all things before they transpire and unveils everything that is hidden.
2. God's Omnipresence. The Holy Spirit is present in all places at all times and at the same time. Nothing is hidden from His sight.

3. God's Omnipotence. The Holy Spirit has the power to hold back, to set forth, to indwell, to make whole, to empower, and to perform the impossible for God's glory.

According to Hebrews 4:13, "There is no creature hidden from His sight, but all things are naked and open to the eyes of Him to whom we must give account." You and I can go to great depths to hide our plans, motives, thoughts and actions from the Lord, do our work in darkness and swim in the swamp of injustice and immorality, but God sees, and God knows. In Isaiah 29: 15-16, we read, "Woe to those who seek deep to hide their counsel far from the Lord, and their works are in the dark; they say, 'Who sees us?' and 'Who knows us?' Surely you have things turned around! Shall the potter be esteemed as the clay; for shall the thing made say to him who made it, 'He did not make me'? Or shall the thing formed say of him who formed it, 'He has no understanding'"? The Potter is God. The "thing" is us. We cannot hide in the darkness or obstruct the Potter from His business.

It is heartening to know that the "eyes of the Lord are on the righteous, and His ears are open to their cry" (Psalm 34:15). What is even more comforting is that God also watches the wicked, extending His grace to them, and pleading with them to turn to Him as He did to Israel when they went astray, "'As I live,' says the Lord God, 'I have no pleasure in the death of the wicked, but that the wicked turn from his way and live. Turn, turn from your evil ways! For why should you die, O house of Israel?'" (Ezekiel 33:11).

Scroll Handed Off

5:7 Then He came and took the scroll out of the right hand of Him who sat on the throne.

Christ takes the scroll out of His Father's hand. Daniel foresaw this moment, "I watched till thrones were put in place, and the Ancient of Days (God) was seated; His garment was white as snow, and the hair of His head was like pure wool. His throne was a fiery flame, its wheels a burning fire. And behold, One like the Son of Man (Jesus), coming with the clouds of heaven! He came to the Ancient of Days, and they brought Him (Jesus) near before Him (God). Then to Him (Jesus) was given dominion and glory and a kingdom, that all peoples, nations, and languages should serve Him. His dominion is an everlasting dominion, which shall not pass away, and His kingdom the one which shall not be destroyed (Daniel 7:9, 13-14).

In His first coming, Christ rode on a donkey into the city of Jerusalem. In His Second Coming, He will appear on a white horse. After the Rapture, the Church Age will be over, and the age of intercession will end. Today we live in a time of grace where we have a High Priest (Jesus Christ) who can sympathize with our weaknesses, since He was tempted as we are, yet He is without sin; we are therefore allowed to "come boldly to the throne of grace, that we may obtain mercy and find grace to help in time of need" (Hebrews 4:15-16). When the Lamb turns into a Lion, this intercession ends! The most feared events in history will begin to unfold and believers will finally rejoice because 6,000 years' worth of grief, sorrow, pain and death will come to an end![11]

God has been so patient. The scoffers have been so crude. They will get to feel their Maker's touch during the dreaded Tribulation (II Peter 3:9). Why has justice been so quiet since the crucifixion? Because of grace! Because God is inviting all to come to Him and be saved! Because God is giving man time to turn from his wicked ways! After the Rapture, it's "hammer" time! Satan and all his plans will ultimately be cast into hell and the clock starts ticking the second the Lamb rises, takes the scroll from his Father, and opens up the seals. The "hour" that is to follow is a seven-year period of Tribulation, also known as Jacob's Trouble, but the second half is called the Great Tribulation. We join the psalmist in Psalm 82:8, "Arise, O God, judge the earth; for You shall inherit all nations."

Please don't "misdiagnose" this point. God is not sleeping. He has not forgotten. He is not oblivious. He has "sedated" His justice so that His grace may touch your soul with His Salvation!

Strike the Harp, Light the Incense

5:8 Now when He had taken the scroll, the four living creatures and the twenty-four elders fell down before the Lamb, each having a harp, and golden bowls full of incense, which are the prayers of the saints.

The four living creatures and the 24 elders fall before the Lamb in reverence, worship and praise. When unbelievers fall before the Beast's image in Revelation 13:15 in fear and bondage, their "adoration" is diabolically opposed to the angels' and the church's devotion to Christ. The psalmist proclaimed, "Know that the Lord, He is God; it is He who has made us, and not we ourselves; we are His people and the sheep of His pasture" (Psalm 100:3). The same adoration is found in Psalm 95:6-7, "Oh come, let us worship and bow down; let us kneel before the Lord our Maker. For He is our God, and we are the people of His pasture, and the sheep of His hand."

If one chooses to bow to Christ today during the Church Age, it is done in devotion and admiration. If one refuses to bow today, he will likely bow the knee to the Antichrist during the Tribulation; anyone who bows the knee to the Antichrist will also bow before Christ after the Millennium at the Great White Throne judgment. But the one who bows the knee at the Great White Throne judgment will be cast into the Lake of Fire. Timing is everything! Today, today, today is your perfect opportunity to devote your life to Christ!

Many in heaven are "armed" with harps: the 144,000 Jewish evangelists (Revelation 14:1-3); all those who have victory

229

over the Beast by refusing to worship him and take his 666 mark (Revelation 15:2); the four creatures and the church worship with harps as well (Revelation 5:8). In the Old Testament, the Levites and the psalmist used harps as they ministered to the Lord and worshiped Him (II Chronicles 5:12; Psalm 33:2; 150:3). "Then I will go to the altar of God, to God my exceeding joy; and on the harp I will praise You, O God, my God" (Psalm 43:4).

Each of the 24 elders also has a golden bowl full of incense, which are the prayers of the saints. Your prayers have not gone unheard. They are continually kept and cherished before God. It is simply too difficult for us to understand that when God says, "No," it is for our benefit and not for our harm! We'll see in Revelation chapter 16 that bowls are used to pour out God's wrath upon the unbelievers. Prior to the sounding of the seventh trumpet, an angel anoints the prayers of the saints with incense on an altar before it reaches God as a sweet aroma. He then takes fire from the altar, places it in the same censer and casts it on the earth as a judgment (Revelation 8:3-5). For the believer, the golden bowl is used to seek God's mercy and grace. For the unbeliever, the bowl will be used to receive God's wrath and judgments.

In Exodus 30:7-8 and 40:26-27, we read that incense was burned on the temple altar of incense in the morning and the evening. The altar was in the Holy Place, in front of the veil which separated the Holy Place from the Most Holy Place. The incense would rise and reach God, "reminding" Him of the prayers of His people. The psalmist earnestly uttered, "Let my prayer be set before You as incense, the lifting up of my hands as the evening sacrifice" (Psalm 141:2). On any given day and time, we are contributors to the contents of the golden bowl, making direct deposits. Just what am I contributing? Just what are you contributing?

The prayers of the saints are actually vital to the Lamb taking the scroll. On a daily basis we speak what Jesus taught us in

Matthew 6:8-10, "Our Father, in heaven, hallowed be Your name. Your kingdom come. Your will be done on earth as it is in heaven."

Worthy is the Lamb; the First Choir

5:9 And they sang a new song, saying, "You are worthy to take the scroll, and to open its seals; for You were slain, and have redeemed us to God by Your blood out of every tribe and tongue and people and nation.

The church, represented by the 24 elders, is singing a new song with great pleasure and delight, adoring, praising and worshiping Christ, the Lamb of God, who is the only One worthy to open the seals and initiate judgment upon the wicked. This is not just 24 people singing. This is thousands upon hundred thousands of saints of all ages joining together in adoration and song! What is the big deal? We were not redeemed with corruptible things such as silver and gold. We were eternally redeemed from damnation by the precious and priceless blood of the Lamb! That's huge!

In II Chronicles 7:5, when Solomon dedicated the temple to the Lord, he slew 22,000 bulls and 120,000 sheep. If a bull has 20 liters of blood and a sheep 5 liters of blood, that would be 440,000 liters (116,000 gallons) of blood for the bulls and 600,000 liters (158,000 gallons) of blood for the sheep! But God, in human form, born in Bethlehem, hung on the cross just outside of Jerusalem, shed 5.5 liters (1.5 gallons) of pure divine blood. The animals' blood covered the sins of the people. The blood of Jesus completely purges the sin of those who come to Him because He is the only effective source! In order for us to be blessed, He not only took on our curse, but He also took on our death. In Galatians 3:13, we read, "Christ has redeemed us from the curse of the law, having become a curse for us (for it is written, 'Cursed is everyone who hangs on a tree'"). Always remember, according to II Peter 3:9, God does not want anyone to perish; He longs for all to come to repentance.

The name "Judah" means "praise the Lord," and the tribe of Judah used to lead all of Israel into battle (Judges 20:18). Isn't it fitting that the Lion of Judah is receiving praise and will lead the saints into the Campaign of Armageddon!

The Lord redeemed believers out of every tribe, tongue, people and nation unto God by His blood, and made them kings and priests, to reign on earth. Slaves of ancient times were controlled by their proprietors. To buy a slave's freedom required a price paid by a benefactor. You and I were born as slaves to sin. Christ bought us with a price paid by His sinless life and His shed blood. He won't force us out of bondage, however. It is up to us whether we remain slaves or escape slavery. The saints who were caught up in the Rapture are praising the Lord, thanking Him for the unimaginable price He paid for their redemption! Peter said it best, "Knowing that you were not redeemed with corruptible things, like silver or gold, from your aimless conduct received by tradition from your fathers, but with the precious blood of Christ, as of a lamb without blemish and without spot" (I Peter 1:18-19).

The mention of Jesus redeeming mankind from all nations reminds me of a song I learned as a child, "Jesus loves the little children, all the children of the world. Red and yellow, black and white. They are precious in His sight. Jesus loves the little children of the world!" The peoples, tribes, tongues, and nations of the world are not distinguished by color in God's eyes. God separates us on the basis of our position. Let me explain. We are either to the left of the cross or to the right. We are either the thief who cursed Christ and said, "If you are the Son of God save yourself and save us," or the thief who said, "Remember me." We are either the saints who bow to God before the Rapture or the unbelievers who will bow at the Great White Throne judgment. But be assured, everyone will bow!

Those who miss the Rapture will either be the redeemed who are martyred during the Tribulation or the rebellious who marvel at the Beast and accept his mark. The Antichrist will have power over every tribe, tongue and nation, yet the Gospel will be preached to every nation, tribe, tongue and people (Revelation 13:7;14:6). There are two sides. This is not political. This is not racial. This is not material. This is eternal. If I may ask, "On which side of the cross are you?"

The Rule and Reign of Believers

5:10 And have made us kings and priests to our God; and we shall reign on the earth."

Christ has made us kings and priests to our God; and we shall reign on the earth with Him during the Millennium. This was mentioned at the beginning of Revelation 1:6, "And has made us kings and priests to His God and Father, to Him be glory and dominion forever and ever. Amen." In Exodus 19:6, Israel was called to be a "kingdom of priests." Peter reminds the saints in I Peter 2:9, "But you are a chosen generation, a royal priesthood, a holy nation, God's special possession, that you may declare the praises of Him who called you out of darkness into His marvelous light."

Because Christ, our High Priest, has conquered sin and can sympathize with our weaknesses, He has given us the right to "come boldly to the throne of grace, that we may obtain mercy and find grace to help in time of need" (Hebrews 4:14-16). Once a year the high priest was able to enter the Holy of Holies where God's glory appeared only during Atonement Day, or Yom Kippur; but now because Christ's perfect work on the cross tore the veil, believers have continual access to God's glory at any time.

Believers belong to Christ and He gives us the privilege to be His priests. In Matthew 5:5, Jesus said, "Blessed are the meek, for they shall inherit the earth." We will be kings and priests, reigning with Christ 1,000 years in the Millennium Kingdom (Revelation 20:4). In order for this to transpire, the seals must first be broken; the Antichrist must temporarily reign on the world stage for seven years and come to his final doom; the sovereignty, power and greatness of all the kingdoms under heaven will be handed over to the holy people of the Most High; and Christ's kingdom will be everlasting, and all rulers will worship and obey Him (Daniel 7:25-27). Our rule has nothing to do with our status, race, creed, merit, money or pedigree; our rule has everything to do with our position in Christ!

The saints will co-rule with Christ (Revelation 2:26-27); they will sit with Him on His throne (Revelation 3:21); they will inherit the earth (Psalm 37:9; Matthew 5:5); they will judge the world and judge angels (I Corinthians 6:2-3); and they will take back dominion over the earth which Adam lost (Genesis 1:26-28). This is not just daily news. It's not temporary relief. It's not a dream. It's freedom from sin and living in the presence of God! The ransomed in heaven sing! They wear golden crowns, kneel at the feet of the Lamb, and with all the prayers of the saints over thousands of years and the declarations of the prophets long ago, they break forth in a song of adoration! Why? Because Christ was able to bring about grace and judgment, peace and goodness, health and well-being, rest and joy!

Physicians are unable to conquer all ailments; scientists are unable to understand everything about the universe; government is unable to legislate the quality of human existence; diplomats are unable to prevent war. But Christ?

 Christ is able, He is willing, and He is the only one worthy to redeem mankind! He takes the scroll and all of heaven bursts out in song. The response is beyond seismographic. It's volcanic. It's atomic. It's euphoric.

Oh, blessed hope! How blessed we are to know Him! Bless His holy name!

Heaven Erupts in Worship; the Second Choir

5:11 *Then I looked, and I heard the voice of many angels around the throne, the living creatures, and the elders; and the number of them was ten thousand times ten thousand, and thousands of thousands*

John now hears the second choir of this chapter, the angels of heaven breaking forth into a song. Their numbers are mind-blowing: ten thousand times ten thousand is "myrias" in the Greek, meaning an innumerable multitude, or hosts with an unlimited number. One third of the angels fell and followed Satan (Revelation 12:4); two thirds remained loyal and their total number must be beyond counting. Job proclaimed it beautifully with a rhetorical question in Job 25:3, "Can His forces be numbered?" The answer is a resounding, "No!" Daniel proclaims that a river of fire was flowing before God, and "thousands upon thousands attended Him; ten thousand times ten thousand stood before Him" in Daniel 7:10.

The blood, the scourging, the bruises, the slashes, the beatings, the brutality that fell upon Jesus offends many on earth. They are tragically on the side of the thief who said, "If you are the Son of God, save yourself and save us."

 The theme in heaven is not war. It is not politics. It is not religion. It is not the Antichrist. The theme in heaven is Christ and Christ alone.

His beauty. His love. His compassion. His gentleness. His grace. His forgiveness. His scars. He accomplished what no man, no leader, no politician, no entrepreneur, no teacher, no professor, no student, no priest, no clergyman, no preacher, no athlete, no intellectual, no activist and no scientist could ever do. He saved! There is no argument. There is no boycott. There is no resistance. There is no rebellion. There is complete reverence! The angels, every single one, from first to last, burst forth in a song!

5:12 *saying with a loud voice, "Worthy is the Lamb who was slain to receive power and riches and wisdom, and strength and honor and glory and blessing!"*

When the Father was worshiped in Revelation 4:10-11, the 24 elders cast their crowns before the throne and said, "You are worthy, O Lord (God), to receive glory and honor and power; for You created all things, and by Your will they exist and were created." The angels now offer the same esteem to the Lord Christ, the Lamb. The Lord God says of Himself, "I am the Lord, that is My name; and My glory I will not give to another, nor My praise to carved images" in Isaiah 42:8. In John 17:5, Jesus prayed, "And now, O Father, glorify Me together with Yourself, with the glory which I had with You before the world was." Yes, the Father will not give His glory to any man or idol images, but according to Colossians 1:15, Christ is the image of the invisible God, and according to Philippians 2:8-9 because Christ humbled Himself and became obedient to the point of death, even the death of the cross, "God also has highly exalted Him and given him the name which is above every name." The "Father and the Son receive the same worship."[12] Why? Because Jesus is God incarnate!

Jesus is receiving full acclaim by innumerable created beings! Yes, worthy is the Lamb who was slain to receive power, riches, wisdom, strength, honor, glory and blessing! When the worthiness of Jesus is acknowledged, it is not independent of His Father! According to Philippians 2:10, "At the name of Jesus every knee should bow, of those in heaven, and of those on earth, and of those under the earth, and that every tongue should confess that Jesus Christ is Lord, to the glory of God the Father.

To Christ belongs power, riches, wisdom, strength, honor, glory and blessing:

1. Power. God raised Christ from the dead and seated Him at His right hand in the heavenly places, "far above all principality and power and might and dominion, and every name that is named, not only in this age but also in that which is to come" (Ephesians 1:20-21).

2. Riches. "But God, being rich in mercy, because of His great love with which He loved us, even when we were dead in trespasses, made us alive together with Christ (by grace you have been saved), and raised us up together, and made us sit together in the heavenly places in Christ Jesus" (Ephesians 2:4-6).

3. Wisdom. "Oh, the depth of the riches both of the wisdom and knowledge of God! How unsearchable are His judgments and unfathomable His ways! For who has known the mind of the Lord? Or who has become His counselor? Or who has first given to Him and it shall be repaid to him?" (Romans 11:34-35).

4. Strength. "And He (Christ) said to me (Apostle Paul), 'My grace is sufficient for you, for My strength is made perfect in weakness.' Therefore, most gladly I will rather boast in my infirmities, that the power of Christ may rest upon me. Therefore, I take pleasure in infirmities, in reproaches, in needs, in persecutions, in distresses, for Christ's sake. For when I am weak, then I am strong" (II Corinthians 12:9-10).

5. Honor. "In the same way, Christ did not take on Himself the honor of becoming a high priest. But God gave Him the honor, saying to Him, 'You are My Son, today I have become Your Father ... You are a priest forever, in the order of Melchizedek'" (Hebrews 5:5-6).

6. Glory. "For of Him and through Him and to Him are all things, to whom be glory forever. Amen" (Romans 11:36).

7. Blessings. "I will bless the Lord at all times; His praise shall continually be in my mouth. My soul shall make its boast in the Lord; the humble shall hear of it and be glad. Oh, magnify the Lord with me, and let us exalt His name together" (Psalm 34:1-3).

What is the common thread? People are looking for signs, seeking after wisdom and debating to demonstrate their relevance and assert their authority. But God has made foolish the wisdom of this world. In fact, the "foolishness" of God is wiser than men, and the "weakness" of God is stronger than men. God has chosen the foolish things of the world to put to shame the wise and He has chosen the weak things of the world to put to shame the things which are mighty. He has chosen the despised and the empty-handed. He has chosen to humble those who exalt themselves. Wisdom, righteousness, redemption, justification and sanctification are all freely given to those who come to Christ so that they may glory not in themselves, but in Christ alone, to whom belongs all power, riches, wisdom, strength, honor, glory and blessings! (I Corinthians 1:20-31).

Global Worship; the Third Choir

5:13 And every creature which is in heaven and on the earth and under the earth and such as are in the sea, and all that are in them, I heard saying, "Blessing and honor and glory and power be to Him who sits on the throne, and to the Lamb, forever and ever!"

We now give ear to the third choir which comprises all of creation, in heaven, on earth, under the earth and in the sea, singing, "Blessing and honor and glory and power be to Him who sits on the throne, and to the Lamb, forever and ever!" The created, no matter who, what or where they are, worship the Creator. Since Christ is the object of worship, He is not created!

The psalmist proclaims in Psalm 148:1-13, "Praise the Lord! Praise the Lord from the heavens; praise Him in the heights! Praise Him, all His angels; praise Him, all His hosts! Praise Him, sun and moon; praise Him, all you stars of light! Praise Him you heavens of heavens, and you waters above the heavens! Let them praise the name of the Lord. For He commanded and they were created. He also established them forever and ever; He made a decree which shall not pass away. Praise the Lord from the earth, you great sea creatures and all the depths; fire and hail, snow and clouds; stormy wind, fulfilling His word; mountains and all hills; fruitful trees and all cedars; beasts and all cattle; creeping things and flying fowl; kings of the earth and all peoples; princes and all judges of the earth; both young men and maidens; old men and children. Let them praise the name of the Lord, for His name alone is exalted; His glory is above the earth and heaven."

The Lamb is about to break the seals and open the scroll. He has stood. Sitting is done. The time has come for the saints to witness the fulfillment of God's promises of redemption, justice, righteousness and vengeance. The redeemed will be rewarded. The mocking wicked will be confounded as they taste God's judgments. And all of His creation is singing! All of creation is worshiping the Father and the Son in unison. "Let the saints be joyful in glory; let them sing aloud on their beds. Let the high praises of God be in their mouth, and a two-edged sword in their hand, to execute vengeance on the nations, and punishments on the peoples; to bind their kings with chains, and their nobles with fetters of iron; to execute on them the written judgment — this honor have all His saints. Praise the Lord!" (Psalm 149:5-9). Seven years after the Tribulation, Armageddon will unfold, and Christ with all His saints shall descend from heaven upon the Mount of Olives and save Israel from the clutches of the Antichrist and save the world from the grip of Satan.

This is not some tradition made up of lethargic chanting, standing, sitting, kneeling, yawning and daydreaming! The party is on! Psalm 150:1-6 gives us a sense of the untainted sound, the untroubled movement, the jubilant vibe, the brilliant colors and the freedom in this anxiety free, pain free, accident free, divorce free, healthcare free, heartache free existence, "Praise the Lord! Praise God in His sanctuary; praise Him in His mighty firmament! Praise Him for His mighty acts; praise Him according to His excellent greatness! Praise Him with the sound of the trumpet; praise Him with the lute and harp! Praise Him with the timbrel and dance; praise Him with stringed instruments and flutes! Praise Him with loud cymbals; praise Him with clashing cymbals! Let everything that has breath praise the Lord. Praise the Lord!"

5:14 *Then the four living creatures said, "Amen!" And the twenty-four elders fell down and worshiped Him who lives forever and ever.*

The choir's voice of praise suddenly stops, and the cherubim burst forth with, "Amen!" In the Hebrew it means, "surely, verily, indeed and truly," from the root form "aman," signifying "to be firm, steady, trustworthy and faithful." The Levitical sacrifices transferred guilt from a sinful man to an unblemished animal, sin being imputed to the animal that was then slain. Christ, the unblemished Lamb of God, was our sacrificial substitute, and our sins were imputed to him (II Corinthians 5:21). Medication can make you better, more money can make you richer, more friends can make you happier, but only Jesus Christ can make your sins whiter than snow and give you life eternal! Amen!

The armies of heaven wholeheartedly embrace what they sing with all their hearts, minds and souls because the Father, the Son, the Holy Spirit and the declaration of their Word, was, is and will always be infallible, reliable and true. The four living creatures say, "Amen!" And everything stops. "There is something majestic in the silence of this phrase. Never will such music have been heard in the universe. Never will so many voices have intoned such mighty praise. The armies of armies come to the last note. The mightiest of God's creatures sound the amen. We gaze upon the scene with no voice for utterance and, prostate, we worship the Lord Jesus Christ who now proceeds to the most awful scenes of judgment with actions that are rooted in His cross."[13]

 Amen! Creation agrees and affirms God's faithfulness.
Amen! The saints praise the Lamb's worthiness.
Amen! The hosts declare God's steadfastness.
Amen! The angels endorse His prophecy with truthfulness.
Amen! So be it! Let it be thus!

REV IT UP & SUM IT UP – CHAPTER FIVE:

After the Rapture, the church will witness a transaction that will initiate the Apocalypse. The Father will hand His Son a tightly sealed scroll that has seven seals. The scroll not only contains the judgments of God on an unbelieving, Christ-rejecting world, but it also serves as the means for Christ to strip Satan of his rights over this earth.

At first John weeps because there is no one he can identify to take the scroll and break its seals. That would be tragic because Satan, the usurper, will otherwise continue his reign over the earth, inciting sickness, sin and death. Then John is told to look at the Lion of the Tribe of Judah, Jesus Christ. When John sees Christ, he does not see the Lion, but sees the Lamb who was slain for our sins. The obedient Lamb. The humble Lamb. The Passover Lamb. The Lamb of God. He is the only One who is worthy to take the scroll and open its seals.

There is a roaring celebration that ensues with a three-fold heavenly choir. Why? Because Christ will make all wrongs right! The church sings the first song, proclaiming that Christ is worthy to open the seals because He was slain, redeeming us with His blood. The angels join in and sing the second song, proclaiming that the slain Lamb is worthy to receive power, riches, wisdom, strength, honor, glory and blessing. All of God's creation joins in the third song, declaring that blessing, honor, glory and power belong to God and His Son, the Lamb of God, forever and ever. Amen! So be it! He is worthy of our praise!

Chapter 6
Tribulation Tremors

The time has come for the dreadful Tribulation. In this chapter we'll review six of the seven seals that Christ will unseal. Chaos, tragedy, wars, famine, death, sorrow and grieving will ensue. The death toll will be shocking. The pain people face will be overwhelming. The horrors will be devastating. How will mankind endure? How will mankind respond?

First Seal: The "Peaceful" Antichrist

6:1 Now I saw when the Lamb opened one of the seals; and I heard one of the four living creatures saying with a voice like thunder, "Come and see."

Below is a list of the seven seal judgments. We will cover them in succession:

First Seal: White horse, "peace" (6:1-2).
Second Seal: Red horse, war (6:3-4).
Third Seal: Black horse, famine (6:5-6).
Fourth Seal: Pale horse, death and pestilence (6:7-8).
Fifth Seal: Martyred saints cry from under altar (6:9-11).
Sixth Seal: earthquake; sun-moon-stars disrupted (6:12-17).
Seventh Seal: Seven trumpet judgments released (8:1-6).

We witnessed the chorus of praise to the Father in chapter

four and to the Son in chapter five. Here we see the Son, who took the scroll from His Father, open each seal, which releases a new judgment. Modern day terrors, horrors, injustices, hurricanes, tornadoes, earthquakes, tsunamis and volcanic eruptions will appear minuscule compared to the calamities mankind will experience during the Tribulation. How could God be in control when chaos reaches such new heights? When the Lamb initiates the cataclysmic events, it should be clear that God is in complete control of the judgments, pestilences, action of demons and even the exact time when the demons carry out their plans. We read in Isaiah 45:7 that God forms the light and creates darkness; He makes peace and creates calamity. Some call the events in the Tribulation cruel. I call it merciful. Why? Because God limits the time of the Tribulation and still allows mankind to repent and come to Him!

We will see the phrase "Come and see" spoken by one of the four living creatures when the first four seals are opened, summoning each horse and its horseman and allowing John to grasp the horrors to come. The first cherub or winged angel, the creature like a lion, speaks in a voice of thunder, indicating that what is to befall mankind will be disastrous.

This chapter is closely tied to Matthew 24, in what is known as the Olivet Discourse, where Jesus sat on the Mount of Olives and explained to His disciples about events that would take place during the end times before His Second Coming. Matthew 24 does not talk about the Rapture. The only time we have a record of Jesus speaking about the Rapture is in John 14:1-4, "Let not your heart be troubled; you believe in God, believe also in Me. In My Father's house are many mansions, if it were not so, I would have told you. I go to prepare a place for you. And if I go and prepare a place for you, I will come again and receive you to Myself, that where I am, there you may be also. And where I go you know, and the way you know."

We don't hear much more about the Rapture until the apostle Paul, who arrived on the scene after the resurrection of Christ, calls it a "mystery" and reveals to us what it is! In I Corinthians 15:51-52, Paul writes, "Behold, I tell you a mystery; we shall not all sleep, but we shall all be changed — in a moment, in the twinkling of an eye, at the last trumpet. For the trumpet will sound, and the dead will be raised incorruptible, and we shall be changed." In our reading, the Rapture already occurred in Revelation 4:1, when John heard a voice like a trumpet speaking to him, saying, "Come up here." As in Matthew 24, our text in Revelation chapter six does not talk of the Rapture, but of the Tribulation and the Second Coming of Christ.

6:2 *And I looked, and behold, a white horse. He who sat on it had a bow; and a crown was given to him, and he went out conquering and to conquer.*

In Matthew 24:4-5, Jesus said to His disciples, "Take heed that no one deceives you. For many will come in My name, saying, 'I am the Christ,' and will deceive many." This correlates with Revelation 6:2, "And I looked, and behold, a white horse. He who sat on it had a bow; and a crown was given to him, and he went out conquering and to conquer." Many believe that the man on the horse is Jesus Christ. That is not the case. The man on this white horse is Antichrist, Satan's "son", tool and pawn. The Lamb just opened the seal; nothing more. "It violates all logic for the same person to be opening the seal and sending himself forth."[1] "The Antichrist is seen riding a white war-horse, and with bow in hand, but with no arrow fitted to it. The symbol suggests bloodless victories."[2] Initially, the Antichrist's government will be established without the need for warfare. His ultimate goal is world domination and his "peace" is short-lived. It is worth repeating. The Lamb of God is in absolute control and the Antichrist is allowed to appear on the scene only after the Lamb opens the first seal.

The fact that the Antichrist rides this horse should not surprise us because we read about the character of Satan in II Corinthians 11:14. He "transforms himself into an angel of light." Satan, the great Dragon, the serpent of old, called the Devil, "deceives the whole world" (Revelation 12:9). We will see Jesus coming down with a white horse for His Second Coming (Revelation 19:11). So, what does Satan do? He fabricates. He devises a plan to deceive the whole world. To the masses, he looks like the real deal, the "Messiah," the economic and political savior of the world. "Although there will be numerous false messiahs down through history, none as convincing and successful as this final figure."[3]

According to II Thessalonians 2:6-7, "And now you know what is restraining, that he (the Antichrist) may be revealed in his own time. For the mystery of lawlessness is already at work; only He (Holy Spirit) who now restrains will do so until He is taken out of the way." When believers are Raptured to heaven, the Holy Spirit leaves as well. Only when the Holy Spirit is removed will the Antichrist be revealed. Mayhem will devastate the globe. Millions of believers will have disappeared from the earth. What will Satan do? He will have the Antichrist ready, to come as a "peacemaker," riding a white horse. In his heart, however, he is a man of war, a murderer and the father of lies; he comes to steal, kill and destroy (John 10:10).

In Daniel 8:23-25, we read "And in the latter time of their kingdom, when the transgressors have reached their fullness, a king (Antichrist) shall arise, having fierce features, who understands sinister schemes. His power shall be mighty, but not by his own power (he is controlled by Satan); he shall destroy fearfully (he is the conqueror of human souls, riding the white horse) and shall prosper and thrive; he shall destroy the mighty (dominions), and the holy people (those who turn to Christ during the Tribulation). Through his cunning (eloquently speaks of peace but skillfully initiates wars), he shall cause deceit to prosper under his rule. And he shall exalt himself in his heart (like his father Satan). He shall destroy many in their prosperity. He shall even rise against the Prince of princes (Jesus Christ); but he shall be broken without human means (God will destroy him)."

The Antichrist will accomplish what in the past seemed impossible: a peace treaty between Israel and the Arab nations as is spoken of in Daniel 9:27, "he (Antichrist) shall confirm a covenant with many for one week (seven years)." But we must remember, Satan, the Antichrist, the False Prophet and all of hell's demons cannot act without God's permission. Each seal will reveal a new judgment, none "arise from chance, but are all under Divine control. The great False Messiah of the first Seal cannot be revealed until the appointed moment shall have come and the voice from the throne gives the permissive command, 'Go!' The judgments cannot fall until the same command is given."[4]

The Antichrist will deceive many as a man of peace as we'll see in the next paragraph. "The coming of the lawless one (Antichrist) is according to the working of Satan, with all power, signs, and lying wonders, and with all unrighteous deception among those who perish, because they did not receive the love of the truth, that they might be saved" (II Thessalonians 2:9-10). Satan will use the Antichrist to deceive mankind with miraculous signs. When people reject the truth, Jesus Christ, they are deceived into embracing any lie, and in this case, the ultimate lie, Satan.

After the Rapture, the Antichrist will appear on the scene, "comforting" people's hearts and minds with his message of peace at the beginning of a perilous time of chaos, unrest, confusion, socio-economic collapse and emotional breakdown.

1. He will deceive the Jews into believing that he is the world's greatest political leader and diplomat and he will guarantee peace in the Middle East. How will they be deceived? They did not believe the Way, the Truth and the Life, Jesus Christ; so, they will believe the father of iniquity, the father of lies, and the father of death, Satan and his unholy trinity.

Jesus prophesied this in John 5:43, "I have come in My Father's name, and you do not receive Me; if another comes in his own name (Antichrist), him you will receive." According to Daniel 8:23, "A king shall arise, having fierce features, who understands sinister schemes." That king is the Antichrist. He will scheme, inspire, charm and win the hearts of mankind.

2. He will manipulate the minds of international leaders into submitting to his universal dictatorship. "Authority was given to him over every tribe, tongue and nation" according to Revelation 13:7. "His military exploits will not be confined to a corner but carried out on a vast scale. He is spoken of as the man who will 'shake kingdoms' and 'make the earth to tremble'" (Isaiah 14:16).[5] According to Daniel 8:24, "he shall destroy fearfully ... he shall destroy the mighty."

3. He will gather the Arab and the Jewish leaders under one roof and convince them of a peaceful co-existence. We see this in Daniel 9:27, where the Antichrist shall prevail and ratify a treaty with many for one week (seven years).

4. He will pave the way for the Jews to build their third temple on the Temple Mount in Jerusalem. The first temple was built by Solomon and destroyed by Babylon in 586 BC. The second was built in 516 BC and destroyed by Rome in 70 AD. The third will be built during the first part of the Tribulation. How do we know? We rely on three verses:

    a. Daniel 9:27, where the Antichrist will stop the temple sacrifices of the temple in the middle of the Tribulation. If he stops the sacrifices of the temple, there must be a temple.

    b. II Thessalonians 2:3-4, where the Antichrist

will enter the temple and desecrate it, again at the middle of the Tribulation. If he enters the temple, there must be a temple.

  c. Revelation 11:1-2, where John is told to measure the third temple. If John is measuring the dimensions of the temple, there must be a literal temple!

How will the Antichrist convince two diabolically opposed religions, cultures, peoples, beliefs, traditions, ways of life and ways of thinking to sign a treaty of peace, which will allow Israel to build its third temple? Perhaps he is so convincing that his speech mesmerizes each group at the negotiating table. Perhaps he will convince the Arabs to concede, secretly keep their mouths shut, and trust him to break the covenant, annihilating the nation of Israel and allowing the Arabs then to move in and possess their land. Perhaps the world, which desperately seeks a savior, will convince themselves that this man is their only hope.

5. He will confirm a treaty that will convince the Jews that they now enjoy in such a confident state, that they will tear down the physical walls that protect them, a "land of unwalled villages, a peaceful people, who dwell safely, all of them dwelling without walls, and having neither bars nor gates" (Ezekiel 38:11). If you've been to Israel and Jerusalem, you will realize that walls and gates certainly exist, and peace and safety with their surrounding neighbors are but fanciful wishes and, at this moment, an impossibility.

6. He will, as we'll see in the middle of the Tribulation, break this covenant, put an end to temple worship, and declare himself to be God by standing on the Temple Mount and declaring that he is the rightful

ruler of the universe. Daniel 9:27, "Then he (Anti-christ) shall confirm a covenant with many for one week; but in the middle of the week he shall bring an end to sacrifice and offering. And on the wing of abominations shall be one who makes desolate." The week Daniel speaks of equals seven years. The middle of the week means three and a half years. When the first three and a half years have concluded, Satan will commit the abomination of desolation. We see the arrogance of Satan in Revelation 13:5, "And he was given a mouth speaking great things and blasphemies, and he was given authority to continue for forty-two months (three and a half years)."

Matthew 24:15 correlates with these verses, stating that you shall "see the 'abomination of desolation,' spoken of by Daniel the prophet, standing in the holy place." We also read about the abomination in II Thessalonians 2:3-4, "The man of sin (Antichrist) is revealed, the son of perdition, who opposes and exalts himself above all that is called God or that is worshiped, so that he sits as God in the temple of God, showing himself that he is God." The Antichrist is blasphemous, bearing the character of wretchedness.

Why would God even allow the Antichrist to rule even for a short time?

1. For the punishment of Israel. This is not an anti-Semitic comment. This is Biblical prophecy by Daniel and Jeremiah. "It shall be for a time (one year), times (two years), and half a time (half a year; the Great Tribulation, the time of Jacob's Trouble, will be three and a half years, the second half of the Tribulation); and when the power of the holy people (Jews) has been completely shattered, all these

things shall be finished" (Daniel 12:7). "Alas! For that day is great, so that none is like it; and it is the time of Jacob's Trouble, but he shall be saved out of it" (Jeremiah 30:7). One of the key reasons for the Tribulation is to bring Israel back to God. Tragically, millions of Jews, along with billions of Gentiles, will die with an unrepentant heart during this time.

2. For the repentance of Israel. After the Abomination of Desolation, the Jews will finally realize that the Antichrist is not the Messiah. The Great Tribulation will begin, and the Jews will take shelter in Petra, an ancient city in Jordan approximately 80 miles south of Jerusalem, where God will protect them for three and a half years. We'll study this further in chapter twelve. Revelation 12:14 recaps the exodus, "But the woman (Israel) was given two wings of a great eagle, that she might fly into the wilderness to her place, where she is nourished for a time and times and half a time, from the presence of the serpent." According to Zechariah 12:10, the remnant Jews will turn to Christ at the end of the Great Tribulation, "And I will pour on the house of David and on the inhabitants of Jerusalem the Spirit of grace and supplication; then they will look on Me (Christ) whom they pierced. Yes, they will mourn for Him (Christ) as one mourns for his only son, and grieve for Him as one grieves for a firstborn."

3. For the judgment of the world. If one rejects God, he by default not only accepts Satan, but also will give Satan the rights to his soul. Not fair? It's about choices! It's a "yes" or "no" "vote" for God, the ambivalent and apathetic defaulting to a "no" status. Choose this day whom you will serve! (Joshua 24:15). Jesus spoke of this in Matthew 24:21-22, "For then there will be great tribulation, such as has not been since the beginning of the world until this time, no, nor ever shall be. And unless those days were shortened, no flesh would be saved; but for the elect's sake those days will be shortened."

4. For the exposure of the world's unbelief. Millions of believers will have been Raptured. Billions of people will die of wars and plagues during the Tribulation. And how will mankind respond? "But the rest of mankind, who were not killed by these plagues, did not repent of the works of their hands, that they should not worship demons, and idols of gold, silver, brass, stone, and wood, which can neither see nor hear nor walk. And they did not repent of their murders or their sorceries or their sexual immorality or their thefts" (Revelation 9: 20-21).

5. For the provocation of the final showdown between Christ and Satan's forces and the defeat of his forces. After the Campaign of Armageddon, the Antichrist and the False Prophet will be cast into the Lake of Fire. After the Millennium, Satan will be cast into the Lake of Fire, along with billions of unbelievers that will resurrect from Hades, be transported to the Great White Throne judgment, then cast into the Lake of Fire. (Revelation 19:20; 20:10-15).[6]

The false peace treaty forged by the Antichrist will launch what we know of as Ezekiel's Gog and Magog war which we'll see when the second seal is opened. While peace is being preached and people are being deceived, sudden destruction is on the horizon (I Thessalonians 5:3). Will the peace treaty work? Only for a short time. People will hunger for peace during the Tribulation, and their frantic desire for an answer in the midst of escalating human suffering will lead them right into Satan's trap, tragically believing that the Antichrist is the way, the truth and the giver of hope and life.

We'll be introduced to the four horsemen in this chapter. As we've just seen, the first horseman, riding on a white horse, is allowed to rule the earth with deceit by introducing peace and safety through his treaty. The second horseman is allowed to take away peace and cause war. The third horseman is allowed to cause a worldwide famine. The fourth horseman, along with Death and Hades, is allowed to kill one fourth of the earth's population. "All of these horrific and terrible realities — the very manifestation and flowering of sin of which God is no author — are harnessed for His purposes. The troubling and yet comforting reality is that there is no creature which ultimately does not serve God's purpose, either willingly or unwillingly. Troubling, because in the inscrutable purpose of God such evil is allowed to continue. Comforting, because everything we suffer is subject to God's approval and purpose."[7]

Second Seal: The Swordsman

6:3 When He opened the second seal, I heard the second living creature saying, "Come and see."

Below is a list of the seven seal judgments. We will now discuss the second seal.

First Seal: White horse, "peace" (6:1-2).
Second Seal: Red horse, war (6:3-4).
Third Seal: Black horse, famine (6:5-6).
Fourth Seal: Pale horse, death and pestilence (6:7-8).
Fifth Seal: Martyred saints cry from under altar (6:9-11).
Sixth Seal: earthquake; sun-moon-stars disrupted (6:12-17).
Seventh Seal: Seven trumpet judgments released (8:1-6).

As Christ opens the second seal, the second living creature, one like a calf, says, "Come and see," summoning the second horse and horseman and inviting John to grasp what shall come after the transient "peace" experienced by mankind at the beginning of the Tribulation. It is important to understand that the seals are not being opened simultaneously, but subsequently to one another. It is also critical to remember who is opening the seals, the only One worthy, the Lamb of God, the Lion of the tribe of Judah, the loving Messiah.

6:4 Another horse, fiery red, went out. And it was granted to the one who sat on it to take peace from the earth, and that people should kill one another; and there was given to him a great sword.

In Matthew 24:4-6, Jesus said to His disciples, "Take heed that no one deceives you. For many will come in My name, saying, 'I am the Christ,' and will deceive many. And you will hear of wars and rumors of wars. See that you are not troubled, for all these things must come to pass, but the end is not yet." This reference about wars correlates with Revelation 6:3-4, where the second living creature shows John that "Another horse, fiery red, went out. And it was granted to the one who sat on it to take peace from the earth, and that people should kill one another; and there was given to him a great sword." After "peace," there will be wars and one in particular, the Gog and Magog War, that will shake the world into realizing that God is truly Lord (Ezekiel 38:23).

Many believe that the war mentioned in Ezekiel 38-39 is the war of Armageddon. That is incorrect. The events of Ezekiel 38-39, along with Psalm 83 and Daniel 11:40 occur soon after the Rapture. After the Antichrist deceives Israel, and has the Jews believing that they can finally "dwell safely," a nation "dwelling without walls" as noted in Ezekiel 38:8, he influences specific nations to attack Israel.

The Antichrist will lure its leader, Gog, from the land of Magog, which is modern day Russia. Due to a vacuum left in the Middle East by America from 2008 to 2016, Russia befriended and worked alongside Arab nations, an alliance once impossible to envision. But God had already prophesied it 2,500 years ago. All nations will serve His purpose! After the Rapture, Gog, the Russian president, will lead a specific coalition of nations to attack Israel.

Gog will gather "Meshech, Tubal, Gomer and Togarmah" (Ezekiel 38:2, 6) which altogether comprise modern day Turkey (West, East, North, and South Turkey respectively). Gog will also draw Persia (Iran), Cush (Ethiopia, Sudan, Somalia), and Put (Libya)

into the coalition. According to Psalm 83:1-6, joining them will also be the Edomites (southwestern
Jordan) and the Ishmaelites (Saudi Arabia) and Tyre
(Lebanon). And according to Daniel 11:40, the king
of the North (north of Israel is Syria) and the king of
the South (south of Israel is Egypt) will also join.

The Euphrates River starts in Turkey and has 21
dams; the Euphrates flows southeast into Syria and
then southeast into Iraq (Babylon). The Tigris River
also starts in Turkey and heads southeast into Iraq.
Both rivers run parallel throughout the land of Iraq
(Tigris runs through the capital city Baghdad), join
at the southeast border of Iraq, and after running
through the city of Al Basrah, spill into the Persian
Gulf. The Euphrates supplies at least one third of the
water supply to Syria. According to the Assyrian International News Agency, author Daniel Pipes writes
that Turkey stopped the water supply into Syria in
2014, made possible by the large reservoir behind
its Ataturk Dam.[8] If left unchecked, this would have
affected millions of lives in Syria and well as Iraq.
Turkey has water. Other nations have oil. Turkey will
get its oil via squeezing, threatening, and blackmail-
ing its neighbors, and will not stand unnoticed.

Russia and Iran have now secured the airways in Syria.
Russia and Iran not only support Syria but have their
army, navy and air force controlling the land of Syria
(including the border just north of the Golan Heights
of Israel)! Russia arms Iran with nuclear weapons.
Iran arms Hezbollah (ruling Lebanon, also north of
Israel) with their weapons of terror.

Russia, Iran and Syria have already formed an "unholy
alliance" and will, along with Turkey, attack Israel in
the first six months of the Tribulation. You may choose

to ignore the facts, but you will come face to face with the truth one day. I pray it will not be too late for you because if you stay on earth for the Tribulation, you will experience hell on earth. If you can't handle the heat and humidity in the summer, or the traffic jam on the freeways, or find yourself traumatized by the Coronavirus Pandemic and the pandemonium of 2020, you won't be able to handle the Tribulation! The day of salvation is today!

How do we know the Gog and Magog War occurs right after the Rapture? Because it will be a time of peace, Israel will have believed a lie, their walls will be taken down and gates will not exist, their minds will be at ease, and their arms will have been laid down (Ezekiel 38:8, 11, 14). This cannot be before the Rapture; the walls are still up today and will remain that way until the Tribulation. This cannot refer to the Campaign of Armageddon because at that time the land will no longer be at peace.

God will put hooks into Gog's jaws (the Russian leader), and lead him out, with all his army, "horses and horse-men, all splendidly clothed, a great company with bucklers and shields, all of them handling swords ... Out of the far north, you (Russia) and many peoples with you (Iran, Syria and all above mentioned nations), all of them riding on horses, a great company and mighty army, will come up against My people Israel like a cloud to cover the land" (Ezekiel 38:4, 15-16). Some scoff at the notion of horses when we're living in a nuclear age. Since everything today is controlled and monitored by computers, cyberattacks will likely force an era of new fighting, with an ancient twist, horses!

According to Ezekiel 38:18-23, this campaign will be singlehandedly contested and spoiled by God. "And it will come to pass at the same time, when Gog comes against the land of Israel,' says the Lord God, 'that My fury will show in My face. For in My jealousy and in the fire of My wrath I have spoken: surely in the day there shall be a great earthquake in the land of Israel, so that the fish of the sea, the birds of the heavens, the beasts of the field, all creeping things that creep on the earth, and all men who are on the face of the earth shall shake at My presence. The mountains shall be thrown down, the steep places shall fall, and every wall shall fall to the ground. I will call for a sword against Gog throughout all My mountains,' says the Lord God. 'Every man's sword will be against his brother. And I will bring him to judgment with pestilence, and bloodshed I will rain down on him, on his troops, and on the many peoples who are with him, flooding rain, great hailstones, fire and brimstone. Thus, I will magnify Myself and sanctify Myself, and I will be known in the eyes of many nations. Then they shall know that I am the Lord.'"

Satan, represented by the fiery red dragon in Revelation 12:3, will have his pawn, the Antichrist, ride on a red horse in Revelation 6:4. Red depicts his true color, for he is fueled with rage, blood and war. He is not the catalyst for peace! Though it is actually Satan through the Antichrist who leads the coalition by riding on a red horse, it is God who "grants to the one who sat on it to take peace from the earth" (Revelation 6:4), and it is God who puts "hooks into your (Russia's leader) jaws, and leads you out, with all your army horses." But the coalition of diverse nations will turn on each other and slaughter each other! They have come to loot, but instead, they will not only kill the people of the same team, but they will also be privy to priceless knowledge: God is God! He always has been; He always will be!

Let's evaluate Israel's history:

1. How did Israel survive Pharaoh? Fast pass tickets through the Red Sea, courtesy of God.

2. How did Israel survive the forty years of wilderness? The cloud by day and the fire by night, God's enduring presence; and daily heavenly manna. (Numbers 14:14; Exodus 16:15).

3. How did Gideon and three hundred men defeat the Midianites, who were "as numerous as locusts?" The three hundred blew their trumpets and the Lord set the enemies' swords against each other. (Judges 7:1-25).

4. How did King Jehoshaphat defeat the Moabites and the Ammonites descending upon Jews from Syria for a massacre? By seeking the Lord. By praying and fasting. By singing, "Give thanks to the Lord for He is good, His love endures forever!" (II Chronicles 20:1-30). A simple song? No, a song of praise that stirs the Lord of Lords!

5. How did Israel survive the Babylonian exile in 586 BC? A miracle orchestrated by God seventy years later through the ungodly King Cyrus! "Thus says the Lord, the Redeemer, of Cyrus, 'He is My shepherd, and he shall perform all My pleasure,' saying to Jerusalem, 'You shall be built,' and to the temple, 'Your foundation shall be laid'" (Isaiah 44:28).

6. How did Israel survive 2,000 years of extinction after the Roman conquest of Jerusalem in AD 70? An incomprehensible miracle! "Who has heard of such a thing? Who has seen such things? Shall the earth be made to give birth in one day? Or shall a nation be born at once? For as soon as Zion was in labor, she gave birth to her children" (Isaiah 66:8).

7. How did Israel become a nation on May 14, 1948?

Not only by a stamp of approval by President Harry Truman, legitimizing its existence to the world, but more importantly, God's hands ushering in a prophecy. "Behold, I will bring them from the north country, and gather them from the ends of the earth, among them the blind and the lame, the woman with child and the one who labors with child together; a great throng shall return there" (Jeremiah 31:8).

8. How did Israel survive the Six Day War of 1967? They were outnumbered three to one! God's hand of intercession.

9. How did Israel survive the Yom Kippur War of 1973? Not only by President Richard Nixon's intervention to combat an Arab attack that was backed by the Soviet Union, but more importantly, God's mercy. A miracle!

10. How will Israel survive the Ezekiel 38 battle after the Rapture? I'm glad you asked! Here is the answer … "'And it will come to pass at the same time, when Gog (Russia's leader) comes against the land of Israel,' says the Lord God, 'That My fury will show in My face … 'Every man's sword will be against his brother (Israel's enemies will attack each other rather than attacking Israel). And I will bring him (Gog) to judgment with pestilence and bloodshed; I will rain down on him, on his troops and on the many peoples who are with him (Gog's allies), flooding rain, great hailstones, fire, and brimstone. Thus, I will magnify Myself and sanctify Myself, and I will be known in the eyes of many nations. Then they shall know that I am the Lord'" (Ezekiel 38:18-23).

"And you, son of man (Ezekiel), prophesy against Gog, and say, 'Thus says the Lord God: Behold, I am

against you, O Gog, the prince of Rosh, Meshech, and
Tubal; and I will turn you around and lead you on,
bringing you up from the far north (Moscow, Russia),
and bring you against the mountain of Israel (and
leave but the sixth part of thee — stated in the King
James Version) ... Then those who dwell in the cities of
Israel will go out and set on fire and burn the weapons,
the shields and bucklers, the bows and arrows, the
javelins and spears; and they will make fires with them
for seven years (the seven years further substantiates
that the Gog and Magog war occurs at the beginning
of the seven-year Tribulation) ... For seven months
the house of Israel will be burying them (Gog and all
his dead allies), in order to cleanse the land. Indeed,
all the people of the land will be burying, and they will
gain renown for it on the day that I am glorified,' says
the Lord God" (Ezekiel 39:1-13).

How do five-sixths of Russia and its allies vanish
with only one-sixth remaining at the end of the Gog
and Magog war, and how does Israel survive? In short,
solely by God's righteous right hand. Miracle upon
miracles!

Do not be deceived. Satan is causing all these ills, but
he is not in control; he is under God's jurisdiction.
God states in Isaiah 46:11, "Indeed I have spoken it;
I will also bring it to pass. I have purposed it; I will
also do it." There is no doubt. There is no hesitation.
When God speaks, it will unfold. It will happen!

Third Seal: Black Famine

*6:5 When He opened the third seal, I heard the third living
creature say, "Come and see." So I looked, and behold, a black
horse, and he who sat on it had a pair of scales in his hand.*

Below is a list of seven seal judgments. We will now discuss the third seal.

First Seal: White horse, "peace" (6:1-2).
Second Seal: Red horse, war (6:3-4).
Third Seal: Black horse, famine (6:5-6).
Fourth Seal: Pale horse, death and pestilence (6:7-8).
Fifth Seal: Martyred saints cry from under altar (6:9-11).
Sixth Seal: earthquake; sun-moon-stars disrupted (6:12-17).
Seventh Seal: Seven trumpet judgments released (8:1-6).

As Christ opens the third seal, the third living creature, one who has the face of a man, says, "Come and see," summoning the black horse and its rider and inviting John to grasp what will occur after the second seal's bloodbath.

The third seal is presented with a black horse and a pair of scales. When Satan committed spiritual suicide, pridefully attempting to be worshiped instead of worshiping God, he who was Lucifer, the light bearer, became evil and represented sin and darkness. Black represents evil, mourning, sorrow, lamentation, affliction, calamity, judgment and famine. Sorcery, mediums and astrology are three practices known as "black magic." In our text, the black horse will deliver the "gift" of famine, represented by a pair of scales, used to weigh food, indicating that this will be a terrible time of scarcity.

The color black is associated with famine according to Lamentations 4:8-9, "Now their (Judah who is exiled by the Babylonians in 586 BC) appearance is blacker than soot; they go unrecognized in the streets; their skin clings to their bones, it has become as dry as wood. Those slain by the sword are better off than those who die of hunger; for these (people) pine away stricken for lack of the fruits of the field." During the Tribulation, food for most people will be scarce and prices outrageously high. Also during the second half of the Tribulation, the Antichrist will unveil the 666 mark, and no one will be able to buy or sell without the mark.

6:6 *And I heard a voice in the midst of the four living creatures saying, "A quart of wheat for a denarius, and three quarts of barley for a denarius; and do not harm the oil and the wine."*

In Matthew 24:7-8, Jesus said to His disciples, "For nation will rise against nation, and kingdom against kingdom. And there will be famines, pestilences, and earthquakes in various places. All these are the beginning of sorrows." This reference about famines correlates with Revelation 6:5-6, the black horse and the pair of scales.

A denarius was a workman's average daily wage, worth approximately 15 cents. The fact that they will work all day for only a quart of wheat or three quarts of barley depicts that people will barely have enough to survive on only a small portion of bread. Usually, sixteen to twenty measures were purchased with one denarius.[9] Bread, considered a bare necessity in our days, will become a luxury during the Tribulation. Not only will people succumb to death by the sword, but also by starving.

Though a common supply of bread will be hard to come by, luxury items such as oil and wine will be available for the rich class. Despite suffering for the poor, there will be the rich who will live in abundance and indulgence. The availability of wine, however, should not minimize the crippling worldwide famine that will crush the poor.

The distinction between the rich, the middle class and the poor will be amplified in the Tribulation. How so? Socialism is a deception that fools the masses into thinking all aspects of their lives will be fair and equal compared to their neighbors'; on the contrary, it gives the politicians, or the establishment in power, more muscle, more money, more privileges and more leeway for engaging in corruption while denying the masses their freedoms. It is a true distribution of wealth from the common people to the pockets of those who are the governing parties. The media strongly supports the establishment and caters to them by speaking their "truth," stigmatizing, demonizing and ostracizing those who do not follow their gospel, their policies and their mandates.

Socialism is a dead-end street that produces hunger, frustration, poverty, long lines and poor health care; it is a system where politicians manage the wealth of a country, rationing healthcare, regulating food supply, restricting individual success, restraining free speech and retarding innovation. The establishment offers everything for free ... in exchange for your freedom. If you are unsure of this fact, just ask Venezuelan citizens about their great social experiment that brought a wealthy nation down to its knees in 2019.

Socialism proposes that what we know now is all we need to know to plan for the future. It is not based on science, but on a doctrine, dogma and ideology. It is not a creation of ideas but a redistribution of wealth, killing steady progress and stifling the surprise of creating fresh ideas, new technologies and brilliant innovations. The very idea of Socialism was not crafted by heaven's hands. Why would I say that? Because Satan is here to steal, kill and destroy (John 10:10). Stealing from those who work and giving to those who largely don't care to work constitutes the backbone of Socialism; its very intention is to control the people being governed: regulating or stealing their speech, their actions, their healthcare and their lives. I am a firm believer in helping the needy who are unable to support themselves, but that is not Socialism. Helping those who are unable is called compassion!

What used to be a small spark of Socialism in economic and political ideology is now catching ablaze in the

United States of America. The explanation is simple. It is preparing the minds and souls of people to accept a Socialist/Globalist/One-World-Government/New-World-Order. How will the establishment finally achieve it? First, proponents will erroneously point to Scandinavian countries as Socialist states but will fail to tell us that they function as a free market economy. Second, a tragic pandemic or disruption may snare the world to unite. Finally, the great lure will likely be "global warming" or its new designation, "climate change," so that we may save the earth. One can be wrong with the term "global warming," but one can never go wrong with the term "climate change" because the climate always changes; in fact, it has done so for thousands of years!

Climate change is the greatest unscientific scam that will ultimately convince the United States of America to become Socialist as the world unites in the name of "saving" itself. China and India, not the United States of America, are two of the greatest culprits in polluting our earth, but the establishment wants to school us, conform us and ultimately force us to embrace their philosophy or face the consequences; their passion is not to save the world; they couldn't care less about you and me; their goal is to gain power over the minds, the monies and the lives of mankind. Though its proponents don't say it, they disdain the Creator but embrace the created. The timing of their agenda is impeccable. The coming of the Lord is so near and the appearance of the Antichrist is dawning. The Lord will take His bride, the church, home while the Antichrist will gather his children under his Socialist/Globalist/One-World-Government/New-World-Order. One thing is for sure: there will literally be global warming like never recorded when the fourth bowl is poured out on the earth at the tail end of the Tribulation, and mankind will be scorched with the sun's great heat (Revelation 16:8-9).

The New-World-Order proponents have hijacked the media and educational system; the innocent minds of children in elementary schools in America are being programed with anti-God and anti-country rhetoric. Preachers are already being told what they are allowed to preach. Social media companies are censoring and banning conservative views and justifying their actions by calling the moderate voices "hate speech." Any opposing debates are being banned by identity politics and cyberbullying. College campuses boast students who vehemently oppose views other than their own distorted opinions. Drugs that were once illegal are now legal and flow in the bloodstreams of the rich and poor, clouding the minds of their users. Legalized abortion and assisted suicide are ironically celebrated as choice, without consideration for the sanctity of life.

 Look and listen closely. Anarchy is not only rising steadily, but it is churning expeditiously.

Warning: The rhetoric against Christ-followers in the United States of America will escalate in this decade and this strong opposition against Christ-followers will ultimately turn into persecution. Even before the Rapture, you will witness the hatred, intolerance, bashing, censoring, imprisoning and slaying of Christ-followers escalate across the globe. Being a Christian in the United States of America will likely become a crime. Why? Because Christ-followers preach the love of Christ, who is the only Way to God, and the establishment's thinking deems that to be narrow-minded speech which is dangerous and hateful. This is not a conspiracy theory. This is reality. If you think it's bad now, you'll be shocked by the future cruelty; it will be exponentially worse in the Tribulation with be-headings of Christ-followers (Revelation 20:4). You can attempt to fight the establishment but once they control all the branches of the government, the rules of our land will change, our sacred Constitution will be trashed, and many will bow down to the establish-ment's religion of conformity.

I do believe that God will allow a certain time of reprieve for us to return to His Word and place our trust in Him, but once the establishment has its way, Socialism in the United States of America will be the rule of the land. Socialism will hand the ball off to Globalism and the New-World-Order. It is inevitable. It is gut-wrenching. It is heartbreaking. A leader will arise who does not believe in people achieving, excel-ling and creating, attempting to equalize all citizens while exempting the elite and politicians. The United States of America will then find it easy to reduce its military power. It will ban Christ-followers from speaking, sharing, and proclaiming the beautiful Gos-pel. Its leaders will become anti-Israel. After the Rap-ture, when the believers leave for heaven, the United States of America will crumble as Europe rises; Amer-ica will become a second-rate nation and submit to the Antichrist's Socialist/Globalist/One-World-Govern-ment/New-World-Order.

When the Rapture occurs, Satan will not have to strong arm our government; the sovereignty of America will be broken by the establishment and people will blindly follow the status quo because it is the "moral" way of existing; those who subscribe to any other system will be labeled as people who are a threat, filled with hate-speech and a detriment to the Antichrist's utopia. Those who do not follow the politically correct belief will be martyred because they will be an enemy of the state.

It is worth noting that after President Woodrow Wilson, many of our presidents from both parties have embraced the New-World-Order. Sadly, it is unknown whether the pawns of Socialism even know what they are doing, that is, ushering in the Antichrist's Socialist/Globalist/One-World-Government/New-World-Order. If any leader attempts to resist the New-World-Order, snubbing the new regime, he will be opposed and taken out. There will finally be a One-World-Government, the Babylonian system, which we'll read about in chapters 17 and 18, that will rule for only a short span of seven years and will be destroyed by Jesus Christ in His Second Coming.

You can play the Game of Thrones all you want to. Who will fall and who will stand? No intellect, no power, no charm, no force, no scheme, no propaganda and no leader will be able to withstand the Lion and the Lamb. Let all the world leaders read and understand: the last throne standing will be that of Christ's, ruling with His righteous right hand!

Again, despite a One-World-Government, there will still be a distinction between social classes in the Tribulation according to Revelation 6:6. Luxurious products will belong to the rich, and poorer quality products will belong to the common. Interestingly, as we'll read in Revelation 18:13, oil and wine are listed among the commercial wealth of Babylon when she is destroyed.

To most people's utter surprise, Socialism/Globalism does not exist in heaven or hell! Every man whose name is written in the Book of Life will be rewarded "according to his work" (Revelation 22:12). The rewards one receives in heaven determine his status for Eternity! "And the dead (the unbelieving, unrighteous and self-righteous standing before the Great White Throne) were judged according to their works, by the things which were written in the books … and they were judged, each one according to his works" (Revelation 20:12-13). Hell, as well, will boast its own hierarchy; not as in who rules, but as in who experiences different degrees of torment!

Fourth Seal: Death Upon Death

6:7 *When He opened the fourth seal, I heard the voice of the fourth living creature saying, "Come and see."*

Below is a list of the seven seal judgments. We will now discuss the fourth seal.

First Seal: White horse, "peace" (6:1-2).
Second Seal: Red horse, war (6:3-4).
Third Seal: Black horse, famine (6:5-6).
Fourth Seal: Pale horse, death and pestilence (6:7-8).
Fifth Seal: Martyred saints cry from under altar (6:9-11).
Sixth Seal: earthquake; sun-moon-stars disrupted (6:12-17).
Seventh Seal: Seven trumpet judgments released (8:1-6).

As Christ opens the fourth seal, the fourth living creature, one who is like a flying eagle, says, "Come and see," summoning the fourth horse and its horseman, and showing John the tragic consequences of famine. Peace led to war. War led to famine. We'll now see that famine triggers the fourth horseman, who brings the cold tidings of worldwide death. As God "Revs It Up," the world's population endures greater hardships and its strength continues to diminish.

6:8 *So I looked, and behold, a pale horse. And the name of him who sat on it was Death, and Hades followed with him. And power was given to them over a fourth of the earth, to kill with sword, with hunger, with death, and by the beasts of the earth.*

In Matthew 24:7-8, Jesus said to His disciples, "For nation will rise against nation, and kingdom against kingdom. And there will be famines, pestilences, and earthquakes in various places. All these are the beginning of sorrows." The Pestilences of Matthew 24:7-8 correlates with the horrific conditions described in Revelation 6:8. The word "pale" is "chloros" in the Greek, denoting a green-yellowish-pale color, having the appearance of sickness and death.

In my cardiology world, there is a condition called vasovagal syncope, which means that someone faints when faced with a traumatic event (such as a blood draw) or sustaining an injury (such as fracturing a bone). When this occurs, an abundance of adrenalin is poured out into one's blood stream. The regulatory part of the body detects the overabundance of adrenalin and activates the vagus nerve found in the neck to secrete a calming hormone. Many times, the calming hormone "overshoots" the adrenalin, causing the person to collapse.

Patients usually bounce back quickly, but they appear pale, ashy and sweaty and feel and look completely drained for the next hour. Their complexion is unmistakable, and at the time of the episode, the patient's appearance looks terminal. In our text, pale is not a favorable color, and it denotes sickness, illness, anemia, disease, a lack, horror, death and despair.

Death is the name of the rider on this anemic, ill and pale fourth horse. He is Satan, the serpent of old, the Devil, Death himself who leads the God-forsaken place named Hades. Power is given to him and the demonic forces of Hades over a fourth of the earth, to kill with sword, with hunger, with death, and by the beasts of the earth.

Since the cross and the resurrection of Jesus Christ, Abraham's side of Hades, known as Paradise, is empty (Hades in the Greek, and Sheol in the Hebrew). We are introduced to Hades in the story of the rich man and poor Lazarus in Luke 16:19-31. Hades is split into two sides: first, the torment side where Christ-haters are "stored" (after they pass through the gates of death) until they are sent to their ultimate destination, the Lake of Fire (Revelation 20:14); second, the Paradise side of Hades where God-fearing men and women awaited the victory of Christ on the cross.

A gulf separates the two sides and no one from either side will ever be able to cross over. The Paradise side is now completely empty and will remain empty. After His death on the cross, Jesus visited the Paradise side and took the redeemed souls who loved His Father to heaven (Ephesians 4:8-10). When a Christ-follower now dies, his soul and spirit go straight to heaven, bypassing the Paradise side of Hades. These souls will receive their new glorified bodies at the Rapture. In spite of the soul-spirit of a person who has died being without its permanent glorified body prior to the Rapture, the soul-spirit is still housed in a temporary body that is compatible with God's mighty presence and is also identifiable.

As the fourth seal is broken, we see that the evil spirits and demons from the tormented side of Hades rise and follow Satan to kill one-fourth of the earth's population. Though we read that Satan, Death and Hades ride recklessly throughout the world, we must remember that according to Revelation 1:18, Christ holds the keys of Hades and Death. According to Psalm 103:19, "The Lord has established His throne in heaven, and His kingdom rules over all." "Indeed, heaven and the highest heavens belong to the Lord your God, also the earth with all that is in it" (Deuteronomy 10:14).

Though world events appear out of control, they are under God's divine control. Though Satan appears to be roaming freely, he is still under God's jurisdiction and will ultimately serve God's purpose.

 Why are Death and Hades associated with one another? They are companions, Death snatching the body and Hades seizing the soul and spirit of an individual that dies.

If the earth's population were eight billion during the Rapture, two billion people would be wiped out when the contents of the fourth seal unfold. How will the disasters occur, where one fourth of the earth's population will die? As mentioned, pestilence is spoken of in Matthew 24:7 and correlates with Revelation 6:8, foreshadowing nuclear and biological warfare, famines, disease and beasts attacking man and killing 25% of the world's population. More than 40 million people died in World War I, more than 80 million in World War II. These tragic deaths will pale compared to the carnage that will cover the earth after the fourth seal is opened.

The opening of the fourth seal empowers the fourth horse-man to release the fourth judgment, issuing a fourfold global decree of sword, hunger, death (pestilence or disease causing death) and wild beasts of the earth, identical to Ezekiel's prophecy regarding Jerusalem in Ezekiel 14:21, "For thus says the Lord God: 'How much more it shall be when I send My four severe judgments on Jerusalem — the sword and famine and wild beasts and pestilence — to cut off man and beast from it!'"

We read in Ezekiel 33:27, "Say thus to them (Judah who had rejected the Lord in 600 BC), 'Thus says the Lord God: as I live, surely those who are in the ruins shall fall by the sword, and the one who is in the open field I will give to the beasts to be devoured, and those who are in the strongholds and caves shall die of the pestilence.'" The prophet Amos outlined the Tribulation judgments of God: "Woe to you who desire the day of the Lord! For what good is the day of the Lord to you? It will be darkness, and not light. It will be as though a man fled from a lion, and a bear met him! Or as though he went into the house, leaned his hand on the wall, and a serpent bit him! Is not the day of the Lord darkness, and not light? Is it not very dark, with no brightness in it?" (Amos 5:18-20).

 This is a powerful and ominous message for Christ-hating, Christ-denying, Christ-mocking and Christ-rejecting

people: they may escape one of the plagues, but they will be smitten by another.

These four judgments occurred on a smaller scale to Judah when Nebuchadnezzar ransacked them. It will happen on a global scale during the Tribulation. How can we be sure of its global scope? First, the cataclysmic number of deaths boast of large-scale figures, eliminating the notion of a local event. Second, the four-fold nature of sword, hunger, death and beasts signifies a global event, the number four pointing to the East, West, North and South. If one escapes the sword, he will starve. If he escapes the famine, he will die of disease. If he escapes disease, he will be attacked by beasts. How will beasts, or ferocious animals, take part in this picture? "Once food becomes scarce, wild animals which generally leave man alone will begin to attack man for food."[10]

In the 2020 Coronavirus Pandemic, the world became aware of its frailty. A small virus, approximately 120 nanometers, which if it were multiplied 5,000 times, would end up being the size of a small green pea, brought nations down to their knees. There was mayhem in New York City's hospitals where a shortage of medical supplies, beds and ventilators sent shockwaves of fear around the nation. Can you imagine that this horrendous and grave plague's victims will seem inconsequential to the deaths during the Tribulation? Can you even imagine the scene of ambulances, firefighters, nurses and doctors in complete bewilderment as they face a death toll rate of two billion? Unimaginable! Horrible! Gruesome!

Horror upon horror. Injury upon injury. Sickness upon sickness. Death upon death! And this is only the fourth seal! More pestilence is on its way. More deaths are inevitable. More hardships will unfold. God continues to "Rev It Up!" Today, as you hear God's voice calling your name, stop and listen, heed his voice and come and follow Him. He will restore your soul, lead you beside peaceful waters, and pour out His goodness and mercy upon you. Whatever you do, choose life!

You may be stuck where you are in life. People in your past may still be haunting your soul. People in your present may be stifling your progress. Your fears of what is to come in the future may be suffocating your hopes. The hardships and heartaches of life tend to beat us up. The mistakes, guilt, and hurts of yesterday can at times bury us. There is a God who hears our cry. There is a God who longs to draw nigh. There is a God who will, with His righteous right hand, hold you up high. You don't have to do anything to "qualify." He simply loves you; He is the only One who can give life, hope, joy and peace, because for you He was willing to die.

Fifth Seal: The Martyrs' Plea

6:9 When He opened the fifth seal, I saw under the altar the souls of those who had been slain for the word of God and for the testimony which they held.

Below is a list of the seven seal judgments. We will now discuss the fifth seal.

First Seal: White horse, "peace" (6:1-2).
Second Seal: Red horse, war (6:3-4).
Third Seal: Black horse, famine (6:5-6).
Fourth Seal: Pale horse, death and pestilence (6:7-8).
Fifth Seal: Martyred saints cry from under altar (6:9-11).
Sixth Seal: earthquake; sun-moon-stars disrupted (6:12-17).
Seventh Seal: Seven trumpet judgments released (8:1-6).

We continue to see the correlation between Revelation and the Olivet Discourse. In Matthew 24:8-12, Jesus said to His disciples, "All these (the first four seals) are the beginning of

sorrows. Then (fifth seal) they will deliver you up to tribulation and kill you and you will be hated by all nations for My
name's sake. And then many will be offended, will betray one
another, and will hate one another. Then many false prophets will rise up and deceive many. And because lawlessness
will abound, the love of many will grow cold." Unlike what we
saw with the first four seals, none of the four creatures state,
"Come and see," when the fifth seal is opened. "There are
no voices of command from heaven under this seal, and no
messengers dispatched from the throne; for the reason that
bloody persecutions of God's servants come from beneath —
not from above."[11]

At this point in our study of Revelation we are still in the first
half of the Tribulation. The Antichrist has not yet committed
the abomination of desolation, (desecrating God's temple
found in Matthew 24:15; II Thessalonians 2:4) which ends the
first three and a half years of the Tribulation and ushers in the
666 mark of the Beast. The False Prophet has not yet resurrected a statue of the Antichrist that will be worshiped by the
world's inhabitants. The believers are being martyred because
their testimony rivals the false New-World-Order of the Antichrist and not because they refuse the 666 mark, which has
not yet been revealed. How will there be converts during these
perilous times? We'll see in chapter seven that there will be
millions of people who will respond to Christ's love because
of the 144,000 thousand Jewish apostles preaching the Gospel worldwide (Revelation 7:1-8).

The first four seals are grouped into one and the
three last seals follow, a common division of the
blessed book of Revelation. These last seals will
constitute a time of unprecedented martyrdom of
Christ-followers, and anti-Semitism will spiral out of
control. Those who attempt to live, speak or act other
than what is prescribed by the New-World-Order

will be killed. If you were to speak out about the love of Christ today, without watering down the Gospel, you would be ostracized, considered "dangerous" in "elite" circles, be censored, fired or sued. This sentiment will only get worse, shifting to visceral hatred, in the coming years in the Land of the Free, and will lead to imprisonment or even worse.

Those who come to Christ, be they Jews or Gentiles, during the Tribulation will be considered enemies of humanity, opponents of progressivism and proponents of free speech, and will be beheaded for high treason (Revelation 20:4). They will likely be placed in mass extermination camps, not by accident, but by sheer calculated cruelty, and face horrible persecutions that will quench the thirst and gladden the hearts of those who hate Christ-followers.

The "assumption" of Christians being persecuted is supported by Luke 21:12-17, when Jesus spoke to the disciples about the Tribulation, "But before all these things, they will lay their hands on you and persecute you, delivering you up to the synagogues and prisons. You will be brought before kings and rulers for My name's sake. But it will turn out for you as an occasion for testimony. Therefore, settle it in your hearts not to meditate beforehand on what you will answer, for I will give you a mouth and wisdom which all your adversaries will not be able to contradict or resist. You will be betrayed even by parents, brothers, relatives and friends; and they will put some of you to death. And you will be hated by all for My name's sake."

The fifth seal reveals that the martyr's souls are under the altar of God, slain for accepting and proclaiming their faith for the Word of God. We hear them crying out for vindication. In Leviticus 4:7, the priest poured the blood of the sacrificed animal at the base of the brazen altar. The blood of the animal is considered to be the life of the animal in Leviticus 17:11-15, and spilling it represents a picture of sacrifice.

The Tribulation martyrs devote themselves to God and sacrifice their lives for Him; their blood is spilled, their souls are taken to heaven, where they call out from the depths of heaven's altar. They are likely under the altar of incense which we spoke of in Revelation 5:8, where the prayers of the saints rise to the throne of God.

How do we know that these martyrs go to heaven? "We are confident, yes, well pleased rather to be absent from the body and to be present with the Lord" (II Corinthians 5:8). We will see them worshiping God in Revelation 7:9-17. They have not yet received their resurrected and glorified bodies as believers did who were in Christ and took part in the Rapture prior to the Tribulation. The martyred souls of the Tribulation will receive their new bodies after the Tribulation and just before the Millennium (Revelation 20:4). They will also receive the crown of life (Revelation 2:10).

Just as Jesus was slain, so will His followers be: "Yet for Your sake we are killed all day long; We are accounted as sheep for the slaughter" (Psalm 44:22). Though their death is celebrated on earth by the godless, their souls are not only present in heaven but are recognized by John, and as we shall see, their cries will be acknowledged by God. "It is altogether a wrong interpretation of the Scriptures which represents the dead in a state of non-existence, unconsciousness, or oblivion."[12] Their bodies (material part) lay on earth but their soul-spirit (immaterial part) are in heaven; though their soul-spirit lives, they are still in an intermediate state, awaiting their future resurrected and glorified bodies.

6:10 And they cried with a loud voice, saying, "How long, O Lord, holy and true, until You judge and avenge our blood on those who dwell on the earth?"

They cry out, not for the forgiveness of those who slew them as Stephen did in Acts 7:60, but for retribution. They ask God when they'll be vindicated; their cries will be answered at the end of the Tribulation, as God proclaims in Isaiah 63:4, "For the day of vengeance is in My heart, and the year of My redeemed has come."

Because the martyrs are asking the question, "How long?" there must still be a consciousness of time in the afterlife. Those in Hades, destined to be cast in the Lake of Fire, will be in conscious anguish as noted in (Mark 9:42-48). Those in heaven will be in conscious blessedness (Philippians 1:23). These martyrs, however, though in the presence of the living God, are waiting for the day of God's vengeance.

The martyrs do not call out for clergy, friends, family, lawyers, politicians or self-help gurus. They call out to the sovereign Lord. Who else can help? Who can do what He does? Who can undo what He does? In Isaiah 43:11, 13, we become aware of God's might, "I, even I, am the Lord, and besides Me there is no savior. There is no one who can deliver out of My hand; I work, and who will reverse it?" "Consider the work of God; for who can make straight what He has made crooked?" (Ecclesiastes 7:13). Who else is holy? Who else is true? According to I Samuel 2:2, "No one is holy like the Lord, for there is none besides You, nor is there any rock like our God."

There will soon by a song of jubilation sung by the martyrs, "Alleluia! Salvation and glory and honor and power belong to the Lord our God! For true and righteous are His judgments, because He has judged the great harlot who corrupted the earth with her fornication, and He has avenged on her the blood of His servants shed by her" (Revelation 19:1-2). However, as we'll see, the earth-dwellers are incorrigible. They will refuse Christ and raise their fists against God and blaspheme Him (Revelation 16:21); refuse to repent (Revelation 9:20-21); worship the Antichrist (Revelation 13:8); and continue to persecute Christ-followers and celebrate their deaths (Revelation

11:10). Go ahead. Be incorrigible. Try to take out the Gospel. Maim and slander Christ-followers and call yourself diplomatic and peaceful. Mocking God may get you airplay now, but your actions in the future will be indefensible. The end for you will be eternally unbearable.

6:11 *Then a white robe was given to each of them; and it was said to them that they should rest a little while longer, until both the number of their fellow servants and their brethren, who would be killed as they were, was completed.*

When Christ was speaking to the church in Sardis, the dead church, He said, "he who overcomes shall be clothed in white garments, and I will not blot out his name from the Book of Life; but I will confess his name before My Father and before His angels" (Revelation 3:5). It is because of God's divine patience that time has lingered as He affords ample opportunity to anyone who will come to Him. As He has numbered the stars and named them individually (Psalm 147:3-4), He has placed an exact number of fellow Christ-followers who will be slain during the Tribulation. He will also avenge their deaths in His time (Revelation 19:2). God is sovereign over time and life, "Since man's days are determined, the number of his months is with You; You have appointed his limits, so that he cannot pass." (Job 14:5).

How will God dress the martyred souls with white, clean and pure garments when they haven't yet received their glorified bodies? I believe they have temporary heavenly bodies until they receive their incorruptible and eternal bodies. When Moses and Elijah appeared on the Mount of Transfiguration, Peter, John and James recognized them (Matthew 17:1-13). Their bodies had long been buried, but their souls and spirits were alive. They weren't wearing name tags reading, "Hello, I'm Mo!" and "Hi, I'm Eli!" They were recognized by the disciples. Even in their temporary bodies, they are distinct and identifiable. Because John saw the souls under the altar, I believe they were "dressed" in their temporary bodies. How else could God clothe them? When the Tribulation and martyrdom ends, heaven will sing, "Alleluia! For the God Omnipotent reigns! Let us be glad and rejoice and give Him glory" (Revelation 19:6-7).

"Oh Lord God, to whom vengeance belongs — O God, to whom vengeance belongs, shine forth! Rise up, O Judge of the earth; render punishment to the proud. Lord, how long will the wicked, how long will the wicked triumph?" (Psalm 94:1-3). The answer is, "Not too much longer!" The Rapture is imminent. The Tribulation will start thereafter.

 The wrath of God will pour down from heaven. God's martyrs will not be forgotten. Earth-dwellers will disdain the Son's invitation. Satan will finally be denied access to heaven's garden. You are free to reject God's mercy now and even during the Tribulation. But you are not free to escape His judgment and discipline!

Sixth Seal: Galactic Disturbances

6:12 *I looked when He opened the sixth seal, and behold, there was a great earthquake; and the sun became black as sackcloth of hair, and the moon became like blood.*

Below is a list of the seven seal judgments. We will now discuss the sixth seal.

First Seal: White horse, "peace" (6:1-2).
Second Seal: Red horse, war (6:3-4).
Third Seal: Black horse, famine (6:5-6).
Fourth Seal: Pale horse, death and pestilence (6:7-8).
Fifth Seal: Martyred saints cry from under altar (6:9-11).
Sixth Seal: earthquake; sun-moon-stars disrupted (6:12-17).
Seventh Seal: Seven trumpet judgments released (8:1-6).

This verse correlates with Matthew 24:7-8, where Jesus said to

His disciples, "For nation will rise against nation, and kingdom against kingdom. And there will be famines, pestilences, and earthquakes in various places. All these are the beginning of sorrows."

Earth-dwellers will be in panic mode, believing the end has come, but to their dismay, "all these are the beginning of sorrows" according to Matthew 24:8. The ugly head of anarchy is on the upswing in the United States of America, where some citizens refuse to follow law and order in the name of fighting fascism, and others refuse to respect barriers. But the country is still divinely restrained by the Spirit of God who is now present on earth. When Satan, the "lawless one," as he is described in II Thessalonians 2:8, takes over in the Tribulation, then a new constitution of unparalleled mayhem will emerge straight out of the corridors of hell! When people turn away from God, unspeakable terror will result. The cosmic events that transpire when the sixth seal is opened are straight from the throne of God.

The "Ring of Fire" is a 25,000-mile-long, horseshoe-shaped string of 452 volcanoes and geologic sites of strong seismic activity encircling the Pacific Ocean. It includes 75% of the world's volcanoes and boasts 90% of its earthquakes. On January 23, 2018, activity along this ring affected Alaska, the West Coast of North America, Japan, the Philippines and Papua New Guinea, all within 24 hours. An earthquake 8.2 in magnitude hit the coast of Alaska, impacting the West Coast, Canada and Hawaii, triggering tsunami warnings. An eruption of Mount Kusatsu-Shirane in Japan darkened the skies with black ash as volcanic rocks rained on people. In the Philippines, Mount Mayan erupted spewing out fountains of red-hot lava 2,300 feet above its crater, as ash plumbs rose up to

2 miles in the sky and rained down on people, affecting 40,000 villages. In Papua New Guinea, a Kaovar Island volcano erupted and caused thousands to evacuate from surrounding islands.[13]

These heart-wrenching disasters, tragically claiming priceless lives, pale against the devastations man will face during the Tribulation! The earth will shake in unprecedented magnitudes, and as we'll see, the governing heavenly bodies such as the sun, moon and stars will plummet. As if the volcanic eruptions, earthquakes and tsunamis weren't enough, nuclear warfare will cause deaths, dust and debris to flood the atmosphere, and showers of asteroids and meteors will deface earth's surface. It is not inconceivable that these horrid events will cause the sun to darken and the moon to become red like blood! The timing of each calamity will be unpredictable, the loss of lives will be irreconcilable, and the whirlwind of disturbances will be unmanageable!

Catastrophic events during the Tribulation will rattle the cosmic realm. The prophet Joel describes this graphically, "And I will show wonders in the heavens and in the earth: blood and fire and pillars of smoke. The sun shall be turned into darkness, and the moon into blood, before the coming of the great and awesome day of the Lord. And it shall come to pass that whoever calls on the name of the Lord shall be saved. For in the Mount Zion and in Jerusalem there shall be deliverance, as the Lord has said, among the remnant whom the Lord calls." (Joel 2:30-32).

Both the black and the bloody red colors demonstrate the judgment of God. An artist can paint on canvases, highlighting the moon and the sun as he desires. A filmmaker can create apocalyptic images digitally and manipulate them with computers. A government can become a world threat by fashioning nuclear arsenals. But only God can darken the sun, bloody the moon and control the very breath of life. God's power will be on full display during the Tribulation. Terror will grip people's hearts. Fear will be a daily companion. Death tolls will rise exponentially. Run. Hide. Curse. Pump your fist at the Creator! The clock will be ticking, and man will meet his Maker!

Be reminded of this, however: Jesus did not come to die on the cross to condemn the world, but He came to save the world. Therefore, it grieves God to see the wicked perish. God longs for the unbeliever to turn to Him, but if the unbeliever rejects Him, God does not take pleasure in his death! (John 3:17; Ezekiel 33:11). During the Tribulation, the intensity of the unbeliever's hatred toward God will magnify and his heart will be seared. God will turn up the heat, "Rev It Up," and man will face deadly cosmic disruption issuing from the throne of God:

1. When the fourth trumpet is sounded in Revelation 8:12, "a third of the sun was struck, a third of the moon, and a third of the stars, so that a third of them were darkened. A third of the day did not shine, and likewise the night."

2. When the fifth trumpet is sounded in Revelation 9:1-2, when Satan, who is temporarily given the key to the Bottomless Pit by God, will open the pit, smoke will rise out of it, and "the sun and the air were darkened because of the smoke of the pit."

3. When the fourth bowl is poured out on the sun in Revelation 16:8-9, "men were scorched with great heat."

 This is the real "global warming." It will be global, and it will definitely be searing hot. But it ain't nurturing gone wrong from Momma Nature and it ain't a natural marvel. It's from Papa God and it's supernatural!

Man declines to worship the everlasting Light of the world, Jesus Christ, and elects to worship the created, the sun, moon and stars. As the atmosphere changes and the sun is dimmed and the moon appears red, the people of this world will taste the dark judgments of God. When one rejects the light, he will embrace the darkness.

Look up! Look up now! When you can see the sky. When you can enjoy the warmth of the sun. When you can gaze at the stars and marvel at their twinkling lights. When you can be in wonder of the moon's calmness. There is coming a day when a thick cloud of ash will cover the earth and fear will fill the hearts of man. There is coming a day when grace turns to wrath and God's long-suffering ends. Look up! Look up now! Turn your heart to God. Fall on your knees and meet the love of your soul, the Father who cares for you, Christ who died for you and the Holy Spirit who longs to embrace you. Look up! Look up now! Before the Day of the Lord falls suddenly upon the earth in an atomic millisecond!

6:13 *And the stars of heaven fell to the earth, as a fig tree drops its late figs when it is shaken by a mighty wind.*

The language presented in our text is not hyperbolic. The events will literally occur! Swarms of asteroids will descend upon the earth as fallen stars. The earth will be smoking, the heavens will be shaking, and the seas will be roaring! There will be a dreadful outpouring of wrath upon the earth! All mankind will recognize that hope is directly related to their dependence upon God and not to their self-sufficient independence. Hope placed anywhere else is empty. However, since many do not want God's order, they will receive disorder and destruction.

Isaiah foretold of these events in Isaiah 13:9-13: "Behold, the day of the Lord comes, cruel, with both wrath and fierce anger, to lay the land desolate; and He will destroy its sinners from it. For the stars of heaven and their constellations will not give their light; the sun will be darkened in its going forth, and the moon will not cause its light to shine. 'I will punish the world for its evil, and the wicked for their iniquity; I will halt the arrogance of the proud and will lay low the haughtiness of the terrible. I will make a mortal more rare than fine gold, a man more than the golden wedge of Ophir (poetic description, scarcity of man makes him more precious than pure gold). Therefore, I will shake the heavens, and the earth will move out of their place, in the wrath of the Lord of hosts and in the day of His fierce anger.'"

Once figs are ripe, they will fall to the ground if not tended. The wind blows, the branches that are burdened with great weight lose their grip and cast the figs to the ground. The time has come. The figs are ripe. The Lord has extended His mercy and grace for thousands of years, only to be mocked and spit upon. The people of the world have snubbed, scoffed and scorned their Maker.

 God has been patient, but the winds of grace are shifting drastically to the winds of wrath! The environmentalist's attempt to save creation falls short because he fails to acknowledge the Creator! How ironic! How egotistic! How myopic! How tragic!

6:14 *Then the sky receded as a scroll when it is rolled up, and every mountain and island was moved out of its place.*

Google maps will no longer be relevant! The seismic disturbances will alter the topography of the earth as we know it. As earth's tectonic plates shift, swing and shuffle, volcanoes erupt, and earthquakes ensue, the landscape of our planet will change drastically. Though this earthquake is great, there will be one greater still in Revelation 16:19 when the seventh bowl is poured, and every island will flee away, and mountains will not be found. God is able to make every mountain low as He declares in Isaiah 40:4. People will think that the end of the world has come. Hysteria will dominate their minds. Despite the horrors of the sixth seal, the last great and terrible day of the Lord will still have not yet arrived for God is just beginning to "Rev it up!"

6:15 And the kings of the earth, the great men, the rich men, the commanders, the mighty men, every slave and every free man, hid themselves in the caves and in the rocks of the mountains,

"Previous judgments have reached some classes of people, but there have always been those who through the advantage of wealth or fortuitous circumstance have been able to find some refuge. But now every class is reached, from kings to slaves."[14] All hearts will be filled with dismay. God is no respecter of persons (Acts 10:34). He will accept all who come to Him, kings, paupers, great men, scorned men, rich men, poor men, leaders, followers, known, unknown, mighty, weak, every slave and every free man. He will also pour His wrath on those who reject Him, rich or poor, powerful or common, educated or uneducated, with status or without status. Low or high, they'll see the signs in the sky, and desperately try to hide, as God will justify His wrath and magnify His Son.

The irony lies in the fact that those who tormented Christ-followers will now experience affliction themselves. Another ironic note is that man prides himself in humanism and abolishing wrongs, but the despicable evil of slavery still remains and flourishes in the form of sex trafficking during the Tribulation. Why? Because the heart of man is deceitful, desperately wicked and beyond cure (Jeremiah 17:9). You can tear statues down in attempts to erase history, but you cannot rid man of his heart which, at best, is odious and vile. Adam and Eve hid from the presence of the Lord God among the trees of the garden when they sinned (Genesis 3:8). So too will mankind hide themselves in caves and rocks of the mountains to try and preserve themselves, while lifting up their fists towards heaven to curse God. They still don't get it! There is only one Rock that can save: He is the Lord, the Rock eternal, Jesus Christ (Isaiah 26:4).

6:16 *and said to the mountains and rocks, "Fall on us and hide us from the face of Him who sits on the throne and from the wrath of the Lamb!*

Just so people have no misunderstanding as to who the author of these disasters is, they will get a glimpse into heaven and gaze upon the Lamb of God, somewhat like Stephen, the martyr, was able to gaze into heaven in Acts 7:56.[15] But for Stephen, it was going home. For these earth-dwellers, the scene is devastating, filled with terror and dread. They have scoffed at God and His prophets as they did in the days of Noah. Yet what is so heartbreaking is that there is no cry of repentance, no prayers calling on God's name for mercy, no hint of humility, no signs of seeking God's face and no attempt to leave their wicked ways. Instead, they cry out to the mountains and rocks, "Fall on us and hide us from the face of Him who sits on the throne and from the wrath of the Lamb!"

 To escape the horrors of the sixth seal does not end in rest or peace for the unrepentant heart; it is not a dead-end; it is not over; it is only the beginning of more terror, trepidation and torment in Hades and the Lake of Fire.

The unbelievers desperately seek to escape. Isaiah prophesied this desperation, "They shall go into the holes of the rocks, and into the caves of the earth, from the terror of the Lord and the glory of His majesty, when He arises to shake the earth mightily" (Isaiah 2:19). They desperately want relief. In fact, they want to die. While Christ-followers want to see His face, Christ-rejecters conversely want to hide themselves from the face of the Lord. David prayed in Psalm 27:4, "One thing I have desired of the Lord, that will I seek: that I may dwell in the house of the Lord all the days of my life, to behold the beauty of the Lord, and to inquire in His temple." Unbelievers can run wherever they please, but nothing in all creation is hidden from God's sight! (Hebrews 4:13). For the reader of this book, there is still time: the door of God's mercy is still wide open for you!

6:17 *For the great day of His wrath has come, and who is able to stand?"*

The wrath of God began at the opening of the first seal, but it is with the opening of the sixth seal that earth-dwellers finally realize vengeance is falling upon them and recognize that God is responsible for it.[16] Unbelievers are crying out that the "great day" of God's wrath has come, but this is not true. In Matthew 24:8, Christ said, "All these are the beginning of sorrows." "Little do they know that all they have seen and experienced is no more than a shadow of the terror which must yet come. These are but the judgments that precede the great day of His wrath."[17] In the unleashing of the sixth seal, the Great Tribulation, the last three and a half years, has not yet begun!

What exactly is the "Day of the Lord?"

1. We are in the "day of man," a period of approximately 6,000 years since Adam's fall, where we live in the land of disease, hospitals, heartaches, depression, divorce, destruction, prisons, psychiatric wards, suicide, rape, homicide, accidents and terrorism. Humanism will plunge man's behavior even to a lower state of morality. Why? Because it has the word "human" in it! That is why Socialism will not work for the good!

2. The "Day of Christ" will soon come, when the church is Raptured to heaven.

3. The Rapture will initiate the "Day of the Lord" where God will intervene in human affairs; this will include time from the Tribulation through the end of the Millennium. But it

is the first seven years, the Tribulation, that is so devastating! During the seven years, there will be an acceleration of devastation, where God will "Rev It Up," until we reach the climax, the "great day of His wrath," in the Campaign of Armageddon.

4. After the Millennium, there will be the "Day of God" where we'll live in a new world and new heaven for all Eternity.

Isaiah prophesied about the Day of the Lord in Isaiah13:6-9, "Wail, for the day of the Lord is at hand! It will come as destruction from the Almighty. Therefore, all hands will be limp, every man's heart will melt, and they will be afraid. Pangs and sorrows will take hold of them; they will be in pain as a woman in childbirth; they will be amazed at one another; their faces will be like flames. Behold, the day of the Lord comes, cruel, with both wrath and fierce anger, to lay the land desolate; and He will destroy its sinners from it."

Many prophets wrote about this "day," as found in Zephaniah 1:14-17, "The great day of the Lord is near; it is near and hastens quickly. The noise of the day of the Lord is bitter; there the mighty men shall cry out. That day is a day of wrath, a day of trouble and distress, a day of devastation and desolation, a day of darkness and gloominess, a day of clouds and thick darkness, a day of trumpet and alarm against the fortified cities and against the high towers. 'I will bring distress upon men, and they shall walk like blind men, because they have sinned against the Lord; their blood shall be poured out like dust, and their flesh like refuse.'" Death will be so common that funerals will be uncommon! Why? Because man's flesh will be like refuse or garbage!

The prophet Malachi also spoke of the utter devastation that will lead to complete barrenness, "'For behold, the day is coming, burning like an oven, and all the proud, yes, all who do wickedly will be stubble. And the day which is coming shall burn them up,' says the Lord of hosts, 'That will leave them neither root nor branch'" (Malachi 4:1-2).

When you look for further evidence of the meaning of a verse, look to the Bible to interpret the Bible! In Isaiah 2:10-21, we read, "Enter into the rock, and hide in the dust, from the terror of the Lord and the glory of His majesty. The lofty looks of man shall be humbled, the haughtiness of men shall be bowed down, and the Lord alone shall be exalted in that day. For the day of the Lord of hosts shall come upon everything proud and lofty — upon everything lifted up — and it shall be brought low — upon all the cedars of Lebanon that are high and lifted up, and upon all the oaks of Bashan; upon all the high mountains, and upon all the hills that are lifted up; upon every high tower, and upon every fortified wall; upon all the ships of Tarshish, and upon all the beautiful sloops. The loftiness of man shall be bowed down, and the haughtiness of men shall be brought low; the Lord alone will be exalted in that day, but the idols He shall utterly abolish. They shall go into the holes of the rocks, and into the caves of the earth, from the terror of the Lord and the glory of His majesty, when He arises to shake the earth mightily. And his idols of gold, which they made, each for himself to worship, to the moles and bats, to go into the clefts of the rocks, and into the crags of the rugged rocks, from the terror of the Lord and the glory of His majesty."

How will man respond? In senseless panic, but not in humble repentance (Revelation 6:16; 9:21; 16:11). Who will be able to stand God's wrath? In Revelation 6:17, John refers to the words of Joel 2:11, "For the Day of the Lord is great and very terrible; who can endure it?" Man is quite resilient, but also repugnant. After the asteroids stop falling and scientists rise to give a plausible explanation to the disasters, as did Pharaoh's wise counselors, mankind will likely rise to rebuild what has been damaged and continue to turn their back to God. Do not mistake this: God is love and gave up the life of His Son to save you and the world. But God is also just, and He does not live in a hall of injustice, but the halls of righteousness. He will send His wrath because man did not receive His love. I do hope you do not find yourself hiding in the rocks. I pray you turn to the Rock of Ages, God, Jesus Christ, the Holy Spirit, and accept His gift of forgiveness before the Day of the Lord dawns!

REV IT UP & SUM IT UP – CHAPTER SIX:

After the Rapture, the Antichrist will strike a deal with the Jews and the Arabs, confirming a treaty that ushers in what is promised to be seven years of "peace." Israel will tear down its walls because they will feel safe and will rebuild their third temple. Christ will open six out of the seven seals, and mayhem will rule the globe. The events in this chapter correlate with Matthew 24, what is known as the Olivet Discourse, when Christ prophesied of the dreadful days of the Tribulation from the Mount of Olives. The correlating chapters are found in Mark 13 and Luke 21 and reveal the following:

1. False Peace. The first seal reveals a horseman riding on a white horse. The horseman is the Antichrist, deceiving the world that he is the promised "Messiah." Revelation 6:1-2 correlates with Matthew 24:4, Mark 13:6 and Luke 21:8.

2. Wars. The second seal reveals a horseman riding on a red horse. The Ezekiel 38-39 war, the Gog and Magog campaign, where Russia, Iran, and Syria, along with many other nations will attempt to ransack Israel. Only one sixth of Russia and her allies will survive because God will rain down terror on them, saving Israel. Revelation 6:3-4 correlates with Matthew 24:5, Mark 13:7, and Luke 21:9.

3. Famines. The third seal reveals a horseman riding on a black horse; in his hand will be a scale, measuring food. War will lead to famine, food will be scarce but the rich will still have their wine and oil, living the life of luxury. Revelation 6:5-6 correlates with Matthew 24:7-8, Mark 13:8 and Luke 21:10.

4. Pestilence and Death. The fourth seal reveals a horseman riding a pale horse. While peace leads to war, and war leads to famine, famine leads to pestilence and death.

One fourth of the world's population will tragically die! Revelation 6:7-8 correlates with Matthew 24:7-8, Mark 13:8 and Luke 21:11.

5. Persecutions and Martyrs. The fifth seal reveals the souls of those martyred during the Tribulation for their newly found faith in Christ. They plead for God to avenge their death. God clothes them with righteous garments and exhorts them to wait just a little longer. Revelation 6:9-11 correlates with Matthew 24:8-12, Mark 13:9-13 and Luke 21:12-17.

6. Cosmic disturbances. The sixth seal unleashes cosmic disturbances, causing even the rich along with the poor to finally acknowledge that the Lamb of God is in charge of the chaos, causing the sun to darken, the moon to turn bloody red and the earth to quake. Even then, man will cling to his obstinate state of unbelief and snub God. The Day of the Lord has come! Revelation 6:12-17 correlates with Matthew 24:7-8, Mark 13:24-25 and Luke 21:11.

We are urged in Proverbs 27:1 not to brag about our future, "Do not boast about tomorrow, for you do not know what a day may bring forth." During the Day of the Lord, bragging rights will dwindle as man's courage continues to crumble. Just for the record: plan A is to kneel now in repentance while plan B is to stand guilty at the judgment!

Chapter 7
Preach with Passion,
Die with Purpose

With all the believers disappearing, tragedy unfolding and the Antichrist appearing, how will people turn to Christ during the Tribulation? Chapter seven gives us a glimpse into salvation during the Tribulation, giving us a short pause from the seals being opened. We will study about the 144,000 thousand Jewish evangelists who preach the Gospel of Jesus Christ during the first half of the Tribulation and see the fruit of their labor.

144,000 Sealed Jewish Evangelists

7:1 *After these things I saw four angels standing at the four corners of the earth, holding the four winds of the earth, that the wind should not blow on the earth, on the sea, or on any tree.*

After these things, "meta tauta" in the Greek, meaning following these things (after the contents of the sixth seal were released resulting in the shaken earth, darkened sun and bloodied moon), John sees four angels, four corners and four winds. The number four denotes divine divisions and foundations such as direction, time, seasons and elements. There are four "corners" or directions of the world, North, South, East, West. There are four seasons in a year, spring, summer, autumn and winter. There are four universal elements: earth, fire, air and water. There are four gospels in the Bible, Matthew, Mark, Luke, John. The throne of God is surrounded by four beasts, images of a lion, ox, man and eagle. Noteworthy is that the New Jerusalem will be foursquare. Because the number four covers all corners of the earth, this verse denotes an all-encompassing global occurrence.

In Revelation 7:1, there is a divine decree issued for peace in the midst of turmoil. The winds are to be held back. This offers us a pause from the chaos as we anticipate the opening of the seventh seal. We'll see a shift from the judgment of the panic-stricken unbelievers to the protection of some of God's people and the martyrdom of those who turn to Christ.

The first six seals have been opened, one fourth of the earth's population has fallen, and not surprisingly, fear has paralyzed the hearts of those remaining on the earth. God intervenes, controlling time, space and matter, and declares calmness until His servants are sealed, as we'll see in verse three. Chapter seven "delays for a brief moment the disclosure of that which is to take place when the seventh and final seal is removed from the scroll of destiny."[1]

God commands four of His angels to control the four winds. This occurs at the four "corners," or the four main compass directions of the world, making it an international event. The politicians, in all arrogance, will jump to their feet and likely try to take credit for the tranquility that arrives. However, they have nothing to do with the calmness and they have no clue that this is just a lull before the next storm.

We see in Revelation 7:1 that the wind is not allowed to blow on the earth, the sea, nor any tree, all of which are life supporting factors. When the seventh seal is opened, the first trumpet will cause one third of the trees and one third of the earth to be burned and the second will cause one third of the sea creatures to die. But this will not begin until God's servants are sealed with His protection. In addition to these actual events there is important symbolism found in this verse:

1. The earth symbolizes Israel. Throughout the Bible, the word "earth" often means land, a people of a particular city or kingdom. In Isaiah 1:1-3, we read, "The vision of Isaiah the son of Amoz, which he saw concerning Judah and Jerusalem in the days of Uzziah, Jotham, Ahaz and Hezekiah, kings of Judah. Hear, O heavens, and give ear, O earth! For the Lord has spoken, 'I have nourished and brought up children, and they have rebelled against Me; the ox knows its owner and the donkey its master's crib; but Israel does not know, My people do not consider.'" Isaiah's audience which is called the "earth" is clearly Israel. Here earth is used in a local sense to refer to Israel.

2. The sea symbolizes the Gentile world. There are many examples in the Bible in which the words sea and waters represent nations. In Isaiah 17:12, we read, "Woe to the multitude of many nations — who make a noise like the roar of the seas, and to the rushing of nations that make a rushing like the rushing of mighty waters!"

3. The tree symbolizes those in authority. In Judges 9:7-15, a parable humorously has a group of trees talking to other trees, desiring to anoint a king over them. The trees talk to the olive tree, the fig tree and the vine, all which reject the notion of being the king of the trees. The group of trees finally turn to a thorn bush, which irrationally boasts that it will provide them with shade and protection.

In Revelation chapter seven, we'll see three groups of people who will "make it through" the Tribulation:

1. We'll find the first group in verses 3-8. They are the 144,000 Jewish evangelists who will be sealed with God's name, will be exposed to the terror of the Tribulation but

will not be harmed, and will be empowered to preach the Gospel, turning millions to Christ.

2. We'll find the second group in verses 9-17. They are the earth-dwellers who were not Raptured, who will turn to Christ during these horrific times and will "make it through" by being martyred, entering into heaven and the presence of God. Each martyr's soul and spirit will be in heaven though their mortal bodies remain mutilated on earth. They will receive their resurrected and glorified bodies at the end of the Tribulation.

3. The third group is "silent" in this chapter. They are the Gentiles who turn to Christ during these horrific times and will somehow physically survive, making it through the Tribulation, bypassing heaven and entering the Millennium in their non-glorified bodies (Matthew 25:31-46). Joining this group will be the remnant of Jews who were hidden and protected in the city of Petra during the Great Tribulation.

The Gentiles are spoken of in Matthew 25:31-46. There will be a judgment of the sheep and goats after the Tribulation, just after the Second Coming of Christ and just before the Millennium. Christ will divide the sheep (those who turned to Him in the Tribulation, physically survived, and were kind to their Jewish brothers) from the goats (those who rejected Him in the Tribulation, physically survived, and neglected their Jewish brothers).

He will say to the sheep, "Come, you blessed of My Father, inherit the kingdom prepared for you from the foundation of the world; for I was hungry and you gave Me food; I was thirsty and you gave Me drink; I was a stranger and you took Me in; I was naked and you clothed Me; I was sick and you visited Me; I was in prison and you came to Me." After these survivors ask Christ when they saw Him, He will answer, "Assuredly, I say to you, inasmuch as you did it to one of the least of these My brethren, you did it to Me." Christ's brethren refer to the Jews, and how Christ-followers treated them during the Tribulation. The "goats" who did not accept Christ during the Tribulation will be condemned to eternal punishment.

What will happen to the believers with non-glorified bodies? They will enter into the Millennium but will not get their glorified bodies until the end of the Millennium, will be able to procreate and will be able to live a thousand years in their transformed, yet non-resurrected bodies. There will be multitudes of their offspring who will refuse to worship the Lord and will end up rejecting Christ; they will join Satan a thousand years later and try to overthrow Christ; they will not succeed and will be cast into the Lake of Fire.

"Now when the thousand years have expired, Satan will be released from his prison and will go out to deceive the nations which are in the four corners of the earth, Gog and Magog (this Gog and Magog is a saga that continues a thousand years later and is not the Gog and Magog of Ezekiel 38-39), to gather them together to battle, whose number is as the sand of the sea (millions of those born during the 1,000 years will reject Christ at the end of the Millennium). They went up on the breadth of the earth and surrounded the camp of the saints and the beloved city (Jerusalem). And fire came down from God out of heaven and devoured them. The devil, who deceived them, was cast into the Lake of Fire and brimstone where the beast and the false prophet are. And they will be tormented day and night forever and ever" (Revelation 20:7-10).

How will these believers live during the thousand years on earth? "No more shall an infant from there live but a few days, nor an old man who has not fulfilled his days; for the child shall die one hundred years old, but the sinner being one hundred years old shall be accursed. They shall build houses and inhabit them; they shall plant vineyards and eat their fruit. They shall not build, and another inhabit; they shall not plant, and another eat; for as the days of a tree (longevity), so shall be the day of My people, and My elect shall long enjoy the work of their hands. They shall not labor in vain, nor bring forth children for trouble; for they shall be the descendants of the blessed of the Lord, and their offspring with them" (Isaiah 65:20-23).

"But everyone shall sit under his vine and under his fig tree, and no one shall make them afraid; for the mouth of the Lord of hosts has spoken" (Micah 4:4). "Thus says the Lord of hosts, 'Old men and old women shall again sit in the streets of Jerusalem, each one with his staff in his hand because of great age. The streets of the city shall be full of boys and girls playing in its streets'" (Zechariah 8:4-5). "They shall not hurt nor destroy in all My holy mountain, for the earth shall be full of knowledge of the Lord as the waters cover the sea" (Isaiah 11:9).

But how can one live to be up to one thousand years old without having a glorified body? "Along the bank of the river, on this side and that, will grow all kinds of trees used for food; their leaves will not wither, and their fruit will not fail. They will bear fruit every month, because their water flows from the sanctuary. Their fruit will be for food, and their leaves for medicine" (Ezekiel 47:12). The waters that flow from Christ's Millennium throne and the trees along its course will provide healing and longevity for the people!

***7:2** Then I saw another angel ascending from the east, having the seal of the living God. And he cried with a loud voice to the four angels to whom it was granted to harm the earth and the sea,*

The angel with the seal of God appears from the East. East is referred to as the direction in which the glory of the Lord either departs in judgment as it did from Solomon's temple in Ezekiel 10:18 or the direction from which the glory of the Lord will return in deliverance as it will in the Millennium, according to Ezekiel 43:2-4. Just preceding Armageddon, the angel will also come from the East. And at the Second Coming of Christ, Jesus comes from the East when He arrives with all His glory,

"For as the lighting comes from the east and flashes to the west, so also will the coming of the Son of Man be" (Matthew 24:27). The East announces the dawning of a new day or a new beginning. In our text, it is the direction from which God's protective seal comes prior to further judgments. A new day dawns: evil runs rampant in Satan's hands … but God will "Rev Up" the message of the Gospel to invite millions to come to Him. Grace upon grace … even during the Tribulation!

The word "seal" in the Greek is "sphragis," and is the same word used for the six seals in chapter six. In the context of the seven seals that Christ opens, it is a cover that not only authenticates a document but prevents unauthorized personnel from opening it. In the context of this verse, it is an impression, inscription or hallmark stamped upon the foreheads of God's chosen, approved, commissioned and empowered to do His work, bearing the name of the Father and the Lamb of God, denoting ownership and protection (II Corinthians 1:22; Ephesians 1:13-14).

The seal is not fabricated by man nor can it be purchased. Its origin is the living God. In Isaiah 46:9-10, God says of Himself, "'For I am God, and there is no other; I am God, and there is none like Me, declaring the end from the beginning, and from ancient times things that are not yet done,' saying, 'My counsel shall stand, and I will do all My pleasure.'" He is the only living God. All others are but idols made by the hands of man.

According to Psalm 103:20, the angels obey the commands of God, "Bless the Lord, you His angels, who excel in strength, who do His word, heeding the voice of His word." Chaos belongs to Satan. Control belongs to God because He is sovereign. But, ultimately, even chaos serves the purposes of God!

7:3 saying, "Do not harm the earth, the sea, or the trees till we have sealed the servants of our God on their foreheads."

In our text, God sends forth an angel who gives a God-given command to the four angels to withhold calamity until His servants are sealed with the stamp of protection. This angel speaks in a loud voice, denoting the urgency of his message. Who is in control? According to Isaiah 45:7, even judgment and calamity are subject to God's demand, "I form the light and create darkness, I make peace and create calamity; I, the Lord, do all these things." According to Isaiah 43:13, God proclaims, "'Indeed before the day was, I am He; and there is no one who can deliver out of My hand; I work, and who will reverse it?'"

In Ezekiel 9:4-6, we read about how an angel was directed by God to place a seal on the foreheads of those who grieved over sin, "And the Lord said to him, 'Go through the midst of the city, through the midst of Jerusalem, and put a mark on the foreheads of the men who sigh and cry over the abominations that are done within it.' To the other angels He said in my hearing, 'Go after the first angel through the city and kill; do not let your eye spare, nor have any pity. Utterly slay old and young men, maiden and little children and women, but do not come near anyone on whom is the mark." God will always mark His own. As we'll see in Revelation 13:16-18, Satan will fabricate his 666 brand and mark his own (Revelation 13:18; 14:11; 16:2; 19:20).

The name of the living God on the foreheads of His elect will serve as a marker for the angel of judgment to "Passover" them as he did when he saw the blood over the doorposts of only the Israelites in the land of Goshen! "As blood was put upon the door of the houses of Israel in Egypt so that the angel of death would pass over these houses and strike only those which were not marked, so the seal of God is put upon the forehead of His own so that the angels of judgment, passing through the world, will know those who are God's."[2]

In our next verse we will be introduced to the elect servants of God, the 144,000 Jewish evangelists who will be sealed; the judgments are placed on hold between the sixth seal

(Revelation 6:12-17) and the seventh seal (Revelation 8:1) until these Gospel messengers are supernaturally sealed with God's name and therefore, His protection.

***7:4** And I heard the number of those who were sealed. One hundred and forty-four thousand of all the tribes of the children of Israel were sealed:*

God always lays claim to His own children, but that does not exempt them from the common hardships of life. He said to Elijah, "Yet I have left seven thousand in Israel who have not bowed unto Baal" (I Kings 19:18); though the seven thousand worshiped and honored God, they were still under the cruel reign of Ahab and Jezebel. However, we must remember that by this time (in the end times), the church has already been Raptured and is exempt from these hard times. Many Jews and Gentiles will come to know Christ during the Tribulation as the 144,000, who will go unscathed, proclaim God's Word, leading people to the Savior during the first half of the Tribulation.

Why would the Apostle Paul refer to himself as "one untimely born" in I Corinthians 15:8? He was dramatically converted while on his way to Damascus in hot pursuit of Christ-followers in order to kill them. He was perhaps implying that he was born 2,000 years before the 144,000 evangelists who will preach the Gospel worldwide. If a single Paul changed this world for Christ, can you imagine what 144,000 Pauls will do!

There are reasons for delays in life. God is in control even when everything around us seems to be out of control. Just as there is a reason for the delay in opening the seventh seal and harming the earth, sea and trees there is a reason for the delay that you and I often face today when pleading with the Lord in prayer.

 Even in His "silence," He is at work and will never neglect you, His child. His Name is Immanuel, and He is with you in the dark, in the pain, in the shortage, in the emptiness,

in the wilderness, in the failure, in the fall and in life's stings and strains. His hands are not too short to save you nor His ears too dull to hear your cry! (Isaiah 59:1).

Those who are sealed will be a thorn in the side of Satan, reminding him that he is on a leash and God will only allow so much of his evil to propagate. Remember, all knees will bow before the living God and not before Satan! Earth-dwellers will bow before the image of the Beast as seen in Revelation 13:15, falling before a false idol. Satan has propagated idols, captivating man's heart, mimicking the living God. But there is only one God. One holy. One good. One true. And the only One who humbly came down to us, giving us the gift of eternal life, if we will receive it, instead of the sham gods who ask you to "go up" to their level and attempt to earn eternal bliss!

Some believe these 144,000 evangelists represent the church. Absurd! The church is taken up in the Rapture and when the Word says 144,000 of all the tribes of the children of Israel, that's what it means! Israel signifies Israel. The church does not have tribes. Israel does. I go back to what I learned from a wise teacher, Ron Rhodes: "When the literal sense makes good sense, seek no other sense, lest it result in nonsense."

Here is a good example of mercy and grace. God chose Israel to be a light to the Gentiles of the world, showing Him to be the true God, in which Israel miserably failed. Israel also failed to follow God. For that they faced two brutal exiles, one by the Assyrians approximately 700 BC and the other by the Babylonians approximately 600 BC. To add insult to the injury, Israel failed to recognize their own Messiah, Jesus Christ, who is the only One God who could heal the blind and cleanse the leper! But during the Tribulation, God will choose 144,000 Jews to proclaim His Gospel and they will do so with boldness, authority and a deep love for God and His Son, Jesus Christ. Grace! Mercy! God's goodness! Giving mankind break after break! Please, don't squander your opportunity!

7:5 of the tribe of Judah twelve thousand were sealed;
of the tribe of Reuben twelve thousand were sealed;
of the tribe of Gad twelve thousand were sealed;
7:6 of the tribe of Asher twelve thousand were sealed;
of the tribe of Naphtali twelve thousand were sealed;
of the tribe of Manasseh twelve thousand were sealed;
7:7 of the tribe of Simeon twelve thousand were sealed;
of the tribe of Levi twelve thousand were sealed;
of the tribe of Issachar twelve thousand were sealed;
7:8 of the tribe of Zebulun twelve thousand were sealed;
of the tribe of Joseph twelve thousand were sealed;
of the tribe of Benjamin twelve thousand were sealed.

According to Ephesians 1:13, Christ-followers are sealed with the Holy Spirit, "In Him you also trusted, after you heard the word of truth, the gospel of your salvation; in whom also, having believed, you were sealed with the Holy Spirit of promise." The 144,000 evangelists will also be sealed with the Holy Spirit.

There are 12,000 from each tribe: Judah, Reuben and Gad; Asher, Naphtali and Manasseh. Simeon, Levi and Issachar; Zebulon, Joseph and Benjamin. Dan and Ephraim (Manasseh's brother and Joseph's son) are left out of the list, perhaps because in the Old Testament, these two were known for immersing themselves in idolatry as we'll see below.

Israel's tribes are said to be "lost," but as Joseph seated his brothers all in order by age during a feast (Genesis 43:33-34), so too God will arrange the Jewish tribes and commission them to preach the Gospel. In God's economy, they are not lost. Even if they were, God gives life to the dead and "calls those things which do not exist as though they did" (Romans 4:17).

John takes great pains to name each of the tribes, indicating the tribes are not lost. A grave error in interpreting these passages is the notion that the ten tribes were lost when the

Northern kingdom of Israel, which began with the civil war between King Jeroboam (took over ten Northern tribes) and King Rehoboam (took over two Southern tribes), were attacked and exiled by Assyria approximately 700 BC. The common unfounded belief is that the ten tribes were assimilated and lost their historical identity.

The Apostle Paul commented on the distinct identity of Israel in Romans 11:25-27, "For I do not desire, brethren, that you should be ignorant of this mystery, lest you should be wise in your own opinion, that blindness in part has happened to Israel until the fullness of the Gentiles has come in. And so, all Israel will be saved, as it is written, 'The Deliverer will come out of Zion, and He will turn away ungodliness from Jacob; for this is My covenant with them, when I take away their sins.'" In James 1:1, the disciple James, the half-brother of Jesus, states, "James, a bondservant of God and of the Lord Jesus Christ, to the twelve tribes which are scattered abroad: Greetings."

John, the author of Revelation, supports the fact that the twelve tribes are not lost when he writes about the New Jerusalem, "Also she had a great and high wall with twelve gates, and twelve angels at the gates, and names written on them, which are the names of the twelve tribes of the children of Israel" (Revelation 21:12). Paul differentiates between Gentiles and Jews, James writes to the twelve tribes and John presents the gates of the New Jerusalem with the names of the twelve tribes. God is able to "surgically" and precisely identify each Jewish tribe. How? We find that representatives from the ten northern tribes migrated south and thus were preserved (II Chronicles 30:1-11; 34:1-9).

 God precisely decrypts "chromosomal language" and He will designate each Jewish evangelist in his distinct tribe!

As mentioned, another common misinterpretation is the concept that the church replaces Israel, known as Replacement

Theology. This view states that because Israel rejected her Messiah Jesus, she has permanently cast aside by God in favor of the church and the church is considered to be the "New Israel." Although Gentile believers are called the spiritual seed of Abraham, they are not from the physical seed of Jacob (Romans 4:12-18; Galatians 3:7-8, 29). "For nowhere in all of Holy Writ — not once — is the church denoted by the word 'Israel.'"[3]

"Blindness in part has happened to Israel until the fullness of the Gentiles has come in" (Romans 11:25). God says in Jeremiah 31:35-36, "Thus says the Lord, Who gives the sun for a light by day, the ordinances of the moon and the stars for a light by night, Who disturbs the sea, and its waves roar, the Lord of hosts is His name, 'If those ordinances depart from before Me, says the Lord, then the seed of Israel shall also cease from being a nation before Me forever." Because God's ordinances will not cease, neither will Israel!

Twelve is a perfect number, symbolizing God's authority as well as perfect governmental foundation. When squared, it indicates completeness; when multiplied by 1,000, it represents vastness.[4] We cannot place a limit as to how many Jews will eventually come to Christ in the Tribulation, but there is a finite number placed on the number of Jewish evangelists during the Tribulation. The 144,000 are described as "first fruits unto God and to the Lamb" in Revelation 14:4. They represent the first stage of the harvest of Jewish souls who are heaven bound.

Why is there a variance in mentioning the twelve tribes at different times in scripture (Genesis 35;23-25; Exodus 1:2-4; Numbers 1:5-15, 26; I Chronicles 2-8)? Jacob had twelve sons who were the heads of the twelve tribes. Joseph, the eleventh son, had two sons, Ephraim and Manasseh, whose names later were added to the list of the tribes. This makes fourteen names and not all same twelve are listed when presenting the truths concerning Israel. Levi, the priestly tribe, was not endowed with military duties and was therefore not given a portion of the land of Canaan; the Lord Himself was Levi's portion (Deuteronomy 18:1-2). A new tribe needed to fill its place both in military affairs and in the land; therefore, Joseph was replaced by his two sons. When the names of Levi and Joseph were left out, twelve names remained.

In the 144,000 evangelists' case, Dan and Ephraim were left out due to reasons mentioned previously; they immersed themselves in idolatry. But we'll now take a closer look as to why these two tribes are omitted from the honor of evangelizing. According to Deuteronomy 29:18-21, if a man, woman, family or tribe turns away from the Lord and serves the gods of the nations, the Lord will separate them from all the tribes of Israel for adversity. The tribe of Dan migrated north of their original location and persuaded a renegade Levite to join them along with his graven image. They overthrew a town named Laish and renamed it Dan. Thereafter, they set up the carved image and a priesthood resided over it.

Consequently, Dan became a center for idol worship, with one of the two golden calves placed in Dan, courtesy of King Jeroboam, who promoted alternate sites of worship rather than the proper site of Jerusalem (Judges 18:19-30; I Kings 12:28-30). King Jeroboam's second idol was placed in the tribe of Ephraim (Bethel) according to I Kings 12:29. Jeroboam, the king of the ten Northern tribes, therefore, covered the northern and southern parts of Israel, tricking his people to worship man-made idols instead of the living God; this way, he would not lose the loyalty of his people to Rehoboam, the king of the two Southern tribes.

In our text, therefore, Levi replaces Dan and Ephraim is replaced by his father Joseph. Manasseh, Ephraim's brother is included and completes the list of twelve. In Numbers 32:23, God says to Israel (as well as to you and me), "Be sure your sin will find you out." That's not just a quote. That's a promise from God!

In Revelation 2:12-29, the churches of Pergamum and Thyatira were warned about

1. Balaam's teachings, who entices Israel toward idolatry (Numbers 31:1-24).

2. Jezebel's teachings, who promoted Baal worship in the Northern Kingdom (I Kings 18; 21:25).

The people of the earth will worship the Dragon and the Beast and kill those who refuse to worship them (Revelation 13:4, 8, 11-17). And as we'll see in Revelation 17-18, adultery and harlotry are images used of idolatry. Those who worship the Beast and take his mark will be judged and damned (Revelation 14:9; 16:2; 19:20-21). Those who refuse to worship the Beast or take his mark will be martyred but then reign with Christ (Revelation 20:4-6).

Who is to be glorified? John emphatically answers in Revelation 15:4, "Who shall not fear You, O Lord, and glorify Your name? For You alone are holy. For all nations shall come and worship before You, for Your judgments have been manifested." God's servant Joshua said it eloquently, "And if it seems evil to you to serve the Lord, choose for yourselves this day whom you will serve, whether the gods which your fathers served that were on the other side of the River, or the gods of the Amorites, in whose land you dwell. But as for me and my house, we will serve the Lord" (Joshua 24:15). One way or other, you gotta choose!

As we've discussed in previous chapters, Matthew 24 speaks of a time after the Rapture, and "this gospel of the kingdom will be preached in all the world as a witness to all the nations, and then the end will come" (Matthew 24:14). The 144,000, along with Moses and Elijah (Revelation 11) will preach the Gospel of Jesus. A revival unlike any other in history will spread like fire worldwide and multitudes from all nations will come to Christ during the Tribulation. The most horrible time known to mankind will also boast the most converts to Christ!

Tribulation Martyrs

7:9 After these things I looked, and behold, a great multitude which no one could number, of all nations, tribes, peoples, and tongues, standing before the throne and before the Lamb, clothed with white robes, with palm branches in their hands,

The Great Commission, found in Matthew 28:18-20, has now been in effect for 2,000 years, "And Jesus came and spoke to them, saying, 'All authority has been given to Me in heaven and on earth. Go therefore and make disciples of all the nations, baptizing them in the name of the Father and of the Son and of the Holy Spirit, teaching them to observe all things that I have commanded you; and lo, I am with you always, even to the end of the age.' Amen." After seeing the lethargic churches of Asia Minor, John may have been pleasantly surprised to see so many people come to Christ during the Tribulation. There is nothing like hardship, lack, loss and the looming threat of death that can get a man down on his knees! The Tribulation will be such a time. And that will translate into millions of people coming to Christ.

Though I am not a movie enthusiast and have never seen the movie, "The Texas Chainsaw Massacre," I am intrigued by its theatrical poster, "Who Will Survive and What Will Be Left of Them?" The Tribulation will be a time of dread, doom, darkness and disasters such as never recorded before in history. By the end of the fourth seal, one fourth of mankind will be killed (Revelation 6:8). By the end of the sixth trumpet, one third of mankind remaining will be killed (Revelation 9:18). These two combined judgments literally take out half the world's population! This onslaught of terror will not be just a local calamity; it will be global. Who will survive? What will be left of them? That remains to be seen and is out of your control. What then is in your control? To answer this question, you must first come to terms with another question … why would you miss the Rapture and be stricken by the excruciating sorrow and suffering of the Tribulation?

The "great multitude which no one could number" in Revelation 7:9 is the countless company of believers who come to faith in Christ during the Tribulation. They will be persecuted and beheaded (Revelation 20:4) by the Antichrist. John will later see "the woman (Babylon), drunk with the blood of the saints and with the blood of the martyrs of Jesus" (Revelation 17:6).

These believers did not fear those who were able to kill the body, but rather reverenced God who is able to destroy both soul and body in hell (Matthew 10:28). The fourfold description of these saints, referring to them as "nations, tribes, peoples and tongues," emphasizes the worldwide reach of the Gospel. These Tribulation saints are martyrs and not the 144,000 evangelists; they come to Christ because of the work of the 144,000 evangelists.

You'll recall in Revelation 5:9 that the Raptured Church sang a song that also described the worldwide scope of salvation, "You are worthy to take the scroll, and to open its seals; for You were slain, and have redeemed us to God by Your blood out of every tribe and tongue and people and nation, and have made us kings and priest to our God; and we shall reign on the earth."

The Tribulation elect stand "before the throne and before the Lamb, clothed with white robes, with palm branches in their hands," and like the martyrs of the fifth seal (Revelation 6:9-11), they are clothed in white. They will receive their resurrected bodies just prior to the Millennium. How then can they be wearing white robes? When the rich man in the book of Luke died, his body was buried, and his soul went to Hades (Luke 16:1, 22-23). Even though his soul and spirit were without its body, Jesus ascribed eyes and a tongue to his bodiless soul (Luke 16:23-24). Angels as well do not have physical bodies by nature, but the Bible attributes wings, faces, feet and hands to them (Isaiah 6:2-6).

During Jesus' First Coming, we read in John 12:13 that the people of Israel "took branches of palm trees and went out to meet Him, and cried out, 'Hosanna! Blessed is He who comes in the name of the Lord! The King of Israel!'" This gesture became a symbol of national liberation and blessing.[5] During the Feast of Tabernacles (Sukkoth), Israel was instructed to take branches of palm trees and rejoice before the Lord their God for seven days; the boughs were used to make booths or tabernacles, reminding them of how God took care of them in the wilderness for forty years (Leviticus 23:40-43). In the Millennium, all nations will go up to Jerusalem each year, commemorating the literal wilderness experience of Moses and also the symbolic wilderness of Israel's dispersion among the nations after rejecting her Messiah (Zechariah 14:16).

John sees these martyrs standing before the throne of the Lamb, clothed with white robes. Their spilled blood did not save them; only the blood of the Lamb rescued them. They will not be disfigured by their scars. They will not have stains. They will be clothed with the white robes of righteousness, given to them for their endurance by the loving Father. They will not be empty handed. They will no longer be tormented. They once stood trembling in front of the Antichrist. Now they stand praising in the presence of the living God. Their suffering is over! They will sing Hosannas to the Highest as they wave their palm branches in complete adoration and celebration of Christ.

7:10 and crying out with a loud voice, saying, "Salvation belongs to our God who sits on the throne, and to the Lamb!"

The martyrs cry out with a loud voice, "Salvation belongs to our God who sits on the throne, and to the Lamb!" This is similar to Revelation chapter four, where the church worships God for His sovereignty, and Revelation chapter five, where the church worships Christ for His sacrifice. The prophet Zechariah prophesied Jesus' First Coming, "Rejoice greatly, O daughter of Zion! Shout, O daughter of Jerusalem! Behold, your King is coming to you; He is just and having salvation, lowly and riding on a donkey, a colt, the foal of a donkey" (Zechariah 9:9). No one is forcing these Tribulation martyrs to shout, sing, and praise; it comes naturally from a heart of rejoicing. They are in the presence of the Father. They've rounded the bases and have safely slid into home. There is only one way of companionship with the Father: through the Son, who gives the unmatchable gift of salvation.

When Jesus rode a donkey into Jerusalem centuries later on Palm Sunday, fulfilling Zechariah's prophecy, the crowd laid palm branches along His path and cried out, "Hosanna to the Son of David!" (Matthew 21:9). The word "Hosanna" is composed of two parts in the Hebrew: 1) "yashah," meaning save, deliver, help, avenge, defend and rescue and 2) "na," meaning I pray, used in petition or encouragement. The word "Hosanna" developed into a shout of praise and worship, "God you are our Savior, our Defender, and we worship You!" The martyrs raise their voices and worship the Lord in awe, recognizing Him as their Savior.

Salvation was completed at the cross, and now the deed of the earth belongs to Christ, but the full manifestation of praise to God awaits as seen in Revelation 19:1, "After these things (Babylon falling), I heard a loud voice of a great multitude in heaven, saying, "Alleluia! Salvation and glory and honor and power belong to the Lord our God!" Salvation is not found in institutions such as universities or court rooms; salvation is by grace through faith, found in God the Father and His Son, Jesus Christ, through the power of the Holy Spirit.

I believe what infuriates many today is their inability to save themselves. Man is full of self-sufficient pride. PhD's, MD's, ThD's, PharmD's, JD's, or an expensive toy like a Mercedes just can't provide full satisfaction! The Father speaks in Isaiah 43:11, "I, even I, am the Lord, and besides Me there is no Savior."

Zacharias saw the infant Jesus and proclaimed in Luke 1:68-70, "Blessed is the Lord God of Israel, for He has visited and redeemed His people, and has raised up a horn of salvation for us in the house of His servant David, as he spoke by the mouth of His holy prophets."

Search. Read. Study. Dig. Explore. Upside, downside, inside and outside. Here, there and everywhere. You will find that in all the clutter, there is still an emptiness in the center of your soul, a void that can only be filled by the Savior, Jesus Christ! Why are billions of souls still running on empty despite living in plenty? Because they believe everything except the Truth, the person of Jesus Christ, and ironically long for the eternal answer that only Jesus can provide to fill their souls!

7:11 All the angels stood around the throne and the elders and the four living creatures and fell on their faces before the throne and worshiped God, 7:12 saying: "Amen! Blessing and glory and wisdom, thanksgiving and honor and power and might, be to our God forever and ever. Amen."

All of heaven's inhabitants, an innumerable host, including the angels, the church, and the four living creatures fell and worshiped God. The word, "worship," in the Greek is "Proskyneo," meaning to fall forward upon the knees and touch the ground with the forehead, as a tribute and an expression of profound reverence. This worship is sevenfold, making it complete and perfect: blessing, glory, wisdom, thanksgiving, honor, power and might. Power and might stem from Him; wisdom is only found in Him; blessing, glory, thanksgiving and honor belong to Him forever and ever. Amen! Blessed be the name of our Lord!

The emphasis placed in my high school chapel meetings was a declaration I shall always remember, "Man's chief and highest end is to glorify God and enjoy Him forever." Worship has a strong emphasis in the book of Revelation. When John first saw Christ in a vision on the Island of Patmos, he fell prostrate in awe. Man was made to worship someone. Kids "idolize" sports heroes. Adults "idolize" famous personalities. Students "idolize" their mentors. Some "idolize" politicians. Most people "idolize" themselves. The unsaved will turn to the Antichrist and "idolize" and worship him (Revelation 13:4, 8, 12, 15). We all have a profound desire in our souls to worship and if we don't know the true and living God, then we'll worship anything and anyone.

God is worthy to be praised. The distractions of our lives lead us into a storm of complaints. There will be no such disruptions in heaven as we worship God:

1. Sovereign God: the four living creatures are in constant worship, singing "Holy, holy, holy, Lord God Almighty, who was and is and is to come!" (Revelation 4:8).

2. God of Creation: the twenty-four elders, signifying the church, raise their voices, "You are worthy, O Lord, to receive glory and honor and power; for You created all things, and by Your will they exist and were created" (Revelation 4:9-11).

3. God of Redemption: the four living creatures and the twenty-four elders worship God's Son as He takes the scroll, "You are worthy to take the scroll, and to open its seals; for You were slain and have redeemed us to God by Your blood" (Revelation 5:8-9).

4. God of Salvation: the angels, four living creatures, the twenty-four elders, and ten thousand upon ten thousand worship the Lamb, "Worthy is the Lamb who was slain to receive power and riches and wisdom, and strength and honor and glory and blessing!" (Revelation 5:11-12).

5. Godhead: every created being joins in unison, "Blessing and honor and glory and power be to Him who sits on the throne, and to the Lamb, forever and ever!" (Revelation 5:13).

6. Mighty God: innumerable martyrs raise their voices and sing to Yahweh, "Salvation belongs to our God who sits on the throne, and to the Lamb!" (Revelation 7:9-10).

7. Everlasting Father: as mentioned above, all of heaven's inhabitants join the martyrs and proclaim that God alone is to be praised, "Amen! Blessing and glory and wisdom, thanksgiving and honor and power and might, be to our God forever and ever. Amen." (Revelation 7:11-12).

8. The Lord of the universe: when the seventh angel sounds his trumpet in Revelation 11, we hear loud voices in heaven worshiping, "The kingdoms of this world have become the kingdoms of our Lord and of His Christ, and He shall reign forever and ever!" (Revelation 11:15).

9. The Judge, Omnipotent and Omnipresent: after the seventh angel sounds his trumpet, the twenty-four elders fall on their faces and worship God, "We give You thanks, O Lord God Almighty, the One who is and who was and who is to come, because You have taken your great power and reigned. The nations were angry, and Your wrath has come, and the time of the dead, that they should be judged, and that You should reward Your servants the prophets and the saints, and those who fear Your name, small and great, and should destroy those who destroy the earth." (Revelation 11:16-18).

10. Sovereign and Omniscient God: before the unleashing of the seven bowls, martyrs who had overcome the Beast, sing, "Great and marvelous are Your works, Lord God Almighty! Just and true are Your ways, O King of the saints! Who shall not fear You, O Lord, and glorify Your name? For You alone are holy. For all nations shall come and worship before You, for Your judgments have been manifested." (Revelation 15:1-4).

11. Omnipotent God: when Babylon falls, all God's servants worship, singing, "Alleluia! For the Lord God Omnipotent

reigns! Let us be glad and rejoice and give Him glory, for the marriage of the Lamb has come, and His wife has made herself ready." (Revelation 19:1-7).

12. Author and Finisher of our Faith: as we wait for the Bright and Morning Star to take us home in the Rapture, the Spirit and the bride (the Church) say, "Come" in reverence and worship. (Revelation 22:17).

I sometimes find myself saying, "My situation may be bad, but my God is good." He is worthy of my praise. He has given me the greatest gift of all, His Son, and has loved me in my darkest moments. At the end of the day, who will I glorify, myself or God? Where do my blessings come from? Who bestows wisdom to me? Who shall I thank? Who shall I honor? Who is my Almighty God and where does my strength come from? Christ is the only One worthy of my worship.

 Stop and think. Assess your life wisely. Who in your life is praiseworthy? Will you spit or bow at Calvary? Who is the author of your faith presently? Whose mark will you carry? Where will you live for all Eternity?

7:13 Then one of the elders answered, saying to me, "Who are these arrayed in white robes, and where did they come from?"

One of the twenty-four elders asks John to identify those standing before the throne and before the Lamb, clothed with white robes, having palm branches in their hands. The elder is referring to the multitudes we saw in verse nine who were singing, "Salvation belongs to our God who sits on the throne, and to the Lamb!" He asks John, "Where did they come from?" This question helps us to understand that they are new arrivals in heaven because they were not present in chapter four during the Rapture. Nor were they among the multitudes of the redeemed worshiping the Lamb when Christ first took the scroll from the Father in chapter five (Revelation 5:9). They arrived after the 144,000 evangelists were mobilized during the Tribulation. They realized that Christ is the true Messiah and were martyred for their faith.

7:14 And I said to him, "Sir, you know." So he said to me, "These are the ones who come out of the great tribulation, and washed their robes and made them white in the blood of the Lamb.

John is certain that the elder knows and states emphatically, "Sir, you know." The elder tells John that these are the martyrs who have arrived from the ongoing persecution of Christ-followers during the Tribulation. They have gone through the hour of trial that greatly tested those who dwell on earth (Revelation 3:10). Harsh times await those who reject the Lord today, especially for the Jewish nation as they face the time of "Jacob's Trouble" (Jeremiah 30:7). According to Daniel 12:1, "there shall be a time of trouble, such as never was since there was a nation, even to that time." But neither trouble nor hardship, persecution nor famine, nakedness nor danger, torture nor sword, death nor life, angels nor demons, present nor future, nor any powers, neither height nor depth, nor anything else in all creation will be able to separate these Christ-followers from the love of God (Romans 8:35-39).

I recall one day being in the emergency room. The patient was in his 40s and he was not responsive. His appendix had burst, and he had dismissed it as indigestion. For the next twenty-four hours, he stayed in bed, squirming in pain. His family begged him to go the hospital, but he refused. When they found him burning with fever and not able to make sense, they called 911. His veins were collapsed, and I had no time to gown up in the emergency room. I made a slit in his neck and placed a triple lumen catheter that led to his heart, hoping to pour intravenous fluids quickly into his dying body before he was rushed to the operating room. When I was placing the catheter, blood trickled down my shirt, tie, pants and shoes. But my patient's life, not the blood stains, were my priority. Miraculously, our patient made it through the surgery and lived. For the record, the red blood stains never came off my clothes!

There is, however, the blood of One who can turn putrid garments into garments white as snow. As we read this verse, we see that the red spilled blood of the slain Lamb made the martyrs' robes white! They not only received salvation, having their sins washed, but they had a complete transformation of their bloodied garments of persecution into clean robes of glorification! Those who come to Christ are justified by His blood. According to Psalm 116:15, precious in the sight of the Lord is the death of his faithful servants, but still, their spilled blood cannot and does not cause redemption. Leave that to the scarred hands, side and feet of the Savior!

You don't have to wait—you wouldn't want to wait—for the Tribulation to come to Christ. I'm sure many are saying, "You don't know me. You don't know my past. You don't know what I'm come through and you don't know what I've done." You're right. I don't. But consider this.

 If you fill all of earth's oceans with ink; turn all the skies into paper; transform all the tree branches of this world into pens; change every living man into a scribe; and try to transcribe the love of God that He has for you on the papers on high; you'd drain the oceans dry, and run out of paper in the sky.

His love for you is rich. His love for you is pure. His love for you is measureless! Come, as you are, and accept His boundless love for you!

7:15 *Therefore they are before the throne of God, and serve Him day and night in His temple. And He who sits on the throne will dwell among them.*

Because the martyrs are washed in the blood of the Lamb, they enter directly into heaven. Who then stays out? Those who hate, reject, despise, ignore, mock or overlook God, the Son of God and the Holy Spirit. You can't have one without the other. You can't pick and choose, saying, "I'm cool with God, but I don't believe that Christ can save me; and what's the deal about this 'Holy Spirit?'" The Trinity is One. God, Christ and the Holy Spirit will not share their glory with anyone else! If you reject one of them, you reject them all. In Isaiah 42:8, we read, "I am the Lord, that is My name, and My glory I will not give to another, nor My praise to carved images."

These souls did not know Christ as their Savior prior to the Rapture. They were steadfast in their faith during the Tribulation and overcame the Dragon, Satan and "his son," the Antichrist. They endured the most difficult time known to man in all history! We'll soon see in Revelation 12:11 that "they overcame him (Satan) by the blood of the Lamb and by the word of their testimony, and they did not love their lives to the death."

There is no Socialism/Globalism in heaven. If there were, it would work on earth. These martyrs that have come through the Tribulation serve Christ day and night in His temple. Though they will live eternally in heaven, they have a different ministry and destiny than that of the believers who made it into heaven through the Rapture. The church who was Raptured is the bride, and Christ is the Bridegroom. The church will sit upon His throne to rule and reign with the Lord. We will be rulers and judges, kings and priests. Paul declared in I Corinthians 6:2-3, "Do you not know that the saints will judge the world? And if the world will be judged by you, are you unworthy to judge the smallest matters? Do you not know that we shall judge angels? How much more, things that pertain to this life?" Peter declared in I Peter 2:9, "But you are a chosen generation, a royal priesthood, a holy nation, His own special people, that you may proclaim the praises of Him who called you out of darkness into His marvelous light."

John declared in Revelation 1:6, "And has made us kings and priests to His God and Father, to Him be glory and dominion forever and ever. Amen." We'll see in Revelation 14:4 that the 144,000 Jewish evangelists will be as "glorious bodyguards" of the Lamb, following Him wherever He goes; and the destiny of the martyred souls is that of servants of God, carrying out "priestly work" in the Temple.[6]

And God who sits on the throne will dwell with the martyrs. The throne is the epicenter of God's mercies and grace. God sent Christ to earth 2,000 years ago and "the Word became flesh and dwelt among us, and we beheld His glory, the glory as of the only begotten of the Father, full of grace and truth" (John 1:14). And in the future, when believers live with God in the new heaven and earth, God will dwell with us, and we shall be His people. "God Himself will be with them and be their God" (Revelation 21:3). Peals of lightning and thunder may arise from the throne, but from His throne God will also cover His saints with His feathers, and under His wings they will all find shelter and security.

Our existence in heaven will not default to a mundane, mechanical and monotonous life. "You (God) will show me the path of life; in Your presence is fullness of joy; at Your right hand are pleasures forevermore" (Psalm 16:11). Don't you worry about being bored! You will be entertained and productive beyond anything this world can offer! It will be a place of refuge. A place of rest. A place of goodness. A place of health. A place of mercy. A place of fun. A place of laughter. A place of true love without loss, without fear, without cyber-attacks, without accidents, without terrorists, without termites, without trouble, without sickness, without death and without heartaches! Joy awaits us! Oh, how the heart will enjoy His pleasures! Jumping, dancing, singing, rejoicing in the presence of God? You bet!

7:16 *They shall neither hunger anymore nor thirst anymore; the sun shall not strike them, nor any heat;*

These martyrs faced starvation, sleep deprivation, confusion, destruction, defamation, destitution, false litigation, prison, oppression, and persecution. We'll see in Revelation 8:10-11 that when the third trumpet sounds, the third of earth's waters will turn bitter, and when the fourth bowl is poured out in Revelation 16:8-9, there will be extreme global warming that will scorch the skin off people's bodies! The unbelievers will curse God, but these martyrs will remain faithful to Him and enter into the glory of God, where they will no longer hunger or thirst, nor will the sun be able to strike them.

In the wilderness, under Moses' leadership, God created a cloud of smoke by day and a glow of flaming fire by night; God's canopy sheltered them, and it was their glory and defense.[7] In the Millennium, "The Lord will create above every dwelling place of Mount Zion, and above her assemblies, a cloud and smoke by day and the shining of a flaming fire by night. And there will be a tabernacle for shade in the daytime from the heat, for a place of refuge, and for a shelter from storm and rain." (Isaiah 4:5-6). The martyrs will no longer be exposed to the intense scorching heat which they faced in the Tribulation. Isn't it time for you to walk into God's loving arms from the heat of the day and the storms of the night?

7:17 *for the Lamb who is in the midst of the throne will shepherd them and lead them to living fountains of waters. And God will wipe away every tear from their eyes.*

The Antichrist is depicted in Zechariah 11:16-17, "For indeed I will raise up a shepherd in the land who will not care for those who are cut off, nor seek the young, nor heal those that are broken, nor feed those that still stand. But he will eat the flesh of the fat and tear their hooves in pieces. Woe to the worthless shepherd, who leaves the flock! A sword shall be against his arm and against his right eye; his arm shall completely wither, and his right eye shall be totally blinded." We'll see in Revelation 13:3, that "one of his (Antichrist's) heads as if it had been mortally wounded, and his deadly wound was healed. And all the world marveled and followed the Beast." The Antichrist is a worthless and wicked shepherd. He, just as his father, Satan, will deceive millions, shatter their hearts, and take away their lives, only for them to find themselves living in eternal hell!

In contrast, it is said of the Good Shepherd, Jesus Christ. "'I will feed My sheep, and give them rest,' says the Lord God. 'I will look for the lost, bring back those that have gone away, help those who have been hurt, and give strength to the sick" (Ezekiel 34:15-16). In John 10:11 we find Jesus saying, "I am the good shepherd. The good shepherd gives His life for the sheep." And in Isaiah 40:11, we find, "He will feed His flock like a shepherd; He will gather the lambs with His arm, and carry them in His bosom, and gently lead those who are with young." There you have it! The bad shepherd takes the life of the sheep. The good shepherd gives His life for the sheep. Once you grasp this, your life will change! Seek Him while He may still be found!

The lyrics of one of my favorite songs growing up was (and still is), "I've got a river of life flowing out of me, makes the lame to walk and the blind to see, opens prison doors, sets the captive free, I've got a river of life flowing out of me." When you walk with Christ, He will lead you to living fountains. King David said it the best in Psalm 23:1-3, "The Lord is my shepherd; I shall not want. He makes me to lie down in green pastures; He leads me beside the still waters. He restores my soul; He leads me in the paths of righteousness for His name's sake." The living water is free both in the Old Testament and the New Testament, and it will be free in the Millennium and in Eternity:

1. Old Testament: "Everyone who thirsts, come to the waters; and you who have no money, come" (Isaiah 55:1).

2. New Testament: "Whoever drinks of the water that I shall give him will never thirst. But the water that I shall give him will become in him a fountain of water springing up into everlasting life" (John 4:14).

3. Millennium: "And in that day it shall be that living waters shall flow from Jerusalem, half of them toward the eastern sea and half of them toward the western sea" (Zechariah 14:8). "Along the bank of the river, on this side and that, will grow all kinds of trees used for food; their leaves will not wither, and their fruit will not fail. They will bear fruit every month, because their water flows from the sanctuary. Their fruit will be for food, and their leaves for medicine" (Ezekiel 47:12).

4. Eternity: "I am the Alpha and the Omega, the Beginning and the End. To the thirsty I will give water without cost from the spring of the water of life" (Revelation 21:6). "And he showed me a pure river of water of life, clear as crystal, proceeding from the throne of God and of the Lamb" (Revelation 22:1).

"Converts during the tribulation will have to face fierce and bestial persecution at the hands of their fellow-men, and also have to endure natural tribulations which God will unleash on all mankind as a consequence of the sins of the human race. Yes, it will be possible to be saved during the tribulation, but it is infinitely better and imminently more sensible to accept Jesus Christ as one's Savior now, before the tribulation."[8]

There remains hope for those left behind, and it is found in Revelation 7:17. Can you perceive it? The Lamb will shepherd them and lead them to living fountains of waters and God will wipe away every tear from their eyes! Those that remain and turn to Christ will face sorrow, suffering, sickness and a horrible death. But as they enter into heaven, there will be no more shame, no more struggles, no more depression and no more unanswered questions because our God will wipe away all tears and make all things new! This is welcome news for the martyrs. In Eternity, former things, including sin, will pass away and the martyrs will be filled with immeasurable joy! Caution! Warning! Beware! Don't be caught in the Tribulation. Awake from your slumber. Come. Come to the living waters of Christ today!

REV IT UP & SUM IT UP – CHAPTER SEVEN:

The Tribulation is a period of successive, incessant and ruthless bombardment of judgments that will rain down from God's throne upon unbelieving, ungrateful and unrepentant earth-dwellers. There will be a sudden and a startling "break" from the barrage of assaults instructed by God in order to seal His 144,000 Jewish evangelists, 12,000 from every tribe. They will be sealed on their foreheads with God's name and will be exempt from experiencing the horrible plagues that will strike mankind.

These evangelists will present the Gospel worldwide and there will be millions who come to Christ. Those who accept Christ will be blacklisted, demonized, and put on the most wanted list by the New-World-Order officials because they will be deemed "dangerous" and labeled as enemies of the integrity of the New-World-Order. They will face death by being beheaded. Though each martyr's body will remain slain on earth, his soul and spirit will be with the Lord in heaven. He will receive his new and glorified body at the end of the Tribulation and the beginning of the Millennium. He will not have the same position as the saints who were Raptured; he will serve at the temple of the Lord while those who were Raptured will reign from God's throne.

There will be those who receive Christ during the Tribulation, but against all odds, will survive through the seven years; they will be able to "walk into" the Millennium without receiving glorified bodies. Because they will be able to live up to a thousand years, there must be some sort of physical modification that allows the material body to endure these long years. In Ezekiel 47:12, we find that the Millennial trees hold the secret; their leaves will serve as healing, restorative and therapeutic remedies for the residents! These survivors will be designated as the sheep whom Christ will accept into His kingdom. The other Tribulation survivors who rejected Christ will be designated as the goats and will receive the judgment of eternal hell. Scripture defines a sheep as a believer who has submitted his heart to Christ and a goat as a rebellious person who has not (Matthew 25:31–46).

A word of caution to all. Let those who reject Christ come to Him now! Let those in Christ who slumber, awake, pray, and rededicate themselves. The Day of your Salvation is today, and the day of the Rapture is indisputably imminent!

Chapter 8
Trumpet Melodies

We witnessed the sixth seal being opened in Revelation 6:12-17, God's evangelists sealed with His protection in Revelation 7:1-8, and God's servants being martyred in Revelation 7:9-17. In the eighth chapter, the seventh and final seal will be opened, and we'll study about the horrible devastations of the first four trumpets.

The Seventh Seal Yields Seven Trumpets

8:1 When He opened the seventh seal, there was silence in heaven for about half an hour.

Below is a list of the seven seal judgments. We will now discuss the seventh seal.

First Seal: White horse, "peace" (6:1-2).
Second Seal: Red horse, war (6:3-4).
Third Seal: Black horse, famine (6:5-6).
Fourth Seal: Pale horse, death and pestilence (6:7-8).
Fifth Seal: Martyred saints cry from under altar (6:9-11).
Sixth Seal: earthquake; sun-moon-stars disrupted (6:12-17).
Seventh Seal: Seven trumpet judgments released (8:1-6).

The seventh seal contains seven trumpets (Revelation 8:2) and we'll soon see that the seventh trumpet contains the seven bowls of God's wrath (Revelation 11:15; 15:1). The seventh seal, therefore, establishes a new series of judgments. Consequently, regarding the seventh trumpet, John writes "in the days of the sounding of the seventh angel, when he is about to sound, the mystery of God would be finished, as He declared to His servants the prophets" (Revelation 10:7). John states this beforehand, knowing that the bowl judgments will be the final judgments that will devastate mankind.

 Everything is measured. Everything is timed. Nothing is random. God is not early. He is not late. He is not unsure. He is not confused. He is patient. He is sovereign. He is in control. And He is always on time.

When the first four trumpets sound, cataclysmic destruction ensues and mars the life-sustaining ecosystem, bringing significant harm to mankind (Revelation 8:7-12). The three to follow, the fifth, sixth and seventh trumpets, will be even more devastating, and will affect man directly, maiming their health and life (Revelation 9:1-20; 11:15-19). Keep in mind that it is the slain and resurrected Lamb who is opening up the seals, who is in charge of initiating all these judgments that befall mankind.

When Christ opens the seventh seal, all of the noise in heaven, the worshiping, the glorifying, the praising, the singing, the jubilee comes to a complete halt for half an hour. Not one sound is heard. The horrible wrath that is to fall upon man is so severe and so intense, that heaven stops and gazes in awe as the Lord begins to purify the earth. The intent of the judgments is for purification, cleansing the earth of man's mess. "Both the redeemed and the angels are reduced to silence in anticipation of the grim reality of the destruction they see written on the scroll. The half an hour of silence is the calm before the storm. It is the silence of foreboding, of intense expectation, of awe at what God is about to do."[1] Scripture speaks in other places of silence when heaven and earth bow before the Lord in reverence, awe and fear:

1. "You caused judgment to be heard from heaven; the earth feared and was still" (Psalm 76:8).

2. "Be silent in the presence of the Lord God; for the day of the Lord is at hand" (Zephaniah 1:7).

3. "But the Lord is in His holy temple. Let all the earth keep silent before Him" (Habakkuk 2:20).

4. "Be silent, all flesh, before the Lord, for He is aroused from his holy habitation!" (Zechariah 2:13).

The silence will usher in a downpour of judgments unlike any recorded in all human history. It is an ominous sign of shattering judgments to follow, and all of heaven's inhabitants experience a surreal wonder in their hearts.

8:2 And I saw the seven angels who stand before God, and to them were given seven trumpets.

 There are rankings in heaven, even among angels; not all angels are of the same agency or dignity or of the same "pedigree."

There are dominions, principalities and powers among the celestial orders. For instance, there are chief princes, archangels, cherubim and seraphim. Three powerful angels are named in the Bible: Michael, who is a mighty warrior, the great prince and the protector of Israel (Daniel 10:13; 12:1); Gabriel, who is the great news bearer, standing in the presence of God (Daniel 8:16; Luke 1:19); Lucifer, who became the fierce and fallen angel, the Dragon (Isaiah 14:12; Revelation 12:3).

It is not known who these seven angels are, but they do stand before God, and seven is the perfect and complete number to accomplish God's work. These seven angels are not the seven Spirits of God that appear before the throne (Revelation 4:5) nor are they the twenty-four elders, representing the church, who sit on thrones, clothed in white robes with crowns of gold on their heads (Revelation 4:4). They are members of a privileged group of powerful angels, as is Gabriel, who stand in the presence of God and have close access to Him.

"In eastern courts the most favored courtiers had the right to enter the king's presence at all times; these angels are angels of the presence; their high rank is thus confirmed."[2] When Gabriel spoke to Zechariah the priest, proclaiming that he and his wife, Elizabeth would have a son, Zechariah doubted and asked, "How can I be sure of this? I am an old man and my wife is well along in years." Gabriel answered, "I am Gabriel. I stand in the presence of God, and I have been sent to speak to you and to tell you this good news" (Luke 1:18-19). As Gabriel dwells in the presence of God, so too are these seven angels, who stand before God. Make no mistake, they are loyal, they are the elect, and they are amongst the elite, having the right to enter the presence of the King! Spanning from angels to humans, there is no Socialism/Globalism in heaven!

Each angel was given a trumpet by divine decree. We are about to witness the next set of seven judgments in the series of seals, trumpets and bowls. As we move towards Armageddon, the judgments intensify. You'll also note that there is an alignment between the trumpet and bowl judgments; one third of life sustaining entities such as trees, seas, springs of water and the sun are destroyed in the first four trumpet judgments, while the same entities are entirely destroyed in the first four bowl judgments, respectively.

In Zephaniah 1:14-18, we read, "The great day of the Lord is near; it is near and hastens quickly. The noise of the day of the Lord is bitter; there the mighty men shall cry out. That day is a day of wrath, a day of trouble and distress, a day of devastation and desolation, a day of darkness and gloominess, a day of clouds and thick darkness, a day of trumpet and alarm against the fortified cities and against the high towers. 'I will bring distress upon men, and they shall walk like blind men, because they have sinned against the Lord; their blood shall be poured out like dust, and their flesh like refuse.' Neither their silver nor their gold shall be able to deliver them in the day of the Lord's wrath; but the whole land shall be devoured by the fire of His jealousy, for He will make speedy riddance of all those who dwell in the land."

The Day of the Lord which begins at the Rapture and includes the Tribulation is beyond all horror! We now see the seven angels sounding seven trumpets of alarm and devastation, that will ultimately lead to the fall of Babylon and ushering in the Millennium. The seven trumpets leading to Babylon's fall parallels the seven rams' horns that were blown to overthrow Jericho in the days of Joshua, allowing Israel to enter the Promised Land (Joshua 6:4-5).

***8:3** Then another angel, having a golden censer, came and stood at the altar. He was given much incense, that he should offer it with the prayers of all the saints upon the golden altar which was before the throne.*

Another angel, who acts as a ministering spirit, has a golden censer full of incense just as the twenty-four elders have golden bowls full of incense, which are the prayers of the saints (Revelation 5:8).[3] Let's review what we see throughout scripture regarding incense:

1. On the day of Atonement (Yom Kippur), Aaron took a censer (a pan suspended by chains) and filled it with burning coals. The fiery coals were first transported from the Brazen Altar to the Altar of Incense, having been saturated by the blood of the innocent lambs. Two handfuls of finely ground fragrant incense were added to the coals. He took the censer behind the veil from the Holy Place into the Holy of Holies and placed the incense before the Lord. This formed a cloud of smoke that covered

the mercy seat that sat on top of the Ark of the Covenant, where God's presence resided. The cloud protected Aaron from the overpowering presence of God, lest he die (Leviticus 16:12-13).

 The atoning incense rises with a plea from sinful man and is embraced with mercy and grace by a holy God.

2.   When Israel was wandering in the wilderness for forty years, men rose up against Moses and Aaron and questioned their authority. A total of 250 rebellious Israelites died, which incited the congregation of the children of Israel to complain against Moses and Aaron and rise up against them, saying, "You have killed the people of the Lord." The Lord spoke to Moses and Aaron, saying, "Get away from among this congregation, that I may consume them in a moment."

Moses said to Aaron, "Take a censer and put fire in it form the altar, put incense on it, and take it quickly to the congregation and make atonement for them; for wrath has gone out from the Lord. The plague has begun." Since the plague had begun, Aaron ran in the midst of the assembly, put in the incense and made atonement for the people, and the plague stopped. A staggering 14,700 people died. The plague would have claimed more lives if it weren't for the atoning incense, the plea, the prayer, the petition, the intercession and the supplication for mercy unto God. (Numbers 16:1-50).

3.   The prayers of the saints, as we saw in Revelation 5:8 (the 24 elders holding golden bowls full of incense signifying the prayers of saints) are the continual cries of God's elect throughout history, many of which have remained unanswered for thousands of years. They are like the fragrance of incense which rises to God and will find their fulfillment in the Campaign of Armageddon, the Millennium

and Eternity. David cried out in Psalm 141:1-2, "Lord, I cry out to You; make haste to me! Give ear to my voice when I cry out to You. Let my prayer be set before You as incense, the lifting up of my hands as the evening sacrifice."

4.   Petitions for justice are made by martyrs under the altar of incense at the opening of the fifth seal; these are the cries of believers against their persecutors (Revelation 6:9-11). Our verse in Revelation 8:3 reminds us again of the importance of past, present and future prayers rising up to God, not ignored, forgotten nor scorned, but landing in the bosom of our God who cares for His children as a Good Shepherd.

5.   In Malachi 1:11, the prophet spoke of a time in the Millennium when incense will be offered to God by all of earth's inhabitants, by both Jews and Gentiles; "'For from the rising of the sun, even to its going down, My name shall be great among the Gentiles; in every place incense shall be offered to My name, and a pure offering; for My name shall be great among the nations,' says the Lord of hosts."

Get your bowl that holds your prayers. Get your incense. Let's cast our cares on God for He cares for us! He will sustain us and will not allow the righteous to be shaken (Psalm 55:22; I Peter 5:7).

8:4 And the smoke of the incense, with the prayers of the saints, ascended before God from the angel's hand.

As the incense of the saints' prayers rise to God, He listens with a compassionate heart and offers His merciful hand. According to Lamentations 3:22-23, "Through the Lord's mercies we are not consumed, because His compassions fail not. They are new every morning; Great is Your faithfulness." Herein lies our great hope: all of the believer's prayers will be shortly answered. The prayers of believers and God's mercies towards His children, and their pleas for justice and God's wrath towards His haters are all interdependent and soon to be revealed!

There were two altars in the tabernacle, a larger one in the outer court called the Brazen Altar where sacrifices were made and a smaller one in the Holy Place called the Altar of Incense where the priests offered incense to the Lord (Leviticus 4:7). The earthly tabernacle was a model of the greater and perfect tabernacle in heaven not made with hands (Hebrews 9:11).

It is the heavenly Altar of Incense that we are seeing in this verse from which prayers are being offered to God. Christ was crucified on the cross, or the Brazen Altar, and rose from the dead. That is why we do not see a Brazen Altar in heaven. We only see the Altar of Incense. The only way our prayers reach the throne of God is through our Mediator Jesus Christ. According to I Timothy 2:5, "For there is one God and one mediator between God and men, the Man Christ Jesus."

In the Old Testament, the daily tasks of the priests were tedious. "After passing the (brazen) altar and the laver the priest entered the main room of the Tabernacle or Temple called the sanctuary (Holy Place). In it he saw, first of all, the seven-branched candlestick, symbol of Christ the Light. Then he found the table of shewbread, Christ the Bread of Life, where the saints feed; then at the far end of the room, a golden altar which is called the altar of incense. No blood sacrifice was offered on this altar, though the incense, which was burned before it had to be lighted with fire, procured from the (brazen) altar where the blood of the lamb had dripped. The fire had originally been lighted from the holy presence of God, and it was the failure on the part of Nadab and Abihu (Old Testament priests) to light their incense with the fire from the altar (without getting the fire from the brazen altar), which caused their death, when they brought strange fire (without the blood of the Lamb) into the presence of God.

This teaches, of course, that all worship must be on the basis of the redemption accomplished by Christ."[4]

The prayers of the saints are an aroma pleasing to God. When Hezekiah reinstated the Passover after the Babylonian exile, the Jews were not able to observe the festival in strict accordance to God's laws because a sufficient number of priests had not consecrated themselves nor had the people gathered together at Jerusalem. Yet, God was pleased with their prayers because of the sincere motivation of their hearts. In II Chronicles 30:1-27 we read, "Then the priests, the Levites, arose and blessed the people, and their voice was heard; and their prayer came up to His holy dwelling place, to heaven." We see in the New Testament that Peter was sent to a devout and generous Gentile, Cornelius the centurion of the Italian Regiment, to proclaim the Gospel. Why? The angel who visited Cornelius explained, "Your prayers and your alms have come up for a memorial before God" (Acts 10:4).

When there seems to be an iron ceiling above you and your prayers seem "trapped" on earth, keep on praying, keep on interceding, keep on asking, keep on trusting, keep on obeying and keep on believing. Your words, your groans, your heart's song and the tears that fall from your eyes are rising to the Father as sweet incense that warms His heart! May His love fall upon you as He crowns you with favor!

8:5 *Then the angel took the censer, filled it with fire from the altar, and threw it to the earth. And there were noises, thunderings, lightnings, and an earthquake.*

The same prayers that rose from believers as a sweet aroma to God will result in judgment of the unbelievers. Incense ascends to heaven, but fire is cast upon earth. "If the world will not have Jesus Christ as its Savior and King, it must have Him as Judge."[5]

Unanswered prayers and petitions are now answered. We read

in Romans 12:19, "Beloved, do not avenge yourselves, but rather give place to wrath; for it is written, 'Vengeance is Mine, I will repay,' says the Lord." Vengeance and wrath are not up to us; it's up to the Father. And here, we see it in full display. The Father is now taking care of all unanswered prayers, sabotage, betrayal, injustice, lies, deceits and coverups. No longer will the sinister haters be able to hide or slide. They will be baptized with judgment and fire.

The noises, thundering, lightning and earthquakes all signify a verdict, people strictly guilty of hating the goodness of God and persecuting His servants. "These terms compose a formula of catastrophe; and the fourfold character here (noises, thundering, lightning, and earthquakes) denotes universality of the catastrophe."[6] The thunder and lightning signify impending judgments that have been withheld since the creation of mankind due to God's great mercy.

How ironic! As I was writing this paragraph, there was a 7.1 earthquake that hit Southern California. It had a rolling motion, almost as if someone were playing tug-of-war on your body, pulling you back and forth. It's awkward to watch the ceiling fan sway like a rocking chair as you ponder if the shaking and rattling will intensify and the slip and slide motion will keep on mounting.

The sheer horror of the trumpets will be a magnitude greater than ten out of ten; the fear, the torment, the cries, the anguish will be unbearable as the courage of the God-hating world dwellers begins to dwindle. Just imagine, these noises, thundering, lightning, and an earthquake from God's throne are mere foreshocks before the trumpets begin to sound and catastrophic seismic events occur!

Before the glory of God departed from Solomon's temple in 586 BC, Ezekiel describes how God commanded that coals of fire be scattered over Jerusalem as a sign of judgment against His people for rejecting Him as their Lord. "And I (Ezekiel) looked, and there in the firmament that was above the head of the cherubim, there appeared something like a sapphire stone, having the appearance of the likeness of a throne. Then He (God) spoke to the man clothed with linen, and said, 'Go in among the wheels, under the cherub, fill your hands with coals of fire from among the cherubim, and scatter them over the city.' And he went in as I watched" (Ezekiel 10:1-2).

It's stunning to think that God allowed the destruction of Jerusalem, His beloved City; that is the price of sin. But what is more staggering is His patience in delivering the blow, waiting and pleading with His people for three hundred years to turn back to Him. God is patient. He is kind. He is forgiving. He is giving. No matter who you are, what you've done and what you're doing, He died for you so that you may live. Come to Him and embrace His love for you! I pray that you raise your voice in humility to Him rather than raising your fist in anger against Him.

8:6 *So the seven angels who had the seven trumpets prepared themselves to sound.*

This is a solemn moment. The prayers of the saints have risen as sweet incense to God's throne and the seven judgments, each preceded by a trumpet blow, are about to fall on earth with added gravity compared to the previous six seal judgments. A trumpet sound can indicate:

1. Judging the wicked, those who have been offered the gift of God's grace, but have chosen to dismiss it:

    a. When Joshua and the Israelites marched around the walls of Jericho the seventh time, trumpets were sounded. "And the seventh time it happened, when the priests blew the trumpets, that Joshua said to the people, 'Shout, for the Lord has given you the city! Now the city shall be doomed by the Lord to destruction, it and all who are in it. Only Rahab the harlot shall live, she and all who are with her in the house, because she hid the messengers that we sent'" (Joshua 6:16-17).

b. When Gideon and one hundred men attacked their oppressive enemies, the Midianites, trumpets were sounded. "When I (Gideon) blow the trumpet, I and all who are with me, then you also blow the trumpets on every side of the whole camp, and say, 'The sword of the Lord and Gideon!'" (Judges 7:18).

c. When the seventh seal is opened in the Tribulation, the trumpet judgments will affect reprobate and unrepentant souls. "It is a fearful thing to fall into the hands of the living God" (Hebrews 10:31). God is gracious, kind and patient, not taking satisfaction in the demise of the wicked, and still extending salvation to mankind even during the Tribulation! And though God will show miraculous signs from heaven, multitudes will still not repent (Revelation 6:12-17). For our text, God's wrath has reached a breaking point and is the most fitting reason for the use of the seven trumpets.

2. Calling to assemble God's people:

a. In the wilderness, the Israelites were called to meet at the tabernacle. "And the Lord spoke to Moses, saying, 'Make two silver trumpets for yourself; you shall make them of hammered work; you shall use them for calling the congregation and for directing the movement of the camps. When they blow both of them, all the congregation shall gather before you at the door of the tabernacle of meeting'" (Numbers 10:1-3).

b. In the Rapture, believers are called up to meet Christ in the air. "For the Lord Himself will descend from heaven with a shout with the voice of an archangel, and with the trumpet of God. And the dead in Christ will rise first. Then we who are alive and remain shall be caught up together with them in the clouds to meet the Lord in the air. And thus, we shall always be with the Lord" (I Thessalonians 4:16-17).

   c. In the Millennium, nations are called to assemble in Jerusalem to worship Christ. "So it shall be in that day: the great trumpet will be blown; they will come, who are about to perish in the land of Assyria, and they who are outcasts in the land of Egypt and shall worship the Lord in the holy mount at Jerusalem" (Isaiah 27:13).

3. Sounding the alarm for war:

   a. An ominous warning such as the announcement of the Day of the Lord (from the Rapture through the Tribulation and Millennium). "Blow the trumpet in Zion and sound an alarm in My holy mountain! Let all the inhabitants of the land tremble; for the day of the Lord is coming, for it is at hand" (Joel 2:1).

   b. The Second Coming of Christ, to engage in the Campaign of Armageddon. "Then the sign of the Son of Man will appear in heaven, and then all the tribes of the earth will mourn, and they will see the Son of Man coming on the clouds of heaven with power and great glory. And He will send His angels with a great sound of a trumpet, and they will gather together His elect from the four winds, from one end of heaven to the other" (Matthew 24:30-31).

4. Resting from normal responsibilities.

   a. The Feast of the Trumpets opens the fall holiday season for the Jews, known today as Rosh Hashanah or the Jewish New Year (usually September or October). It precedes the Day of Atonement (Yom Kippur, tenth day of the Jewish seventh month, Tishri, a day of rest and confession, Leviticus 23:27) and the Feast of Tabernacles (Sukkot, 15th day of the seventh month, eight days of rest, commemorating the exodus from Egypt).

"Speak to the children of Israel, saying, 'In the seventh month, on the first day of the month, you shall have a sabbath-rest, a memorial of blowing of trumpets, a holy convocation. You shall do no customary work on it; and you shall offer an offering made by fire to the Lord'" (Leviticus 23:24-25).

b. After 6,000 years of trials, toils and troubles of mankind's history, the saints who are Raptured and those will be martyred in the Tribulation will finally rest with the Father after distinct trumpets are sounded!

5. Mobilizing God's people.

a. The Israelites at Mount Sinai under Moses' leadership. "When the trumpet sounds long, they shall come near the mountain" (Exodus 19:13).

b. In the wilderness. "When you sound the trumpet, the camps that lie on the east side (of the tabernacle) shall then begin their journey. When you sound the trumpet the second time, then the camps that lie on the south side shall begin their journey; they shall sound the call for them to begin the journeys" (Numbers 10:5-6).

c. God will "mobilize" His saints in the Rapture and call them home! John's sudden ascent to heaven symbolized this in Revelation 4:1, "After these things I looked, and behold, a door standing open in heaven. And the first voice which I heard was like a trumpet speaking with me, saying, 'Come up here, and I will show you things which must take place after this.'"

We will now witness the work and ministry of the seven angels with the seven trumpets, remembering that the seventh seal opened by Christ releases the seven trumpet judgments. "The seals and trumpets are still in the phase of the beginning of sorrows."[7]

We are still in the first half of the seven-year Tribulation at this point in the book. For many, God is looked upon as a monster. That is far from the truth! God's heart is so tender and kind, "'For I have no pleasure in the death of one who dies,' says the Lord God. 'Therefore, turn and live!'" (Ezekiel 18:32). God's cry to Israel holds true to everyone today and extends to the Tribulation period, "'Say to them, 'As I live,' says the Lord God, 'I have no pleasure in the death of the wicked, but that the wicked turn from his way and live. Turn, turn, from your evil ways! For why should you die, O house of Israel?'" (Ezekiel 33:11).

 Listen to God's heart! Though the wrath of God is pouring, He is still pleading and His hand of grace is still pardoning!

According to II Peter 3:9, God is not willing that any should perish but that all should come to repentance. The word, "all," in the Greek is "pas," meaning every, all men, whosoever, everyone, all manner of, each and the whole. God is no respecter of persons; come to Him all who are weary, and He will give you rest! (Acts 10:34; Matthew 11:28).

Don't pull a Pharaoh: "'Who is the Lord, that I should obey His voice to let Israel go? I do not know the Lord, nor will I let Israel go!'" (Exodus 5:2). Pharaoh not only ended up letting God's people go, but he also got to know God!

First Trumpet: The Vegetation Spoiled

8:7 The first angel sounded: And hail and fire followed, mingled with blood, and they were thrown to the earth. And a third of the trees were burned up, and all green grass was burned up.

Below is a list of the seven trumpet judgments. We will now discuss the first trumpet.

First Trumpet: 1/3 of trees & grass burned (8:7).

Second Trumpet: 1/3 of sea life & ships destroyed (8:8-9).
Third Trumpet: 1/3 of rivers poisoned–Wormwood (8:10-11).
Fourth Trumpet: 1/3 of sun, moon, stars struck (8:12).
Fifth Trumpet: demonic locusts torment the ungodly (9:1-12).
Sixth Trumpet: four angels at Euphrates lead army (9:13-21).
Seventh Trumpet: seven bowls of wrath released (11:15-19).

Many subscribe to the theory that the description in verse
seven is solely symbolic. I disagree. I believe that there will be
physical demolition of our earth unlike anything seen in the
past. The devastating and heart wrenching California Camp
Fire of 2018 that tragically claimed so many lives will appear
as a mere flicker compared to the first trumpet. Egypt and
all its inhabitants faced physical, tangible and measurable
disasters and so will the inhabitants of the earth during the
Tribulation.

We read in Exodus 9:23-26 that "Moses stretched out his rod
toward heaven; and the Lord sent thunder and hail, and fire
darted to the ground. And the Lord rained hail on the land
of Egypt. So there was hail, and fire mingled with the hail, so
very heavy that there was none like it in all the land of Egypt
since it became a nation. And the hail struck throughout the
whole land of Egypt, all that was in the field, both man and
beast; and the hail struck every herb of the field and broke
every tree of the field. Only in the land of Goshen, where the
children of Israel were, there was no hail." In our text, when
the first angel sounds the trumpet, "hail and fire followed,
mingled with blood, and they were thrown to the earth."
According to Job 38:22, God has access to His "treasury of hail"
and has reserved it for the "time of trouble."

When the five kings of the Amorites attacked Joshua, they
were overcome and fled before Israel from Beth-Horon, and
"the Lord cast down large hailstones from heaven on them
as far as Azekah, and they died. There were more who died
from the hailstones than the children of Israel killed with the
sword." Then Joshua asked for a miracle, and the "sun stood

still in the midst of heaven and did not hasten to go down for about a whole day" (Joshua 10:1-15). Large hailstones were seen as God's handiwork in the past; they will reappear as we see in our text in Revelation 8:7 and will also reappear and strike man at the tail end of the Great Tribulation (Revelation 16:21).

Under the Mosaic Law, if anyone blasphemed the name of God, "all the congregation shall certainly stone him, the stranger as well as him who is born in the land" (Leviticus 24:10-16). Also, if anyone led another to worship other gods, he was to be killed, "and you shall stone him with stones until he dies, because he sought to entice you away from the Lord your God, who brought you out of the land of Egypt, from the house of bondage" (Deuteronomy 13:6-10). Whether it was for blasphemy or idolatry, they were to be stoned. In the Tribulation, the inhabitants of the earth continue to blaspheme God and worship idols, and as the first trumpet is sounded, hail mingled with fire will "stone" them.

The "formula" for judgment includes the three elements of hail, fire and blood, forecasting a dismal future. In Matthew 3:12 we read that God will "gather His wheat (believers) into the barn but He will burn up the chaff (unbelievers) with unquenchable fire." Blood is an essential "ingredient" in this mix as well to remind the unbelievers of the martyrs' blood that they have shed. Volcanic activity along with nuclear arsenals may take part in this devastating display of disarray, but the Lord is more than capable of setting in motion this pandemonium with a "simple" word from His mouth.

When the first trumpet sounds, proponents of Earth Day are not going to have a good day! Today, many have fallen at the feet of "Mother Nature" and have snubbed Father Creator. We should all protect our earth, we should all be compassionate towards animals and we should all decrease waste and pollution. It seems to me, however, that the extreme view of some has become a religion and instead of worshiping God, the environmentalists and global warming-climate change activists worship the creation and reject the power and beauty of the Creator, God, His Son and His Spirit. The 144,000 Jewish evangelists, who are exempt from these judgments, will preach the Gospel as hail, fire and blood emerge from God's storehouse and put a huge dent in what is being worshiped, the earth.

And a third of the trees were burned up, and all green grass was burned up. We are not dealing with a house, or street, or city, or county, or state or a country; we are dealing with the incineration of one third of the world! Each trumpet plague will affect one third of man's physical environment. First, plant life, the primary source of food. Second, the sea, a major source of food. Third, water, which sustains life. Fourth, light, which also sustains life. Just as we saw in Egypt and recorded in Psalm 105:33 where God "struck their (Egypt's) vines also, and their fig trees, and splintered the trees of their territory," so too one third of the trees and grass will be splintered and die. Consequently, a food shortage will follow, causing a great famine in the land.

What is to come was prophesied in the Old Testament in Joel 1:15-20, "Alas for the day! For the day of the Lord is at hand; it shall come as destruction from the Almighty. Is not the food cut off before our eyes, joy and gladness from the house of our God? The seed shrivels under the clods, storehouses are in shambles; barns are broken down, for the grain has withered. How the animals groan! The herds of cattle are restless, because they have no pasture; even the flocks of sheep suffer punishment. O Lord, to You I cry out; for fire has devoured the open pastures, and a flame has burned all the trees of the field. The beasts of the field also cry out to You, for the water brooks are dried up, and fire has devoured the open pastures."

When one third of the trees and grass are destroyed, this cataclysmic event will not only affect the landscape of earth, but the people and animals who are its residents.

The plagues that were isolated to the Egyptians during Pharaoh's time will now be all inclusive, involving all mankind in the Tribulation; what occurred on a "small" scale will play out on the world stage; what was remembered as history now becomes front page headlines; what was local will go global. Before we proceed, let's observe the supernatural alignment of Egypt's plagues with those of the Tribulation:

1. Water becomes blood (Exodus 7:20; Psalm 105:29; Revelation 8:8-9, 11:6).
2. Frogs infiltrate (Exodus 8:1-15; Psalm 105:30; Revelation 16:13).
3. Lice intrude (Exodus 8:16; Psalm 105:31; Revelation 11:6).
4. Flies encroach (Exodus 8:24; Revelation 11:6).
5. Livestock destroyed (Exodus 9:6; Revelation 8:9).
6. Boils spring up (Exodus 9:10; Revelation 16:2).
7. Hail pours down (Exodus 9:23; Psalm 105:32; Revelation 8:7, 16:21).
8. Locusts ravage (Exodus 10:13; Psalm 105:34; Revelation 9:3).
9. Darkness resides (Exodus 10:22; Psalm 105:32; Revelation 8:12, 9:2).
10. Firstborn dies (Exodus 12:29; Psalm 105:36; Revelation 6:15-17).[8]

Second Trumpet: The Seas Marred

8:8 Then the second angel sounded: And something like a great mountain burning with fire was thrown into the sea, and a third of the sea became blood. 8:9 And a third of the living creatures in the sea died, and a third of the ships were destroyed.

Below is a list of the seven trumpet judgments. We will now discuss the second trumpet.

First Trumpet: 1/3 of trees & grass burned (8:7).
Second Trumpet: 1/3 of sea life & ships destroyed (8:8-9).
Third Trumpet: 1/3 of rivers poisoned–Wormwood (8:10-11).
Fourth Trumpet: 1/3 of sun, moon, stars struck (8:12).
Fifth Trumpet: demonic locusts torment the ungodly (9:1-12).
Sixth Trumpet: four angels at Euphrates lead army (9:13-21).
Seventh Trumpet: seven bowls of wrath released (11:15-19).

"Something like a great mountain" is not a mountain; it is "something like" a great mountain. It is not a volcanic eruption. It is a great rock, a "fireball" from space, specifically targeting the sea and causing a third of it to turn into blood. "This is evidently a giant meteorite or asteroid, surrounded by flaming gases set ablaze by the friction of the earth's atmosphere, on a collision course with the earth. The current doomsday scenarios about an asteroid hitting the earth will come true with a vengeance.'"[9]

The Father is methodically eliminating every life-sustaining resource to teach man that he is not independent of the one and only true and living God. God has received much ingratitude for His gifts; now man will receive another "stone" falling into the seas, from which man arrogantly, blindly and erroneously believes we evolved. "As the text does not say the sea became 'like' blood but that it 'became' blood, and, as the same word is used in Revelation 16:6, this should not be taken as only describing the color of the oceans, but must be understood either literally, or with its secondary meaning of 'death.'"[10]

Man's second source of food is now under attack; the sea not only provides food, but oxygen, produced by the phytoplankton and algae in the oceans; as He has devastated the landscape of the earth, God now devastates the sea.[11] With the mountain-like stone falling into the ocean, there will be a titanic disturbance in the ocean, creating deadly tsunamis. These gigantic tidal waves will sink one third of the ocean's ships; one third of the ports will collapse, paralyzing commerce and transportation, as economic chaos results.

Visiting Pearl Harbor is heartbreaking, seeing the devastation that America witnessed as all eight U.S. Navy battleships were damaged. With all due respect and well-deserved honor and gratitude to our great military and the heroes, both men and women, who died and those who serve today, Pearl Harbor will seem minuscule compared to one third of all ships in the world being destroyed.

 The death tolls will be shocking, the scene baffling, and the stench, maddening.

Will people continue to turn their backs to God? Remember, multitudes are coming to Christ, but just as Pharaoh refused to repent, multitudes will also follow course and will reject God during the Tribulation (Revelation 6:16-17; 9:20; 16:9, 11, 21). As Pharaoh hardened his heart, man will harden his heart. God says of Pharaoh, "For this very purpose I have raised you up, that I may show My power in you, and that My name may be declared in all the earth" (Exodus 9:16; Romans 9:17).

People may not accept God during the Tribulation, but they will know Him! Just as the plagues during Moses' leadership caused the fall of Egypt and the birth of the theocratic kingdom of Israel, the plagues of the Tribulation will cause the downfall of the Antichrist and birth the Millennial Kingdom of Christ!

Third Trumpet: The Waters Poisoned

***8:10** Then the third angel sounded: And a great star fell from heaven, burning like a torch, and it fell on a third of the rivers* *and on the springs of water. **8:11** The name of the star is Wormwood. A third of the waters became wormwood, and many men died from the water, because it was made bitter.*

Below is a list of the seven trumpet judgments. We will now discuss the third trumpet.

First Trumpet: 1/3 of trees & grass burned (8:7).
Second Trumpet: 1/3 of sea life & ships destroyed (8:8-9).
Third Trumpet: 1/3 of rivers poisoned–Wormwood (8:10-11).
Fourth Trumpet: 1/3 of sun, moon, stars struck (8:12).
Fifth Trumpet: demonic locusts torment the ungodly (9:1-12).
Sixth Trumpet: four angels at Euphrates lead army (9:13-21).
Seventh Trumpet: seven bowls of wrath released (11:15-19).

This astronomical body, a great star, may also be a meteor or comet like the great mountain in verse eight. It may even be a nuclear catastrophe. It is "burning like a torch" from outer space. As noted in Isaiah 14:12, Satan, son of the morning, fell from heaven. In Revelation 12:4, Satan and his demons (one third of the stars) fell from heaven. The great star in our text is not a spiritual being, but a cosmological event describing an enormous physical object producing poignant physical calamities.

Man can survive about three weeks without food, but only one week without water. Lack of water will lead to extreme droughts and countless deaths will ensue. God continues to destroy what He created originally to show man that he is completely dependent on Him.

 Man can say there is no God; he can wish there were no God; he can even curse God; but that does not change the existence and sovereignty of God.

Tragically, multitudes will refuse to call on His name as their only hope and saving grace.

Contrast this with the martyrs we saw in the previous chapter.

The martyrs spilled their blood, but "they shall neither hunger anymore nor thirst anymore; the sun shall not strike them, nor any heat; for the Lamb who is in the midst of the throne will shepherd them and lead them to living fountains of waters. And God will wipe away every tear from their eyes" (Revelation 7:16). The earth-dwellers who remain during the Tribulation have likely participated, whether by direct commission or indirect omission, in the deaths of martyrs. Those who murdered and spilled blood, will now drink blood. Those whose blood was spilled are now drinking from living fountains of water in the presence of God.

We find the name of this great star to be Wormwood. I was surprised to find this word a total of seven times in the Bible before reading Revelation 8:11. The word signifies an idolatrous and apostate heart (Deuteronomy 29:17-18); a trap leading to death (Proverbs 5:4); judgment, affliction and misery (Jeremiah 9:15; 23:15; Lamentations 3:15, 19); injustice and unrighteousness (Amos 5:7). It is "apsinthion" in the Greek, signifying bitterness and calamity.

Wormwood is an herb and its bitter dark green oil is used for medicinal purposes such as intestinal pain, spasms and killing intestinal worms.[12] Some believe that the disaster at Chernobyl, which is translated to "wormwood," is the star that fell from the sky causing bitterness. The city was evacuated on April 27, 1986, thirty hours after the nuclear power plant accident and is mostly a ghost town today. The Wormwood spoken of in our text occurs during the Tribulation, which is after the Rapture. Neither the Rapture nor the Tribulation have occurred, and therefore we have not yet seen Wormwood fall, which will affect one third of this world's rivers and springs of waters.

People being exposed to bitter water parallels an Old Testament story where Aaron made a grave mistake, forming a golden calf for the Israelites to worship while Moses "delayed" coming down from Mount Sinai with the Ten Commandments.

Moses' anger raged, and "he took the calf which they had made, burned it in the fire, and ground it to powder; and he scattered it on the water and made the children of Israel drink it" (Exodus 32:20). This was a form of punishment.

So too will God cast the Wormwood and expose idolatrous man to drink of the bitter waters. But God is kind. In Marah, where the waters were bitter, Moses cast a tree into the waters and made it sweet to the taste. Jesus' completed work on the cross, the tree of Calvary, provides for anyone who is willing to come and drink of living and life-giving waters (Exodus 15:25; John 4:10; 7:38-39). "If the tree represents the cross of Jesus Christ, then the waters without the tree would be religion without redemption."[13] During these difficult times, many will die of bitter and poisoned water because they intentionally disregarded God and tragically scorned Him and His gift of redemption, even in their misery and death.

Fourth Trumpet: The Lights Dimmed

8:12 Then the fourth angel sounded: And a third of the sun was struck, a third of the moon, and a third of the stars, so that a third of them were darkened. A third of the day did not shine, and likewise the night.

Below is a list of the seven trumpet judgments. We will now discuss the fourth trumpet.

First Trumpet: 1/3 of trees & grass burned (8:7).
Second Trumpet: 1/3 of sea life & ships destroyed (8:8-9).
Third Trumpet: 1/3 of rivers poisoned–Wormwood (8:10-11).
Fourth Trumpet: 1/3 of sun, moon, stars struck (8:12).
Fifth Trumpet: demonic locusts torment the ungodly (9:1-12).
Sixth Trumpet: four angels at Euphrates lead army (9:13-21).
Seventh Trumpet: seven bowls of wrath released (11:15-19).

To better understand the book of Revelation, one must first examine the Old Testament. Isaiah prophesied the darkening of these light sources in Isaiah 13:9-10, "Behold, the day of the Lord comes, cruel, with both wrath and fierce anger, to lay the land desolate; and He will destroy its sinners from it. For the stars of heaven and their constellations will not give their light; the sun will be darkened in its going forth, and the moon will not cause its light to shine."

In Isaiah 5:30 we read, "In that day they will (Israel's enemies) roar against them (Israel) like the roaring of the sea. And if one looks to the land, behold, darkness and sorrow; and the light is darkened by the clouds." We do not know by what means it will be done, but the darkness will be distinct in its manifestation. We've witnessed God stop time as the sun stood still (Joshua 10:12-13). To "dim the lights" would be child's play for Him. The Creator is not only the Author of Life but also the Judge of the World. Not only can he create order, but disorder. Not only does light bow before Him, but so does darkness. Not only does the beginning belong to Him, but also the end!

Pharaoh and the Egyptians can attest to the darkness. We read in Exodus 10:21-23, "'Stretch out your hand toward heaven, that there may be darkness over the land of Egypt, darkness which may even be felt.' So Moses stretched out his hand toward heaven, and there was thick darkness in all the land of Egypt three days. They did not see one another; nor did anyone rise from his place for three days. But all the children of Israel had light in their dwellings." No candle could trump this darkness and no automated timer will be able to trump the darkness that will come.

As you recall, we read in Revelation 6:12-13, "I (John) looked when He (Christ) opened the sixth seal, and behold, there was a great earthquake; and the sun became black as sackcloth of hair, and the moon became like blood. And the stars of heaven fell to the earth, as a fig tree drops its late figs when it is shaken by a mighty wind." There are terrible consequences that will occur: plants will die, animals will perish, the global temperature will decrease, food supply will be reduced, and people will mourn in their wretched anguish.

Despite the darkness' horrible effect, two thirds of the sunlight, moonlight and starlight will still exist. The darkening may be due to smoke from physical disruptions such as volcanoes erupting with dust and ashes rising, or clouds looming, or the great lights inherently dimming, hiding or eclipsing. No matter how the darkness will appear, the originator is God. What kind of God would do such a thing? A God who so loved the world that He gave up His own Son to save us from ourselves, to save us from sin, to save us from hell. Even in the darkness, His voice will be heard. Those who come will walk in the light. Those who don't will die in the darkness.

The Warning Sounded

8:13 And I looked, and I heard an angel flying through the midst of heaven, saying with a loud voice, "Woe, woe, woe to the inhabitants of the earth, because of the remaining blasts of the trumpet of the three angels who are about to sound!"

An angel, like a flying eagle, will fly in the midst of heaven, proclaiming, "Woe, woe, woe to the inhabitants of the earth, because of the remaining blasts of the trumpet of the three angels who are about to sound!" The angel warns that the next three trumpet judgments will be even more horrifying:

1. The fifth trumpet, or first woe, will unleash locusts from the pits of hell (Revelation 9:1-12).
2. The sixth trumpet, or second woe, will unleash four fallen angels who will lead an army from the Far East (Revelation 9:13-21).
3. The seventh trumpet, or third woe, will unleash the final seven bowls of wrath (Revelation 11:15; 16:1-21).

All three woes will focus on the inhabitants of earth and not objects of nature as their direct aim of destruction. The number three signifies the completeness of God's wrath. God's eternality is expressed as the One who is and who was and who is to come in Revelation 1:8, indicating His complete oversight of events within the confines of time. A significant mention of three is in reference to the Trinity (Revelation 16:13). There is a threefold repetition of "Holy" referring to each of the persons of the Trinity (Revelation 4:8). The fact that the Beast uses "six" three times for his mark signifies his desire to mimic the perfect Trinity. The three woes to follow will complete the judgment cycles in the form of trumpets and bowls.

Isaiah used the word "woe" 22 times, more than any other author in the Bible.[14] In our text, "woe" is mentioned three times in one verse! What is to come is so atrocious that it takes three woes to announce it.

 These horrors are incessant, rampant, violent, permanent and a chastisement. A hard head will lead to trouble. But a hard heart will lead to death eternal.

REV IT UP & SUM IT UP – CHAPTER EIGHT:

When Christ opens the seventh and final seal, seven trumpet judgments are released and when the seventh trumpet sounds, seven bowl judgments will be released. In this chapter we'll witness the sound of the first four trumpets.

It's been six thousand years since the creation of Adam and Eve and since the first prayer was whispered to God. All subsequent prayers have "accumulated," rising up as a sweet aroma from the Altar of Incense to our Father who hears, listens and accepts our prayers. In this chapter, an angel of the Lord not only delivers our prayers to God, but also takes fire from the Altar of Incense and casts the fire on earth, manifesting as the seven trumpet judgments upon God-rejecting man during the Tribulation.

We heard the sound of the first four trumpets in this chapter:

1. The first trumpet initiates the destruction of a third of the world's trees and grass, terribly hampering the substance of life.

2. The second trumpet initiates the destruction of a third of the world's seas, sea life and ships, terribly hampering commerce and a critical source of food.

3. The third trumpet initiates the destruction of a third of the world's rivers and waters, causing drought and famine.

4. The fourth trumpet initiates the destruction of a third of the sun, moon and stars, striking the light that sustains life.

I am astonished when I read Genesis and compare it to Revelation. Everything God created in Genesis chapter one, He is systematically destroying in Revelation chapter eight.

1. On the first day, God created light (Genesis 1:3-5); He

"dims" one third of light by sounding the fourth trumpet.

2. On the second day, God created the heavens (Genesis 1:6-8); He covers the skies with darkness by sounding the fourth trumpet.

3. On the third day, God created earth, dry land, grass, trees, waters and the sea (Genesis 1:9-13). He destroys one third by sounding the first three trumpets.

4. On the fourth day, God created the sun, moon and stars (Genesis 1:14-19). He destroys one third of these bodies' lights by sounding the fourth trumpet.

5. On the fifth day, God created the sea creatures and birds of the air (Genesis 1:20-23). He destroys one third of the sea creatures by sounding the second trumpet.

6. On the sixth day, God created the cattle, creatures of the earth and man (Genesis 1:24-31). He allows man and animals to die in each of the first four trumpets.

How can God allow such atrocities? He wishes all of mankind to accept Him and live eternally; man is the one who rejects Him and prefers darkness over light and death over life. God simply obliges, giving a God-hating, Christ-rejecting, Holy Spirit-mocking generation of people what they desire.

Chapter 9
Trumpet Maladies

In this chapter we'll witness the first two of the final three woes, also known as the fifth and sixth trumpet judgments. When the fifth seal is broken, demonic locusts will hound and torment earth's inhabitants who do not have God's seal of protection. We'll also study about an army of 200 million soldiers, released when the sixth trumpet is sounded, who will ultimately kill one third of earth's remaining population.

Fifth Trumpet: Demonic Locusts

9:1 Then the fifth angel sounded: And I saw a star fallen from heaven to the earth. To him was given the key to the bottomless pit.

Below is a list of the seven trumpet judgments. We will now discuss the fifth trumpet.

First Trumpet: 1/3 of trees & grass burned (8:7).
Second Trumpet: 1/3 of sea life & ships destroyed (8:8-9).
Third Trumpet: 1/3 of rivers poisoned–Wormwood (8:10-11).
Fourth Trumpet: 1/3 of sun, moon, stars struck (8:12).
Fifth Trumpet: demonic locusts torment the ungodly (9:1-12).

Sixth Trumpet: four angels at Euphrates lead army (9:13-21).
Seventh Trumpet: seven bowls of wrath released (11:15-19).

Here, John does not see a star that is falling but a star that has already fallen as the fifth angel sounds the trumpet. This star is not a comet or meteor as we witnessed in the second and third trumpet calls; this "star" is Satan, in his fallen state. We find in Isaiah 14:12, 15, "How you are fallen from heaven, O Lucifer, son of the morning! How you are cut down to the ground, you who weakened the nations! Yet you shall be brought down to Sheol, to the lowest depths of the Pit." Jesus said of Satan in Luke 10:18, "I saw Satan fall like lightning from heaven."

Satan, as we saw in Isaiah's reference above, was called Lucifer, son of the morning. He was beautiful and perfect in beauty according to Ezekiel 28:12, but he became proud and corrupted in his wisdom and was therefore cast out of heaven by God (Ezekiel 28:11-19). When Satan fell to the earth, he made God's beautiful earth (Genesis 1:1) void and without form, spurring on darkness (Genesis 1:2). After God started renewing the earth (Genesis 1:3-31), Satan deceived Eve and Adam, causing a curse to fall upon the earth and mankind, giving birth to pain, tears, toils, sickness and death (Genesis 3:1-24).

In our text we don't see Satan falling, but we see him in his fallen state. When we study Revelation chapter 12, which brings us to the midpoint of the Tribulation, we'll see Satan, who has been allowed to converse with God in heaven up to that point, cast down for the last time without the privilege of entering God's presence ever again.

You'll remember from Revelation 1:18 that the "keys of Hades and of Death" belong to Christ and are in His possession. Satan does not have the authority, nor does he have the key to unlock the Bottomless Pit. The terror that is to be unleashed by the fifth trumpet is allowed only because of God's sovereign rule and permission. "The fact that the key of the abyss is given to him is in keeping with the fact that during the tribulation period God allows him free rein and suffers him to do his worst."[1]

The Bottomless Pit is not the Lake of Fire (ultimate and eternal hell) because no one is yet cast into hell. The pit is the abyss, which means seemingly without a bottom, deep under the surface of the ground in the very center of the earth, where demons are locked in solitary confinement so that they will not be able to harm mankind. Satan will actually be locked up in this compartment for 1,000 years during the Millennium as we'll see in Revelation 20:1-2.

I am unsure of the exact location of the Bottomless Pit but believe it is associated with Hades and likely a separate "high security" compartment, pit or reservoir kept for the most notorious demons. There are two classes of demonic spirits: The first is free to roam and oppose God's children (Luke 8:30-21; Ephesians 2:1-3) and the second is confined for being guilty of monstrous sins, having sexual relations with humans (Genesis 6:2-4). We will be discussing the confined demons later in our text. There is a great gulf or chasm that separates the tormented side of Hades from the Paradise side of Hades; the gulf or chasm is where these demons may reside in a place called the "Bottomless Pit."

The demons in Luke 8:30-31 begged Jesus not to be cast into the horrific abyss, but rather to be cast into the swine. The demonic forces which are about to be released in this fifth trumpet judgment will be escorted by Satan to earth's surface only under God's authority and jurisdiction. In Jude 1:6-7, we read about their dwelling, "And the angels who did not keep their proper domain, but left their own abode, He (God) has reserved in everlasting chains under darkness for the judgment of that great day; as Sodom and Gomorrah, and the cities around them in a similar manner to these, having given themselves over to sexual immorality are gone after strange flesh, are set forth as an example, suffering the vengeance of eternal fire."

At first glance the text in Jude appears confusing, but it is important to recall that some demonic angels actually stepped beyond the bounds prescribed to them by God, had sexual encounters with humans, bore giants, or Nephilim, and tainted the world's population during Noah's days (Genesis 6:1-4). This was Satan's grand attempt to corrupt the entire human race and prevent the coming of the Messiah! God destroyed the earth to cleanse it of these giants and the prevalent wickedness of man, sparing Noah and his family, who were the only unaffected humans, and therefore righteous, surviving the great flood (Genesis 7:1-24).

The demons who acted beyond the parameters of rule of law lost their sphere of influence and were bound in chains. They will one day be judged by God and sent forever to the Lake of Fire. But here, we'll see that they may be released from the bottomless pit under the direction of God's sovereignty as agents of torment and cause unbearable pain to those who continue to spit on God's face! Since these demons are "reserved in everlasting chains under darkness" according to Jude, their counterparts of "lesser wickedness" may be the ones released. Either way, as we'll see in the next two verses, they are demons appearing like locusts and their bite will be horrendous. You definitely want to skip this event.

Hell Bound?

9:2 *And he opened the bottomless pit, and smoke arose out of the pit like the smoke of a great furnace. So the sun and the air were darkened because of the smoke of the pit.*

There is a world that is immersed in complete darkness, inhabited by the most repugnant and revolting spirits. By reading the book of Job, we get a glance at the power of God and a place called "Sheol," the temporary holding place of permanently damned departed souls.

"Sheol" is the term in Hebrew, and "Hades" in the Greek, one and the same, both denoting the temporary holding place of souls who are permanently damned. The unbelieving souls, who are in the "tormented side" of Hades will ultimately end up in hell, or the Lake of Fire. Hell, the Lake of Fire, in the Bible is referred to as "Hinnon" in the Hebrew and "Gehenna" in the Greek. No one can change their destiny by prayer, chants, wishes or money, and no one can "work" themselves out of going to hell after they land in Hades and ultimately face the Great White Throne judgment.

Before the resurrection of Christ, believers used to be "housed" in Paradise, or Abraham's bosom, the "happy side" of Hades. Paradise is now emptied, and the souls of all believer's go directly up to heaven at the time of their bodily death. The Bottomless Pit appears to be adjacent to the tormented side of Hades and its proper name is "Tartarus," found in II Peter 2:4, for God did "not spare the angels who sinned but cast them down to Tartarus and delivered them into chains of darkness, to be reserved for judgment." It is from Tartarus, or the Bottomless Pit, that the demonic spirits will rise during the fifth trumpet judgment.

In Summary:

1. Sheol (Hebrew) = Hades (Greek). It is not controlled by Satan! "Sheol is naked before Him (God), and Destruction (death and Hades) has no covering" according to Job 26:6, meaning God sees all and nothing escapes Him.

    Hades has two parts:

    a. Tormented side — where the souls and spirits of unbelievers who have physically died throughout history are housed awaiting judgment at the Great White Throne before being sent to eternal hell.

    b. Paradise side, or Abraham's bosom — where the souls and spirits of believers who died before the resurrection of Jesus used to be housed. After the cross, these souls were taken up to heaven, and now, when a believer dies, his soul and spirit goes straight to heaven. The Paradise side is currently and forever completely empty.

2. Tartarus = the Bottomless Pit. Adjacent to, or far below Hades is Tartarus, or the bottomless pit, where fallen angels are chained and are reserved for judgment, meaning they will be let loose to inflict suffering and torment on unbelievers during the Tribulation. "Tartarus would seem to be more terrible than Hades … it is as far beneath Hades as earth is below Heaven."[2]

3. Hell = Hinnon (Hebrew) = Gehenna (Greek) = Lake of Fire. It is the eternal, ultimate and final stop for the wicked who hate or reject God's Son.

We will study this further in the coming chapters such as Revelation chapter 20:5 (Matthew 25:41; Luke 16:19-31; 23:43; II Corinthians 5:8; 12:3-4; Philippians 1:23; II Peter 2:4).

 One of the most difficult circumstances for a medical doctor in the ICU (intensive care unit) is when a son, daughter, brother, sister, spouse, mother or father lays unconscious after a trauma and is declared by the medical team as "brain dead." It is incredibly sad to see their heart rhythm ticking away, in sync, on time, without skipping a beat, knowing at the same time that their brain has no recorded activity.

As long as their heart is beating, their body is still "alive," and I personally believe that they can still hear because their mind (soul) and their conscience (spirit), which are immaterial, will never die. Therefore, I am very cautious when I utter a word by the bedside, wanting to honor the patient and their family.

Once the heartbeat stops, then the body dies. But the soul and spirit will continue to live forever. The individual's soul and spirit will either go to the tormented side of Hades or to heaven. The soul that ends up in Hades will be housed until it receives its resurrected body at the Great White Throne judgment and then is sentenced to spend Eternity in the Lake of Fire. The soul and the spirit that rises to heaven will be with the Lord and will be united with its glorified body in the Rapture. The only difference between the two souls is the presence or the absence of the blood of Christ which wipes away all sin.

Regarding the place of torment, death and hell, God asks Job, "Have you entered the springs of the sea? Or have you walked in search of the depths? Have the gates of death been revealed to you? Or have you seen the doors of the shadow of death? Have you comprehended the breadth of the earth? Tell Me, if you know all this" (Job 38:16-18). The answers to these test questions are no, no, no, no and no! Job has not. You have not. I have not. No one has, or is, or will, except the sovereign Lord God. Demons know of this place. Satan, their king, knows of this dwelling place and is permitted solely by God to release the abyss-bound, malignant satanic beings upon mankind.

When Satan opens the shaft of the abyss, smoke arises out of the pit like the smoke of a great furnace. We are familiar with the terminology in the Old Testament. When Abraham looked toward Sodom and Gomorrah, and toward all the land of the plain, he beheld "the smoke of the land which went up like the smoke of a furnace" (Genesis 19: 27-28).

 In Cardiology when we place electrodes and leads on a patient's chest, we usually place the red lead on the bottom and the black on top, remembering it as "smoke above fire." If there is smoke, look for the fire.

The abyss is deep underground, and like a volcano spewing out its fire, it also spits out dark smoke as if it arises from a "great furnace." The smoke literally covers the sun and brings darkness over the land, and no brand-name latest antidepressant will lift the gloom out of man's heart!

 Here is the bottom line: if one rejects the Light, Jesus Christ, his heart will bleed with sorrow, his day will turn to night, his sunlit sky will become pitch black and his destiny will be eternally hopeless.

9:3 *Then out of the smoke locusts came upon the earth. And to them was given power, as the scorpions of the earth have power.*

The locusts that emerge are not the normal insects we are accustomed to in nature; no insect or animal would be able to withstand the intense temperature of the abyss. These are satanic beings. During prophet Joel's days, natural locusts under God's sovereign rule devoured the land of Israel. The locusts also symbolized Assyria's invasion of Israel. But more importantly, Joel's words looked through the telescope of prophecy and spoke of the Tribulation.

In our text, the demonic army of locusts will also be under the jurisdiction of God. Make no mistake about it: it is God who gives these demonic forces the right to march as He "Revs It Up" another notch. "The Lord gives voice before His army, for His camp is very great; for strong is the One who executes His word. For the Day of the Lord is great and very terrible; who can endure it?" (Joel 2:11).

Joel's prophecy aligns with the book of Revelation:

1. The Day of the Lord gives rise to the Tribulation (Joel 1:15-2:11 and Revelation 4:1-19:10).

2. The Tribulation gives rise to the judgment of the nations, or the Campaign of Armageddon (Joel 3:1-17 and

Revelation 19:11-21). "'Let the nations be wakened and come up to the Valley of Jehoshaphat; for there I will sit to judge all the surrounding nations. Put in the sickle, for the harvest is ripe. Come, go down; for the winepress is full, the vats overflow—for their wickedness is great.' Multitudes, multitudes in the valley of decision! For the day of the Lord is near in the valley of decision" (Joel 3:12-14).

3. Armageddon gives rise to the Millennium (Joel 3:18-21 and Revelation 20:1-10).

Can you imagine imprisoned fallen demonic angels, restrained by God for centuries, being set loose in the form of infernal and fuming locusts, reserved for a specific time, being used as instruments of judgment upon an ungodly world? To further support this attack, we'll turn to scripture in Jude 1:6, "And the angels who did not keep their proper domain, but left their own abode, He (God) has reserved in everlasting chains under darkness for the judgment of the great day." We see in Revelation 6:17 that it will be unbearable, "For the great day of His wrath has come, and who is able to stand?"

What is so stunning is that the Lord calls this demonic force "His army," meaning that these fallen spirits who reject Him, malign Him, undermine Him, are not only chained up by Him, but will be released by Him, and used by Him for His purposes! "The Lord gives voice before His army, for His camp is very great; for strong is the One who executes His word. For the day of the Lord is great and very terrible; who can endure it?" (Joel 2:11). Like it or not, believe it or not, accept it or not, every knee will bow before the Lord!

Because these locusts have the power of scorpions, they are not "natural" locusts from the face of the earth. These fallen angels originated from heaven, followed Satan to his demise, broke God's rules and boundaries set for them even on earth, ended up in solitary confinement in the Bottomless Pit, and will be released with the first woe or the fifth trumpet. Here is an emboldening word spoken by Jesus to all believers, "Behold, I give you the authority to trample on serpents and scorpions, and over all the power of the enemy, and nothing shall by any means hurt you" (Luke 10:19). Please do not find yourself hanging out during the Tribulation. This ain't no video game where you get to zone in on the villain locust, take it down, earn mega points and advance to an expert's level; this is physically tangible; and without God's divine protection during the Tribulation, this plague will be brutally unbearable! Woe to those who are unbelievers.

9:4 *They were commanded not to harm the grass of the earth, or any green thing, or any tree, but only those men who do not have the seal of God on their foreheads.*

Though these forces are demonic in nature, they still are under the command of God, being instructed not to harm the grass or trees or any green thing. You'll recall that this first woe targets people instead of vegetation. These cannot be natural locusts because natural locusts would harm vegetation as they did in Egypt, "for they covered the face of the whole earth, so that the land was darkened; and they ate every herb of the land and all the fruit of the trees which the hail had left. So there remained nothing green on the trees or on the plants of the field throughout all the land of Egypt" (Exodus 10:15). When natural locusts attack, their sound resembles that of rain, the skies darken, the sun's light dims due to their ominous cloud, and the trees are laid bare. The demonic locusts avoid the very thing that the natural locusts devastate.

Let's revisit the sound and devastation of the first trumpet, "the first angel sounded: and hail and fire followed, mingled with blood, and they were thrown to the earth. And a third of the trees were burned up, and all green grass was burned up" (Revelation 8:7). How could all green grass be burned up in the previous trumpet judgment and there still remains green grass? It may be that all of the third of the green grass was burned up or even if all of earth's green grass were burned up, the time span between the first trump and the fifth trump allowed grass to grow again in season. If vegetation will not be affected by the locusts, who then will be? "Only those men who do not have the seal of God on their foreheads." God's evangelists have already been safely sealed as we saw in Revelation 7:4. Please do not confuse the seal of God on the forehead of believers in this verse as compared to the Antichrist's 666 mark which we will study in Revelation 13:16-18. The only thing Satan originated was sin; otherwise, he is a counterfeit, a liar, a thief and a murderer.

Does it fascinate you that the demonic locusts are able to differentiate between those with God's seal and those without? I'm always thankful to see how great my God is! Do you remember when Jesus was on earth and demons shrieked? Do you recall the poor soul in the country of the Gadarenes, possessed by Legion? When the demonic forces who possessed this man saw Jesus, the man spoke but it was the voice of the demons that declared, "What have I to do with You, Jesus, Son of the Most High God? I implore You by God that You do not torment me" (Mark 5:7). When Jesus healed many who were sick with various illnesses, he also cast out many demons; "and He did not allow the demons to speak, because they knew Him" (Mark 1:34). The demonic locusts will be able to identify those marked with the name of God, the Christ!

A question rises as to those who become believers in Christ during the Tribulation. Will they too be "sealed" as were the 144,000 Jewish evangelists? A hint to the answer is found in II Timothy 2:19, "Nevertheless the solid foundation (believers who do not waiver) of God stands, having this seal: 'The Lord knows those who are His,' and 'Let everyone who names the name of Christ depart from iniquity.'" Let me make it clear that Christ-followers have never been exempt from harm; in fact, John wrote in Revelation 1:9, "I, John, both your brother and companion in the tribulation (hardships, and not the Tribulation) and kingdom and patience of Jesus Christ, was on the island that is called Patmos for the Word of God and for the testimony of Jesus Christ." John was being persecuted for proclaiming Christ! It appears that those who turn to Christ will be exempt from the demonic locusts, but I am unsure of this. I am confident, however, of this: there is no reason for you or I to be there because believers alive at the Rapture will escape the Tribulation!

9:5 *And they were not given authority to kill them, but to torment them for five months. Their torment was like the torment of a scorpion when it strikes a man.*

There is a repetition throughout these verses concerning the authority and power of God; He not only created and rules the universe, but He is the One who sets standards and limits. Many ask, "Why then is this world so messed up?" That's simple. It's because of people like me. It's because of people like you. The sooner we realize it, the better citizens of this planet we'll become!

The time span given to the locusts is five months. Interestingly, the lifespan of a natural locust, usually May through September, is five months. The unbelievers will be unable to escape the torment of the demonic locusts, which sting like scorpions.

A scorpion's neurotoxin can cause swelling, pain, cardiac arrhythmia, seizures, paralysis and even death. Neither Norco, marijuana, cocaine, heroin nor any other drug will be able to soothe the pains, aches, misery, grief, headache, heartache or hardships of the victims, even for a brief second.

The locusts' torment is just a preview of Hades and is nothing compared to the Lake of Fire. The locusts are not allowed to kill the unbelievers but only to aggravate their suffering. This seems so sadistic, yet, I believe it is an act of mercy by God. How so? God is allowing the unbelievers to live in order that they may come to the end of themselves, repent, turn to

Him, and ultimately live an eternal life instead of suffering an eternal death. On the other hand, Satan's desire is to kill the unbelievers in order to prevent them from repenting and drag them down to the Lake of Fire!

The number "five" is significant because it signifies God's grace in scripture. There were five offerings the Israelites offered to the Lord; the tabernacle in the wilderness contained five curtains (Exodus 26:3) and five crossbars (Exodus 26:26-27), five pillars and five sockets (Exodus 26:37), an altar made of wood that was five cubits long and five cubits wide (Exodus 27:1); the height of the curtains within the tabernacle was five cubits (Exodus 27:18). The anointing oil that was used to consecrate the furniture of the tabernacle was comprised of five parts: olive oil, myrrh, cinnamon, calamus and cassia (Exodus 30:23-25). As the 144,000 evangelists preach, the locusts sting and the people cry out in agonizing pain for five months. The grace of God is still available. The people will either cry out and curse God or they will cry out, fall to their knees and embrace their Creator, their Shield and their Savior, the lover of their souls!

9:6 *In those days men will seek death and will not find it; they will desire to die, and death will flee from them.*

Constant and excruciating pain results in a breaking point for every man. Men will seek death in those days but will not be able to die. Job conveys these feelings of hopelessness when he loses everything, including his health, and cannot understand why he can't die. "Why is light given to him who is in misery, and life to the bitter of soul, who long for death, but it does not come, and search for it more than hidden treasures; who rejoice exceedingly, and are glad when they can find the grave? (Job 3:20-22). "When I say, 'My bed will comfort me, my couch will ease my complaint,' then You (God) scare me with dreams and terrify me with visions, so that my soul chooses strangling and death rather than my body. I loathe my life;

I would not live forever. Let me alone, for my days are but a breath" (Job 7:13-16).

My friend, Daniel, a missionary to Ivory Coast, Africa, once asked God to show him what hell was like; he was not prepared for God's feedback and did not expect God to answer his request in such a vivid manner. While traveling to Sri Lanka and proclaiming the gospel of Jesus Christ, he was plagued with a severe heat stroke. The days that followed were filled with torment caused by excruciating pain and itching. He longed to tear the skin off his back, feeling like bugs and mites were crawling under his skin. The inability to sleep and the futile attempts to find a comfortable position for even a simple second, pushed him to imagine if he could just die, the bloodcurdling torture would end. To add to the insult, the suffering was not only physical but gripped his very psyche, driving him to the point of turmoil and hopelessness. God revealed to him that what he experienced was an insignificant and minuscule fraction of the "comforts" of hell.

When one of my patients faces a health condition that poses the inability to breathe, usually due to a severe asthma attack or chronic obstructive pulmonary disease, it is a terrifying event. The struggle to gasp for air sets off an internal alarm that propels him into an anxiety attack, gripped with dread, with the dire possibility of death. As we place the endotracheal tube down his mouth and allow a respirator to breathe for him, we see chaos and death turn into calmness and life as our patient rests under sedation.

There will be no respirators in hell. There will be no endotracheal tubes. There will be no 911 calls. There will no emergency rooms with on-call doctors and a respiratory team that will tend to the dying residents. There will be no rest. There will be no relief. There will be no hope. There will be no goodness because

God is not there. Think about that for a moment—
God is not there! There will be gasping for air. There
will be groaning. There will be wailing. There will be
sobbing. There will be heart wrenching screaming.
What is worse, in a place void of God's love, there will
be perpetual death upon death without end. Though
the five-month period on earth will seem unbearable
with the sting of the locusts, hell will be inconceivably,
exponentially and terrifyingly worse!

During these horrid days, those who are stung by the demonic
locusts will have a burning desire to die or commit suicide,
but all their wishes will be unfulfilled and thwarted by God.
Not only will the locusts sting, but they will not allow their
victims to kill themselves, perhaps paralyzing them and thereby incapacitating them from doing so. The scorpions' poison-
ous stings will lead to madness. Joel described the agony in
Joel 2:6, "Before them (the attacking army) the people writhe
in pain; all faces are drained of color."

It is in Mark's writings where we find how demons capsize
a life. When a father presented his demon-possessed son to
Jesus and the demon recognized the Messiah, "the spirit con-
vulsed him, and he fell on the ground and wallowed, foaming
at the mouth. So He (Christ) asked his father, 'How long has
this been happening to him?' And he said, 'From childhood.
And often he has thrown him both into the fire and into the
water to destroy him. But if You can do anything, have compassion on us and help us" (Mark 9:20-22). Jesus commanded
the unclean spirit to leave, and the spirit made the boy con-
vulse as he came out and left the boy as if he were dead. But
Jesus took him by the hand and lifted him up, and he arose.
(Mark 9:25-26). Only Jesus!

 *Satan wishes ill, wants to kill, and longs to steal. Jesus
gives goodness, mercy, healing and favor. To force the*

*love of God on you would be no love at all. That makes
receiving His love a choice. Your choice.*

**9:7 The shape of the locusts was like horses prepared for
battle. On their heads were crowns of something like gold,
and their faces were like the faces of men.**

The first woe, or the fifth trumpet spoken of in our text with
demons "like horses prepared for battle" (Revelation 9:1-11)
parallels the passage in Joel 2:4-5, "Their appearance is like
the appearance of horses; and like swift steeds, so they run.
With a noise like chariots over mountaintops they leap, like
the noise of a flaming fire that devours the stubble, like a
strong people set in battle array." Joel not only speaks of an
event of natural locusts invading Israel in his time but also of
an end time event from the Bottomless Pit. This is not just a
past event, nor is it a symbolic event, it is a future event that is
both literal and dreadful.

John describes a vision of locusts which exceeds what he has
witnessed in the past and uses similes to explain and uses the
word "like" nine times. I will not spiritualize these passages;
they are what they say and should be interpreted literally.
What fascinates me is that there are angels knows as Cherubim in heaven in the likeness of a lion, an ox, a man, and a
flying eagle (Revelation 4:7). The demonic consist of fallen
angels, and as we will soon see, they will have the look of
locusts, scorpions, horses, lions and men.

John's description is not far-fetched when you consider looking at natural insects under an electronic beam microscope,
with antennas covered with hair, a head with thousands of
eyes, and a body with thousands of scales and legs that look
like spears."John apparently would have us understand the
locusts to be of considerable size. Otherwise the description
of hair, face, teeth, etc. would tend toward the comic."[3]

Why would John equate a locust to a horse? If you were to

compare the heads of each animal, you'd be surprised that they are very similar in appearance! In Italian, the word "locust" means little horse. Locusts are swift, bolting like horses and advancing in waves like human armies. The crowns that the demonic locusts wear depict the rank of the fallen angels as they enjoy their brief victory over mankind. With faces like men, these demonic beings show that they are unyielding, crafty, methodical and strong-minded.

9:8 *They had hair like women's hair, and their teeth were like lions' teeth.*

The locusts are marching like an army. They have a feminine trait such as women's hair, which may indicate a captivating characteristic. These demons will lure earth's inhabitants into their realm and then consume their dignity, their health and their souls! Though they may at first intrigue the human heart, their lion-like teeth reveal their true identity: ravenous, ravaging and ruthless spirits who long to demoralize the soul of mankind. God describes the natural locusts of Joel's day in the same manner, having divine vision of the Tribulation, "For a nation has come up against My land, strong, and without number; his teeth are the teeth of a lion, and he has the fangs of a fierce lion. He has laid waste My vine and ruined My fig tree; he has stripped it bare and thrown it away; its branches are made white" (Joel 1:6-7). As we'll see in verse ten, the locust will not ravage with their teeth; they will instead sting with their tails as a scorpion.

9:9 *And they had breastplates like breastplates of iron, and the sound of their wings was like the sound of chariots with many horses running into battle.*

The Greek word for "breastplate" is translated into "thorax," the chest, the part of the body between the neck and diaphragm; it is an osseous-cartilaginous (bony-cartilage) cage, guarding the heart and lungs with a protective cage called the ribs. The demons' chests were like iron, serving as a shield and an impenetrable armor. According to Ephesians 6:14, Christ-followers wear a "breastplate of righteousness," protecting their hearts from corruption. The demonic locusts wear the "breastplate of iron," a metal that can easily rust, depicting the depravity in the hearts of its bearers.

These demons do not come quietly! Their wings will be like the "sound of chariots with many horses running into battle," causing commotion, disorder and havoc. Joel describes them clearly in Joel 2:3-5, "A fire devours before them, and behind them a flame burns; the land is like the Garden of Eden before them, and behind them a desolate wilderness; surely nothing shall escape them. Their appearance is like the appearance of horses; and like swift steeds, so they run. With a noise like chariots over mountaintops they leap, like the noise of a flaming fire that devours the stubble, like a strong people set in battle array." This is not a computer-generated video or a Hollywood horror show. This is real, where the enemy, Satan, who hates mankind's soul, is coming individually after each person who does not bear the seal of God. There is no get-out-of-jail card. There is no escape. There is no mercy. There is only pain, sorrow and untold distress.

***9:10** They had tails like scorpions, and there were stings in their tails. Their power was to hurt men five months.*

We read in verse three "to them was given power, as the scorpions of the earth have power." We also read in verse five that their "torment was like the torment of a scorpion when it strikes a man." The sting of a scorpion causes pain, numbness and swelling around the area of the sting, but can also cause difficulty in breathing, an accelerated heart rate, restlessness and inconsolable discomfort. These demons are swift, cunning, skilled, devious—showing themselves as attractive (alluring long hair)—yet are full of rage and mischief, ministers of deception, poison and dread.

Both parties will be given five months: the demons will have five months of freedom; the victims will have five months of torment; but the victims will graciously also have the same five months to consider their plight and repent with the opportunity to become Christ-followers.

9:11 And they had as king over them the angel of the Bottomless Pit, whose name in Hebrew is Abaddon, but in Greek he has the name Apollyon.

According to King Solomon, "The locusts have no king, yet they advance in ranks" (Proverbs 30:27). According to Joel 2:7-9, both the natural locusts and the demonic locusts are not in disarray, "They run like mighty men, they climb the wall like men of war; everyone marches in formation, and they do not break ranks. They do not push one another; everyone marches in his own column. Though they lunge between the weapons, they are not cut down. They run to and fro in the city, they run on the wall; they climb into the houses, they enter at the windows like a thief."

In contrast to the natural locusts, the demonic locusts have a king; he is the angel of the abyss or bottomless pit, Satan, named "Abaddon" and "Apollyon." The reason we are given his name in both Hebrew and Greek is because he will destroy both Jews and Gentiles. In Hebrew, his name is "Abaddon," meaning ruin, destruction, perishing, the angel of infernal roots, the minister of greed, guilt, lies, theft, havoc, murder, sickness and death. In Greek, his name is "Apollyon," meaning the destroyer.

Why give the Hebrew name, Abaddon, first? It may be because Jesus Christ came first to the Jews and then the door of salvation was opened to the Gentiles. To the one who is self-seeking and does not obey the truth but desires the paths of unrighteousness—tribulation and anguish will be poured on every soul who does evil, first for the Jew and then for the Gentile. But to the one who seeks God and obeys Him, and follows in the paths of righteousness—glory, honor and peace will be his reward, first for the Jew and then for the Gentile. "For there is no partiality with God" (Romans 2:8-11).

This angel from the Bottomless Pit is Satan and not the Antichrist, for the Antichrist is:

1. Human. "I (Daniel) was considering the horns, and there was another horn, a little one (Antichrist), coming up among them, before whom three of the first horns were plucked out by the roots. And there, in this horn, were eyes like the eyes of a man, and a mouth speaking pompous words" (Daniel 7:8).

2. Like his father, Satan. "And in the latter time of their kingdom, when the transgressors have reached their fullness, a king shall rise, having fierce features, who understands sinister schemes. His power shall be mighty, but not by his own power (his power comes from Satan, his father); he shall destroy fearfully and shall prosper and thrive; he shall destroy the mighty, and also the holy people. Through his cunning He shall cause deceit to prosper under his rule; and he shall exalt himself in his heart. He shall destroy many in their prosperity. He shall even rise against the Prince of princes (Jesus); but he shall be broken without human means" (Daniel 8:23-25).

3. A man of idolatry. "Then the king (Antichrist) shall do according to his own will. He shall exalt and magnify himself above every god, shall speak blasphemies against the God of gods, and shall prosper till the wrath has been accomplished; for what has been determined shall be done. He shall regard neither the God of his fathers nor the desire of women, nor regard any god; for he shall exalt himself above them all. But in their place, he shall honor a god of fortresses; and a god which his fathers did not know he shall honor with gold and silver, with precious stones and pleasant things. Thus, he shall act

against the strongest fortresses with a foreign god which he shall acknowledge, and advance its glory; and he shall cause them to rule over many and divide the land for gain" (Daniel 11:36-39).

4. A man filled with deceit and abomination. "Then he (Antichrist) shall confirm a covenant with many for one week (seven years); but in the middle of the week (three and a half years) he shall bring an end to sacrifice and offering (no more animal sacrifices will be allowed in the third Jewish temple at the midpoint of the Tribulation). And on the wing of abominations shall be one who makes desolate (the Antichrist will claim that he is God in the Holy of Holies), even until the consummation, which is determined, is poured out on the desolate" (Daniel 9:27).

5. An impersonator of the living God. "Let no one deceive you by any means; for that Day (Second Coming of Christ) will not come unless the falling away comes first, and the man of sin is revealed, the son of perdition, who opposes and exalts himself above all that is called God or that is worshiped, so that he sits as God in the temple of God, showing himself that he is God" (II Thessalonians 2:3-4).

9:12 *One woe is past. Behold, still two more woes are coming after these things.*

After five months, the first of the three woes, the fifth trumpet, will come to a halt and will give way to the final two woes, or the sixth and seventh trumpets. The last two woes are even worse than the first woe. Demonic locusts tortured man in the first woe, but in the second woe, an army led by demons, unlike any military power in history, will be released upon the earth (Revelation 9:13-21). God's final woe will "Rev It Up" to an unbearable level of unequaled horror by releasing the seven bowls of His final wrath (Revelation 11:15; 15:7; 16:1-21).

Sixth Trumpet: The Euphrates Angels

9:13 *Then the sixth angel sounded: And I heard a voice from the four horns of the golden altar which is before God,* **9:14** *saying to the sixth angel who had the trumpet, "Release the four angels who are bound at the great river Euphrates."*

Below is a list of the seven trumpet judgments. We will now discuss the sixth trumpet.

First Trumpet: 1/3 of trees & grass burned (8:7).
Second Trumpet: 1/3 of sea life & ships destroyed (8:8-9).
Third Trumpet: 1/3 of rivers poisoned–Wormwood (8:10-11).
Fourth Trumpet: 1/3 of sun, moon, stars struck (8:12).
Fifth Trumpet: demonic locusts torment the ungodly (9:1-12).
Sixth Trumpet: four angels at Euphrates lead army (9:13-21).
Seventh Trumpet: seven bowls of wrath released (11:15-19).

With each successive trumpet, the judgments are escalating in severity. According to Isaiah 26:9, when God's judgments are in the earth, the inhabitants of the world will learn righteousness. But there are those who will remain obstinate, unyielding, haughty and bent on their evil ways, who continue to curse God; however, as they stiffen their necks, they'll taste the upsurge and the growing intensity of the judgments. "No doubt, therefore, each succeeding judgment will uncover a few reluctant 'learners,' but those that remain unconverted are still more stubborn and thus each visitation must increase in severity."[4]

The petitions of martyred saints were made under the Altar of Incense at the opening of the fifth seal (Revelation 6:9-11) and the cries of the saints were offered upon the same altar which is before God's throne at the opening of the seventh seal and the initiation of the sounding of the seven trumpets (Revelation 8:1-5). God's compassions and mercies will not fail. He is encouraging believers that vengeance is finally being dispensed righteously from His throne.

The command given to the sixth angel comes from the Father, "Release the four angels who are bound at the great river Euphrates." The Old Testament depicts the horns of the altar as a sign of mercy, for a man could run to the sanctuary and cling to the horns, begging for mercy as when Adonijah begged King Solomon to spare his life (I Kings 1:50-51). But at this time, mercy, compassion and grace are restrained, and now judgments of wrath pour down sequentially on mankind. As it was in the days of Noah, so too it will be true during the Tribulation: God's Spirit will not strive with man forever! (Genesis 6:3).

The sixth angel who sounds the trumpet is instructed to release the four angels, who are supernaturally bound at the Euphrates River. These four are wicked and fallen angels reserved by God in bondage for a special purpose, a special time and a special place during the Tribulation. Despite this event being "localized" or occurring only at the Euphrates River, it will be a cataclysmic worldwide event given that there is the release of four bound angels, the number four symbolizing a global effect.

Not only are these angels to be judged as the angels who are bound in the Bottomless Pit, but they too will be released to exercise judgment on mankind. I group these four angels with the fallen because God would not bind His heavenly angels who minister to Him and to us. The mention of the Euphrates here and during the sixth bowl (Revelation 16:12-16) further supports the fact that the emergence of the real historical city of Babylon, where the Euphrates River runs, will occur. It is the longest river of Western Asia, 1,800 miles, running its course through ancient cities such as Ur and Babylon, giving rise to the birth of pagan and idolatrous religions. "The river is a double frontier, that of the land promised to Israel and that of the future empire of the Antichrist (Babylon, Iraq). Satan's kingdom is to be divided against itself and therefore it shall not stand. The Euphrates is a most significant border of this division in Satan's kingdom."[5]

The cradle of civilization began at the banks of the Euphrates River where complex urban centers began to grow, and the coffin of civilization will occur at the same place where supernatural judgments continue to rain down. Sin originated there; it is where pride was inoculated into the human DNA by its father, Satan; it's where Satan deceived mankind in the Garden of Eden; it's where the first murder was committed as Cain killed his brother, Abel; it's where the tower of Babel was built; it was the eastern boundary of the Promised Land; it's where Israel suffered exile for 70 years (Psalm 137:1-4).

The Euphrates River is the epicenter of human wickedness. Babylon, along its banks, will once again be the world's material center during the Tribulation; it is where a woman named Wickedness is returned back in a basket to Shinar or Babylon as noted in Zechariah 5:5-11; Babylon will be destroyed at the end of time as noted in Revelation 17-18. It's where God's enemies and worldwide armies will cross in all their pomp to descend upon Megiddo and engage in the Campaign of Armageddon (Revelation 16:12-16; 19:17-21).

***9:15** So the four angels, who had been prepared for the hour and day and month and year, were released to kill a third of mankind.*

It is God who reserves these angels for a specific period of history. In Job 38:31-33 God asks Job a set of questions, "Can you bind the cluster of the Pleiades, or loose the belt of Orion? Can you bring out Mazzaroth (the twelve constellations) in its season? Or can you guide the Great Bear with its cubs? Do you know the ordinances of the heavens? Can you set their dominion over the earth?" The response to all these rhetorical questions without Job having the opportunity to answer is a resounding, "No!" Paul writes in Ephesians 1:11, "In Him (Christ) also we have obtained an inheritance, being predestined according to the purpose of Him who works all things according to the counsel of His will." Even an atheist honors the name of Christ! How so? If you were to ask him what year it is, for example, 2050, he'd say, "2050." That would be 2050 years after the birth of Christ!

These four demonic angels are pent up in agony, rage and revenge. When they are loosed at a precise and preordained time by God, they will unleash mayhem on mankind. They will lead an army that will kill one third of the earth's population. You'll recall that one fourth of the earth's population was killed with sword, hunger, pestilence and wild beasts in Revelation 6:8 when the fourth seal, which released the pale horse, was opened. If 25% of the people are killed, there is only 75% left. If one third is killed with the sixth trumpet, then one third of 75% is 50%. It is sobering to think that after the sixth trumpet judgment less than 50% of the earth's population as compared to the beginning of the Tribulation will remain as man persists to obstinately reject God.

9:16 Now the number of the army of the horsemen was two hundred million; I heard the number of them.

Two hundred million is a specific number and not an indeterminant number as some believe. If it were a "multitude" of people, then John would have so indicated. Joel describes the army as a people, "great and strong, the like of whom has never been; nor will there ever be any such after them" (Joel 2:2).

 According to Ecology.com,[6] the world population was estimated and projected by the following numbers:

1. in 1 AD, 170 million;
2. in 500 AD, 190 million;
3. in 1000 AD, 254 million;
4. in 1500 AD, 425 million;
5. in 1800 AD, 813 million;
6. in 1900 AD, 1.55 billion;
7. in 1930, 2.07 billion;
8. in 1950, 2.56 billion;

9. in 1980, 4.45 billion;
10. in 2000, 6.09 billion;
11. in 2010, 6.87 billion;
12. in 2020, 7.66 billion;
13. in 2030, 8.3 billion;
14. in 2040, 8.87 billion;
15. in 2050, 9.3 billion.

If we lived in the 1500s and read the book of Revelation, we may have had a difficult time deciphering how half of the world's population could be in an army! Worse yet, if we lived during the time when Revelation was written, approximately 100 AD, there might not have even been 200 million people on the face of the earth! But today, an army of 200 million is possible. Compared to this coming war, and in no way discounting the tragedy of lives lost, all the world wars put together will seem insignificant.[7]

I believe the sixth trumpet initiates and prepares the way for the sixth bowl that we'll encounter in Revelation 16:12-16, where we see the kings from the Far East arrive at the Campaign of Armageddon by crossing the Euphrates River. China's population is 1.5 billion and they have already boasted of tallying 200 million in their army. What seemed far-fetched in the past has come to fruition in our days, and will embolden nations to wreak havoc on other nations!

9:17 *And thus I saw the horses in the vision: those who sat on them had breastplates of fiery red, hyacinth blue, and sulfur yellow; and the heads of the horses were like the heads of lions; and out of their mouths came fire, smoke, and brimstone.*

The fifth trumpet unleashed locusts that appeared like horses. In the sixth trumpet John states that he saw horses, not animals that were like horses. John may be referencing a military arsenal such as tanks and helicopters that were not present in his day, but he uses vocabulary that the readers of his time would understand.

The soldiers' breastplates were fiery red, dark sapphire blue (hyacinth) and sulfur yellow. The horse's heads were like lions, meaning that they are likened to merciless beasts. We'll soon read that the two witnesses in Revelation 11:5 will have fire come from their mouths to devour their enemies. Fire, smoke and brimstone depict God's judgment. For instance, in Genesis 19:24 we read, "Then the Lord rained upon Sodom and upon Gomorrah brimstone and fire from the Lord out of heaven."

The Bible speaks of one creature, known as a serpent, portraying Satan, named Leviathan, "Flames stream from its mouth; sparks of fire shot out. Smoke pours from its nostrils as from a boiling pot over burning reeds. Its breath sets coals ablaze, and flames dart from its mouth" (Job 41:19-21).

I believe that this is a human army, possessed, steered and manipulated by satanic powers to invade the city of Jerusalem.

9:18 By these three plagues a third of mankind was killed—by the fire and the smoke and the brimstone which came out of their mouths.

Can you imagine the human crisis the world will face? Even a Category-2 hurricane can blast the shores of the East Coast and destroy the lives and homes of many. If not for federal and state funds with the assistance of humanitarian aid such as the Red Cross and Samaritan's Purse, many would lose their lives.

Who will help these people during the Tribulation? It is inconceivable. Who will bury the dead? Those who live will be inconsolable. Who will be responsible for rebuilding? The stench of the dead will be unbearable. How will life exist? Many parts of the world will be unreachable. More than half of the world's population will be lost. Grotesque videos will go viral on social media platforms. God's time to change this world draws ever so nigh as He "Revs It Up!" Fiction? Fabrication? You've got a right to your opinion. However, when these events come to fruition, make sure you meet and greet the locusts and the army of 200 million horsemen!

9:19 *For their power is in their mouth and in their tails; for their tails are like serpents, having heads; and with them they do harm.*

The power of the horses is in their mouth and tails. Fire will come out of their mouths devouring what is before them. Unlike the locusts who had tails of scorpions (Revelation 9:10), these horses have tails of serpents with heads. Approaching these horses either from the front or the rear will cause harm. This may be a description of a modern military arsenal, including tanks, helicopters and jets. Because of the real threat of modern-day cyber-attacks, a majority of equipment and aircraft will likely be grounded. Horses will have to be used. No matter what the means, the force behind the attack is Satan himself, unleashing his demons to lead the way.

9:20 *But the rest of mankind, who were not killed by these plagues, did not repent of the works of their hands, that they should not worship demons, and idols of gold, silver, brass, stone, and wood, which can neither see nor hear nor walk.*

Those who somehow survive the onslaught of judgments refuse to give up their idols, their crumbling material world and their meager possessions, refuse to bow to God and refuse to repent of their ways. In Revelation 2:21 we see that God gave Jezebel time to repent of her immorality, but she was unwilling. By reading Joel 2:12-13, we see God's tender heart and desire for His created to turn to Him: "'Now, therefore,' says the Lord, 'Turn to Me with all your heart, with fasting, with weeping, and with mourning.' So rend your heart, and not your garments; return to the Lord your God, for He is gracious and merciful, slow to anger, and of great kindness; and he relents from doing harm."

As the time span for life on earth shortens, the wicked inclination of man's heart worsens.

Earth-dwellers continue to be tested, but they are defiantly displaying deranged hearts that will go to any length to spit in God's face. This is reminiscent of Moses dealing with Pharaoh in Egypt. As the plagues intensified, so too Pharaoh's heart hardened all the more. "When Pharaoh saw that the rain and hail and thunder had stopped, he sinned again: He and his officials hardened their hearts" (Exodus 9:34). But Pharaoh and his army ended up buried in the Dead Sea. A defiant stance, brazen rage and dogmatic opposition against God will not lead to victory for the inhabitants of earth; it will lead to their eternal burial.

One can do whatever he wishes; that is called free will. Many chose to hate God and they are allowed to do just that because they are free to exercise their will. However, remember that choices have consequences. Just as God did in Egypt, He will do in the Tribulation: deal harshly with earth's inhabitants so that they may know that the earth is the Lord's and that His "name will be declared in all the earth! (Exodus 9:16).

Idols and gods are the works of man's hands. Man honors man. Man honors animals. Man honors the earth. Man honors the constellations. Man will even go to any length to honor everything except his Creator. Man, in all his frailty, professes to be wise, yet plays the part of the fool (Romans 1:22).

We will soon see in our reading that the False Prophet will entice earth's inhabitants to make an idol in the image of the Antichrist. "And he (the False Prophet) deceives those who dwell on the earth by those signs which he was granted to do in the sight of the beast (Antichrist), telling those who dwell on the earth to make an image to the beast who was wounded by the sword and lived. He was granted power to give breath to the image of the beast, that the image of the beast should both speak and cause as many as would not worship the image of the beast to be killed" (Revelation 13:14-15).

Though idols in themselves are lifeless, the disposition to worship them is demonically inspired. We see this in Deuteronomy 32:17, "They sacrificed to demons, not to God, to gods they did not know, to new gods, new arrivals that your fathers did not fear." During these dreadful days, man will regress, not progress. Idol worship is more prevalent than we think or imagine, even in America. Occultism, astrology, spiritualism and religion lead to eternal hell. The Word of God leads to eternal life.

In I Timothy 4:1 we read, "Now the Spirit expressly says that in latter times some will depart from the faith, giving heed to deceiving spirits and doctrines of demons." If you are shocked at what you see in the news, take a look at what was prophesied 2,000 years ago in II Timothy 3:1-5. These verses are worth reviewing to shock us into reality. "But know this, that in the last days perilous times will come: for men will be lovers of themselves, lovers of money, boasters, proud, blasphemers, disobedient to parents, unthankful, unholy, unloving, unforgiving, slanderers, without self-control, brutal, despisers of good, traitors, headstrong, haughty, lovers of pleasure rather than lovers of God, having a form of godliness by denying its power." If you can't stand the heated times of today, you definitely won't be able to handle it during the Tribulation!

According to Psalm 115:4-8, it is incomprehensible to have idols: "Their idols are silver and gold, the work of men's hands. They have mouths, but they do not speak; eyes they have, but they do not see; they have ears, but they do not hear; noses they have, but they do not smell; they have hands, but they do not handle; feet they have, but they do not walk; nor do they mutter through their throat. Those who make them are like them; so is everyone who trusts in them."

If one continues to accept a lie as the truth, there comes a breaking point when God muddles his mind and hardens his heart. We read in II Thessalonians 2:9-12, "The coming of the lawless one (Antichrist) is according to the working of Satan, with all power, signs, and lying wonders, and with all unrighteous deception among those who perish, because they do not receive the love of the truth, that they might be saved. And for this reason, God will send them strong delusion, that they should believe the lie, that they all may be condemned who do not believe the truth but had pleasure in unrighteousness."

9:21 *And they did not repent of their murders or their sorceries or their sexual immorality or their thefts.*

The Antichrist will have millions of followers and will have his hypnotized cronies purge the land of the treacherous, treasonable and two-timing Christ-followers! It is said of the Antichrist in Revelation 13:6-7, "Then he opened his mouth in blasphemy against God, to blaspheme His name, His tabernacle, and those who dwell in heaven. It was granted to him to make war with the saints and to overcome them. And authority was given him over every tribe, tongue, and nation."

Sorcery, seduction, voodoo, divination, witchcraft and rampant drug use will only soar during this dreadful time. The Greek root for the word "sorcery" is "pharmakeia," from which we get our English word pharmacy. Drugs are a "habit-forming addiction which destroys the will of its victims."[8] Those who remain on earth will be tragically signed over to the Antichrist and drugs will make it effortlessly possible. How so? Those who use illicit drugs or even those who are prescribed narcotics in excess are not in the right frame of mind. One who does not have focus, is easily misinformed, helplessly and tragically following the orders of his New-World leader.

As we'll see in chapters 17-18, Babylon, the city, the religion and the economy will be ruling the minds of the people and will boast, "'I am, and there is no one else besides me; I shall not sit as a widow, nor shall I know the loss of children.'" (Isaiah 47:8). But Babylon, Satan's very tool, will be defeated according to the prophet Isaiah, "But these two things shall come to you in a moment, in one day: the loss of children, and widowhood. They shall come upon you in your fullness because of the multitude of your sorceries, for the great abundance of your enchantments. Stand now with your enchantments and the multitude of your sorceries, in which you have labored from your youth — perhaps you will be able to profit, perhaps you will prevail. You are wearied in the multitude of your counsels. Let now the astrologers, the stargazers, and the monthly prognosticators stand up and save you from what shall come upon you. Behold, they shall be as stubble, the fire shall burn them; they shall not deliver themselves from the power of the flame; it shall not be a coal to be warmed by, nor a fire to sit before!" (Isaiah 47:9, 12-14).

Practicing sorcery, consulting mediums, conjuring spells, calling up the dead is an abomination before God (Deuteronomy 18:10-11). With several "innocent" television series and countless video games and movies promoting witchcraft, many are being indoctrinated into the demonic world, conditioned into a belief that will make them seem like zombies following the demands of the Antichrist. Sorcery and hallucinogenic drugs work synergistically to delve into the malevolent spirit world. The road taken may seem better, fancier, richer, happier and laced with freedom, but it leads right into Satan's playbook: indescribable desolation. Earth-dwellers will continue in their ways. They will not be following any moral laws; they will be deranged, and they will not be running to Christ. They will be running to their daddy, the Antichrist.

Prostitution and human trafficking will be at an all-time high. Lewdness will rule the land. Desires will be unchecked. Promiscuity will become a religion. Hedonistic behaviors will be celebrated all the more. Moral distinctions will fade. Disregard for a neighbor's rights will vanish. The absence of theft, fraud and deception will be the exception. It will be as in the days of the Judges, "In those days there was no king in Israel; everyone did what was right in his own eyes" (Judges 21:25). False prophets will still declare peace. Antichrist-followers will still follow their desire for violence. Though God's Word will still be preached, there will be millions who become "mini-Pharaohs." They will hear the truth. They will see the power of God. They will live through the devastations. And they will still choose to harden their hearts against God and end up drowning in the fire of death.

While describing the hearts of the Israelites, the prophet Jeremiah also poetically defined all of mankind's heart, "O, Lord, are not Your eyes on the truth? You have stricken them, but they have not grieved; you have consumed them, but they have refused to receive correction. They have made their faces harder than rock; they have refused to return. Therefore, I said, 'Surely these are poor. They are foolish; for they do not know the way of the Lord, the judgment of their God'" (Jeremiah 5:3-4).

The prophet Amos also spoke of God's view of Israel's heart. "'I sent among you a plague after the manner of Egypt; your young men I killed with a sword, along with your captive horses; I made the stench of your camps come up into your nostrils; yet you have not returned to Me,' says the Lord. 'I overthrew some of you, as God overthrew Sodom and Gomorrah, and you were like a firebrand plucked from the burning; yet you have not returned to Me,' says the Lord. 'Therefore, thus will I do to you, O Israel; because I will do this to you, prepare to meet your God, O Israel!' For behold, He who forms mountains, and creates the wind, who declares to man what his thought is, and makes the morning darkness, who treads the high places of the earth—the Lord God of hosts is His name" (Amos 4:10-13). And the consequence? Ten of the twelve tribes of Israel ended up being ravaged by Assyria and exiled. During the Tribulation, the earth's inhabitants may rage against God, but they will surely meet Him at the Great White Throne judgment, and will acknowledge on bended knee that He is the one and only Almighty God!

If someone asks for more signs and wonders, it is usually a smoke screen for a rebellious heart that has no intention of submitting to God. If it is signs the earth-dwellers look for, they will get it. The bowls of God's wrath will be released after the seventh trumpet is sounded. The fool will still say in his heart, "There is no God" (Psalm 14:1). It is mind blowing that after all the suffering, the 144,000 Jewish evangelists preaching (Revelation 7:1-17), the two prophets proclaiming God's Word (Revelation 11:1-13), the angel in the sky professing the truth (Revelation 14:6-7), there will be a multitude of survivors during the Tribulation who will still snub God.

 It's simple; man wants to live independently of God, and Satan promises complete freedom from God. Ironically, Satan's promise is a deception for bondage. Regrettably, unbelievers get their wish. Tragically, they meet their fate ... the eternal Lake of Fire.

REV IT UP & SUM IT UP – CHAPTER NINE:

After the fourth trumpet judgment, there remain three woes, or the fifth, sixth and seventh trumpets. Chapter nine covers the first two woes, or the fifth and sixth trumpets.

While the first four trumpets devastated the earth and the heavens, which indirectly affected mankind, the fifth and sixth trumpets affect mankind directly.

The fifth trumpet allows Satan to open up the abyss and release demonic locusts that will sting ungodly earth-dwellers during the first half of the Tribulation. Those stung will be utterly miserable, not being able to relieve themselves of the wretched discomfort. Nothing over the counter or even a prescription from the local doctor will relieve their pain. They will seek to die but will not be allowed to do so. There is mercy dispensed after all from the living God: He allows them to live, giving them the opportunity to turn to Him and evade eternal hell.

The sixth trumpet releases four satanic angels who are bound at the banks of the Euphrates River, who in turn mobilize an army that numbers two hundred million to gather at Megiddo in Israel for the Campaign of Armageddon. These angels are given permission to kill one third of the earth's population. We will see this army marching in full force when the sixth bowl is poured out in Revelation 16:12-16.

The escalation of judgments and their severity is unbearable but what is inconceivable is that mankind will continue in their ways of idolatry, drug use and pride, snubbing God, accepting the Antichrist, and choosing eternal death over eternal goodness, joy and life!

Chapter 10
The Silent Speech of Thunder

By the time we get to the end of chapter nine, the world's status becomes absolutely grim. Six trumpets have already sounded, and we await the seventh. The world is burnt, bloodied, bruised, and battered. The waters are poisoned. People are plagued with sores. Scorpions sting. People cry. Souls die. But amid all this, God is seated on His throne and orchestrates all the affairs of the Tribulation. His Son will soon take complete reign over this world and rule with righteousness and justice. John, seeing all this in a vision, is in distress, deserted on an island, persecuted for his faith. Jesus is in control and in this chapter, appears to John to assure him of his and all believers' secure future.

The Mighty "Angel" Roars

***10:1** I saw still another mighty angel coming down from heaven, clothed with a cloud. And a rainbow was on his head, his face was like the sun, and his feet like pillars of fire.*

Before we hear the blowing of the seventh trumpet, we are introduced to the interlude of the seven thunders found in this chapter. Chapter ten is given to John as a flash-forward to the end of the Tribulation, to assure us that God is still and always will be in power, His Word will stand, and evil will be shut down permanently and eternally. Just as chapter seven (144,000 Jewish evangelists) was an interlude between the sixth and seventh seals, chapter ten serves as an interlude between the sixth and seventh trumpets.

John sees a "mighty angel" coming down out of heaven. The angel holds the Word of God, and in so, the title deed to the world. The Psalmist praised God by singing, "The earth is the Lord's, and all its fullness, the world and those who dwell therein. For He has founded it upon the seas and established it upon the waters. The heavens are Yours; the earth also is Yours; the world and all its fullness; You have founded them" (Psalm 24:1-2; 89:11). The Apostle Paul declares it loud and clear by restating, "For the earth is the Lord's and all its fullness" (I Corinthians 10:26). The "mighty angel" puts one foot on land and the other in the sea and lifts the title deed in the air as a symbol of God ruling over all creation.

For some time, I have struggled with the first verse. Who is this "mighty angel?" Is it Michael, the great warrior? Is it Gabriel, the great messenger? Is it another mighty angel, unknown to us? Is it really an angel or is it Jesus who, in His pre-incarnate state, is called the "Angel of the Lord" in the Old Testament?

At first, I was convinced that this angel is not Jesus. The words "another mighty angel" essentially confirms the fact that the angel is not Jesus. Why would the author call Jesus "another" angel? Why would he even call him an angel? Jesus is distinct. He is God. He is mighty and sovereign. He is unmistakably holy, glorious, full of grace and truth, shining brighter than the sun. One cannot pin Him down as an "angel" or as "another" angel!

Angels are created beings and worship Christ (Hebrews 1:6). "'Angel' is the ordinary Greek word for messenger. To call Christ an angel would be the deepest error. Angels are created beings. The Lord Jesus is the creator of the angelic beings. There is no reason, however, that He cannot act in the capacity of a messenger as He already has acted in the capacity of a servant."[1] I was once convinced that it must be Michael or Gabriel, who are among God's highest-ranking angels. But one thing I heard in my heart repeatedly is to let the Bible interpret the Bible. So, let's look at the Bible.

Jesus appeared in the Old Testament 56 times as the "Angel of the Lord," the Son of God appearing in the form of a human body, known as a Christophany.

The first reference is found in Genesis 16:7-12 where it says that "the Angel of the Lord" appeared to Hagar as she was fleeing in the wilderness from the rage of Abraham's wife. The "Angel of the Lord" appeared to Moses in the burning bush (Exodus 3:2). In Exodus 23, we are told that God spoke to Moses and said He would send an angel to guide and protect the Israelites in the wilderness. He refers to this angel as "My angel" and states that "My name is in Him" (Exodus 23:20-23). This is no ordinary angel; it is Jesus, God's Son. When the "Angel of the Lord" appeared to Moses (Exodus 3:1-5) and Joshua (Joshua 5:14-15), He told both to remove their sandals for they were standing on holy ground.

It is also believed that Melchizedek, the mysterious priest seen in Genesis 14:18-20 and Hebrews 7:1-28, was a manifestation of Christ. I agree. Why else would Melchizedek offer bread and wine to Abram? This is a symbol of communion! By Christ's stripes, His body, represented by the bread, we are healed; by His blood, represented by the wine, we are redeemed.

There are four Biblical facts that reveal the identity of the mighty angel in verse one: 1) clouds, 2) rainbow, 3) shining face like the sun, and 4) feet like pillars of fire.

First, the mighty angel mentioned in verse one was clothed with a cloud. Christ, in His deity, is surrounded by a cloud. "Clouds and darkness surround Him; righteousness and justice are the foundation of His throne" (Psalm 97:2). In Exodus

19:9, after Israel escaped the death grip of Egypt, the Lord said to Moses, "Behold, I come to you in the thick cloud, that the people may hear when I speak with you and believe you forever." During the 40-year journey in the desert, the cloud of the Lord was above the tabernacle by day, and the fire was over it by night (Exodus 40:38).

On the Mount of Transfiguration, a bright cloud overshadowed them and suddenly a voice came out of the cloud, saying, "This is My Beloved Son, in whom I am well pleased. hear Him!" (Matthew 17:5). When Christ ascended to heaven, "He was taken up, and a cloud received Him out of their sight" (Acts 1:9). Jesus said about His Second Coming, "Then they will see the Son of Man coming in a cloud with power and great glory" (Luke 21:27). When He returns at the end of the Tribulation, known as His Second Coming, He will come with the clouds and every eye will see Him (Revelation 1:7).

Second, there is a rainbow on the "angel's" head. God made a covenant with Noah, placing a rainbow in the sky as a symbol of His mercy. The rainbow pictures mercy in the midst of judgment. Who but the Lord could wear a garland or rainbow of mercy? It reminds us of his faithfulness in keeping His covenant; He will never again cover the entire earth with a flood (Isaiah 54:9).

In Revelation 4:3, John is taken up to heaven, and when he sees God sitting on the throne, he states, "And He (God) who sat there was like a jasper and a sardius stone in appearance and there was a rainbow around the throne, in appearance like an emerald." God will not share His glory with an angel, but He has "highly exalted Him (Jesus) and given Him (Jesus) the name which is above every name" (Philippians 2:9).

Third, Christ is pictured as One who has a shining face like the sun. Saul of Tarsus met Him and was blinded by the same bright light (Acts 9:3-6). When Jesus was on the mountain with Peter, James and John, He was transfigured before them. His face shone like the sun, and His clothes became as white as the light (Matthew 17:1-2). In Revelation 1:16-17, "His (Jesus') countenance was like the sun shining in its strength. And when I (John) saw Him, I fell at His feet as dead."

Finally, this angel has "feet like pillars of fire." We read in Revelation 1:15, "His (Jesus') feet were like fine brass, as if refined in a furnace." When Jesus spoke to the church in Thyatira, we read, "These things says the Son of God, who has eyes like a flame of fire, and His feet like fine brass" (Revelation 2:18). An angel does not have the authority to judge; only Jesus does.

Jesus is clothed in a cloud, crowned with a rainbow, and has a face like the sun—all of which are symbols of deity. His feet were like pillars of fire, indicating He has come in judgment—all judgment has been given to Jesus (John 5:22).

It is worth noting that Jesus appeared as the "Angel of the Lord" in his pre-incarnate state in the Old Testament, and in Isaiah 9:6, was specifically called Wonderful, Counselor, the Mighty God, the Everlasting Father and the Prince of Peace. Though He is not called the "Angel of the Lord" in the New Testament, He is the same and is unmistakably called "the faithful witness, the firstborn of the dead, and the ruler of the kings of the earth; the living One; Lion of the tribe of Judah, the Root of David; the Lamb; Word of God; King of Kings, and Lord of Lords (Revelation 1:5; 1:18; 5:5; 7:17;19:13; 19:16).

Daniel also had a similar encounter with a "certain man" in a vision found in Daniel 10:4-6, "Now on the twenty-fourth day of the first month, as I was by the side of the great river, that is, the Tigris, I lifted my eyes and looked, and behold, a certain man clothed in linen, whose waist was girded with gold of Uphaz! His body was like beryl, his face like the appearance of lightning, his eyes like torches of fire, his arms and feet like burnished bronze in color, and the sound of his words like the voice of a multitude." You can call this "certain man" Michael,

Gabriel or another angel. The salient characteristics of eyes of fire and feet of bronze signify the person of Christ.

However, it is not reckless or unreasonable to argue that this mighty angel is not Jesus Christ. Although I am convinced it is Jesus Christ, we will not know assuredly until we see our Father face to face. We accept that the Word of God came to John. We accept that the Word is true. We accept that the "messenger" speaks inspired words from the throne of God. We accept that we are flawed, and His Word is faultless. The fact remains, that whether it is Christ or not, it does not change the truth of the message nor its application.

10:2 *He had a little book open in his hand. And he set his right foot on the sea and his left foot on the land*

In Revelation chapter five, we learned that Jesus is the only one in all the universe who is qualified to take the scroll from God's hand. I believe the "mighty angel" in chapter ten is Jesus, holding God's victorious Word: He claims possession of the earth and reminds us to persevere because all will be well in the end. This interlude is timely because Satan, the "god of this world," seems to have the upper hand in today's economy, society and policies as it will appear during the Tribulation (II Corinthians 4:4). God is reminding us, however, that the earth and the sea and all of the universe belongs to Him and is under His sovereignty. When Christ held the scroll in chapter six, it was sealed. This scroll or little book is open. Interestingly, the closed scroll was opened, and its contents were revealed while the contents of this open book are concealed.

When Moses spoke to the Israelites who were ready to cross the Jordan River and take possession of the Promised Land, he encouraged them by saying, "Every place on which the sole of your foot treads shall be yours: from the wilderness and Lebanon, from the river, the River Euphrates, even to the Western Sea (Mediterranean), shall be your territory. No man shall be able to stand against you; the Lord your God will put the dread of you and the fear of you upon all the land where you tread, just as he has said to you" (Deuteronomy 11:24-25). In our text, "The setting or planting of his feet on sea and land is the formal taking possession of both; or the formal expression of the purpose to do so."[2]

His right foot is set on the sea, representing the Gentile world and the left foot is set on the land, representing the earth, and more specifically Israel. If we are to regard the left side as an ill-fated sign as was done so by the Greeks,[3] then its placement of the left foot on the land may indicate that judgment will not only begin with the Jewish nation, but it will devastate the land and its people. Israel was given the law, the prophets, and the Messiah, and will be held responsible for these great revelations. There are consequences for rejecting the Messiah.

We have discussed the text from Romans 2:8-9 before, "But to those who are self-seeking and do not obey the truth, but obey unrighteousness—indignation and wrath, tribulation and anguish, on every soul of man who does evil, of the Jew first and also of the Greek." Israel will never be forgotten, and the church will never replace Israel. God says of Israel in Isaiah 44:21, "I have formed you, you are My servant; O Israel, you will not be forgotten by Me!" But remember two things: first, "for whom the Lord loves He chastens" (Hebrews 12:6); second, "for everyone to whom much is given, from him much will be required; and to whom much has been committed, of him they will ask the more" (Luke 12:48). The Tribulation will be a horrible time for all people alive at that time, including the Jews, but in its midst, there still flows an offer of salvation from God's throne; and at its finale, there will be redemption for the remnant of Israel.

10:3 *and cried with a loud voice, as when a lion roars. When he cried out, seven thunders uttered their voices.*

Jesus is going to return in triumph to claim the earth for the

Christ-followers! The earth and the sea are rightfully His. He created them, "All things were made through Him (Jesus), and without Him nothing was made that was made" (John 1:3). Two thousand years ago, the incarnate Christ was born, and 33 years later, He was rejected, crucified, and rose from the dead. Today He sits at the right hand of the Father, interceding for us (Hebrews 7:25; Romans 8:34). During the Tribulation, He will stand, take the sealed scroll from His Father and unleash the wrath of God upon the earth (Revelation 6-19). After the Tribulation, He will reign as King of Kings and Lord of Lords (Revelation 19:16).

According to Psalm 2:8-9, God tells His Son Jesus, "Ask of Me (God), and I will give You (Jesus) the nations for Your inheritance, and the ends of the earth for Your possession. You (Jesus) shall break them with a rod of iron; You shall dash them to pieces like a potter's vessel." Jesus will take over holding the deed to the earth in His hand. He will rule as the King of Kings. He will place His left foot on the land; His right foot on the sea; and He will roar like a lion.

Jesus is the Lion of the tribe of Judah in Revelation 5:5, "Behold, the Lion of the tribe of Judah, the Root of David, has prevailed to open the scroll and to loose its seven seals." In Joel 3:16, prophecy states, "The Lord also will roar from Zion, and utter His voice from Jerusalem; the heavens and earth will shake; but the Lord will be a shelter for His people, and the strength of the children of Israel." And in Amos 1:2, "The Lord roars from Zion, and utters His voice from Jerusalem; the pastures of the shepherds mourn; and the top of Carmel withers." According to Psalm 29:5, "The voice of the Lord breaks the cedars, yes, the Lord splinters the cedars of Lebanon." The roaring as a lion further characterizes this "angel" as Jesus Christ.

The prophet Jeremiah spoke of the ferocious roar of the Lord during the Tribulation. "The Lord will roar from on high and utter His voice from His holy habitation; He will roar mightily against His fold. He will give a shout, as those who tread the grapes, against all the inhabitants of the earth. A noise will come to the ends of the earth—for the Lord has a controversy with the nations; He will plead His case with all flesh. He will give those who are wicked to the sword" (Jeremiah 25:30-31).

Joel also spoke of the Lord's roar at the end of the Tribulation, at the Campaign of Armageddon, "'Let the nations be awakened, and come up to the Valley of Jehoshaphat (translated as "Jehovah has judged" in Hebrew);[4] for there I will sit to judge all the surrounding nations. Put in the sickle, for the harvest is ripe. Come, go down; for the winepress is full, the vats overflow—for their wickedness is great.' Multitudes, multitudes in the valley of decision! For the day of the Lord is near in the valley of decision. The sun and moon will grow dark, and the stars will diminish their brightness. The Lord also will roar from Zion and utter His voice from Jerusalem; the heavens and earth will shake; but the Lord will be a shelter for His people, and the strength of the children of Israel" (Joel 3:12-16).

In Isaiah 53:7 the Lamb was led to the slaughter, and as a sheep before its shearers is silent, Jesus did not open his mouth. But here? No way! Jeremiah 25:30-31, Joel 3:1-2 and Amos 1:2 speak of the days of the Lion, the Lord roaring from on high, and all the forces bowing down in silence!

 Jesus will not be denied. He will not be vilified. He will not once again be crucified. His reign shall come to pass as it was prophesied.

He will govern as the risen King, the Lion, the ruler of all creation. He will cry out, and seven thunders will utter their voices. These thunders are not just the usual noise we hear when lightning strikes but are thunder-like voices communicating an ominous message. The Greek word translated "thunder" means "to roar." What did each thunder utter? When lightning strikes, thunder follows. When thunder rolls, the storm unfolds. By now, the seven seals are opened. The six trumpets have sounded. The seventh trumpet is about to sound, unleashing the seven bowl judgments.

These thunders speak words of prophecy, but they are not to be fully disclosed until the set time in the first half of the Tribulation. They are the roars and the warnings that will introduce us to the wretched cries of the haunted souls who will face the judgments of the horrible bowls.

 Though we cannot hear the speech the thunders utter, we will know the horror they will usher.

Six days prior to the Passover, Jesus came to Bethany and Mary anointed the feet of Jesus with costly perfume and wiped His feet with her hair (John 12:1-8). The next day, Jesus entered Jerusalem riding a donkey while multitudes cried out, "Hosanna! Blessed is He who comes in the name of the Lord! The King of Israel!" (John 12:12-13).

Jesus felt sorrow, knowing He was soon to be crucified as seen in John 12:27-32. He stated, "Now is my soul troubled; and what shall I say? Father save me from this hour: but for this cause came I unto this hour. Father glorify Your name. Then came there a voice (God's voice) from heaven, saying, 'I have both glorified it, and will glorify it again.' The people therefore, that stood by, and heard it, said that it thundered: others said, 'An angel spoke to Him.' Jesus answered and said, 'This voice came not because of me, but for your sakes. Now is the judgment of this world: now shall the prince of this world be cast out. And I, if I be lifted up from the earth, will draw all men unto Me.'"

 God's voice thunders. It is the language of grace and goodness to those who love Him. It is the language of horror and judgment to those who reject Him.

***10:4** Now when the seven thunders uttered their voices, I was about to write; but I heard a voice from heaven saying to me,*

"Seal up the things which the seven thunders uttered, and do not write them."

The seven thunders are the only words in Revelation that are sealed. The same throne of God that issues forth the lightning and peals of thunder in Revelation 4:5 issues a command to keep secret what the voices have revealed. When Daniel was given a vision of the Antichrist, he was told, "And the vision of the evenings and mornings which was told is true; therefore, seal up the vision, for it refers to many days in the future" (Daniel 8:23-26). Twice more Daniel was told to seal up the words given to him, "But you, Daniel, shut up the words, and seal the book until the time of the end; many shall run to and fro, and knowledge shall increase" (Daniel 12:4); "And he said, 'Go your way, Daniel, for the words are closed up and sealed till the time of the end'" (Daniel 12:9). The prophecies revealed to Daniel are better understood in our day as knowledge has increased. However, the prophecies revealed by the seven thunders will not be decrypted in our day because what God has shut no one can open (Isaiah 22:22).

Thunder is often a mark of judgment in Scripture as seen in I Samuel 2:10 and Revelation 16:18. Is the message of the thunders too terrifying? Is it too troubling? Or is it all about the timing? The reason is not given. My guess would be inaccurate. The only logical statement I can make is that the thunders indicate more ominous storms loom over the horizon in the form of the seven bowl judgments. And the command is clear, "Do not write them."

"Here is a definite commandment from God that no indication shall be given as to the correct interpretation of the seven thunders. In spite of this, however, some commentators have attempted to do that which God forbade John to do. It seems to me that the reverent student of the Word of God can do nothing more but to pass on to that which follows. A great grammarian says that the verb "seal" is in the tense of urgency,

'Seal up at once.' Paul saw glory in heaven that was not lawful to utter (II Corinthians 12:4). John sees judgment as the power and majesty of God in action. We bow with reverence before the seal and pass on."[5]

When you, however, are in the midst of your tribulation here and now, and God speaks to you in a thunderous way, keep it to yourself, treasure His words, ponder on it, pray about it, pray through it, pray in it, and let it be your sacred and sweet hour with Him!

10:5 The angel whom I saw standing on the sea and on the land raised up his hand to heaven 10:6 and swore by Him who lives forever and ever, who created heaven and the things that are in it, the earth and the things that are in it, and the sea and the things that are in it, that there should be delay no longer, 10:7 but in the days of the sounding of the seventh angel, when he is about to sound, the mystery of God would be finished, as He declared to His servants the prophets.

If this "angel" were Jesus standing, how could He raise His hand and do the unthinkable: swear by God? In Hebrews 6:13 we are told that when God made His promises to Abraham that "He swore by Himself" because "He could swear by no one greater." We witness the same in Jeremiah 22:5 where God says, "I swear by Myself."

Have you ever noticed when people use "Jesus Christ" as a swear word, even though they may not believe in Him, some even abhorring Him, they don't evoke the name of any other god? Why? Because there is no name higher in the sea, on earth or in heaven! God has "highly exalted Him (Jesus) and given Him the name which is above every name, that at the name of Jesus every knee should bow, of those in heaven, and of those on earth, and of those under the earth, and that every tongue should confess that Jesus Christ is Lord, to the glory of God the Father" (Philippians 2:9-11).

People may use Christ's name as a curse word now and think nothing of it. But they will bow the knee, gaze at the holiest Spirit they've ever beheld, and utter words of worship. At that time, it will not be by choice. It will involuntarily flow from their lips. But their horrible reality will be an eternity without God. There is no goodness, no hope, no peace, no laughter, no wellness and no joy in their destiny! But even now, God extends His love and whoever wishes can come to Him!

The hand raised to heaven implies an oath. It is made simultaneously not only by, but also to the Author of Life, heavens, earth and the sea and all that is in them. According to I Corinthians 10:26, "The earth is the Lord's and all its fullness." In I Chronicles 29:11, King David boasted, "Yours, O Lord, is the greatness, the power and the glory, the victory and the majesty; for all that is in heaven and in earth is Yours; Yours is the kingdom, O Lord, and You are exalted as head over all." Job also sang of God's praises, "I know that You can do everything, and that no purpose of Yours can be withheld from You" (Job 42:2). The oath is made. It cannot be broken. It will be fulfilled, and nothing will stop our God.

The oath indicates that there will be no more delay. The interlude between the sixth and seventh trumpets is almost over. The time has come for the seventh trumpet to be sounded and nothing can hinder its execution. We will see the seventh angel sound his trumpet in Revelation 11:15. When this occurs, all the warnings of the prophets concerning judgment will be fulfilled. Then the mystery of God will no longer be a mystery but a reality. The prophets of old could not understand all the scriptures concerning this mystery. They prophesied about the Messiah; they prophesied about the Millennium; but they, including Daniel, were blinded to the 2,000-year church period that will shortly come to an end.

Christ-followers, including the Apostle Paul, have believed that Christ would come back in their day, but the Lord has not yet come. Many have incorrectly predicted the day of His return; the sheer attempt is foolish since we are too finite to know the mind of our infinite God. "Shall we allow the failure of men's figures and prognostications to shake our confidence or obscure our hope? Shall we suffer the many and long delays that have occurred, or that ever may occur, to drive us into the scoffers' ranks?"[6] The answer is a definite, "No!"

The good news announced to the prophets will be fulfilled and realized to the dismay of those who oppose Christ and to the joy of those who adore Him. Christ will return. The church will be Raptured. The ungodly will meet their hero, the Antichrist. The Lord shall return and crush His enemies in the Campaign of Armageddon. Satan will be bound. Christ will rule on earth. The ungodly will be judged. And we will live forever in peace and goodness for all Eternity. The word God spoke by the mouth of all His holy prophets since the world began (Acts 3:21) will be in play.

Habakkuk described the fulfillment in a beautiful way, "For the vision is yet for an appointed time; but at the end it will speak, and it will not lie. Though it tarries, wait for it; because it will surely come, it will not tarry" (Habakkuk 2:3). It's all in God's good time. God's terms. God's way. God's will!

Bitter-Sweet Little Book

10:8 *Then the voice which I heard from heaven spoke to me again and said, "Go, take the little book which is open in the hand of the angel who stands on the sea and on the earth."*

The voice from the throne of God that instructed John not to write down what the thunders uttered now instructs John to take the book from the hand of One who holds the book. The "little book" is the prophetic and living Word of God, the Bible, which in and of itself is not only a written text, but contains the DNA of God, His love, His mercy, His goodness, His tender heart, and His good plan for those bought by the blood of the Lamb, and His punishment for the wicked. It has been criticized. It has been censored. It has been contorted. But it will never be crushed! In His younger years, John not only heard the Word, but he walked with the Word, Jesus Christ. Here, he is told to go and take the Word.

10:9 *So I went to the angel and said to him, "Give me the little book." And he said to me, "Take and eat it; and it will make your stomach bitter, but it will be as sweet as honey in your mouth."*

John did as he was told. He went to the angel and asked for the book. He was told to take it and eat it. The word "eat" in the Greek is "katesthio," meaning to "consume, devour and swallow."[7] John was not to glance at the book; he was instructed to take it, read it, embrace it, digest it, meditate on it and preach it. The book has a sweet message of God's wonderful plan for mankind including salvation—Jesus on the cross; redemption—man receiving the gift of the cross; justification—through the atonement of Christ at Calvary, we are considered righteous and just; sanctification—dying to self but alive in Christ; and glorification—being free of sin for all Eternity because of Jesus' complete work on the cross. It also contains a bitter message of God's judgment regarding sinners who do not repent and come to Him, and their ultimate destiny in a place of eternal grief and death.

When Jeremiah ate God's Word, he exclaimed, "Your words were found, and I ate them, and Your word was to me the joy and rejoicing of my heart" (Jeremiah 15:16). David ate God's Word, "How sweet are Your words to my taste, sweeter than honey to my mouth" (Psalm 119:103). John is told to take the book and eat it, and that he does, finding it bittersweet: Sweet because those who accept the blood of the Lamb receive eternal life; bitter because many will reject the blood of the Lamb and tragically accept eternal death in hell. That is not hate speech. That is the speech of love. Love warns. Hate blinds. Love speaks when it is beneficial to the other person. Hate speaks when it desires to harm the other person.

Ezekiel was also told to eat the Word of God and share the Word with his people who were taken as exiles to Babylon, "Moreover He (God) said to me, 'Son of man (Ezekiel), eat what you find; eat this scroll, and go, speak to the house of Israel.' So I opened my mouth, and He caused me to eat that scroll … So the Spirit lifted me up and took me away, and I went in bitterness, in the heat of my spirit; but the hand of the Lord was strong upon me" Ezekiel 3:1-3,14. That is the beauty of God's truth, it may offend, but it will heal; it may chastise, but it will correct; it may show our stains, but it will make us new! Come! Taste and see that the Lord is good! (Psalm 34:8).

***10:10** Then I took the little book out of the angel's hand and ate it, and it was as sweet as honey in my mouth. But when I had eaten it, my stomach became bitter.*

When John tasted the book, it was sweet as honey, as previously recorded by David, "The law of the Lord is perfect, reviving the soul. The statutes of the Lord are trustworthy, making wise the simple. The precepts of the Lord are right, giving joy to the heart. The commands of the Lord are radiant, giving light to the eyes. The fear of the Lord is pure, enduring forever. The ordinances of the Lord are sure and altogether righteous. They are more precious than gold; than much pure gold. They are sweeter than honey; than honey from the comb. By them your servant is warned and in keeping them, there is great reward" (Psalm 19:7-11).

How could these sweet words become bitter to the stomach? When a believer comprehends the mercilessness of eternal death, he should fall to his knees and cry for the unsaved. This is not the time to find his church pew and make himself comfortable, calloused and critical. This is not the time of unbridled entertainment. This is not the time of revelry. This is the time to share the treasure, Jesus Christ, whom the believer is so privileged to have received! Wake up church! Wake up Pastor! Wake up Christian! Wake up and eat the Book of Life!

10:11 And he said to me, "You must prophesy again about many peoples, nations, tongues, and kings."

John remained faithful as a disciple; he was the only one present when His Lord was crucified. John remained faithful as a pastor; he preached to the seven churches. John remained faithful on an abandoned island; his writings still ring in our hearts today. He was asked to prophesy and so he did. John was condemned to labor on the Island of Patmos by Caesar Domitian. When Domitian died, all his judgments were dismissed. "And John being dismissed from the mines, thus subsequently delivered the same Apocalypse which he had received from God."[8] When John returned to Asia Minor, he shared the book of Revelation faithfully as instructed and prophesied.

We are all asked to share. It's a simple choice. Share the Word of God in the kindest manner, evangelize, give people hope, and taste the sweetness of people coming to Christ. If the Word kept to oneself, it brings bitterness to the keeper's own soul. Sharing is not only a command, but it prevents you and me from being a bitter, angry, discouraged, depressed, sour and ungrateful follower of Christ. After all, who can stand an ornery, irritable and grouchy believer? And if that describes you, it's time to fall on your knees and repent!

Father, as we face trials and tribulation, bitterness, and brokenness of soul, we ask that your comforting Word guard our hearts and minds. Instruct and guide us as you counsel and watch over us. We place our trust in You and Your inerrant Word. Help us to share your life-giving Word with the world. Restore our souls and bless us indeed. In Jesus' name, Amen!

REV IT UP & SUM IT UP – CHAPTER TEN:

This chapter describes an interlude between the sixth and seventh trumpets' judgments. As the Tribulation unfolds, John sees Jesus, the Creator and ruler of the earth, sea and heavens and all its creatures. How do we know it's Jesus standing with one foot on the sea and the other on the land, holding a "little book"? He is radiant like the sun; He is the judge of the universe; He roars as the Lion of the Tribe of Judah; He swears by His Father's name. Angels don't judge, and angels don't roar; God does.

As Christ roars, seven thunders utter their speech. John is first instructed not to write the contents of the speech. The discourse, though its specific words are hidden, is a forerunner of the seven-judgment bowls that are to be poured out on the earth. John is then instructed to ask for the book and eat it. It is sweet to his taste because of the Savior's life-giving sacrifice for us. However, it becomes bitter in his stomach because those who reject the Savior recklessly reject eternal life. John will ultimately be freed from the Island of Patmos and continue to preach, prophesy and proclaim God's inerrant Word.

In your hardest moments, no matter how dreadful your life may be, and whatever hell has thrown your way, Jesus is in the midst of the whole thing. He is on scene. His eyes are on you, not to harm you, but to give you hope.

Your soul may be dismayed. You may ask, "Why did he dump me? Why did she betray me? Why did I lose my job? Why did I lose my spouse? Why did I lose the one I love? Why did I never make it? Why did this tragedy happen to me? Why am I being persecuted? How can they repay me with bad when I have done good?" In Psalm 40:1-3, the psalmist proclaims, "I waited patiently for the Lord, and He inclined to me, and heard my cry. He also brought me up out of the horrible pit, out of the miry clay, and set my feet upon a rock, and established my steps. He has put a new song in my mouth—praise to our God; many will see it and fear and will trust in the Lord."

Allow God's Word to be your counselor (Psalm 119:24). Allow God's Word to be your healing (Psalm 107:20). Allow God's Word to be your guide (Psalm 119:105). Love Him. Trust Him. Praise Him. Share Him. Watch Him do great works in you! Remember, He is not mad at you. He is madly, madly, madly in love with you!

Chapter 11
Two Die or Not Two Die

Chapter 11 deals with Israel's spiritual life while chapter 12 takes us to the midpoint of the Tribulation and describes the persecution Israel will face at that time. In this chapter, we'll see the temple of God being built in Jerusalem during the Tribulation. We will also visit with the prophets of old, Moses and Elijah, as they return to the land of Israel.

The Two Prophets of Old

11:1 Then I was given a reed like a measuring rod. And the angel stood, saying, "Rise and measure the temple of God, the altar, and those who worship there.

Israel's first temple was built by Solomon approximately 960 BC (I Chronicles 22, 28, 29 and II Chronicles 2-7). The second temple was built by Zerubbabel the Governor and Joshua the High Priest approximately 515 BC, 70 years after Israel was exiled to Babylon by King Nebuchadnezzar. The second temple was renovated by King Herod over a period of 40 years and completed by 64 AD, but was destroyed by Rome only a few years later in 70 AD. Note that Israel has been without a temple for 2,000 years and it will be the Antichrist who will deceive Israel into confirming a peace treaty with the Arab nations and will level the ground for Israel to build the third temple during the Tribulation. Negotiating this temple's existence near the Dome of the Rock, the third most holy site in Islam, will not be difficult after the peace treaty takes effect. The Tribulation temple will be followed by the fourth temple that will be built during the Millennium period (Ezekiel 40-48).

Revelation 11:1 refers to the third temple which will be built at the beginning of the Tribulation hour. When we read about the third temple in the Bible, it is usually referred to as the temple where the abomination of desolation will occur, when the Antichrist will desecrate the Holy of Holies:

1. "Then he (Antichrist) shall confirm a covenant with many for a week; but in the middle of the week, he shall bring an end to sacrifice and offering (that means sacrifices were made at this temple prior to its halt). And on the wing of abominations shall be one who makes desolate, even until the consummation, which is determined, is poured out on the desolate" (Daniel 9:27).

2. "And from the time that the daily sacrifice is taken away, and the abomination of desolation is set up, there shall be one thousand two hundred and ninety days" (Daniel 12:11).

3. Jesus said, "Therefore when you see the 'abomination of desolation,' spoken of by Daniel then let those who are in Judea flee to the mountains" (Matthew 24:15-16).

4. The temple will be defiled and used sacrilegiously by the Beast who will claim to be God "and the man of sin (Antichrist) is revealed, the son of perdition, who opposes and exalts himself above all that is called God or that is worshiped, so that he sits as God in the temple of God, showing himself that he is God" (II Thessalonians 2:3b-4).

The Jews will build the third temple in the name of God, without knowing Him. Why else would they believe in the false messiah, the Antichrist? This temple has nothing to do with the church! Christ-followers are already in heaven by this time, having been caught up in the Rapture (Revelation 4:1). The Tribulation is not for the church. It will become the greatest catalyst to bring the Jews the revelation that Jesus Christ is the true Messiah.

God is specific and orderly. John is asked to measure the temple (the Holy of Holies), the altar (likely the brazen altar of sacrifice), and those who are God's own people, the Jews. He will measure it with a light and rigid bamboo-like reed; John is measuring a temple that has not yet been built, but God is God and there is none like Him, declaring the end from the beginning and prophesying future events before their birth or their occurrence (Isaiah 46:9-10).

"They (the Jewish nation) are yet in unbelief at the time of this measuring, but they are known to God with all their doings. Just as in their stubborn rejection of Messiah in His first com-ing, they will continue in their unbelief to the very end of the Tribulation period. A sealed remnant will be saved, and others will be undoubtedly brought to the Lord, but it is not until they have looked upon Messiah whom they have pierced (Zechariah 12:10) that their national salvation will come."[1] "The measuring of the temple and the worshipers, therefore, shows that the Father is watching over those whom He has separated unto Himself."[2]

We don't hear God instructing John to document the temple's dimensions as we'll see in Revelation 21:16-17, when the Lord gives the measurements of the New Jerusalem which will exist during the Millennium. When Israel was in exile, the Spirit of the Lord lifted Ezekiel to the New Jerusalem where he met a man who had "a measuring rod in his hand" and meticulously measured the Millennium temple (Ezekiel 40-46). As we'll see in the next verse, John is instructed to exclude the outer court of the third temple.

***11:2** But leave out the court which is outside the temple, and do not measure it, for it has been given to the Gentiles. And they will tread the holy city underfoot for forty-two months.*

This instruction not to measure the non-Jewish section describes God's pending judgment against Gentile nations who will sink deep into idolatrous worship. The rod can therefore be a judgment stick instead of a measuring stick; it signifies God's judgment against the idolater, and at the same time, God's staff of protection and preservation for the true worshiper.

Once the Antichrist desecrates the temple, the Gentiles will tread underfoot the holy city, Jerusalem, for three and a half years, and persecute the Jews. But they too will be trampled upon, not by nations, but by God! In God's economy, the punishment always fits the crime. God will cast out this unmeasured section of Gentiles and trample on it in the winepress of His wrath in His second coming; He will "ekbale ezothen" in the Greek, or "throw outside, cast out or expel outside;" the Holy City, Jerusalem, will be trampled on by the Gentiles for the last three and a half years in the Tribulation but these Gentiles will be trampled on by God.[3]

This is in stark contrast to the church that existed prior to the Rapture. "In the church there is neither Greek nor Jew, Barbarian, Scythian, bond nor free; but all nationalities and conditions in life yield to one common brotherhood and heirship. The text, therefore, tells of a new order of things; the Jew is again in the foreground for the Fathers' sakes, and the Gentiles are thrust back."[4]

According to Isaiah 62:7, Jerusalem will be a "praise in all the earth," meaning it will have great honor worldwide. When the American Embassy in Israel was officially moved to Jerusalem on May 14, 2018, a palpable venomous uproar erupted around the globe. Not only do the nations of the world refuse to acknowledge God's purpose for Jerusalem today, but they will refuse to do so during the Tribulation, and will set their hearts on devouring Jerusalem.

Even though God has allowed His chosen people to taste utter hardship such as slavery under Pharaoh's rule and has diminished the city of Jerusalem to nothing after uprooting and exiling its people to Babylon under Nebuchadnezzar's reign, He has placed Jerusalem as the centerpiece of the whole world and will not forget her. "Thus says the Lord God, 'This is Jerusalem; I have set her in the midst of the nations and the countries all around her'" (Ezekiel 5:5).

God also declares ownership of Jerusalem and that is why it will be impossible for any nation or culture to annihilate it or eradicate it off the map, "Yet I (God) have chosen Jerusalem, that My name may be there" (II Chronicles 6:6). God said to David and to Solomon his son, "In this house (His temple) and in Jerusalem, which I have chosen out of all the tribes of Israel, I will put My name forever" (II Chronicles 33:7).

It's actually very simple. The church does not replace Israel. The world doesn't own Israel. God watches over Israel. Israel will remain Israel because God has full and final ownership over Israel.

After the Antichrist desecrates the temple, there will be forty-two months (second half of Daniel's last week of the seventieth week) left in the Tribulation, and he will elevate himself to the throne of a One-World-Order (Daniel 7:25, 12:7, 11-12; Revelation 13:1-8). As we'll see in Revelation 12:1-14, the remnant Jews will flee to the wilderness where God will protect them. The Gentiles will subsequently have free reign to move into Jerusalem and plunder it. This too is simple.

Satan hates Jesus Christ, who will reign from Jerusalem in the Millennium; if Satan can take down and obliterate Jerusalem, he believes he can stop Christ from reigning; he will therefore lead multiple coalitions to annihilate Israel, Jerusalem and the Jews. Once again, it will appear that the Gentile nations have taken over Jerusalem, but it will be short-lived, lasting only 1,260 days. The Second Coming of Christ will set all the records straight, humbling the Gentile nations, while rescuing the Jewish remnant.

The end times of the Gentiles will be unveiled with the Second Coming of Christ. Jeremiah 30:6-9 foretells us that the Lord will save Israel from "the time of Jacob's Trouble." Don't underestimate God's love as well as justice for Israel as seen in Jeremiah 30:10-11, "'Therefore do not fear, O My servant Jacob,' says the Lord, 'Nor be dismayed, O Israel; for behold, I will save you from afar, and your seed from the land of their captivity. Jacob shall return, have rest and be quiet, and no one shall make him afraid. For I am with you,' says the Lord, 'to save you; though I make a full end of all nations where I have scattered you, yet I will not make a complete end of you. But I will correct you in justice and will not let you go altogether unpunished.'"

11:3 And I will give power to my two witnesses, and they will prophesy one thousand two hundred and sixty days, clothed in sackcloth."

The voice in this verse is likely from God's throne as He is the One who gives power to His witnesses. Why two? Two is the number required by the law of Moses to authenticate the account of an eyewitness (Numbers 35:30). Who are these two? As we'll soon see, their ministries resonate the ones of Moses and Elijah, the two prophets of old, for they have the power to cause rain to stop, turn water to blood and strike the earth with all plagues.

Two prophets will appear for 1,260 days (the Jewish calendar has 360 days in one year), or forty-two months, or three and a half years to proclaim God's message of salvation. Their "headquarters" will be in Jerusalem, but their message will be "broadcast" to all the world. They talk, they walk, they wear sackcloth, they have breath, they die and rise by the power of God. "By no stretch of the imagination, then, can an interpreter regard these witnesses as other than real persons.[5]

The witnesses' reign is during "the first half of the final week of the seventy weeks of Daniel, before the Beast reaches ascendancy and is able to overcome them (Revelation 11:7)."[6] Their ministry cannot occur during the second half of the Tribulation. The simplest way of clarifying this is that the Beast will be defeated at the end of Daniel's seventieth week, or at the end of the seven years, and will be cast into the pit. If the Beast kills these two witnesses (Revelation 11:7) at the end of the seven years, there will be no time for celebration as the world will be gearing up for the Campaign of Armageddon. Overthrowing the prophets would logically contribute to the rise and fame of the Beast and not his fall and imprisonment; "their martyrdom will be the first persecuting act of the Beast, after he breaks his covenant with the Jews."[7] The two witnesses will therefore prophesy during the first three and a half years of the Tribulation.

They wear sackcloth, a coarse cloth made of black goat hair, depicting sorrow, mourning and repentance. When Jacob thought his son Joseph was killed, he tore his clothes, put on sackcloth and mourned for his son (Genesis 37:34). Repentance is God's petition to man to turn to Him and be saved under His loving arms. Any other way leads to deception in the putrid arms of Satan. This is likened to the bitterness that John felt deep in his belly when he ate God's Word, which translated into doom for those who reject it.

The prophets who wore sackcloth such as Isaiah were heartbroken over the message of judgment that they proclaimed.

The two prophets of old will warn those who remain on earth of the impending judgments and plead with them to turn to Christ. It seems peculiar that these two prophets appear in Revelation chapter 11 and not before; perhaps their time on earth will be a very small window; perhaps the 144,000 Jewish evangelists have to do their work first before the two prophets appear. Whatever the reason, their message is on point and does not change: repent for the Kingdom of God is near!

11:4 These are the two olive trees and the two lampstands standing before the God of the earth.

There is a great deal of discussion as to the identities of the two witnesses. But remember, we are not studying Revelation to identify the Antichrist or these two prophets; we are studying Revelation to know Jesus Christ. No matter who the two witnesses are, they are men of God, anointed, directed by the Spirit of God and speaking God's Word. The reason I believe that these two prophets are Moses and Elijah is threefold:

1. As seen in Matthew 17:1-13, Moses, representing the Law, and Elijah, representing the prophets, appeared on the Mount of Transfiguration with Jesus Christ. Peter wanted to immortalize all three, but God told Peter, James and John to listen to His Son. Jesus is above the Law. He is above the prophets. He is above all. God did not send Enoch, John the Baptist or two new prophets; He sent Moses and Elijah, two of the most well-known and influential figures in Jewish history.

   It is the ultimate expression of grace on behalf of God to call upon Moses to appear at the Mount of Transfiguration and also during the Tribulation. Moses struck the rock, representing Jesus Christ, twice and subsequently was not allowed access to the Promised Land (Numbers 20:11). He lived in luxury, he lived in isolation, he took on the "Antichrist" of his day, Pharaoh, and was able to govern one and a half million of his countrymen; he will be back to conduct God's business during the Tribulation.

It is fascinating that God mentions both of these prophets in the last three verses of the Old Testament. "Remember the law of Moses, My servant, which I commanded him in Horeb for all Israel, with the statutes and judgments. Behold, I will send you Elijah the prophet before the coming of the great and dreadful day of the Lord. And he will turn the hearts of the fathers to the children, and the hearts of the children to their fathers, lest I come and strike the earth with a curse" (Malachi 4:4-6). Just as these two were with Jesus on the mount, they will be His two witnesses during the Tribulation.

2. Moses turned the Nile River into blood and struck Egypt with plagues using the rod God handed to him (Exodus 7-10). Elijah shut up the dew of heaven for three and a half years with his prayer, and there was no rain in Israel (James 5:17-18). The two will do the same in the Tribulation.

3. Moses died, and his body was taken up to heaven as seen in Deuteronomy 34:5-6 (like the dead in Christ will rise during the Rapture). Elijah did not die a physical death and his body was taken up to heaven by a whirlwind as seen in II Kings 2:9-11(like those Christ-followers who are alive will be taken up during the Rapture).

Many assume the second witness is Enoch and not Moses, quoting Hebrews 9:27, "It is appointed unto men once to die." Since Enoch did not die and was resurrected, they believe that Enoch must come back to die. But there will be millions of Christ-followers during the Rapture who will not die and will be caught up with the Lord. The argument regarding necessary death does not hold because the death spoken of in Hebrews 9:27 is not physical, but spiritual; "Enoch is a picture of the Church of Jesus Christ, taken out of the world before the tribulation shall come upon it."[8]

The two witnesses are called olive trees (literally trees of oil) and lampstands to signify that their work is not by their own might. In Zechariah 4:1-14, an angel gave the prophet Zechariah a vision, showing him a solid gold lampstand with an oil container above it. On the lampstand stood seven lamps, each with seven flames. An olive tree was on the right side of the oil container and another olive tree was on the left, both pouring oil into the container, which subsequently fueled the burning lamps to shine. This was during the days of Joshua the high priest and Zerubbabel the governor, both dumbfounded with the overwhelming task of rebuilding Solomon's temple that was destroyed by the invading armies of Babylon.

The oil symbolizes the Holy Spirit, who gave Joshua and Zerubbabel the zeal to accomplish their task, not by might, not by power, but "'by My Spirit,' says the Lord" (Zechariah 4:6). When Zechariah asked the angel about the two olive branches that poured oil into the bowl, the angel answered, "These are the two anointed ones (or literally the two sons of oil), who stand beside the Lord of the whole earth" (Zechariah 4:14). As God's servants were empowered by the Holy Spirit to rebuild the temple, so will these two anointed witnesses, who carry the oil and shine the light of Christ in the midst of darkness also complete God's work in the first half of the Tribulation. How wonderful! We see two chosen vessels, anointed by the power of the Holy Spirit, proclaiming the message of God's beautiful light in the midst of a sin-laden, plague-burdened, dark-covered world during the Tribulation.

In Revelation 1:12, we saw seven golden lampstands, representing the church. In this chapter, we only see two. Why not seven? Because the church has been caught up in the Rapture! In Zechariah 4:14, we read, "These are the two anointed ones, who stand beside the Lord of the whole earth" and in Revelation 11:4, we read, "These are the two olive trees and the two lampstands standing before the God of the earth." Coincidence? Ghost writer? No, more like the Holy Ghost!

***11:5** And if anyone wants to harm them, fire proceeds from their mouth and devours their enemies. And if anyone wants to harm them, he must be killed in this manner.*

These two witnesses will be hated by the world. Why? Because when God sheds His light on evil, it screams, riots, vandalizes, and becomes ungovernable. Assassins will attempt to destroy these two, but God's sovereign protection will have the last word. Forget about Batman and Robin: that's fantasy. These two prophets are real people with supernatural anointing. I don't believe that they are an apparition, or phantom-like figures. I believe the Lord sent them back as they were before they left earth.

There will be an encore ensemble in the Tribulation of what Moses achieved 3,500 years ago and what Elijah performed 2,800 years ago. But the "fireworks" at this concert will far surpass the events of the past. Fire will come out of the mouths of the two witnesses and devour those who desire to hurt them. Fire is a sign of judgment and destruction. It is said of Jesus in Isaiah 11:4, "He shall strike the earth with the rod of His mouth, and with the breath of His lips He shall slay the wicked." God told the prophet Jeremiah, "Because you speak this word, behold, I will make My words in your mouth fire, and this people wood, and it shall devour them" (Jeremiah 5:14). It seems likely that literal fire will come out of the two witnesses' mouths because their miraculous powers must exceed those of the demonic world.

***11:6** These have power to shut heaven, so that no rain falls in the days of their prophecy; and they have power over waters to turn them to blood, and to strike the earth with all plagues, as often as they desire.*

According to James 5:17-18, "Elijah was a man with a nature like ours, and he prayed earnestly that it would not rain; and it did not rain on the land for three years and six months. And he prayed again, and the heaven gave rain, and the earth produced its fruit."

James refers to I Kings 17:1, when Elijah said to Israel's wicked King Ahab, "As the Lord God of Israel lives, before whom I stand, there shall not be dew nor rain these years, except at my word." The famine revealed the apostasy of Israel and exposed the 450 false prophets of Baal and 400 prophets of Asherah, who competed with Elijah on Mount Carmel. The prophets called out to their god to consume their sacrifice with fire; no word; no fire; then Elijah called out to the true God to consume his sacrifice and God intervened with fire; the people of Israel fell on their faces and exclaimed, "The Lord, He is God! The Lord, He is God!" (I Kings 18: 19-40).

The seven-year Tribulation will bring an end to idolatry and will ultimately force God's enemies to bow before Him as conquered foes. Elijah will once again set the stage in the first half of the Tribulation by calling for a drought, this time globally. Do you recall what the Pharisees asked John the Baptist when they inquired as to who he was in John 1:21? "Are you Elijah?" As prophesied in Malachi 4:5, Elijah will return.

According to Psalm 105:26-41, God sent Moses His servant who performed His signs among the Egyptians. "He (God) sent darkness and made it dark. He turned their waters into blood and killed their fish. Their land abounded with frogs, even in the chambers of their kings. He spoke, and there came swarms of flies, and lice in all their territory. He gave them hail for rain, and flaming fire in their land. He stuck their vines also, and their fig trees, and splintered the trees of their territory. He spoke, and locusts came, young locusts without number, and ate up all the vegetation in their land, and devoured the fruit of their ground. He also destroyed all the firstborn in their land, the first of all their strength. He also brought them (Israel) out with silver and gold, and there was none feeble among His tribes. Egypt was glad when they departed, for the fear of them had fallen upon them. He spread a cloud for a covering, and fire to give light in the night. The people asked, and He brought quail, and satisfied them with the bread of heaven. He opened the rock, and water gushed out; it ran in the dry places like a river."

Just as God performed wonders through Moses in Egypt, He will do so again through His chosen servants in the Tribulation. And just as God protected His people in Egypt and led them through the wilderness, feeding them, guiding them and protecting them, He will do so again in the Tribulation by feeding, guiding and protecting His chosen people in Bozrah-Petra (modern day Jordan).

The Two Prophets Taken Out

11:7 *When they finish their testimony, the beast that ascends out of the bottomless pit will make war against them, overcome them, and kill them.*

The two prophets cannot be killed unless God ordains it. Nothing can happen to a child of God without the Lord's divine permission. In fact, God's children are immortal until their work is done. Even Christ was slain, but not before He finished His work; He said to His Father, "I have glorified You on the earth. I have finished the work which You have given Me to do" (John 17:4).

The Beast, known as the Antichrist, the second person of the evil trinity, raises his ugly head and ascends out of the Bottomless Pit to war with the two prophets. "The 'Lamb' is the Savior of sinners; the 'Beast' is the persecutor and slayer of the saints. The 'Lamb' calls attention to the gentleness of Christ; the 'Beast' tells of the ferocity of the Antichrist. Under the Law lambs were ceremonially clean and used in sacrifice, but beasts were unclean and unfit for sacrifices."[9]

The Beast will come out of the Bottomless Pit, fight against the two witnesses, and kill them. He possesses his father's, or Satan's, demonic character and features as Paul described in II Thessalonians 2:9, "The coming of the lawless one (Antichrist) is according to the working of Satan, with all power, signs, and lying wonders."

He rises from the deep well within earth's belly where deviant angels are restrained until they are cast into the Lake of Fire. A defining attribute of the Beast and his father Satan is their fierce opposition to God's people, including the two witnesses, God's saints, and the Jews (Daniel 7:21, 25; Revelation 7:9-16; 11:7; 12:11; 13:7; 20:4; Jeremiah 30:7). This is the Beast that rode on the white horse in Revelation 6:2. Ironically, he rides forth to conquer and kill saints, but it is he who will be conquered by Christ and it is the saints who are the true overcomers!

The witnesses will preach and accomplish their work. The Antichrist, however, will attempt to interrupt and terminate their work. We will soon find that the Antichrist will be mortally wounded in Revelation 13:3; he will then arise, counterfeiting a Christ-like resurrection, and kill the two witnesses, receive great fame, and prophetically accomplish God's will for the next three and a half years, or the second half of the Tribulation.

Because no one has been able to overcome the two witnesses in the first half of the Tribulation, the world will be in awe of the Beast's powers, "And all the world marveled and followed the beast (Antichrist). So they worshiped the dragon (Satan) who gave authority to the beast; and they worshiped the beast, saying, 'Who is like the beast? Who is able to make war with him?" (Revelation 13:3-4).

"He (the Antichrist) will come back from the Abyss by means of his resurrection by Satan. Along with his resurrection, the act of killing the Two Witnesses will provide another reason why mankind will worship him. All previous attempts to kill the Two Witnesses fail."[10] The events will be as follows:

1. The Antichrist will be alive and will perpetuate his work starting with the peace agreement to kick off the Tribulation.

2. The 144,000 Jewish evangelists will preach.

3. The two witnesses will preach and perform miracles in the span of the three and a half years).

4. The Antichrist will receive a deadly wound and die, possibly inflicted by the two witnesses.

5. The Antichrist will rise from the abyss, staging a resurrection similar to the true Messiah, Jesus Christ. He will kill the two witnesses solely because God will allow it.

6. The world will be in awe of the Antichrist, the Beast, and worship him because he was dead and now is alive, and he alone was able to kill the two witnesses. The two witnesses, however, to the dismay of the whole world, will rise from the dead and ascend up to heaven in plain sight because God's breath enters into them three and a half days after their death.

7. The Antichrist will then rule for forty-two months (chapter 13: verse 19), or three and a half years during the second half of the Tribulation, called the Great Tribulation, or the time of "Jacob's Trouble."

11:8 And their dead bodies will lie in the street of the great city which spiritually is called Sodom and Egypt, where also our Lord was crucified.

The two witnesses will lay where the Lord was crucified, Jerusalem, the Holy City. Why then, does the writer call Jerusalem Sodom and Egypt? The depraved spiritual conditions that existed in Sodom before its destruction and the idolatrous environment that abounded in Egypt before the plagues are found infiltrating Jerusalem during this period. "To call it Sodom and Egypt is to indicate that it is utterly given over to the devil and to the vicious practices of sin which result where God takes His hand from a nation, people or city, and allows men to go to the extremes of their desire."[11] The city Jerusalem has the spiritual attributes of Sodom and Egypt, but its physical identity is undoubtedly Jerusalem, the place of Christ's crucifixion. For those who argue that the city is not Jerusalem, Bullinger states, "A Sunday-school child could tell us where the Lord was crucified; but these learned men cannot."[12]

The two prophets will not be given a proper burial. In fact, their dead bodies will be left on the streets. The absence of a burial is particularly repugnant to the Jews and is an act of humiliation, disgrace and dishonor.[13] According to Jeremiah 22:19, it is likened to the burial of a donkey, "He (Jehoiakim, the king of Judah) shall be buried with the burial of a donkey, dragged and cast out beyond the gates of Jerusalem." The Beast will be glorified by mankind as they stare at his two trophies!

***11:9** Then those from the peoples, tribes, tongues, and nations will see their dead bodies three-and-a-half days, and not allow their dead bodies to be put into graves.*

How wretched! The two witnesses lay dead on the streets of Jerusalem, exposed to heat, birds that prey and the eyes of men who hate for three and a half days. The mention of fourfold "peoples, tribes, tongues and nations" depicts the global significance of this event. Ayatollah Khomeini of Iran did the same to American servicemen, by displaying them in the streets of Tehran following the April 1980 hostage rescue attempt. If it were not for God's intervention as we'll see in verse eleven, the two witnesses would be left to rot on the streets. They will lay there for three and a half literal days, three signifying death followed by life, relating to the resurrection of our Christ on the third day.

The death of the two witnesses will be seen by the whole world. Years ago, this was a common laughing point for unbelievers, asking how the whole world could possibly observe one event at the same time! The answer is in modern communication technology and the smartphone; their death will go viral; it will have millions of views and "likes" in seconds. "The older commentators might have felt a difficulty in understanding how the whole earth could rejoice at an event happening in Jerusalem. But in these days of electric inventions, telephones, and wireless telegraphy, we all know how the next day the whole world sympathizes or rejoices together."[14]

It's not hard to believe human depravity will reach new depths when you see blatant acts of anarchy on college campuses and on our city streets these days. At present, the fight is against "conservatives." There is coming a day in America, before the Rapture of the church, when a lashing will be the plenty for anyone who believes in the Lord Jesus Christ. Many will scoff at this sentence but pay attention when the police are told to stand down as anarchists physically attack law enforcement agents, conservatives and God-fearing people in the name of tolerance and political correctness. Why are they allowed to be so violent without repercussions? It is because mayors and police chiefs of cities are so politically aligned that they allow beatings, vandalism, hate speech and bullying, and justify their stance by stating they are fighting against racism and fascism.

The bullying has actually risen to a higher level in the United States of America; it is called labeling the opposing view as racists and bigots; it is called targeting them; it is called silencing them by threatening to physically harm them and boycotting their businesses; it is called lulling the masses to accept a New-World-Order under the irresistible auspices of equality, harmony, prosperity, everything free, stability and security … all which leads to the ugly reality of misery, poverty, disparity, dependency and despondency. These "enlightened elites" are tolerant with anyone who agrees with their Socialist/Globalist/One-World-New-World-Order view. Fighting a different world view with hatred and violence, however, is not fit for a civilized society. This violence, fueled with enmity, will only intensify during the Tribulation. People who turn to Christ during the Tribulation will not be tolerated, and they will be despised to the point that anyone who kills them will be celebrated and rewarded. I do believe, however, that there will be a reprieve, a revival, a recourse and a return to God's Word in these days before the Rapture and the Tribulation! Get ready!

11:10 And those who dwell on the earth will rejoice over them, make merry, and send gifts to one another, because these two prophets tormented those who dwell on the earth.

Those who dwell on earth, who detest God and who worship the Beast, will rejoice over the death of the two witnesses. When I was growing up in Chattanooga, Tennessee, I had some friends who were avid soap opera watchers. When a "beloved" actor, the character in the story line, got hurt, shot or died on the set, these friends would send condolence cards to each other; they would also exchange congratulations cards when someone on the set got married.

During the Tribulation, the God-hating, Jesus-despising, Holy Spirit-rejecting earth-dwellers will rejoice in the death of the two witnesses, believing that a time of "peace" and "calm" will follow, and their days of torment are coming to an end. There will likely be a declaration of a new holiday such as "Beast Day," where fellow earth-dwellers will rejoice and exchange gifts because their tormentors are finally ousted! Their celebration will be short lived.

This is the only time the book of Revelation records a time of rejoicing on earth during the Tribulation; it will be the earth-dwellers' new Halloween! People have made it through the seven seals and six trumpets, half of the earth's population is dead, the two witnesses are slain, and the earth-dwellers feel a sense of pending relief. They will carouse and socialize until they realize that their celebration is fleeting, and their souls will forever be dying.

The Two Prophets Taken Up

11:11 Now after the three-and-a-half days the breath of life from God entered them, and they stood on their feet, and great fear fell on those who saw them.

In Genesis 2:7 we read, "And the Lord God formed man of the dust of the ground and breathed into his nostrils the breath of life; and man became a living being." Job declared that "The Spirit of God has made me, and the breath of the Almighty gives me life" (Job 33:4). In the same way, the breath of God, the Spirit of the Living God, resuscitates the two dead witnesses, and the parties around the world come to a screeching halt! How could two lifeless corpses stand on their feet? Viral images on social media will permeate the hearts of mankind and fear will dominate their souls.

The Lord took the prophet Ezekiel to a valley of dry and dead bones and asked him if the bones could once again live. Ezekiel answered, "O Lord God, You know." God told Ezekiel to prophesy to the bones and say to them, "O dry bones, hear the word of the Lord! Thus says the Lord God to these bones, 'Surely I will cause breath to enter into you, and you shall live." The bones revived! (Ezekiel 37:1-14). This is a picture of the prophetic rebirth of Israel as a nation which was fulfilled on May 14, 1948. God always fulfills His promises and the breath of God gives life. It gives life to you and me. It gives life to Israel. And it will give life to the two prophets of old, witnesses of God's sovereign power over all the earth!

When Belshazzar, King Nebuchadnezzar's grandson, was king and organized a lavish party in honor of his gods, there was an abundance of wine that was consumed in revelry … until the handwriting on the wall appeared. We read that King Belshazzar's "countenance changed, and his thoughts troubled him, so that the joints of his hips were loosened, and his knees knocked against each other" (Daniel 5:6). We read in Daniel 5:1-31, that Daniel was summoned to read and interpret the writing on the wall, "Mene, Tekel, Peres," which meant that King Belshazzar's days were numbered (Mene), he was weighed in the balances and was found lacking (Tekel), and his kingdom was to be divided (Peres) and given to the Medes and Persians.

This too will be the handwriting on the wall, or the canvas of the sky, for the earth-dwellers: two witnesses who were loathed, were killed, were mocked, will rise from the dead demonstrating the power of God and then expose the depravity of man. It will be "Mene, Tekel, Peres" repeated, and earth's dwellers will sink into the pits of fear and face the ongoing horrors of the Great Tribulation as their days are numbered, they have been weighed and found to be lacking, and their Antichrist's kingdom will soon be divided and their souls doomed.

11:12 And they heard a loud voice from heaven saying to them, "Come up here." And they ascended to heaven in a cloud, and their enemies saw them.

Moses and Elijah, the two witnesses, will hear God's voice, rise from the dead and be caught up into heaven as the world watches. John heard the same voice in Revelation 4:1, when the Lord said, "Come up here, and I will show you things which must take place after this." "Come up here!" What glorious words! It is God calling His children home, where it is debt-free, tear-free, illness-free, sad-free and death-free! And most importantly, it is filled with hope, with God's holy presence and with His glory!

This is a series of the "first" resurrection; "for as in Adam all die, even so in Christ all shall be made alive. But each one in his own order: Christ the first fruits, afterward those who are Christ's at His coming" (I Corinthians 15:22-23). This is the "carpool" we spoke of in Revelation 4:1, the Christ-follower being resurrected at his appointed time. The two witnesses' resurrection provides an unparalleled testimony that God is all powerful and sovereign as the world watches in awe.

11:13 In the same hour there was a great earthquake, and a tenth of the city fell. In the earthquake seven thousand people were killed, and the rest were afraid and gave glory to the God of heaven.

As the world observes, God sends a quick and clear judgment upon the blasphemous people who were rejoicing over the death of the two witnesses. There is nothing good to report as mankind stands in the sewage-infested field of utter desolation. Two men come to life and vanish in a cloud. An earthquake hits Jerusalem and 7,000 people are killed. It is interesting that an exact number of 7,000 is recorded. The number seven in the Bible depicts perfection; God's flawless plan is so detailed that it is precise to the last number, whether in the tens, hundreds, thousands, millions or ten to the power of Eternity.

This is one of the four earthquakes mentioned in the book of Revelation:

1. We saw the first with the opening of the sixth seal (Revelation 6:2).

2. The second is mentioned here, when the two witnesses are resurrected there is a devastating earthquake, where a tenth of the city crumbles and 7,000 people die (Revelation 11:13).

3. The third occurs when the seventh trumpet is sounded and "there were lightnings, noises, thunderings, an earthquake, and great hail" (Revelation 11:19).

4. The fourth is even greater in magnitude than the one

mentioned after the two witnesses resurrect and occurs at the pouring out of the seventh and final bowl (Revelation 16:17).

News alert! Those alive will be so frightened that they will praise God; not out of converted hearts, but out of astonishment and alarm; strictly lip service. Their reaction is like the Pharisees who saw a paralytic healed, were amazed, praised God, and yet were filled with fear (Luke 5:26). They did not get saved; they just got scared.

Some people will quickly acquire a spiritual lingo quickly, especially if nuclear warfare is the topic of the day! Since the 666 mark has not yet been implemented, there is still hope for those who remain to turn from their evil ways and look upon the Lord for repentance. There is a possibility that the "rest were afraid and gave glory to the God of heaven" means just that … repentance.

 Offering lip service to God will not reach His ears but speaking the language of humility and responding to the Holy Spirit's conviction reaches God's heart.

11:14 The second woe is past. Behold, the third woe is coming quickly.

We now come to the third woe. The angel in Revelation 8:13 said, "Woe, woe, woe." Each woe was a different judgment, one worse than the previous. The first woe was the fifth trumpet blast, the second woe the sixth trumpet sound. At this point, the final woe, the seventh trumpet, is about to sound. It is worth noting again that between the sixth and seventh seal, there was an interlude, where we saw the 144,000 Jewish evangelists sealed and millions being martyred for their faith (Revelation 7). Between the sixth and seventh trumpet, a "mighty angel" stood straddling the sea and the earth, John ate the book of prophecy, and the two witnesses ministered upon the earth from Jerusalem (Revelation 10-11).

Seventh Trumpet: The Kingdom to Come

***11:15** Then the seventh angel sounded: And there were loud voices in heaven, saying, "The kingdoms of this world have become the kingdoms of our Lord and of His Christ, and He shall reign forever and ever!"*

Below is a list of the seven trumpet judgments. We will now discuss the seventh trumpet.

First Trumpet: 1/3 of trees & grass burned (8:7).
Second Trumpet: 1/3 of sea life & ships destroyed (8:8-9).
Third Trumpet: 1/3 of rivers poisoned–Wormwood (8:10-11).
Fourth Trumpet: 1/3 of sun, moon, stars struck (8:12).
Fifth Trumpet: demonic locusts torment the ungodly (9:1-12).
Sixth Trumpet: four angels at Euphrates lead army (9:13-21).
Seventh Trumpet: seven bowls of wrath released (11:15-19).

The seventh trumpet reveals God's final sentences upon the earth, unveiling the seven bowl judgments seen in chapters 15-16. The last of the seven trumpets is not to be confused with the "last trump" of the Rapture, where believers shall be changed "in a moment, in the twinkling of an eye, at the last trumpet. For the trumpet will sound, and the dead will be raised incorruptible, and we shall be changed" (I Corinthians 15:51-52).[15]

"In the book of Revelation, the seventh trumpet is never called 'last.'"[16] Furthermore, the seventh trumpet covers a long span of time and includes the seven bowls of judgments on the unbelieving, making it impossible for it to be sounded "in the twinkling of an eye" event as noted for the Rapture. Because some continue to equate the seventh trumpet with the last trumpet sound, they erroneously believe that the Rapture occurs with the seventh trumpet sound at the mid portion of the Tribulation (Mid-Tribulation theory).

Though this seventh trumpet does not align with the last trump, it does coincide with the trumpet of the Day of the

Lord found in Joel 2:1-2, "Blow the trumpet in Zion, and sound an alarm in My holy mountain! Let all the inhabitants of the land tremble; for the day of the Lord is coming, for it is at hand: a day of darkness and gloominess, a day of clouds and thick darkness."

These verses (Revelation 11:15-19) are a preview of Jesus' Millennial coronation from heaven's perspective. The events of Revelation chapters 12-18 describe the transition of earth's ownership from Satan to Jesus Christ, the King of Kings and Lord of Lords. Though this will not occur until the end of the Tribulation, the inhabitants of heaven are already proclaiming with certainty what Daniel prophesied in Daniel 2:44, "And in the days of these kings (earthly kingdoms) the God of heaven will set up a kingdom which shall never be destroyed; and the kingdom shall not be left to other people; it shall break in pieces and consume all these kingdoms, and it shall stand forever."

The kingdoms of this world are under Satan's authority now and will be during the Tribulation though he lost all rights when Christ spilled His precious blood, died and rose from the grave; Satan is allowed to rule solely by God's permission, and all authority has been given to Christ in heaven and on earth (John 12:31; Matthew 28:18). "But even if our gospel is veiled, it is veiled to those who are perishing, whose minds the god of this age has blinded, who do not believe, lest the light of the gospel of the glory of Christ, who is the image of God, should shine on them" (II Corinthians 4:3-4). Satan is the god of this age, but God has ultimate authority, and will strip all rights from Satan. Satan is not an equal rival to our triune God and is defeated. God has given Satan only temporary rights while he is creating, propagating and instilling chaos on earth and in the hearts of man.

Do you ever wonder why we have wars, hospitals, sickness, brokenness, thefts, corruption, greed, homicides, murders, addictions and depravity? Did you know that none of these existed in Genesis chapters 1-2, and none of these will exist in Revelation 21-22 and beyond? What's the common denominator?

 Where Satan is, there is evil, war and brokenness. Where Satan is not, there is goodness, peace and wholeness.

So, do we need more reform, more regulations, more institutions, more universities and more hospitals? No, we need Jesus! But many do not want Jesus, and during the Tribulation, "the rulers take counsel together, against the Lord (God) and against His Anointed (Christ, the Messiah), saying, 'Let us break Their bonds in pieces and cast away Their cords from us.'" Rest assured, this wicked plot will never succeed. God says of Christ, "You shall break them (kings and rulers of the earth) with a rod of iron; You shall dash them to pieces like a potter's vessel." Those who reject Christ will perish, but blessed are those who put their trust in the Son! (Psalm 2:1-12).

***11:16** And the twenty-four elders who sat before God on their thrones fell on their faces and worshiped God*

During the fifth seal opening (6:10), we saw the martyred saints of the Tribulation cry out in vengeance, "How long, O Lord?" The vengeance they sought is now coming to fruition. The twenty-four elders, symbolizing the Raptured Church in heaven, recognize the grandeur of this event and fall on their faces and worship God as we observe in Revelation 4:10, 5:8-14, 7:11, 11:16 and 19:4. Christ does not come to set His foot on earth until the Second Coming, which at the point of this verse is about three and a half years away. Therefore, the rejoicing in heaven is due to an anticipation of Christ's nearing Millennium reign.

***11:17** saying: "We give You thanks, O Lord God Almighty, The One who is and who was and who is to come, Because You have taken Your great power and reigned.*

Seven hundred years before Christ's birth in Bethlehem, Isaiah saw the Lord sitting on a throne, "high and lifted up, and the train of His robe filled the temple. Above it stood seraphim; each one had six wings: with two he covered his face, with two he covered his feet, and with two he flew. And one cried to another and said, 'Holy, holy, holy is the Lord of hosts; the whole earth is full of His glory!'" Isaiah went on to proclaim Christ's reign, "Of the increase of His government and peace there will be no end, upon the throne of David and over His kingdom, to order it and establish it with judgment and justice from that time forward, even forever. The zeal of the Lord of hosts will perform this" (Isaiah 6:1-3; 9:7). The prophets have foretold of Christ's reign and heaven foretells it as they see the seventh trumpet blown and grasp the impending doom of Satan and the commencement of the righteous reign of Christ.

Truly, He was. He, the Master Craftsman, created the world with God (Proverbs 8:22-31). Truly, He is. He, the High Priest, petitions His Father on our behalf. Truly, He will be. He, the King of Kings and Lord of Lords. Yes, we join the Psalmist in awe, "Lord, you have been our dwelling place in all generations. Before the mountains were brought forth, or ever You had formed the earth and the world, even from everlasting to everlasting, You are God" (Psalm 90:1-2). It would be better for us to bow the knee now in humble repentance because at the Great White Throne judgment, all the unbelievers will bow in sorrowful defeat and confess He is Lord. Tragically, they will be a day late and a dollar short!

11:18 The nations were angry, and Your wrath has come, and the time of the dead, that they should be judged; and that You should reward Your servants the prophets and the saints, and those who fear Your name, small and great, and should destroy those who destroy the earth."

The twenty-four elders continue to worship God, speaking of the future events with anticipatory language, as if they were present realities. We'll look at Psalm 2:1-12 again as it will be a recurring theme:

1. The nations will rage, and their leaders will be furious.
2. They will plot to overthrow God, but their plans will be in vain.
3. They will unite, exchange ideas, and encourage one another.
4. They will seek freedom from God's laws and love.
5. God will laugh at their schemes.
6. God will scorn their One-World-Order.
7. God will speak to them with judgment.
8. God will pour out His wrath upon them.
9. God will set Christ on His holy hill of Zion.
10. God will call Christ His Son.
11. God will grant His Son any wish.
12. God will give His Son the nations as His inheritance.
13. God will give His Son the ends of the earth to possess.
14. God will allow His Son to break nations with a rod iron.
15. Christ will dash the rebellious nations to pieces.
16. God will counsel the kings of the earth to be wise.
17. God will instruct the judges of the earth.
18. God will advise them to serve the Lord with fear.
19. God will encourage them to kiss the Son.
20. If they do not, they will perish.
21. Blessed will be those who trust God.

According to Revelation 11:18-19, seven events will transpire during the rest of this book, as Christ the King returns and deals with earth's rebels, His saints, and the invisible forces of Satan:

1. The nations will be angry as stated above in Psalm Two and will gather at Megiddo for the Campaign of Armageddon in an attempt to permanently destroy Israel and obliterate the name of God and His existence.

2. The day of God's wrath is unleashed during the Tribulation but not fully displayed until His Second Coming in the Campaign of Armageddon.

3. At the conclusion of Jesus' reign on earth which will be at the end of the thousand-year Millennium, the wicked are judged at the Great White throne (Revelation 20:11-15). We read in Genesis 49:10 that the Messiah will come from the tribe of Judah and reign as King. In II Samuel 7:16, the promised Messiah, Jesus Christ, is prophesied to reign on an eternal throne. In Daniel 7:13-14, we read that the Messiah will have an everlasting dominion. In Luke 1:32-33, Mary is told that she will give birth to a son who will reign over the house of Jacob forever, and of His kingdom there will be no end!

4. The faithful Old Testament prophets and saints are Raptured at the end of the Tribulation and will rule for all Eternity with Christ (Daniel 12:1-2). "This term (the saints) is the common one in the New Testament to designate the general body of believers and is nowhere used in the New Testament Scriptures to express a select company. It is the common appellation of the redeemed in both Testaments."[17] It doesn't matter if you are rich or poor, educated or uneducated, famous or common, strong or weak, great or small. What matters is the blood of the Lamb and your acceptance or rejection of His precious blood as the payment for your sins.

5. Those who destroyed the earth will be destroyed in eternal death. According to Hebrews 9:27, "It is appointed for men to die once, but after this the judgment" (for the unsaved and unbelieving). "The word 'destroy' is the same, actually, as 'corrupt.' Man had destroyed the earth by corrupting the earth, using it not for God's glory, but instead to satisfy his own greed and lust."[18]

 It's vital to save the environment. But it's foolish to ignore man's soul that gravitates toward immorality while passionately trying to save the earth. In the end, you'll lose both.

6. The temple of God opens and the "lost" ark is seen! See verse 19.

7. Earthquake and great hail will ensue because of the seven bowl judgments. See Revelation 11:19.

***11:19** Then the temple of God was opened in heaven, and the ark of His covenant was seen in His temple. And there were lightnings, noises, thunderings, an earthquake, and great hail.*

The temple of heaven is opened, and the Ark of the Covenant is seen, which is a seal of God's very presence, His faithfulness to a stiff-necked people and His atonement for the idolatrous heart.

According to Exodus 26:33, the Ark was kept in the Most Holy Place. The lid of the Ark was called the mercy seat and signified an atoning cover because on the Day of Atonement, the high priest sprinkled the blood of an innocent animal on it to signify Israel's repentance and God's redemptive power. (Leviticus 23:27; Numbers 29:7).

The last time the Ark was seen was when it was placed in Solomon's temple (II Chronicles 35:3). Archaeologists to date are unsure of its whereabouts. Was it destroyed when King Nebuchadnezzar burned the temple of God in 586 BC? Was it destroyed during the Babylonian captivity? That is unknown and a controversial point; but greater than the Ark of Moses' days is the heavenly Ark. "Christ has not entered the holy places made with hands, which are copies of the true, but into heaven itself, now to appear in the presence of God for us" (Hebrews 9:24). Christ changed it all!

1. The Ark of the Covenant is seen in heaven's temple. The Ark contained the ten commandments, manna, and Aaron's rod that budded. Jesus is the law and has fulfilled the law. Jesus is the true manna, the Bread of Life (John 6:35). Jesus is the rod that budded; He rose from the

dead on the third day as the flowers and almonds "rose" from a dead rod!

2. Lightning, thunder, earthquake and hail will ensue because the great bowl judgments are about to be cast upon mankind, Satan, the Antichrist and the False Prophet in the Great Tribulation.

3. Heaven's residents explode in joy, anticipating the dawning of the Millennial Kingdom of Christ.

REV IT UP & SUM IT UP – CHAPTER ELEVEN:

Two anointed witnesses and prophets of old, Moses and Elijah, will prophesy for 1,260 days, during the first three and a half years of the Tribulation. They will have the power to shut the heavens so there will be no rain and strike the waters and turn them into blood. Those on earth will hate the two witnesses and will try to harm them, but fire will come out of the two servants' mouths and devour them.

After sustaining a mortal wound (Revelation 13:3), the Antichrist will miraculously resurrect, emulating Christ, from the Abyss and kill the two prophets; the world will refuse their burial because the two tormented them. The Antichrist will gain world acclaim because no one else was able to kill the two prophets. Their bodies will lie on the streets of Jerusalem as the world watches and celebrates, sending gifts to each other. But in three and a half days, God breathes life into the two dead prophets, and they rise from the dead and are taken up to heaven while the world watches in a paralyzed state of awe and fear.

The seventh trumpet, which is not what is referred to as the "last trump" by the Mid-Tribulation proponents, is sounded and all of heaven cheers, anticipating Christ's imminent Millennial reign which will put an end to the Tribulation chaos; the seventh trumpet will release the seven bowl judgments in the Great Tribulation, or the last three and a half years of the Tribulation as we'll see in the chapters 15-16.

Separating the two half periods of the Tribulation will be the Abomination of Desolation, where the Antichrist will be standing in the Holy of Holies, proclaiming that he is God. Though the Gentiles will trample the temple of God, heaven's multitude will rejoice when it hears the seventh trumpet sound, anticipating Christ's victorious reign on earth and for all Eternity.

*The Verse by Verse discussion
continues in
Volume II*

REFERENCES

Endnotes, Volume I

Introduction

1 Ron Rhodes, *Bible Prophecy Answer Book* (Eugene, OR: Harvest House Publishers, 2017), 29.

Chapter 1

1 Robert L. Thomas, *Revelation 1-7* (Chicago, IL: Moody Press, 1992), 61.

2 Robert L. Thomas, *Revelation 1-7* (Chicago, IL: Moody Press, 1992), 130.

3 Gregory K. Beale, *The Book of Revelation: A Commentary on the Greek Text* (Grand Rapids, MI: William B. Eerdmans Publishing Co., 1999), 58.

4 Walter L. Wilson, *A Dictionary of Bible Types* (Peabody, MA: Hendrickson Publishers, 1999), 363.

5 Gregory K. Beale, *The Book of Revelation: A Commentary on the Greek Text*, (Grand Rapids; MI: William B. Eerdmans Publishing Co., 1999), 59.

6 Robert L. Thomas, *Revelation 1-7* (Chicago, IL: Moody Press, 1992), 66.

7 J.A. Seiss, *The Apocalypse: Lectures on the Book of Revelation* (Grand Rapids, MI: Zondervan Publishing House, 1966), 29.

8 John MacArthur, *Revelation 1-11: The MacArthur New Testament Commentary* (Chicago, IL: Moody Press, 1999), Rev. 1:7.

9 J.A. Seiss, *The Apocalypse: Lectures on the Book of Revelation* (Grand Rapids, MI: Zondervan Publishing House, 1966), 35.

10 Tertullian, *The Prescription of Heretics*, volume 3, chapter 36.

11 http://distancebetween2.com/patmos/ephesus

12 Robert L. Thomas, *Revelation 1-7* (Chicago, IL: Moody Press, 1992), 87.

13 J.A. Seiss, *The Apocalypse: Lectures on the Book of Revelation*, (Grand Rapids, MI: Zonervan Publishing House, 1966), 86.

14 Robert L. Thomas, *Revelation 1-7* (Chicago, IL: Moody Press, 1992), 87.

15 A.R. Fausset, "The Revelation of St. John the Divine," in Robert Jamieson, A.R. Fausset, and David Brown, *A Commentary, Critical and Explanatory, on the Old and New Testaments* (Oak Harbor, WA: Logos Research Systems, Inc., 1997, 1877), Rev. 1:9.

16 Alan F. Johnson, *Revelation: The Expositor's Bible Commentary* (Grand Rapids, MI: Zondervan Publishing House, 1966), 23

17 E.W. Bullinger, *Commentary on Revelation* (Grand Rapids, MI: Kregel Publications, 1984, 1935), 72.

18 John Hartnett, "Pleiades or Orion, Bound or Unbound" (TJ 18 (2), 2004), p 44. https://creation.com/images/pdfs/tj/j18_2/j18_2_44-48.pdf

19 Richard Chenevix Trench, *Commentary on the Epistles to the Seven Churches in Asia* (Eugene, OR: Wipf and Stock Publishers, 1861), 33.

20 J.D .Hays, John Imbric, NJ Shackleton, "Variations in the earth's Orbit. Pacemaker of the Ice Age," December 10, 1976, Volume 194, 4270, *Science*

21 Richard Chenevix Trench, *Commentary on the Epistles to the Seven Churches in Asia* (Eugene, OR: Wipf and Stock Publishers, 1861), 45.

22 Richard Chenevix Trench, *Commentary on the Epistles to the Seven Churches in Asia* (Eugene, OR: Wipf and Stock Publishers, 1861), 47.

23 John F. Walvoord, T*he Revelation of Jesus Christ* (Chicago, IL: Moody Press, 1966), 48.

Chapter 2

1 G.L. Borchert, "Ephesus," in Geoffrey W. Bromiley, ed., *International Standard Bible Encyclopedia* (Grand Rapids, MI: William B. Eerdmans Publishing Co., 1979, 1915), 115.

2 Daymond R. Duck and Larry Richards, *Revelation* (Lancaster, Pennsylvania: Starburst Publishers, 1998), 27.

3 David Jeremiah, *The Seven Churches of Revelation* (San Diego, CA: Turning Point, 2016), 23.

4 Robert L. Thomas, *Revelation 1-7* (Chicago, IL: Moody Press, 1992), 129.

5 https://www.allaboutfollowingjesus.org/early-christian-persecution-faq.htm

6 William R. Newell, *Revelation: Chapter by Chapter* (Grand Rapids, MI: Kregel Publications, 1994, 1935), 39-40.

7 William R. Newell, *Revelation: Chapter by Chapter* (Grand Rapids, MI: Kregel Publications, 1994, 1935), 40.

8 John F. Walvoord, *The Revelation of Jesus Christ* (Chicago, IL: Moody Press, 1966), 58.

9 Arnold G. Fruchtenbaum, *The Footsteps of Messiah*, rev ed. (Tustin, CA: Ariel Ministries, 2003), 755-756.

10 Robert L. Thomas, *Revelation 1-7* (Chicago, IL: Moody Press, 1992), 158.

11 Colin J. Hemer, *The Letters to the Seven Churches of Asia in Their Local Setting* (Grand Rapids, MI: William B. Eerdmans Publishing Company, 1989), 60.

12 Monty S. Mills, *Revelations: An Exegetical Study of the Revelation to John* (Dallas, TX: 3E Ministries, 1987), Rev. 2:8.

13 Robert L. Thomas, *Revelation 1-7* (Chicago, IL: Moody Press, 1992), 159.

14 J.B. Lightfoot and J.R. Harmer, *The Apostolic Fathers*, 2nd ed. (Grand Rapids, MI: Baker Book House, 1989), 119-122.

15 Colin J. Hemer, *The Letters to the Seven Churches of Asia in Their Local Setting* (Grand Rapids, MI: William B. Eerdmans Publishing Company, 1989), 65.

16 J.B. Lightfoot and J.R. Harmer, *The Apostolic Fathers*, 2nd ed. (Grand Rapids, MI: Baker Book House, 1989), 110.

17 David Jeremiah, *The Seven Churches of Revelation* (San Diego, CA: Turning Point, 2016), 37.

18 J. Willard Willis, *The Revelation of Jesus Christ* (http://toulonbaptist.com/Revelation/990131.htm)

19 Colin J. Hemer, *The Letters to the Seven Churches of Asia in Their Local Setting* (Grand Rapids, MI: William B. Eerdmans Publishing Company, 1989), 67.

20 Grant R. Osborne, *Revelation* (Grand Rapids, MI: Baker Academic, 2002), 11.

21 Daymond R. Duck and Larry Richards, *Revelation* (Lancaster, Pennsylvania: Starburst Publishers, 1998), 33.

22 http://www.biblestudy.org/bibleref/meaning-of-numbers-in-bible/10.html

23 Colin J. Hemer, *The Letters to the Seven Churches of Asia in Their Local Setting* (Grand Rapids, MI: William B. Eerdmans Publishing Company, 1989), 69.

24 Jerome Smith, *The New Treasury of Scripture Knowledge* (Nashville, TN: Thomas Nelson Publishers, 1992), Rev. 2:12.

25 Monty S. Mills, *Revelations: An Exegetical Study of the Revelation to John* (Dallas, TX: 3E Ministries, 1987), Rev. 2:12.

26 http://www.biblestudy.org/bibleref/meaning-of-numbers-in-bible/2.html

27 Monty S. Mills, *Revelations: An Exegetical Study of the Revelation to John* (Dallas, TX: 3E Ministries, 1987), Rev. 2:13.

28 R. North, "Pergamum," in Geoffrey W. Bromiley, ed., *International Standard Bible Encyclopedia* (Grand Rapids, MI: William B. Eerdmans Publishing Co., 1979, 1915), 3:768.

29 Tim Lahaye, *Revelation Unveiled* (Grand Rapids, Michigan: Zondervan, 1999), 58.

30 Mal Couch, "Ecclesiology in the Book of Revelation," in Mal Couch, ed., *A Bible Handbook to Revelation* (Grand Rapids, MI: Kregel Publications, 2001), 138.

31 Arnold G. Fruchtenbaum, *The Footsteps of Messiah*, rev ed. (Tustin, CA: Ariel Ministries, 2003), 56.

32 Matthew Henry, *Matthew Henry's Commentary on the Whole Bible : Complete and Unabridged in One Volume* (Peabody, MA: Hendrickson, 1996, c1991), Rev. 2:17.

33 Monty S. Mills, *Revelations: An Exegetical Study of the Revelation to John* (Dallas, TX: 3E Ministries, 1987), Rev. 2:18.

34 Colin J. Hemer, *The Letters to the Seven Churches of Asia in Their Local Setting* (Grand Rapids, MI: William B. Eerdmans Publishing Company, 1989), 109.

35 Richard Chenevix Trench, *Commentary on the Epistles to the Seven Churches in Asia* (Eugene, OR: Wipf and Stock Publishers, 1861), 140.

36 James Strong, *The Exhaustive Concordance of the Bible* (Ontario: Woodside Bible Fellowship, 1996), G4105.

37 Monty S. Mills, *Revelations: An Exegetical Study of the Revelation to John* (Dallas, TX: 3E Ministries, 1987), Rev. 2:20.

38 William R. Newell, *Revelation: Chapter by Chapter* (Grand Rapids, MI: Kregel Publications, 1994,1935), 57.

39 Gregory K. Beale, *The Book of Revelation: A Commentary on the Greek Text* (Grand Rapids, MI: William B. Eerdmans Publishing Co., 1999), 32.

40 Colin J. Hemer, *The Letters to the Seven Churches of Asia in Their Local Setting* (Grand Rapids, MI: William B. Eerdmans Publishing Company, 1989), 125.

Chapter 3

1 P.J. Rhodes, *A History of the Classical Greek World 478-323 BC.* 2nd edition. Chichester: Wiley-Blackwell, 2010, p. 6.

2 David Jeremiah, *The Seven Churches of Revelation* (San Diego, CA: Turning Point, 2016), 73.

3 Monty S. Mills, *Revelations: An Exegetical Study of the Revelation to John* (Dallas, TX: 3E Ministries, 1987), Rev. 3:1.

4 David Jeremiah, *The Seven Churches of Revelation* (San Diego, CA: Turning Point, 2016), 73.

5 David Jeremiah, *The Seven Churches of Revelation* (San Diego, CA: Turning Point, 2016), 73.

6 Donald Grey Barnhouse, *Revelation* (Grand Rapids, MI: Zondervan Publishing House, 1971), 68.

7 J.A. Seiss, *The Apocalypse: Lectures on the Book of Revelation* (Grand Rapids, MI: Zondervan Publishing House, 1966), 73.

8 Loraine Boettner, *The Reformed Doctrine of Predestination* (Phillipsburg, NJ: Presbyterian and Reformed Publishing Company, 1932), 61-62.

9 Donald Grey Barnhouse, *Revelation* (Grand Rapids, MI: Zondervan Publishing House, 1971), 70.

10 Monty S. Mills, *Revelations: An Exegetical Study of the Revelation to John* (Dallas, TX: 3E Ministries, 1987), Rev. 3:3.

11 Jerome Smith, *The New Treasury of Scripture Knowledge* (Nashville, TN: Thomas Nelson Publishers, 1992), Rev. 3:7.

12 https://orthodoxwiki.org/Philadelphia_(Asia_Minor)

13 David Jeremiah, *The Seven Churches of Revelation* (San Diego, CA: Turning Point, 2016), 88.

Endnotes, Volume I

14 Donald Grey Barnhouse, *Revelation* (Grand Rapids, MI: Zondervan Publishing House, 1971), 75.

15 Gregory K. Beale, *The Book of Revelation: A Commentary on the Greek Text* (Grand Rapids, MI: William B. Eerdmans Publishing Co., 1999), 94.

16 Arnold G. Fruchtenbaum, *The Footsteps of Messiah,* rev ed. (Tustin, CA: Ariel Ministries, 2003), 155.

17 Donald Grey Barnhouse, *Revelation* (Grand Rapids, MI: Zondervan Publishing House, 1971), 78.

18 Arnold G. Fruchtenbaum, *The Footsteps of Messiah,* rev ed. (Tustin, CA: Ariel Ministries, 2003), 66.

19 David Padfield, *Colosse,* Hierapolis, Laodicea, 2014, p 5.

20 David Padfield, *Colosse,* Hierapolis, Laodicea, 2014, p 6.

21 Colin J. Hemer, *The Letters to the Seven Churches of Asia in Their Local Setting* (Grand Rapids, MI: William B. Eerdmans Publishing Company, 1989), 188.

22 Robert L. Thomas, *Revelation 1-7* (Chicago, IL: Moody Press, 1992), Rev. 3:14, 300.

23 Michael J. Svigel, "Christ as Arche in Revelation 3:14," in *Bibliotheca Sacra,* vol. 161 no. 642 (Dallas, TX: Dallas Theological Seminary, April-June 2004), 225.

24 Arnold G. Fruchtenbaum, *The Footsteps of Messiah,* rev ed. (Tustin, CA: Ariel Ministries, 2003), 66.

25 Richard Chenevix Trench, *Commentary on the Epistles to the Seven Churches in Asia* (Eugene, OR: Wipf and Stock Publishers, 1861), 195-196.

26 Henry Barclay Swete, *The Apocalypse of St. John* (Eugene, OR: Wipf and Stock Publishers, 1998, 1906), lxi.

27 Henry Morris, *The Revelation Record* (Wheaton, IL: Tyndale House Publishers, 1983), Rev. 3:21.

28 Donald Grey Barnhouse, *Revelation* (Grand Rapids, MI: Zondervan Publishing House, 1971), 84.

Chapter 4

1 Donald Grey Barnhouse, *Revelation* (Grand Rapids, MI: Zondervan Publishing House, 1971), 88.

2 Jerome Smith, *The New Treasury of Scripture Knowledge* (Nashville, TN: Thomas Nelson Publishers, 1992), Rev. 4:1.

3 Mark Hitchcock, *The End* (Carol Stream, Illinois: Tyndale House Publishers, Inc, 2012), 145.

4 Donald Grey Barnhouse, *Revelation* (Grand Rapids, MI: Zondervan Publishing House, 1971), 89.

5 A.R. Fausset, "The Revelation of St. John the Divine," in Robert Jamieson, A.R. Fausset, and David Brown, *A Commentary, Critical and Explanatory, on the Old and New Testaments* (Oak Harbor, WA: Logos Research Systems, Inc., 1997, 1877), Rev. 4:2.

6 Robert L. Thomas, *Revelation 1-7* (Chicago, IL: Moody Press, 1992), 343.

7   Robert G. Gromacki, "Twenty Four Elders of Revelation," in Mal Couch, ed., *Dictionary of Premillennial Theology* (Grand Rapids, MI: Kregel Publications, 1996), 377-378.

8   J.A. Seiss, *The Apocalypse: Lectures on the Book of Revelation* (Grand Rapids, MI: Zondervan Publishing House, 1966), 104.

9   Donald Grey Barnhouse, *Revelation* (Grand Rapids, MI: Zondervan Publishing House, 1971), 91.

10 Donald Grey Barnhouse, *Revelation* (Grand Rapids, MI: Zondervan Publishing House, 1971), 92.

11 Walter L. Wilson, *A Dictionary of Bible Types* (Peabody, MA: Hendrickson Publishers, 1999), 180.

12 Donald Grey Barnhouse, *Revelation* (Grand Rapids, MI: Zondervan Publishing House, 1971), 96-97.

13 Robert L. Thomas, *Revelation 1-7* (Chicago, IL: Moody Press, 1992), 361.

14 Alan F. Johnson, *Revelation: The Expositor's Bible Commentary* (Grand Rapids, MI: Zondervan Publishing House, 1966), Rev. 4:8.

15 E.W. Bullinger, *Commentary On Revelation* (Grand Rapids, MI: Kregel Publications, 1984, 1935), 231.

Chapter 5

1   E.W. Bullinger, *Commentary on Revelation* (Grand Rapids, MI: Kregel Publications, 1984, 1935), 233.

2   Ron Rhodes, *Bible Prophecy Answer Book* (Eugene, OR: Harvest House Publishers, 2017), 66.

3   Renald E. Showers, *The Pre-Wrath Rapture View* (Grand Rapids, MI: Kregel Publications, 2001), 96.

4   John MacArthur, *Revelation 1-11 : The MacArthur New Testament Commentary* (Chicago, IL: Moody Press, 1999), Rev. 5:2.

5   Merrill C. Tenney, *Interpreting Revelation* (Peabody, MA: Hendrickson Publishers, 1957), 126.

6   Robert Anderson, *The Coming Prince* (Grand Rapids, MI: Kregel Publications, 1957), 173.

7   Renald E. Showers, *Maranatha, Our Lord Come* (Bellmawr, NJ: The Friends of Israel Gospel Ministry, 1995), 92.

8   Robert H. Mounce, *The Book of Revelation* (Grand Rapids, MI: William B. Eerdmans Publishing Co., 1977), 144.

9   Harold D. Foos, "Christology in the Book of Revelation," in Mal Couch, ed., *A Bible Handbook to Revelation* (Grand Rapids, MI: Kregel Publications, 2001), 106.

10 David Baron, Zechariah: *A Commentary on His Visions and Prophecies* (Grand Rapids, MI: Kregel Publications, 1918), 116.

11 J.A. Seiss, *The Apocalypse: Lectures on the Book of Revelation* (Grand Rapids, MI: Zondervan Publishing House, 1966), 117.

12 Jerome Smith, *The New Treasury of Scripture Knowledge* (Nashville, TN: Thomas Nelson Publishers, 1992), Rev. 5:12.

13 Donald Grey Barnhouse, *Revelation* (Grand Rapids, MI: Zondervan Publishing House, 1971), 113.

Chapter 6

1 https://www.biblestudytoos.com/commentaries/revelation/revelation-6/revelation -6-2.html (v.2 "he who sat on it.")

2 Arthur Walkington Pink, *The Antichrist* (Oak Harbor, WA: Logos Research Systems, 1999, 1923), s.v. "The Career of the Antichrist."

3 Randall Price, *Jerusalem In Prophecy* (Eugene, OR: Harvest House Publishers, 1998), 192.

4 E.W. Bullinger, *Commentary on Revelation* (Grand Rapids, MI: Kregel Publications, 1984, 1935), Rev. 6:17.

5 Arthur Walkington Pink, *The Antichrist* (Oak Harbor, WA: Logos Research Systems, 1999, 1923), s.v. "The Genius and Character of the Antichrist."

6 Renald E. Showers, *Maranatha, Our Lord Come* (Bellmawr, NJ: The Friends of Israel Gospel Ministry, 1995), 108-109.

7 https://www.biblestudytoos.com/commentaries/revelation/revelation-6/revelation -6-2.html (v.2 "was given to him.")

8 AssyrianInternationalNewsAgency.org (AINA.org); www.aina.org/news/20140604200113.html

9 A.R. Fausset, "The Revelation of St. John the Divine," in Robert Jamieson, A.R. Fausset, and David Brown, *A Commentary, Critical and Explanatory, on the Old and New Testaments* (Oak Harbor, WA: Logos Research Systems, Inc., 1997, 1877), Rev. 6:6.

10 Arnold G. Fruchtenbaum, *The Footsteps of Messiah*, rev ed. (Tustin, CA: Ariel Ministries, 2003), 219.

11 J.A. Seiss, *The Apocalypse: Lectures on the Book of Revelation* (Grand Rapids, MI: Zondervan Publishing House, 1966), 140.

12 J.A. Seiss, *The Apocalypse: Lectures on the Book of Revelation* (Grand Rapids, MI: Zondervan Publishing House, 1966), 142.

13 https://nypost.com/2018/08/22/ring-of-fire-hit-with-70-earthquakes-in-just-48-hours/

14 Donald Grey Barnhouse, *Revelation* (Grand Rapids, MI: Zondervan Publishing House, 1971), 140.

15 Monty S. Mills, *Revelations: An Exegetical Study of the Revelation to John* (Dallas, TX: 3E Ministries, 1987), Rev. 6:14.

16 Arnold G. Fruchtenbaum, *The Footsteps of Messiah*, rev ed. (Tustin, CA: Ariel Ministries, 2003), 221.

17 Donald Grey Barnhouse, *Revelation* (Grand Rapids, MI: Zondervan Publishing House, 1971), 140.

Chapter 7

1   Robert H. Mounce, *The Book of Revelation* (Grand Rapids, MI: William B. Eerdmans Publishing Co., 1977), Rev. 7:1.

2   Donald Grey Barnhouse, *Revelation* (Grand Rapids, MI: Zondervan Publishing House, 1971), 144.

3   Alan F. Johnson, *Revelation: The Expositor's Bible Commentary* (Grand Rapids, MI: Zondervan Publishing House, 1966), Rev. 7:1-3.

4   A.R. Fausset, "The Revelation of St. John the Divine," in Robert Jamieson, A.R. Fausset, and David Brown, *A Commentary, Critical and Explanatory, on the Old and New Testaments* (Oak Harbor, WA: Logos Research Systems, Inc., 1997, 1877), Rev. 7:4.

5   John MacArthur, *Revelation 1-11 : The MacArthur New Testament Commentary* (Chicago, IL: Moody Press, 1999), John 12:13.

6   Donald Grey Barnhouse, *Revelation* (Grand Rapids, MI: Zondervan Publishing House, 1971), 153.

7   Walter Scott, *Exposition of the Revelation* (London, England: Pickering & Inglis, n.d.), 165.

8   Monty S. Mills, *Revelations: An Exegetical Study of the Revelation to John* (Dallas, TX: 3E Ministries, 1987), Rev. 7:17.

Chapter 8

1   John MacArthur, *Revelation 1-11 : The MacArthur New Testament Commentary* (Chicago, IL: Moody Press, 1999), Rev. 8:1.

2   Monty S. Mills, *Revelations: An Exegetical Study of the Revelation to John* (Dallas, TX: 3E Ministries, 1987), Rev. 8:2.

3   A.R. Fausset, "The Revelation of St. John the Divine," in Robert Jamieson, A.R. Fausset, and David Brown, *A Commentary, Critical and Explanatory, on the Old and New Testaments* (Oak Harbor, WA: Logos Research Systems, Inc., 1997, 1877), Rev. 8:3.

4   Donald Grey Barnhouse, *Revelation* (Grand Rapids, MI: Zondervan Publishing House, 1971), 156.

5   Donald Grey Barnhouse, *Revelation* (Grand Rapids, MI: Zondervan Publishing House, 1971), 158.

6   Walter Scott, *Exposition of the Revelation* (London, England: Pickering & Inglis, n.d.), 173.

7   Donald Grey Barnhouse, , *Revelation* (Grand Rapids, MI: Zondervan Publishing House, 1971), 162.

8   https://www.biblestudytools.com/commentaries/revelation/introduction/the-plagues-of-egypt-and-the-tribulation.html#2.13.7

9   John MacArthur, *Revelation 1-11 : The MacArthur New Testament Commentary* (Chicago, IL: Moody Press, 1999), Rev. 8:8.

10 Monty S. Mills, *Revelations: An Exegetical Study of the Revelation to John* (Dallas, TX: 3E Ministries, 1987), Rev. 8:8.

11 John MacArthur, *Revelation 1-11 : The MacArthur New Testament Commentary* (Chicago, IL: Moody Press, 1999), Rev. 8:8.

12 Timothy Friberg, Barbara Friberg, and Neva F. Miller, *Analytical Lexicon of the Greek New Testament* (Grand Rapids, MI: Baker Books, 2000), 85.

13 Donald Grey Barnhouse, *Revelation* (Grand Rapids, MI: Zondervan Publishing House, 1971), 165.

14 Ron Rhodes, *Bible Prophecy Answer Book* (Eugene, OR: Harvest House Publishers, 2017), 111.

Chapter 9

1 Arthur Walkington Pink, *The Antichrist* (Oak Harbor, WA: Logos Research Systems, 1999, 1923), s.v. "Antichrist in the Apocalypse."

2 Donald Grey Barnhouse, *Revelation* (Grand Rapids, MI: Zondervan Publishing House, 1971), 168.

3 Robert H. Mounce, *The Book of Revelation* (Grand Rapids, MI: William B. Eerdmans Publishing Co., 1977), Rev. 9:17.

4 Henry Morris, *The Revelation Record* (Wheaton, IL: Tyndale House Publishers, 1983), Rev. 9:13.

5 Donald Grey Barnhouse, *Revelation* (Grand Rapids, MI: Zondervan Publishing House, 1971), 175.

6 http://www.ecology.com/population-estimates-year-2050/

7 Monty S. Mills, *Revelations: An Exegetical Study of the Revelation to John* (Dallas, TX: 3E Ministries, 1987), Rev. 9:16.

8 Donald Grey Barnhouse, *Revelation* (Grand Rapids, MI: Zondervan Publishing House, 1971), 178.

Chapter 10

1 Donald Grey Barnhouse, *Revelation* (Grand Rapids, MI: Zondervan Publishing House, 1971), 179.

2 E.W. Bullinger, *Commentary on Revelation* (Grand Rapids, MI: Kregel Publications, 1984, 1935), Rev. 10:2.

3 Timothy Friberg, Barbara Friberg, and Neva F. Miller, *Analytical Lexicon of the Greek New Testament*(Grand Rapids, MI: Baker Books, 2000), 4:182.

4 James Strong, *The Exhaustive Concordance of the Bible* (Ontario: Woodside Bible Fellowship, 1996), H3092.

5 Donald Grey Barnhouse, *Revelation* (Grand Rapids, MI: Zondervan Publishing House, 1971), 183.

6 J.A. Seiss, *The Apocalypse: Lectures on the Book of Revelation* (Grand Rapids, MI: Zondervan Publishing House, 1966), Rev. 10:6.

7 Frederick William Danker and Walter Bauer, *A Greek-English Lexicon of the New Testament and Other Early Christian Literature* (Chicago, IL: University of Chicago Press, 2000), 442.

8 Mark Hitchcock, "The Stake in the Heart—The A.D. 95 Date of Revelation," in Tim LaHaye and Thomas Ice, eds., *The End Times Controversy* (Eugene, OR: Harvest House Publishers, 2003), 133.

Chapter 11

1 Donald Grey Barnhouse, *Revelation* (Grand Rapids, MI: Zondervan Publishing House, 1971), 194.-

2 Donald Grey Barnhouse, *Revelation* (Grand Rapids, MI: Zondervan Publishing House, 1971), 195.

3 Jerome Smith, *The New Treasury of Scripture Knowledge* (Nashville, TN: Thomas Nelson Publishers, 1992), Rev. 11:2.

4 J.A. Seiss, *The Apocalypse: Lectures on the Book of Revelation* (Grand Rapids, MI: Zondervan Publishing House, 1966), Rev. 11:2.

5 Daniel Wong, "The Two Witnesses in Revelation 11," in *Bibliotheca Sacra*, vol. 154 no. 615 (Dallas, TX: Dallas Theological Seminary, July-Sep 1997), 348.

6 Jerome Smith, *The New Treasury of Scripture Knowledge* (Nashville, TN: Thomas Nelson Publishers, 1992), Rev. 11:3.

7 J. Dwight Pentecost, *Things to Come: A Study in Biblical Eschatology* (Grand Rapids, MI: Zondervan Publishing House, 1958), 309

8 Donald Grey Barnhouse, *Revelation* (Grand Rapids, MI: Zondervan Publishing House, 1971), 201-202.

9 Arthur Walkington Pink, *The Antichrist* (Oak Harbor, WA: Logos Research Systems, 1999, 1923), s.v. "The Beast."

10 Arnold G. Fruchtenbaum, *The Footsteps of Messiah*, rev ed. (Tustin, CA: Ariel Ministries, 2003), 250.

11 Arnold G. Fruchtenbaum, *The Footsteps of Messiah*, rev ed. (Tustin, CA: Ariel Ministries, 2003), 250.

12 E.W. Bullinger, *Commentary on Revelation* (Grand Rapids, MI: Kregel Publications, 1984, 1935), Rev. 11:8.

13 J.B. Payne, "Burial," in Geoffrey W. Bromiley, ed., *International Standard Bible Encyclopedia* (Grand Rapids, MI: William B. Eerdmans Publishing Co., 1979, 1915), 1:556.

14 E.W. Bullinger, *Commentary on Revelation* (Grand Rapids, MI: Kregel Publications, 1984, 1935), Rev. 11:9.

15 J. Dwight Pentecost, *Things to Come: A Study in Biblical Eschatology* (Grand Rapids, MI: Zondervan Publishing House, 1958), 188-192

16 Jerome Smith, *The New Treasury of Scripture Knowledge* (Nashville, TN: Thomas Nelson Publishers, 1992), Rev. 11:15.

17 Walter Scott, *Exposition of the Revelation* (London, England: Pickering & Inglis, n.d.), Rev. 11:18.

18 Henry Morris, *The Revelation Record* (Wheaton, IL: Tyndale House Publishers, 1983), Rev. 11:18.

Index

Index, Volume I

Index, Volume I

Other books by Dr. Sam

Playing on Your Last String

Mirror, Mirror on the Wall

Not on My Shift

I Got a Big But(t)

Absolute Hope

Life Prescriptions

Mad Love

When Hope Finds You

God Knows Your Address

Children's Books with CDs

Friends With Tommie Bear

Tommie Bear Goes to School

Revelation series by Dr. Sam

Rev It Up - Verse by Verse (Volumes I and II)

Rev It Up - Step by Step (Chronological order)

Rev It Up - Rhyme by Rhyme (Poetry book)

Rev It Up - Image by Image (Illustrated book)

Rev It Up - for Kids (Children's book)

Rev It Up - Rap It Up (CD)

Dr. Sam Online

BeaconOfHearts.org
MenderOfHearts.org

Instagram: @DrKojoglanian

Twitter: @BeaconOfHearts
              @MenderOfHearts

Facebook: BeaconOfHearts
           MenderOfHearts

Dr. Sam Offline

Samuel Kojoglanian, MD, FACC
Interventional Cardiologist

Mender of Hearts, Inc
24868 Apple Street #103
Santa Clarita, CA 91321